THE FINE PRINT

My Life as a Deskman

Jack Schwartz

ACKNOWLEDGMENTS

Every book has more than one progenitor. This one is no exception. What started out as a personal recollection for a circle of intimates became a book largely due to the encouragement of a few newspaper friends who insisted that it merited a wider audience. Foremost among them was my old boss at Newsday, Tony Marro, who read the original manuscript and contributed many significant correctives to my early efforts, helping me where memory failed and when enthusiasm faltered. I also owe a debt of gratitude to Sandee Brawarsky whose quiet and gentle encouragement has been a source of inspiration over the years. And special thanks go to my erstwhile colleagues Joseph Berger of The New York Times and Ari Goldman of the Columbia University Journalism School for their careful reading of my work and helpful suggestions in offering a rounded characterization of some of the personalities depicted here. All four are mentioned in dispatches, along with the writers Phillip Lopate and Julie Salamon, among the men and women of letters who shared some of the events recounted here. A special note of thanks goes to the gifted Isaac Peterson who designed and produced this book. Finally, let me begin and end my tale with a humble note of thanks to my wife, Nella, who steered me through a sea of doubts, inspired me when my spirits flagged and served as the best deskman I could ever hope for.

I describe not Men, but Manners; not an Individual, but a Species.

—HENRY FIELDING, *Joseph Andrews*

CONTENTS

THE LEAD

Newspaper memoirs usually fall into two categories: the revelations of an intrepid reporter or the reflections of a celebrity editor. To my knowledge, there is very little about life on a news desk from the mid-level toilers who worked there. But in the words of one knowledgeable observer: "The most useful man on a newspaper is one who can edit. Writers there are galore. Every profession offers them. But the editor is a profession apart." That was Times publishers Adolph Ochs, speaking at the Columbia Journalism School in 1925. I believe his words still ring true and that the "profession apart" also has a story to tell about the news business. It is in this voice that I choose to speak.

When I started working for newspapers a lifetime ago, city rooms flaunted spittoons, lacked air conditioning and dispensed with décor. Everyone seemed to be smoking, drinking or growling—some simultaneously. Certainly no one appeared to have a problem with these categories. News was cast in lead and so were some of the editors; the men played at being Hemingway, the few women, at Jean Arthur. For better or worse that world is gone. Before it fades altogether, I hope it might be of some interest to leave a small record by someone who was there.

I was fortunate to work in the heyday of American print journalism—a period of roughly 40 years starting in the late 50's. The second half of the 20th century provided a brief window when newspapers gained respectability before their subsequent decline. World War II wrought tremendous changes in the way Americans saw themselves and the world, and news coverage reflected this transformation, gaining repute with enterprising local, national and foreign coverage. Reporters were better educated and so were readers. America was on the move and on a roll.

Newspapers had evolved from political pamphlets, three-penny gazettes, personal fiefdoms, merchandising vehicles, urban raffishness and static broadsheets to become dynamic, influential, powerful disseminators of news and opinion. Everybody read one; in big cities, sometimes two, "a morning" for the news and "an afternoon" for sports and scandal. And in any given town, everyone was reading from the same page—or two or three. The American newspaper had come of age. If you were working for one you had the feeling that you were at the center of things. With it, came a new-found stature, a break with the yellow past.

The new unwritten contract between a paper and its readers was a sense of trust. "Fairness," if not objectivity, was the watchword and papers strove to be even-handed in a good-faith effort to earn the confidence of their readers. Newspapers could write with authority, the mainstream media represented a general public consensus and competition was limited. Radio was Top Forty and television, whatever its inroads, still lacked the gravitas of print. The owners were flush with cash, which fostered ambitious reporting and led to a sense of independence in the boardrooms and confidence in the newsrooms. There was a lot wrong with this picture as well. But there is no doubt that to have worked in that era was a heady experience.

I should stress at the outset that this will not be an analysis or an overview. I hope simply to evoke my own experience, or the bits and pieces of it that will have to serve as a record. Consequently, I must work with the elisions and illusions of memory plus whatever scraps of paper or moldering clips I could gather. Others may recall things differently but this is my own take on that time rendered as honestly as I can remember. The result is not a memoir but rather a longish rewrite job. In this case, I am phoning in the story to myself. As such it may be pasted together, a little long on the imagination, full of inserts and revises and cross-outs, with lots of second-guessing, and doubtless eyeball rolling by knowledgeable readers familiar with aspects of the story.

While I've made a good-faith effort to get things right, one could always use a deskman. By way of apology I invoke another newspaperman, Mark Twain, who has Huck Finn observe about his rendering of "Tom Sawyer": "There was things which he stretched, but mainly he told the truth."

THE ULTIMATE TABLOID

My first job for a newspaper came in the spring of 1957 with The Daily Mirror. The Hearst flagship paper in New York, it was a flagrant tabloid, unregenerate, unreconstructed, unrepentant. I loved it. The Mirror pandered shamelessly to the worst impulses of its readers; it brazenly celebrated the excesses of the yellow press. It was at once irreverent and irrelevant, outrageous, wantonly corruptible—and great fun to read. It offered a far better rough-and-tumble education for a novice than any journalism school could provide.

Like most of my fellow copy boys I was a college student by day, lackey by night. I was also an editor of The City College Campus, a full-time calling in itself. I would generally show up for classes in the morning, devote my energies to the school paper in the afternoon and take the D Train downtown to The Mirror for the 6 P.M.–1 A.M. shift. I'd take the subway back to the Bronx, catch some sleep and be back in school for classes the next morning. In the summer, I worked days at The Mirror, a morning paper, and got a weekend job at the afternoon New York Post working the 1-8 A.M. trick on Friday and Sunday nights.

What struck me right off at The Mirror was that the copy boys spent their spare time reading and the rewrite men spent their spare time drinking. The newspaper was located on 45th Street between Third and Second Avenues, three blocks north of The Daily News, the sun in whose yellow light The Mirror glinted. Presumably, the name of the paper alluded to holding up a glass to the city it covered, but to us, the only meaning of the Mirror was that it served as a moon to reflect the dominant rays of the Daily News, then in its heyday. One of our first tasks of the evening was to make our way to the News truck ramps at 7 P.M. as its first edition—which hit the streets at 8 —was rolling off the presses. There, through an arrangement with the News's paper handlers, we were slipped a bundle of copies which we raced back to The Mirror offices. Our editors appropriated the relevant stories they'd missed, tossed them to the rewrite bank and fed them re-processed into our second edition, which came out at 11 and was a near reflection of The News's first edition. The News probably did the same thing although I never thought it had to bother.

Afternoon papers made their livings by rewriting the mornings, but The Mirror was a morning paper that rewrote the mornings.

The editors banked on no one taking them seriously, not the competition, not the readers and most certainly not themselves. Which is not to say that they weren't touchy about their status. They were forever taking umbrage at one another or terrifying underlings for some breach of journalism, personal etiquette or due respect. It was like being in the Mafia: at the mercy of a collection of crude bruisers sensitive to the honor due them and merciless in punishing infractions.

One evening, Selig Adler, the senior and meanest of the three Adler brothers who de facto ran The Mirror, found that someone had sat on his fedora—most men wore hats in those days. The fedora, perched atop the hat rack, was slightly caved in on the left side—not permanently crunched or flattened; a few taps from the inside would have restored the blocking. But Adler took this as a personal affront. In full throat, he bellowed: "Who the hell sat on my hat?" It was clear in Adler's mind that only a copy boy could have given such offense. There were eight of us cowering on the copy-boy's bench, and there were eight more possible culprits on the dayside who could have committed the act between the time Adler returned from lunch and the start of the night shift. No one owned up and he grew apoplectic. "No one leaves here tonight until we find the son-of-a-bitch who sat on my hat!"

Did anyone actually sit on Adler's hat? Probably not. More likely someone had brushed by, or cuffed it while reaching for their own hat (which copy boys generally didn't wear but logic wasn't a factor here). What was palpably real, however, was Adler's power to terrify his lessors unchecked, his freedom to imagine that his hat, and thereby his dignity, had been affronted, and his license to throw a fit without anyone saying him nay.

No one in that room, except for perhaps a few reflective spirits, thought Adler might be making a fool of himself, and if they did they weren't saying. The office was divided into three camps on this: The Sheep who quavered and hoped that Grendel wouldn't lumber their way; The Implementers who actually believed the hat had been sat on because Selig declared it so, who bridled on his behalf that so dastardly an act could have been perpetrated and who were casting beady eyes about to unearth the miscreant; and the Pragmatists who, while not denying the justice of Selig's rage, sought a way to distract him (including tossing him a sacrifice if need be) in order to get on with the evening's business. I have found this division of institutional response to be generally in

4

keeping at most of the papers I've worked for, the ratios and harmonies in relative concordance with the one described here.

You're probably waiting for the outcome but the truth is I don't quite remember the exact disposition except that a full investigation was promised and that no one ever confessed. The idea of any of us stepping forward and declaiming "I am Spartacus" was not a serious option for kids who needed the work. My general recollection is that, like a hurricane that expends itself and roars out to sea, Selig was distracted by something—a phone call, a girlfriend, hunger—and blew off toward the elevator banks. What I do remember is the sheer pleasure he took in his wrath and his ability to inflict it with impunity.

The title of head copy boy at The Mirror, like everything else about the place, was a misnomer. The man who held the job didn't carry copy and wasn't a boy. He was probably well past 70 by the time I got there, and he grew meaner with each year. His name was Jack Flynn and, according to office lore, he was supposed to have been Hearst's chauffeur, rewarded for his services with this lifetime sinecure. Just a few rungs above those he supervised, Flynn's well-being depended on appeasing his bosses and oppressing his charges. Often, he did his masters one better, stirred by a dose of age and class resentment, since he knew that not only would we outlive him, but that most of us would move beyond him.

The system was simple enough. We sat on a long wooden bench against a wall at the far end of the city room between the news desk and the banks of rewrite men who polished stories phoned in by reporters and re-crafted the wire-service news rattling in on teletype machines. If a writer finished a piece of copy—stories were done in takes, a page or two at a time, between editions—he'd yell "Boy!" and the copy boy on the far right, or front seat of the bench, would leap up, grab the copy from the writer, move it to the news desk, strip the carbons and distribute the copies to the in-baskets of the appropriate editors. When the boy's turn was done, he would go to the end of the bench and become No. 8, or last in line, waiting as the invisible conveyer belt moved along until he was No. 1 again. Should the copy boy not hop to it with sufficient alacrity, Flynn would again bark "Boy!" and fix the offender with a baleful stare.

5

Since many of us were in college and doing our homework while this was going on, it was possible that some poor soul could be absorbed in a book when his turn came, or daydreaming, or exhausted, or occasionally drunk. Most, however, got the rhythms down and knew that when we were two bodies from the head seat to shift into vigilant mode. If things proceeded normally, there were about three minutes of uninterrupted study time before one had to go on alert. This may seem like a distracting method of doing homework but actually it was just another way of focusing. I recall reading "Death of a Salesman" for the first time on that bench. I was in the No. 1 seat just at the moment when Uncle Charlie is explaining Willy to Biff. I was able to suspend my emotion, like a ping pong ball over an air gun, move the copy, sit back down at the end of the bench and then resume reading as if I'd just emerged from a time warp with no seconds elapsed between. Studying this way must have had some efficacy because the lines stuck although I didn't get to see the play till years later.
Some of us laugh at Chaplin scrambling through the machinery in "Modern Times" without realizing that what made him funny for millions was that it was their real experience.

Jack Flynn relished rewarding his pets and harrying his goats. He had refined the disbursement of petty rewards and punishments to an art. When an editor on the news desk had done marking up a piece of copy, he'd hold the take aloft in his hand, from which we'd snatch it. Sometimes, if the editor had sufficient rank he'd simply stare at Flynn. This gave Flynn one of his pleasures. It allowed him to simply yell "You!" and point, picking on any of us arbitrarily. This tossed the rhythm of the bench out of order and threw us off stride, setting each against all. It thoroughly delighted Flynn. As a countermeasure, one had to keep an occasional eye on the editors to make sure a nod was not in the offing. More practically, we set up a sub-rhythm where every eighth turn someone was the designated eyes and if the nod was given, a quick elbow along the line alerted us all to look up.

To move the copy from the news desk out of turn also meant an extra trip to the composing room, located on the second floor, and then back up to the newsroom on the third floor. The composing room was a maelstrom of grousing printers, clacking linotype machines and harried assistants known as "devils" who seemed to be perennially about to drop the heavy type-filled chases they were carrying. Our job was to bring the stories to the copy-cutter, a superannuated printer who would distribute the copy to his men at the linotype machines, ostensibly in a rational manner but more likely than not giving the easy stuff to his friends, the onerous jobs to the vulnerable and the up-front stories to the steadiest hands or whoever was most sober.

The copy-cutter himself usually reeked of alcohol and foul cigars. His attitude toward copy boys ranged from casually contemptuous to overtly hostile. Our brief encounters were exacerbated when an editor marked something RUSH, a red flag for the copy-cutter who used it as an opportunity to hold forth on the manhood and intelligence of the editors and their minions and guarantee that the story would wend its way snail-like through the process. The editor, of course, never had to countenance this and could turn on the copy boy if the type didn't readily appear. Somehow, the copy boy, who had as much clout as an enemy messenger before a pagan king, was responsible to plea for the copy. It was like an Irish funeral where two sets of feuding relatives send increasingly vitriolic messages back and forth through an anxious child. On the plus side, once out of sight of Flynn we could disappear down the back elevator, sneak outside for a smoke, kill five minutes and blame it on a copy-cutter who'd kept us waiting. Flynn always had to cede to someone else who was beating on us. And it was impossible to monitor anyone in the chaos of the composing room.

Oddly enough, Flynn's greatest delight turned out to be mine as well: extra duty on the food run. The newspaper was surrounded by a network of saloons and a food run at the paper involved making the rounds of several hash houses plus separate detours for rum which, for many of The Mirror's denizens, was a primary source of nourishment. The result, if one wasn't careful, could be a mix-up of orders, food coming late or booze not delivered or served wrong. Any such misdemeanor might result in a concordance of angry writers demanding the head of the poor wretch responsible. You could misplace a page proof and survive but God help anyone who got someone's burger medium instead of rare.

The booze runs were particularly dicey. For a time, when too many liver ailments decimated the rewrite bank, liquor was proscribed at The Mirror, which was like banning oxygen from the Earth. So we had to stop off at the adjacent Mirror Bar, a dense, narrow oval emanating fumes of tobacco, alcohol and greasy fries. It was frequented by the printers but resorted to in extremis by reporters and a few of the gamier photographers. I never actually saw the bar. It was lined two and three deep with men in blue coveralls wearing paper hats. They'd pass your order overhead hand over hand from the bartender who was hidden somewhere in the back. We had to order squirts, or coke bottles filled with gin, rum or whiskey in precise quantities for each needy soul upstairs. By an improvised marking system of stickers, we assigned each squirt to the appropriate scribe. Considering that the order was given in a smoky crowd of noisy, mettlesome, inebriated printers it was nothing short of miraculous that it came out straight.

I liked going out on the food runs because you could be gone for a very long time and there was no way that Flynn could keep track. It was a throw-me-in-the-briar-patch situation. You wanted to be out just long enough to catch the night air but not so long that the natives turned on you. I enjoyed noodling around Second Avenue—much more raffish then than today. I was fond of strolling by places like The Pen & Pencil and imagining all the great journalistic chat going on at the tables (actually no one ordered from there and I never knew a newspaperman who admitted to going inside). But it was the desolate spots that most fascinated me. The streets around The Mirror, certainly toward Third Avenue, were then still somewhat shabby, commercial, abandoned in the evening, murky. The shadow of the torn-down Third Avenue El hovered over the neighborhood. A remnant of the Irish poor had not yet been rooted out. At the Mirror Bar there was one old lady who took a shine to me because she thought I looked like a young Owney Madden, the notorious Irish criminal and local folk hero who she fancied had red hair, as I did. The printers liked the old girl and some of it rubbed off on me so they treated me well enough and the bartender—who I'm not sure I ever did see, but must have seen me— made sure I got the right order.

On foggy, mildewed nights, which it often seemed to be, the lampposts emitted a murky violet glow bathing the streets in an eerie purple, like a precursor for Gotham in "Batman." It was faintly oppressive and, with a little imagination, menacing. The place that epitomized this for me was the Bickford's on 45th and Second. Going inside there was like walking into the interior of an Edward Hopper. It made "Nighthawks" look like the Stork Club. I went there for a writer named Dick Wilson who liked the eggs — they laid on a lot of ketchup which made me slightly nauseous. Although it troubled me to go to Bickford's because it was so dreary, the place had its perverse fascinations. I've seen pictures of

8

the eatery's cantilevered white facade in architecture books evoking nostalgia for the years around the war. The authors should have been inside one of these joints on a weekday midnight in January.

My peers at The Mirror could have been the crew of an urban Pequod. Val Cardinale, cherub-cheeked and earnest from St. John's, would submit high-minded treatises to the editorial page (The Mirror was the only major newspaper where the copy boys could write editorials.) Russ Tansey, a part-time philosophy major who did not seem hopeful about the human condition, would disappear every so often on a bender. (Flynn gave Russ a lot of slack, recognizing a kindred spirit who'd gone down the track a bit faster with less control.) Phil Nicolaedes, the Greek actor, an Apollo look-alike, a bit older than the rest of us, dipped in and out of the job as his roles required. One day, in an altercation whose origins I forget, Phil denounced Flynn as a bully and a bootlicker which brought down the curtain on his copy-boy career but not his acting one—I read his obit recently and was glad to see that Phil achieved a life in the theater. Then there was Nick Basile who, at the time, showed no particular interest in journalism and was the only one of our night crew besides myself to make it to The New York Times, where he had a long and honorable career as a makeup editor.

There was another fellow who, because of seniority, sycophancy or a bit of both, was allowed to work the police radio till one day he breathlessly reported that a Roosevelt had been rushed to Lenox Hill Hospital, sending a squad of Mirror Radio cars there to discover that it was actually someone named Lenox who'd been rushed to Roosevelt Hospital. No one mourned for him.

The level-headed one was Artie Oshins who seemed to have earned the confidence of the news desk. Had The Mirror not folded, he might have actually had a career on the paper if a life there could be considered such. He knew everyone's tics and was the Charles Bickford character in the prison movies who would warn you at the outset about which screws to watch out for.

And there was my friend Tom Hyland who reminded me of the movie actor Richard Conte. Tom didn't look like him—quite the opposite—he was rangy, crew-cut, an Irish, pug-nosed, blue-eyed boy, but he had that immeasurable cool that Richard Conte exuded whether playing a G.I. or a gangster. Tom let you know that he could finesse his way into and out of any situation, and he had great knowledge of the world.

I liked Tom's attitude and I tried to model myself after him. We hung out together and on Saturday nights I'd walk over with him to attend the printers' mass at St. Agnes on 43rd Street off Third. It was held at 2 A.M. after the pressmen got off work from The Mirror and The News so they wouldn't have to wake up in the morning for Sunday services. It is in such humane ways that The Church kept its flock in the fold. The pews, well named in this case, reeked like a distillery. Distributing the wine—even symbolically—struck me as redundant. But the printers found the service agreeable; it made everyone feel good and Tom, although he affected to not having much use for the Church, attended for atavistic reasons. I came to appreciate the scene, all the mysteries and the chalices and the vestments and the priest and the whiff of incense, which I considered more pagan than Christian.

Hazing was not limited to copy boys. It was ubiquitous. People on top were expected to abuse their underlings, most particularly those directly below, to remind them who the boss was; failure to do so was a sign of weakness, a loss of nerve that could lead to disrespect and breakdown. The paradigm for such dynamics— Human Relations 101 in The Mirror School of Journalism—was the relationship between the city editor, Ed Markel, and his deputy, Norman Miller. They sat opposite each other along the news desk and it was Miller's task to pre-read the copy before handing it to Markel for final approval. Markel was a growler whose rumble grew by decibels like a train coming through a tunnel. You could hear the wheels churning as he stoked his anger, the inevitable roar as he rolled over his victim and then a hiss of steam at the end. Markel would generally start a conversation with his deputy by gingerly lifting a piece of copy Miller had just handed him as if it were bat guano, then toss it back toward Miller paper-airplane style with a snort. Markel had this down so that the paper wafted glider-like toward Miller's side of the desk. Then he'd fix Miller with a stare of withering contempt, stage-sigh in exasperation and begin, low and slow (but not low enough to miss being heard by anyone within earshot): "You dumb, stupid, son-of-a-bitch . . . " And then, in rising four-letter crescendo, he'd detail why Miller had failed yet again, allowed this or that to get through; that it was a wonder anything got done with Miller around.

Depending on the infraction, Miller might briefly try to defend himself but this only got Markel into higher dudgeon, so eventually, Miller desisted and just sat there, smiling—it was a death's head grin—while Markel eviscerated him. Miller was an ex-Marine, stocky, bull-necked, still in good shape; he could have leaped over the desk and throttled Markel but never did. He just sat there, taking it. His being an ex-Marine actually helped Markel since Miller was trained to respect authority, accept intensive abuse from on high without flinching and take pride in his ability to do so without whining, which to him was a sign of manhood.

It was said that Markel owed Miller money and that he dealt with his guilt by defying his creditor. Was Miller a lousy editor? Doubtful. He was neither more nor less competent than most of his peers and certainly met the standards of his time and place. Of course, Markel never fired Miller. He relished having Norman around. If Miller left, Markel would have had to find a new Norman. And the qualities of character for such work—fear, guilt, cravenness, uncertainty, expediency, stoicism, desperation—are qualifications that are not on a resume and can't be taught but must be intuited by managers and then developed gradually. Editors love their punching bags. This was a timeless and universal truth on every newspaper I worked for. Markel and Miller were archetypes, not exceptions.

Oddly enough, the night editors were a little more collegial, or less choleric, than the day shift. The nicest of the lot were Pete Berrechia and Mark Marchesi who filled the same slots in the evening that Miller and Markel did earlier, playing the good angels to the dayside demons. Generally, the night side, where a great deal of the nitty-gritty got done, had a less frenetic atmosphere than the dayside. There were, in effect, two newspapers and the feeling of the night side when the day editors went home was generally a sigh of relief that they were gone "and now we can put the paper out." Mind you, we copy boys weren't going to get a "thank you" or a "please"—such politesse would have been mistrusted and misinterpreted; these people, after all, were giving us orders—but the edge was off and if there was upset, it was usually tied to a reason, not the eruption of some personal volcano.

The Adler brothers were replaced at night by Cy Stern— a phlegmatic fellow who smoked a Sherlock Holmes pipe and reminded me of Sparks, the laconic radio operator of a doomed vessel, playing chess on the wireless as the ship went down—and

Mort Ehrman, the night managing editor. Mort, a little guy, half bantam, half bird-dog, became a star at the Mirror when, legend had it, he spotted the fighter Gene Tunney emerging from City Hall amid one of his marriages, and tried to conduct an interview while pulling open a limousine door that the ex-champ was attempting to slam closed on Mort's foot. It was The Mirror way. I'm not sure if Ehrman got the interview, unless the stream of vituperation issuing from Tunney counted—and why shouldn't it at The Mirror?—but the image of the paper's intrepid gamecock going mano a mano with the former heavyweight demonstrated sufficient acuity and reportorial prowess to vault Ehrman to high editorial office. Doubtless what impressed the powers was Ehrman's calculation that if Tunney took a poke at him he would have killed Ehrman on the spot and been charged with murder on his wedding day. Love and Death, what a story.

By my time, Ehrman had aged a bit and was now a sage character, balding (everybody went bald differently at the Mirror), ferret-eyed and sporting a gravelly Brooklyn accent. One of the consolations of most newspapers in those days was that they were produced by people who were at one with their readers. The editors didn't need focus groups because they were focus groups. Like their readers, they played the horses, went to the fights and read the funnies. They studied The Mirror racing form, devoured Dan Parker on boxing and followed Joe Palooka in the comics. If they liked it, so would the readers.

The top of The Mirror food chain was Hinson Stiles, the managing editor, and Glen Neville, the editor-in-chief. I always thought they were WASP ringers brought in for the sound of their names to give the tab respectability and deal with the corporate types at Hearst. For several weeks after my arrival, I spotted a scruffy, white-maned, beefy codger in sneakers, lurking around the elevator banks taking home bags of food and newspaper bundles. I thought he was one of the crazy old types who hung out at The Mirror and got handouts from the staff. It was only after I noticed him one evening rummaging in the front-lobby waste basket and asked one of the night-siders if they wanted me to shoo him off that I was told it was Hinson Stiles, that he was the managing editor and to let him alone. No one ever explained his behavior to me or thought they had to. It might have been a small compulsion or he could have been a bit of a pack rat. It was harmless enough, he never got in anyone's way and, given the level of pathology in that place, it was a tick that people took in stride. Some years later,

I read in the trade journal Editor and Publisher that Stiles had been injured after being dropped by an elephant on a visit to Ceylon. The elephant was picking up the visitor with its trunk, a trick performed for the benefit of tourists, but the portly Stiles seemed to be too much for the creature who dispensed with its burden summarily. While this item might have given one pause, I found it perfectly in keeping with the mystique that emanated from the Mirror in its various permutations.

Glen Neville was a different matter. With a countenance that would not have been out of place on Mount Rushmore, Neville was as perfect-looking an editor-in-chief as I've ever seen. Most of the others were out-of-shape, cartoonish types, but Neville was the real thing. I never was quite sure what Neville actually did; once I saw him mark up a few galleys, and I was told that he composed some of the editorials that Val Cardinale didn't write. But it wasn't for the likes of me to question the doings of the great.

Actually, my relationship was not with Neville, but with his daughter, Mousey, who was about five years old at the time. One of my jobs was to carry the first edition down to the Neville residence—apartments on the first floor of a toney building on the southeast corner of Gramercy Park. Since The Mirror was too cheap to pay for a subway, much less a cab, I'd hike down the 22 blocks from the office to the Nevilles, rain or sleet, always making sure to keep the papers dry. When I arrived at the building, I would stamp my boots on the hallway mat, trek down the corridor and ring the bell; after a pause, while I stood there damp, Mousey materialized and, deftly ignoring me, would snatch the papers from my glove, trill a "thank you" into the air ever so politely, and shut the door in my face. What Mousey understood perfectly even then, bless her five-year-old Waspy heart, was that there was a world of distinction between her class and mine and, at her tender age, she was giving me a lesson in that difference.

The columnists were an outsize version of the editors; they were expected to act out and be bigger than life. They didn't spend much time in the office and it was rare that we got to see their faces. One night while answering the phones on the city desk, I got a call from a drunk who wanted to know the winner of the third at Rockingham. I responded in the time-honored fashion by telling the caller he could find out by buying the paper. Sometimes, if they were nice, we'd go look but if we were busy or they were nasty, we'd hang up. This one was nasty; also he was so far gone that it was hard to hear him, which was probably a good thing because he was assaulting the English language and threatening to do likewise to me. I hung up. He called back. He told me he was our celebrity columnist Nick Kenny—a common ploy—and asked who I was. I told him I was Ed Sullivan and hung up. He called back again and told me he'd have me fired if I didn't give him the winner of the third at Rockingham. I told him it was Whirlaway and hung up.

By chance, Jack Flynn chose that moment to send me on an errand. I came back a short while later and that's when I first got a look at Nick Kenny in the flesh. He appeared not only older than the standing photo in his column—they all did—but like a grotesque of it. His cheeks were a blotch, further reddened by the fact that he was in high choler. In my absence, he had charged the phone desk and threatened to disembowel the wretch who had replaced me and had no idea why he was being attacked. Because innocence was irrelevant in these situations the poor devil was simply trying to appease the dragon. Flynn himself was confused, knowing neither the source nor the nature of the infraction and, since Kenny was spouting a froth of obscene gibberish, he was only adding to the confusion. All they could make out was that something bad had happened to Nick Kenny in the general vicinity of the phones but the old who-what-why-and-how was something Kenny, in his rage, or out of it probably, was incapable of conveying. I returned in time to see Kenny's nephew, Rich —one of the wags on the copy desk whose imitations of his uncle I subsequently grew to savor—steer the old boy out of the city room with the promise that the miscreant would be duly impaled. No one ever figured out what happened, ascribing it to one of Nick Kenny's boozy rages.

Lee Mortimer was another stalwart Mirror columnist in whose circles I didn't travel. Mortimer's claim to infamy was a vindictive, score-settling column that festered into "New York Confidential," the forerunner of the modern tell-all poisonography. When it came to character assassination, innuendo and sexpose, Mortimer wrote the book. My dealings with Mortimer consisted of dropping the Bulldog Edition off at his place at the Beaux Arts apartments. I usually rang the bell and left the paper on the doormat although I recall one time he (or someone who looked like him) appeared in a dressing gown and nodded brusquely by way of acknowledgment. I don't know why these people didn't use their doormen but, for whatever reason, they insisted on getting their papers direct from the copy boys. Maybe it gave them a sense of connectedness to the paper, that we somehow or other left a whiff of the city room. Mostly, it was just power, having the clout to make The Mirror send a boy over to their place with the paper.

Then there was Walter Winchell. By the time I got to see him he was over-the-hill and well on his richly deserved slide into oblivion at a paper that was itself well into a state of decline. What was sad was that he pretended nothing had changed. And, as far as I could tell, he actually believed all that stuff about the romance of journalism. On a newspaper that was cynical even by the standards of city-room cynicism, Winchell was like a wide-eyed high-school girl from Kansas. He actually used words like "scoop" in the city room and sounded excited about it. Though I'm not sure that at this stage he was doing much more than signing off on the fluff, flummery and flackery that made up his column.

Early one spring evening as the first edition was closing, the great man came roaring in with his Winchell hat cocked, tie akimbo, planted himself in front of the copy desk, one hand out in front of him like an oath-taking Horatio and yelled: "Stop the Presses!" All heads went down—it was like a take-cover drill flawlessly executed—but not before a few incredulous stares. Sam Susskind, the copy chief, was a prudent man who handled Winchell with the tact that the sanitarium doctor shows to Blanche DuBois. He asked matter-of-factly what the news event was and Winchell breathlessly went into a lather about a little girl who'd just been run over on Second Avenue and got her legs banged up; he'd seen it himself.

Given The Mirror's votive commitment to rape, mayhem, disaster, divorce, scandal, spicy sex, the peccadillos of the rich, the misfortunes of the poor and racy photos (our daily blondes were generally chestier; the News's blondes were leggier), this was not exactly front-page news by our standards, or anyone else's. But Susskind was a prince. "We'll send a reporter right over, Walter," he said. "And a photographer," Winchell reminded him. "Before the ambulance comes." "And a photographer," Sam said. "We'll make the bulldog?" Winchell asked. "We'll give it our best shot," Sam said. Winchell hopped out of there like a rabbit on coke. Everyone on the desk was staring straight down at their pencils. There were a few sniggers but Susskind stared them down. After Winchell had trotted off, Sam walked over to the news desk and had a word with Cy Stern. The next day, we actually carried a small item deep in the well of the paper on the accident. Many years later I learned from Winchell's biographer Neal Gabler while he was writing his book that, as a kid, Winchell had been hit by a car and got his leg banged up. Winchell was, by all accounts, an awful human being, but he was like one of those producers who believed every line in his own movies even though he'd seen all the artifice and muck that had gone into their making.

As at any tabloid worth its spice, the soul of the Mirror was the rewrite bank, a cranky, capricious, tormented and talented collection of dissolute spirits. Their names out of central casting— Jim Donohue, Pete Houlihan, Dick Wilson—they slouched over their typewriters like a travesty of Melville's harpooners. There was also Don Paneth who was considered the house intellectual because he read novels instead of the racing form. Also he didn't drink but brought a sandwich from home. This would have made him an object of derision except that The Mirror, in its tolerance of aberrant behavior, allowed even for the deviance of primness.

And there was the legendary Harry Altshuler, master of the rewrite bank, who could turn the dross of other papers into tinsel in a twinkling. Harry looked as if he'd been embalmed by an inept apprentice. Slicked hair, deadpan eyes, a face drained of emotion, Altshuler had a pallor that was meant for the blue fluorescence of poolrooms; it was as if he had lived indoors for 50 years. If Harry smiled he kept it to himself. But that bleached neutrality provided a perfect conduit for whatever muck The Mirror was serving up that day. While the great rewrite men have different styles, they all maintain that distance from the news, a certain emotional asbestos that enables them to get close to the heat of a story but not consumed by it. Al Aronowitz could affect a Jewish, schmaltzy sensibility at The Post, Bob McFadden had a more cerebral approach at The Times, Like piano virtuosos, although their interpretations were idiosyncratic, their command of the craft emanated from a special talent that is as teachable at journalism schools as writing string quartets. Harry Altshuler had the touch. He burned with the cold fire of a lesser hell.

At The Mirror there was a lot to rewrite. There were reasons for the familiar double bylines of that era. Most of our police reporters were more policemen than reporters. They hung out in the police shacks which were then in all the boroughs, played cards with the cops or each other, tried to do as little work as possible and knew their way around. When something big happened or, more likely, if another paper was on to something that might get them embarrassed, they scrambled to cover their hides. Better yet, to knock down the piece—demonstrate that it was invalid, that the opposition had gotten it wrong. This could backfire. The wisest course was to leave it for the night side to follow with just sufficient dust to prove they'd worked the story, but not so much effort that they'd get sucked into following it themselves. They could then repair to the nearest watering hole, priding themselves on having started the engine. The front-page nonsense was for the movies.

There was a certain blue-collar pragmatism in their approach abetted by the idea that newspapers were just another industry where you worked your shift as light as possible and clocked out as soon as you could. You owed the bosses nothing and they owed you less. It was only a later generation of more affluent dedicated journalists for whom the profession was "fun" and a calling, who soldiered on into the wee hours for glory. In this world they would have been considered oddballs. The pattern held true at City Hall and most other beats. Few of these reporters considered themselves writers, much less stylists, and their job was simply to feed whatever they had over the phone as quickly and imaginatively as possible to whoever was on the other end, who was in turn supposed to transform it deftly into saleable newspaper copy.

Accuracy was relative and on The Mirror, it was more relative than elsewhere, with both reporter and rewriter adding novelistic seasoning according to taste. No one's ego was hurt if the rewrite man changed the words because the reporter wasn't writing anything in the first place; he was reporting. This resulted in a reasonable division of labor. The guy who sliced the pastrami didn't expect to be the waiter. It was only in later years when the two jobs were collapsed into one that "writers" became touchy about their prose being altered. A reporter who thought himself a stylist whose copy was sacrosanct would've been marked as a prima donna. The double byline was, at the low end, a two-man donkey act, but at the high end, an acrobatic team of great skill and daring.

The Mirror reporting staff was composed of not so much writers as characters. Oddly enough, the paper had kept a number of women reporters after the war when more "responsible" papers, such as The Times gave the jobs back to the returning men. At the time this was seen not as a badge of progress but a mark of further fecklessness. The Mirror, because of its very perverseness, utilized its women not as sob sisters like The Post's Fern Marja Eckmann but as real reporters like the redoubtable Ara Piastro. Not being "serious" gave The Mirror a lot more freedom than its more austere competitors.

One of the most memorable characters on the paper's staff was Jim Donohue who will remain, for me, the model of a rewrite man—at least The Mirror version. To be sure, Jim didn't have a particularly light touch at the keyboard or a deft way with leg men. I can't recall that he did any memorable stories; his name certainly doesn't come to mind when Mirror alumni invoke the past. But Jim—a lanky Irishman who clanked doggedly at the typewriter, kept his whiskey defiantly in the open bottom drawer of his desk and shouted into a headset out of the Nuremburg trials that never fit properly on his curly red hair—epitomized for me the inspired hacks and frustrated talents who in those days made up the core of the rewrite ranks. Jim sported a coat that, like its owner, had a distinct personality: frayed, scruffy, dangling, field-green with brownish tweeding threatening to unravel. It looked as if it had been lifted from a dead German grenadier in World War I and then recycled through several pawn shops before landing on Jim. Generally, he hung it up and people didn't hang their coats right next to it so it always had a lot of room on the rack. Jim could be testy and editors gave him a wide berth. Half dervish, half-drudge, Jim would chafe at the reporter on the other end of the phone while simultaneously staring down the editor who was nagging him to produce a story.

As indicated, Jim drank a lot and sometimes a little more than a lot. For this to be noticed at The Mirror meant a prodigious amount. In those days, downing a few on the job didn't raise any eyebrows. Jim O'Neill, the police reporter at Newsday would often have liquor on his breath but it was treated convivially and with a certain bonhomie. Several years later at a much prissier New York Times, Al Clark, an old cop reporter, too often had too much and was considered embarrassing. I never had a problem talking to Al—I understood that whatever his chemical disabilities, he thought the place, not he, had gone crazy, and he acted this out. He became the very Mr. Hyde that a new breed of editors dreaded. At some level he relished playing the bogeyman of their worst overachieving nightmares. At Newsday, the editor-in-chief, Bill McIlwain, would engage staffers at three-martini lunches that were short discourses on the art of writing and the craft of journalism. I don't know how good his judgment or energy level was when he got back. As times changed it cost him his job; he went on the wagon and proceeded to run some other papers with greater rigor. ("I no longer suffer fools gladly," he observed.)

Not everyone could always handle it, although Donohue acquitted himself well enough while working. Off-duty was sometimes another matter. One of the tales told of Jim was an after-hours foray into Penn Station where, as legend had it, he was sighted at a revolving General Motors display featuring a Cadillac, a Buick and a Chevy. Jim, always top of the line, was driving the Caddy. According to the cops who told our guys the story, he was shouting "News-Mirror! News-Mirror!" No one could quite make out what this meant but it obviously had some import for Donohue. In those days, a newspaperman on a binge would get no worse than a Dutch-uncle talk and some black coffee. And what's the harm in driving drunk without a license if the car can't move? When it was discovered that Jim was a Mirror rewrite man, the cops reportedly gave him an escort home.

The Mirror managed to cover world events for its million daily readers in its own inimitable way. While The Times fussed with foreign bureaus and diplomatic correspondents, The Mirror perfected the craft of rip-read-and-rewrite. Moreover, practicing recombinant journalism on prose that was already partially in English was a light lift. Getting a foreign story off the wires provided a bon-bon for the rewrite bank. The trick was to make it short and colorful. While the broadsheets concentrated on news of political and economic import, The Mirror kept its eye out for juicy political scandals abroad—and there was always a British cabinet minister with a racy sex life who was willing to oblige. If the general rule for the serious papers in their foreign report was to stress politics and downplay natural disasters, The Mirror reversed the process. A train wreck in Jakarta or a hotel fire in Singapore was something that Mirror readers could identify with. In effect, it treated the world as one great police blotter.

Typical was the Mirror's coverage of a state visit to the U.N. in December 1957 by the Saudi monarch Ibn Saud. While The Times and The Trib were worrying themselves about the balance of power in the Middle East and the price of oil, The Mirror focused its energies on Ibn Saud's harem at the Waldorf. Under a headline that read, "Y'Know About U.S. Girls? / Well, Harems Scare 'Em," the Mirror ran a story by an intrepid woman reporter who'd putatively investigated harem life. Should any female Mirror reader have illusions of an idyllic existence as odalisque to a pasha, our Nellie Bly debunked the myth of exotic harem life, warning instead that the reality was more akin to "cell-block A in the women's penitentiary." Accompanying the story was a prominently displayed photo of an Arab potentate, identified as Ibn Sam glaring out at the reader, with a bushy black mustache, fiery dark eyes, a white kaffiyeh somewhat askew and an uncanny resemblance to Sam Susskind, the Mirror copy chief. Perhaps this was a near-relative of the Saudi ruler if not the King himself, in a caption that could have easily been misread by The Mirror audience as Ibn Saud.

Now Susskind, a Brooklyn native, had what in those crustier times might have been considered a somewhat Semitic face. Presumably, so did the King, whatever he looked like. Moreover, they would have been about the same age, and shared a certain portly dignity, a weightiness and substance that were attributes of maturity, authority and good living. Moreover, Sam was a good company man and would do whatever was necessary to advance the paper's interests. Ever since then, Susskind was known as Ibn Sam or, to the more literate, Susskind of Arabia. Years later, when I was City Editor at Newsday, long after The Mirror's demise, I got a call from the publicity director of Nassau Community College complaining about some malfeasance we had inflicted on the school. My secretary told me the PR man's name was Sam Susskind. I got on the phone and said, deadpan: "Is this Ibn Sam?" End of complaint.

Each of New York City's seven newspapers back then had its delivery trucks painted in distinctive colors. The Mirror's color was red. I got to ride in one of these vehicles during a transit strike in the winter of 1957–58. The subways and buses were out, I couldn't get a cab at 1 A.M. to drive to the Bronx and I couldn't afford one in any case. If The Mirror made accommodations for its staff, no one told me, and I'd doubt it. In those rough-and-tumble times it was every man for himself. So I waited an hour and hitched a ride with one of the truck drivers going up to the Bronx. His route started at West Farms and continued along White Plains Road taking him within a few blocks of my building. In exchange, we agreed on the fiction that I'd help him toss out the papers along his route.

For the late edition the trucks went out from 2 to 3 A.M. Between 4 and 5 A.M. the morning papers were dropped in front of candy stores, subway kiosks and newspaper stands through the farthest reaches of the outer boroughs so they'd be there when the owners opened for business at 6 A.M. Most candy stores had a little wooden newspaper stand attached to their façades so customers could pick up their morning paper and toss the change into a cigar box on the outside window counter. Everyone had their own favorite store and their own favorite paper, sometimes two. Theft—of either the bundles or the boxes—did not seem to be a problem, or at least a sufficiently pressing one, to change the system. Later on, when safety became an issue, the unions pressed for two men on a truck, which management considered featherbedding and the drivers insisted was security. They were probably both right. But at this time, at least in the trucks I rode, there was only a driver so he didn't mind a little company.

I made sure to wind up quickly during those nights so as not to miss my ride, making a dash for the delivery bins where the last papers were still rolling off the presses. Subway stoppages usually took place in January to greet a new mayor and for maximum public discomfiture. The paper's bin platforms were open to the street so that coming down from the editorial department you were greeted by a blast of cold air that I found liberating because it signaled freedom from the coils of the city room. The ramps were a scene of controlled chaos. Mailers were sorting the bundles and tossing them onto the trucks where the drivers stacked them. The union was rigorous about who could do what. An assortment of security cops, pressmen, union reps, paper handlers and various hangers-on all milled about in heavy sweaters and thick jackets, smoking and joking, rubbing their open-tipped gloved hands for warmth, shouting orders decipherable only to themselves. When my truck was full I climbed aboard a block away, and we were off.

There was snow on the ground which seemed to get fresher and deeper as we left Manhattan and rumbled into the Bronx. The cab of the truck had a sliding door to make it easier for the operator to toss the bundles but my driver preferred to keep it closed, maintaining that he got fewer drafts that way. We trundled along at a brisk pace, our breaths steaming, the moon waning, the wheels crunching over new snow. The empty streets glistened along Morris Park Avenue where the Christmas lights tarried after the holiday, and the cab offered a certain coziness. I made a final drop near White Plains Road and walked the rest of the way, adrenaline pumping and oblivious to the cold.

If The Mirror's trucks were fun, the real thrill was riding in its radio cars. They looked like police cars with a siren on the roof except they were painted a deep red to distinguish them from the two-tone cop vehicles. There was less distinction between them and the fire-chief wheels and The Mirror used this to good advantage in getting an edge on the competition at fire stories, or just getting back to the office quicker. One got a great rush careening down city thoroughfares with The Mirror siren howling at full blast and traffic making way on either side, while racing toward an assignment—usually having no urgency whatsoever.

I had the chance to enjoy such a ride on the occasion of a Hearst Milk Fund benefit. The Mirror sponsored an annual gala to raise money for the city's poor, which was only fair since it spent the rest of its time exploiting them. This year's extravaganza was to be held at a black-tie premiere at Radio City. The movie was "The Prince and the Showgirl" starring Marilyn Monroe and Laurence Olivier as a noble who falls for a commoner—one of his more forgettable roles. The Mirror had thrown its entire culture staff— admittedly, a contradiction in terms—into this one. Film critics, society writers and, most importantly, its formidable photographers, which is where I came in. The event was supposed to take up the entire picture centerfold of the next day's Mirror and the paper had assigned one of its camera aces, Barney Coons, for the job. Even among the photographers, an anarchic lot whose world-view bordered on terminal nihilism, Barney was a hard case. He fancied himself a recorder of mayhem—the grizzlier the better—and disdained the celebrity assignments which he considered the purview of poofters. To say he bridled at this task put it mildly.

Barney's job was to shoot all the celebrities as they entered the Radio City lobby for the premier with his Speed Graphic flash. To accomplish this, the newspaper provided Coons the aforementioned Mirror radio car, and me. My job was two-fold: first, to identify the celebs as they pulled up on Sixth Avenue so Barney could position himself and not waste shots; second, midway through this exercise of flash and flesh, I was to grab the plates from his camera and run them back to the office for an early edition, while Barney soldiered on, roaming inside the building for more targets. The job was literally a milk run, since there was no competition and not much of a challenge. But at The Mirror nothing was a sure thing.

Barney liked to lift a glass even more than most of his breed and, at show time, he seemed to have disappeared. I was sent to find him. I made the rounds of a few of his favorite saloons. By a stroke of luck, I actually stumbled upon him in The Gondola Bar on Third Avenue. He was stretched out on a red leather banquette in the back of the establishment, where he seemed quite at home. I tried to urge Coons up but he shook me off, which made me anxious fearing that I'd be blamed if he failed to show. But the old adage about God looking after fools and drunkards proved true and the manager of the Gondola came to my rescue. With the alacrity of someone who had performed this drill more than once, he bent over Barney and murmured in his ear. Like something out of a horror movie, Coons bolted upright as if he'd been zapped by lightning and, without blinking, turned to me and snapped: "Come on sonny! Whaddaya waiting for?" He slurped a coffee awaiting him at the bar, grabbed his camera and we were on our way.

A Mirror radio car was double-parked around the corner on 45th Street. We took off with a whoosh. It was like being in the Batmobile. Siren blowing, elbow on the horn, Barney was barreling through midtown traffic. We only had nine blocks to traverse but I thought even this was too far to go without a crackup. The only thing that saved us was that cars actually did pull over in the mistaken belief that Coons was a fire chief on his way to a three-alarmer. I realized with awe and queasiness that Coons had done this before. In the midst of our trip we were stopped at a light—itself a miracle—when who should pass by but Eddie Condon, one of my jazz idols, who was weaving around Sixth Avenue. "Mr. Coons," I said. "That's Eddie Condon." "Well get out of the car and help him," he ordered. "Can't you see the man is drunk." I emerged from the car and offered my services to Condon but he waved me off and weaved on. "Some people can't hold their liquor," Coons observed.

The episode seemed to have calmed him down because we arrived at Radio City without further incident and Barney became a testy but competent professional. He double-parked near a police barrier and we barreled through to the clearing under the theater's marquee. (Although righting wrongs is what many journalists say drew them to the profession, it's safe to say that more than a few are driven by the sheer high of access—getting past police barriers or on the presidential plane or to opening night.)

The police had set up saw-horses all around the entrance and a crowd was already milling beyond them. The Mirror had sprung for klieg lights, which lit up the sky above Radio City. The first starlets started drifting in and Barney sent me to check out the talent as the cavalcade of limousines slowed down and backed up. My task was to spot the license plates of hired cars for wannabes and stick my neck inside likely limos looking for big fish. Ava

Gardner was supposed to show up and I was to alert Coons the minute she appeared.

But the prize catch was Marilyn Monroe. She had recently left Joe DiMaggio and married Arthur Miller, and was at the height of her fame and notoriety. The crowd was milling and lowing in anticipation. One did not get the impression of individual faces, but rather a many-headed beast, pawing the ground before a charge. A few Hearst executives, be-frocked wives in tow, glided through, followed by a cluster of the usual society types who always seemed to turn up at such things. In their wake came a smattering of minor actors and the feeder fish of publicity and production folk who glom on to these events, all drifting through with airs of alternating self-consciousness and self-importance.

Still no Marilyn and, as the evening wore on the herd grew restless. A few shouts of "Where's Marilyn," went up, followed by chants of "We Want Marilyn." The crowd now felt it had earned the right to catch a glimpse of the star and the management was somehow reneging on its part of the bargain. Rhythmic applause began, akin to the audience in a movie theater demonstrating when the projection machine falters. Any late-coming minor celebs who had the misfortune to arrive now were startled by a chorus of disconcerting boos, unaware of what they'd done to antagonize their audience. The cops, growing edgy, were fingering their clubs.

And then, like Venus rising from her shell, Marilyn emerged from a caramel-custard limo. She was sheathed in a green-sequined gown with deep cleavage. Her sleevelessness was a costume in itself: white shoulders, creamy bare arms melting into long green gloves. Her flaxen hair fluffed out in a sunburst. She smiled, showing those glistening teeth, vamping for an adoring throng. She was gorgeous and she knew it. This was, after all, not a movie but the real thing, a live performance, a prologue to the rock concerts of a generation later where talent was overtaken by an otherworldly persona imposed on the superstar so that entertainment was no longer diversion but worship.

Marilyn seemed to understand all this intuitively and toy with it, like a knowing vestal. Trailing three feet behind her, a net hanging aft a trawler, was her latest spouse, Arthur Miller. He wore a summer white tuxedo jacket and looked as dazed as she looked dazzling. His horn-rimmed glasses, the mark of an intellectual, seemed out of place in all that eye-popping density. So here he was, one of America's greatest living dramatists, playing second-banana— make that tenth banana—to a movie queen. I wondered what he was thinking.

At the time, it was all I could do to keep abreast of Barney who was kneeling down to snap Marilyn as she swept through. She was only a few feet from us when she gave her fans a little toss of the head, so that a zephyr managed to flick through her golden hair. The crowd went wild and a few of the more brazen and agile and younger devotees broke through, whether to touch her or get autographs or snatch a sequin. The cops closed in and there was a brief scuffle. Marilyn, emerged unscathed and sailed past as if nothing happened. Arthur Miller followed on. Coons, meanwhile, was cursing the proverbial blue streak. In the melee, someone had knocked into him and he'd muffed the shot of Marilyn making her grand entrance. From The Mirror's point of view, we had next to nothing. Near apoplectic, he gave me his photo plates and ordered: "I gotta go in and get Marilyn. Wait 10 minutes for Ava; if she shows, spot her and tell me. If not, go back with the plates."

I was about to set off for my post when I heard a commotion behind me. I turned around to see that Barney was trying to struggle past a young usher at the lobby door. It seems that he had somehow lost his press pass in the confusion and the usher was telling him: "Sorry sir, but I can't admit you without a ticket or press identification." Barney was beside himself. Using every four-letter-word and combination thereof in his salty vocabulary, Coons threatened to have the usher's cojones hanging from the majestic chandeliers in Radio City's carpeted lobby if he didn't let him through. The usher was dutifully holding him at bay and they were doing a little belly dance with Coons trying to slide through the glass door and his nemesis struggling to prevent him. Finally, Coons tore lose, but in so doing somehow tore his pants above the fly; I can't figure out how this happened; it must have snagged on the usher's belt buckle, but there you have it. When last I saw Coons, he was hanging on to his zipper with one hand, his Speed-Graphic with the other, and hopping toward the Grand Staircase. Ava never showed.

I went back to The Mirror with what I had and Coons appeared about two hours later. In my absence, Barney's luck had not much improved. His only hope for recouping the evening was a staged shot after the screening. Since the movie featured Olivier playing a Ruritanian prince to Monroe's chorus girl, the publicity department at Warner's dressed up a squad of young men as chocolate soldiers and had Marilyn review each of them as they saluted her. As a parting gift she gave the last of the lot a nub on the chin and a kiss on the cheek.

It was this shot that saved the day for Barney. Or so he thought. As it turned out, he got more than he'd bargained for. The story goes that when Marilyn chucked the Ruritanian Guardist under the chin, he became discernably tumescent—at least in the photo with those tight-fitting Rudolf Friml trousers that he was required to wear. Whether or not Marilyn noticed—it was after all, a brief encounter—her soldier was definitely standing at attention. Barney loved it and so did his fellow photographers. The anxious photo editor caught between offending the publisher and a near-rebellion of his staff, passed the buck to the managing editor, Mort Ehrman. Mort, a sensible man, knew that even at The Mirror, we could go only so far, particularly with a Hearst charity event to collect money for the city's deserving poor. He decided to retouch the photo. The next day a shot of Monroe and the guardsmen made the centerfold of The Mirror, but what our readers didn't see was the original which showed that the soldier was very glad to see Marilyn.

In addition to covering cultural events, The Mirror had its own way of reporting scientific achievements. When the Russians launched their space shot with the dog Laika aboard, beginning what was to become the space race, The Times was ready with an opus by Walter Sullivan and a constellation of sidebars; the Tribune countered with Earl Ubell's memorable opening: "There'll be two moons in the sky tonight." The Mirror, of course, was blissfully unaware of any of this. The paper had already been put to bed, most of the editors had decamped, the rest—including what passed for a lobster shift—were playing poker upstairs with the photographers and were not to be disturbed. I was on the late shift and doodling about the wire room where I was gathering copy for the perusal of the morning crew. Suddenly, the bells began ringing urgently. In those days, the wire room, was an important part of any newspaper, since most papers were run on the cheap and depended in large measure for their national and foreign coverage on reports from the various news services. At The Mirror, the title of foreign editor was an oxymoron.

The wire room was a large glass-enclosed space off the city room with scores of teletypes clacking away incessantly so that the doors always had to be kept closed. Inside, there were banks of teletype machines with pride of place going to the Associated

Press (black print), followed by the United Press (a bluish purple), the International News Service, Reuters and a host of others including a separate wire for radio broadcasts. All of the big ones had separate foreign, national and local wires. The job of the copy boy entrusted with the wire room was to sort out the various files and distribute them appropriately and, most importantly, make sure that the paper roll did not run over or run out. Should either of these things happen, the reaction was not dissimilar to cave dwellers discovering that the keeper of the flame had let it expire. I had nightmares about letting a roll of paper run out without replacing it in time. Such weight was given to this task that we were usually absolved from all other chores while on wire-room duty, and if things got hot, a second boy was sent in as well.

The wire room worked on straight Pavlovian principles. When the bells went off on a machine we were alerted that something important was happening. While the ostensible reason for this was one of speed - to get one to the machine quickly - a latent assumption was that many of those charged with wire-room monitoring were incapable of judging a news story and therefore had to be guided by bells. It was like Vespers for Dummies. This rule obtained throughout the year except on Christmas Eve when those lucky enough to be working the night shift got treated to a medley of Christmas songs from the bells on the wires, accompanied by figures of Santa and Yule trees pecked out by the X's being punched on the wire. I wondered what would happen if a war broke out on Christmas Eve but it was usually a slow night.

In any case, on this evening the bells started up and I went to a wire machine to read that the Russians had just propelled a dog into the heavens; the space age was upon us. I grasped that, while not a Mafia slaying, this was still a story of some import, even for The Mirror. I also realized that there was virtually no one around. I had about as much company as Laika. Then, far up the row of private offices at the rear, I saw a flicker of light. Mort Ehrman was inside watching The Late Show. I knocked on the door waving the wire copy and Ehrman motioned me in, not able to hide a slight annoyance at being interrupted. "Whaddaya want, kid?" he asked. "Mr. Ehrman, it says here the Russians have sent a rocket into space with a dog in it." I could see it was taking a while to penetrate. After some thought, he said: "It'll wait. Let's watch the movie. You can stay." So we watched till the end of the film. Then Ehrman picked up the wire and read it again, with the fervid concentration of a primitive islander trying to make sense of a crashed B-52. I could see that what interested him was not so much the space shot as Laika. A dog whirling around in space. Better than a mobster getting thrown off a roof. This wasn't Ehrman's kind of story but he knew viscerally that we somehow had to show the flag. "All right kiddo, I'll take care of this," he said, and marched off to the wire room with me in tow.

By now, the machines were bursting with the coverage. Ehrman perused the wires, more sniffing them than reading and then said: "O.K., just give me the top of the AP. Then you stay here until I tell you to go." He trundled toward the composing room, almost pawing the wire copy and disappeared. About a half hour later he came back, holding a proof of our new front page. Not to be outdone by its more austere competition The Mirror would herald the advent of the space age with a reverse plate— giant bold white type on a black background. The blaring headline declared: "Ruskies Loft Dog." Following this on the revamped Page One were about three paragraphs of wire copy giving a general idea of what had happened. And at the end were the words: "For Further Coverage, See Mirror Exclusive, Page 5." There was, of course, no exclusive, but presumably, it would have sold a lot of papers. I didn't stick around long enough to learn whether Ehrman, in a lapse of sanity, would kick it upstairs and cooler heads would prevail. But at the Mirror there were few cooler heads, and so it remains fixed in my brain.

When a big-city paper folded, most of its editorial survivors were picked up by other newspapers —like a rule of the sea. At least this obtained when there were enough other papers around to do the rescuing. When the Herald-Tribune went down it was like the explosion of the planet Krypton with scores of supermen dazzling the firmament of the various journalistic worlds where they landed. The glorious diaspora of the Trib men and its impact on newspapering is legendary. When The Mirror folded virtually everyone went into public relations. The road was natural. A cozy relationship already existed with whomever its writers were covering in the first place; now they could drink in the daytime and get paid for it. There was then more honesty about dishonesty. Sports writers had their hotel—and bar—bills paid for by the teams they were covering, auto writers got to "try out" cars and movie writers got junkets to Hollywood.

All this was somewhat "cleaned up" in a subsequent era of journalistic rigor. The result was less to effect reform than to foster a climate of hypocrisy in which the corruption was practiced more subtly and people became experts at denial. In a later day, fashion editors still did not dress on their own dime, political reporters remained chummy with their sources, and top editors threw their weight around to get the usual perks. The need to curry and use favor is ubiquitous in human affairs. It can be curbed, perhaps controlled, but never eliminated. The only difference between the older breed and their successors is that the former were more forthcoming.

If there were any distinguished newspaper careers that came out of The Mirror's demise, I'm not aware of them—the copy boys may have done better than the rest with a few of us winding up at The Times— but the world of P.R. was fructified. The Mirror did leave one enduring legacy: Selig Alder later decamped for Florida and helped make The National Enquirer a must-stop on our nation's checkout lines. Many of the tabloid skills learned at The Mirror went into The Inquirer and then some since the few strictures that still limited a New York daily were unnecessary in the Brave New World of supermarket journalism. The Mirror's demise in 1963 was barely a blip on the radar screen of my life. The Mirror held fabled reunions and Larry Van Gelder, a Times colleague and one of the erstwhile Mirror copy boys who worked on an earlier watch than I had, told me in later years how he fell down laughing from all the outrageous stories that the paper's veterans would tell about the bad old days. But I had no desire to go back. I don't know that Dickens ever wanted to return for a blacking-factory reunion.

I remember a decent man, a southerner, named Knowles. He was silver-haired and dignified and was among the human flotsam that swept ashore at The Mirror. He was far too classy for such a tab, but there he was. Knowles had a mid-level job on the night desk and when the Adlers yelled at him (probably growled in deference to his years) he just took it like a beat-up old fighter by then quite inured to body blows. He was always courtly to me, or at least cordial, which at The Mirror passed for kindness, behavior that under the circumstances I found remarkable. Knowles called me Jackanapes. When I came to work, I'd sometimes notice him loitering in an alcove a few doorways down from the building entrance, finishing a cigarette and waiting for the last possible moment to enter.

One winter night, it was pouring and I spotted Knowles lighting up in the doorway. The alcove wasn't much protection and the rain was sluicing off his fedora. The sky was ether-colored and the downpour engulfed everything in a sodden wire mesh. Usually, I

29

pretended not to see the man, but this time I approached him and said: "It's almost time, Mr. Knowles. Don't you think you should come up." He exhaled and looked at me wistfully: "Thanks son, but I've got to finish my smoke you know. There's still a little while." For some reason this stayed with me, shaping my vision of newspapers in a fatalistic way, tinctured with negative romanticism and tinted by rain scenes from the movies. There was something about this calling that made me want to distance myself from it even as I embraced it. I could never quite shake the image of being on a darkling plain.

During this period, I also got a job at The New York Post. It was unthinkable to turn down newspaper work that was available. It doubled one's chances of being hired after college. Luckily, I started in early summer when school had ended, making it easier to juggle two jobs. I was working day sports hours at The Mirror during the week as well as two nights at The Post—a part-time deal on the weekend. Friday evenings, I'd go home to the Bronx, nap and take the subway back downtown to The Post which was then on Vesey Street along the Hudson. I'd work the 1-8 A.M. shift, subway home, sleep, party, return Sunday night for a similar vigil and be back at The Mirror at 10 Monday morning. With luck, there was usually enough time to hang out and stoke up on breakfast at one of the greasy spoons around The Post before heading uptown to 45th Street.

My debut at The Post was not an auspicious one. A little after midnight, I met a City College pal, Vic Ziegel, who was starting on the night shift as a sports copy boy. We rode up to the city room in a creaky, gated lift, accompanied by a gnome-like creature whom I mistook for the elevator operator but who turned out to be the night news editor. We must have done something in our banter to tick him off because he gave us the fish eye and, although he never said anything, this did not advance our career opportunities. Vic, luckily, came under the aegis of the sports editor, Ike Gellis, although he labored a while before getting a crack at reporting and going on to a legendary career.

The Post at the time was the New York liberals' darling, the domain of publisher Dorothy Schiff, exuding civic virtue at every pore. It's pantheon boasted Jimmy Wechsler whose broadsides of conscience emanated daily from its editorial pages; Ted Poston, the first— and for a long time virtually the only —black reporter on a New York newspaper, and Murray Kempton in his prime— actually Murray Kempton was always in his prime. The paper entered the lists early against McCarthyism, became the target of red-baiting by Winchell & Co., cast itself as friend of the poor and downtrodden, exposer of gouging landlords and grafting pols. With the PM, The Compass and The Star gone, The News and Journal-American somewhere to the right of the Vatican, the World-Telegram waffling, the Tribune still rock-ribbed Republican and getting too hip too late, and The Times carrying the laundry for the Establishment, The Post was, by default, the only game in town for left-of-center New Yorkers except for the dwindling faithful who held fast to The Worker. The Post's bleeding heart, however, ended at the door, where it treated its employees as badly as any of its right-wing rivals and probably worse than some. In the grand tradition of the trade, when it came to the help, The Post was exploitive, overbearing and mean-spirited. What attracted us as copy boys was not its vaunted liberalism but the fact that it had the best rewrite bank in the city.

This was made possible by the fact that there were two Posts, the Post of Jimmy Wechsler and the Post of Paul Sann. By day it was Wechsler's, by night—or at least in the early morning hours— it was Sann's. One paper crusading for justice, the other cruising for sleaze. The genius of that bygone Post was that it made its readers feel good and bad at the same time. The art of synthesizing these dialectics was the task of a team of writers who brought new dimensions to cynicism. Their names were then legendary in the narrow world of rewrite-men: Normand Pourier, elegant in his prose if not his conduct; the deft Ernest Tidyman who bailed out to write the Shaft novels; the puckish Gene Grove, a Peck's bad boy among a sea of them; a young Don Forst who later brought the spirit of The Post to papers he presided over in Los Angeles, Boston and New York; a youthful Ed Kosner, my old City College friend, who learned his trade at The Post before moving on to run Newsweek, New York magazine and a much-altered Daily News; Pete Hamill who cut his teeth there, and the redoubtable Al Aronowitz who flew nightly on quicksilver wings. They were consummate wordsmiths: quick, sure, arrogant, armed with dazzling superficiality and blessed with perfect pitch for the ripe cliche, the ability to turn it around and make it come up sounding almost new. It was their own form of jazz— fitting mayhem to a theme and improvising on a riff that got the juices flowing with everyone trying to top each other in whatever was coming down that night.

The evening was a concert with Sann wielding the baton. Clearly the master of the revels, he'd ease in at dawn, orchestrate the front page, and make it all come out smoothly. He played to a quick-witted audience of sharpies whose agile pens added bite to the news. Sometimes, they were too clever by half. Gene Grove got into hot water for writing a story in which the initial letters of each paragraph spelled out an obscene acrostic. But for the most part, their prose was disciplined, whatever the disarray of their lives.

My perspective on this —in a strict Hobbesian sense—was short, nasty and brutish. The operative spirits in my netherworld were Stan Opotowsky who oversaw Friday night/Saturday morning and Al Davis who ran the show the rest of the week. The polarities of Oppo, as he was called (not by me) and Davis are instructive. Stan ran the night city room like the Island of Lost Boys. A lanky fellow, he would slouch with his legs propped on the desk and flip methodically through a pile of girlie magazines in his drawer. Opotowsky seemed to be intent on nothing other than the contours of the ladies he was studying. Occasionally, a reporter would come by and share his view and they might exchange observations on the various anatomies displayed. Such behavior today would probably cost an editor his job or at least bring him up on charges of rampant sexism and indifference to staff sensibilities. In this pre-enlightened time, however, Opotowsky's behavior was revered because it sent a message to the troops that the news should be taken with a grain of salt, and that the atmosphere in his city room would be relaxed, urbane and civil. (He had enough sense to later leave newspapers and make a career as an executive at ABC-News.) But what appeared to be a benign, almost cavalier approach, belied a tough competitor who, by example, defused the natural tension of the city room and got more out of people in a relaxed atmosphere than others did in a turbulent one.

The idea that a city editor has to give ulcers to get results is a myth that is much abused. The outstanding newsroom leaders may have been explosive or not, but this wasn't the axis along which their talent lay. Resourcefulness, imagination, audacity, tenaciousness, a sixth sense for where the story was—and wasn't; these were the attributes of great editors. Perhaps most important was the ability to inspire and handle the troops. Temper was incidental to their success.

If Opotowsky was the good cop, Al Davis was the bad one. Davis was talented and ambitious, with an eye toward succeeding Paul Sann. He was also austere, tyrannical and driven. His targets were generally the younger writers, people on tryout or the occasional wretched copy boy. Anything could set him off: Failure to sharpen pencils to a fine point, misplaced carbons in a copy book, taking too long on a food order. Infractions generally prompted a snide rebuke about how inept the culprit was. Davis didn't explode; he dismembered. He preferred the ice-pick with short, sharp stabs.

Copy boys, however, were small beer. Davis enjoyed best to lean into vulnerable writers. I remember for weeks he worked over a young reporter until the poor guy was trembling whenever he handed in copy. What made Davis particularly intimidating was that he was smarter than his targets—and he was usually right. It is, of course, not hard for an editor to catch errors in the work of a writer—that's why there are editors. The point is how to respond. Davis used lighter fluid. During the new man's travail Davis would publicly take him to task for his gaffes, read the poor devil's mistakes aloud and deride him for his putative incompetence. Since Davis was in charge, and he was "right," there was virtually nothing the victim could do except swallow it. There was always a certain amount of hazing in newspaper offices but under Opotowsky it took the form of banter—a good-natured, if edgy raillery with a give-and-take quality; under Davis it was like bear-baiting with the crowd enjoying it, turning ugly. The operative idea being that if you couldn't absorb it, you didn't belong. As for Davis, his fortunes eventually foundered and he never quite reached the pinnacle he'd sought. Years later, I would sit next to a humbled Davis—by then I called him Al—on The New York Times Metro desk. But that is another story.

My experience at The Post was generally limited to the lower depths. Jimmy Wechsler never called me in to discuss editorial policy and Paul Sann never regaled me with anecdotes at the bar. If I ever had any contact with him it was with his left hand, holding aloft a piece of copy to move somewhere; I don't think he ever looked at me. On the other hand, he was perfectly businesslike. I was simply one of those hot-chocolate handles at the Horn & Hardart. You pull it and the cocoa comes out. My relations were mostly with the other copy boys whom I found meaner and more cliquish than their peers uptown. At the Mirror it was Us against Them; at The Post it was Each against All. Perhaps breaking in at The Mirror was so fruitless and the favors so few that the senior boys could afford to be more generous to their lessors. At The Post, whether illusory or not, there was the hope of being noticed, and this created a rat-race atmosphere. There was a definite pecking order and a hierarchy of assignments as opposed to a sharing of tasks.

The best job, operating the police radio, went to the son of the man who owned the coffee shop downstairs. The worst jobs, the food runs, fell inordinately to the new boys. At The Post, this was a particularly onerous task. As opposed to The Mirror with a variety of night-time fooderies to choose from in Midtown, The Post had rather limited options in the early morning hours of the Wall Street area. The favorite, by default, was a place known as

The Greek's (I have no idea what the real name was or if it had one), about six blocks away on what was a bleak trudge in the summer heat and a blustery wind-tunnel in winter with gusts coming in off the Hudson threatening to blow the food bags from one's clutch. By the time I returned half-frozen to the lobby it was impossible not to have a running nose. Should the food order be wrong by a hair's-breadth, roast beef coming up on white instead of rye, back you went out into the street accompanied by the appropriate contumely from the wronged reporter. By 8 A.M., the coffee shop downstairs would open, which was good news because I didn't have to walk outside, but bad news because there was an additional food run at 7:30 and if anything went wrong I had to stick around on my own time until I got it straight. The Post's editors were great defenders of union rights except when it came to their own.

When histories of journalism are written, no one has a chapter on eating but food is a very important component of life in the city room. There is a Sid Caesar routine about an executive meeting that deteriorates into the chaos of ordering lunch. Outlandish as it seems, this is not too far off the mark concerning what obtained in newspaper offices in a troglodyte age when there were set feeding times. Every institution (I use that word advisedly) and each hierarchy within it, got the feeding it deserved. The Mirror food runs were always bibulous, diverse and anarchic, Falstaffian revels of gastronomy, chaos and excess. The Post food runs were gluttonous, desperate and mean-spirited. The Long Island Press didn't have food. At the Paris Herald-Tribune the food-run was the high point of the evening: Staffers piled into cabs at the office— then located off the Champs-Elysees — and conducted a grand prix across Paris, descending on a bistro of choice. There, thanks to the French unions and the five-hour time difference with the States, they indulged in a Rabelaisian between-editions feast returning choleric and not quite malleable, until the first hours of the next edition. The Times had a cafeteria but depended for crunch-time nourishment on a portable coffee wagon run by the ubiquitous Fernando, more about which later.

That summer, I had an opportunity to earn a trifecta as a scrub, juggling three copy-boy jobs at once. In response to an earlier application, I got a telegram from The New York Times, offering me an opportunity to work Saturdays at the Times magazine. Since my Friday night task at The Post ended at 8 A.M., the Magazine job didn't begin till 10, and I was free Sundays, I could have carried it off—a triple crown of subservience. It was the only time my immigrant mother, who deferred to me in all such matters, put her foot down. Two jobs was enough. And I already had them. Of course, the question was, which two? It only dawned on me years later that I could have dropped my night duties at The Post—where my full-time prospects were dim—for daytime hours at the tonier Times. It's the counsel my older self would have given my younger one but, alas, I had the benefit of this wisdom only in hindsight. I often wondered what my career might have been like if I'd caught the eye of the Sunday editors and managed to move up the ladder at The Paper of Record without all the vicissitudes my career subsequently took before actually becoming the Magazine's copy chief 20 years later.

My first full-time reporter's job came with The Long Island Press in the fall of 1959 after I graduated City College. I had heard baleful stories of loneliness and boredom and surrender from friends who had worked on out-of-town papers—most of them later went into P.R. or trade mags—and I determined to avoid this fate by staying local. I sent letters to a surfeit of newspapers within driving range of New York (there were lots in various shapes and sizes in those days) and got roundly rejected by the few that bothered to answer. Undeterred, I proceeded methodically to knock on doors, county by county. Lacking a car, or the ability to drive one, I utilized public transit. In my assault on Westchester's Macy chain (which devolved into the better-run but just as parsimonious Gannett chain) I took the Dyre Avenue line in the Bronx up to the last stop. There I boarded the morning buses for my various venues in Westchester. At this hour of the day, the only other passengers heading north from the city were maids who looked about as happy going to their destinations as I did. At least they had jobs. For a few weeks I became a regular and chatted them up, more about where to find things in the downtown areas of wherever I was going than anything else, but they seemed more accommodating than the bus drivers who eyed me as something out-of-kilter.

I made the rounds of virtually every daily up there: The Mount Vernon Argus, The Mamaroneck Times, The Yonkers Herald-Statesman, The White Plains Reporter-Dispatch, on and on. Since I had bothered to actually show up, someone at the doorkeeper level usually appeared to see me; I think a few may even have glanced at my college clips. The answer, of course, was always the same. Come back when you've got some experience. I expected no less. I only hoped to be lucky. Still, it was a dispiriting affair, not because I couldn't find work but because of the prospect that I might actually get hired. They were all such dim, sorry little places. I had read their papers carefully before approaching each one and the copy was pedestrian and uninspired. I knew I couldn't learn much at such venues. It was a matter of doing time and acquiring the bona fides to move on to something more substantive. After the New York papers where I'd worked, even as a copy boy, these offices—I couldn't call them newsrooms—seemed listless, the copy lifeless.

I imagined I was in one of those Depression movies where the hero can't find work as the camera keeps panning between a montage of office managers giving him the thumbs-down and the worn soles of his shoes as he trudges up the stairs of one seedy employment bureau after another. An office of The Reporter Dispatch is currently located in Yorktown Heights opposite a street where New York state administers driving tests. It is a flat, squat, boxy building that forms an apostrophe to a mini-mall. Some years ago, while waiting for my son to complete his driver's test, I fantasized what it might have been like had I been hired there— and had I stayed. The feeling was somewhat akin to the pre-waking nightmare that I'd been drafted again.

My travels took me south to New Jersey where I actually managed an interview at the Bergen Record, and eastward where I was called in at The Long Island Press. The Record seemed interested and said they'd get back to me. The Press, using the term Long Island in its broader geographical context, was actually located on Jamaica Avenue in Queens. Although its purview extended to the far reaches of Long Island, as I was to learn, it was anchored in Queens and moored in some Brooklyn dockings as well. I considered it at least a semi-New York paper because you could still get there by subway, even if it took three trains to arrive from the Bronx. I appeared clutching my City College clips in a Clorox-blue scrap book and was ushered in to the office of the managing editor, David Starr. Perhaps made for better things, Starr had chosen to be a big fish in this brackish pond. Solid, slick-haired, he had a squarish demeanor and brimmed with self-possession. He was the best of a certain managerial type. To him I was probably a hungry kid from the Bronx, willing, exploitable, capable enough. They had a big turnover, an open slot and I was a cheap investment.

To his credit, Starr picked out the best of my City College clips and homed in on one piece in particular, a story I'd written a few years before about Herb Stempel who had a brief reign as champ of the NBC quiz show "Twenty One." Dan Enright, the program's producer, was packaging Stempel as the prototype of a poor but brilliant City College nebbish. Stempel would eventually take the fall for the smoother Charles Van Doren of Columbia, which eventually led to the exposure of the program as being fixed, providing further entertainment as the 1994 film "Quiz Show." While "Twenty One" was still riding high, I called Stempel for an interview but he wasn't home so I wound up talking to his wife, Toby, who told me she'd be glad when the whole thing was over, asserting that they were moderately well off and that Herb didn't have to wear the chintzy outfit in which he appeared on the program. She said that she came from a well-to-do family and Stempel's trademark blue suit was a publicity stunt cooked up by the show to make him look more deprived and sympathetic.

Starr asked me what had happened with the piece and I told him that NBC took umbrage and threatened to sue. The school's P.R. department told us we could get the college into a libel suit and that we were betraying our alma mater which was basking in great publicity from the show. The fact is, we were doing our job. But the college authorities leaned on the editors who caved. Several had been suspended the previous spring for a raucous April Fool's issue and did not want to risk further testing the school's patience. Along with a few others, I protested—what were we after all correcting?—but we were overruled. Our paper, The Campus, ran a retraction, which was probably the most craven action I'd ever been part of in journalism and I hadn't even started yet. Had we had the presence of mind and the gumption, alerting any of the dailies where we worked as stringers and copy boys, to pursue this loose thread might have unraveled the show's hokum sooner. But it was not to be. Nevertheless, my earlier enterprise served me well because Starr liked the story enough to ask only two more questions: "Can you drive?" I looked him dead in the eye. "Sure," I said. A fib. "You got a car?" "I can get one." This was at least possibly true. "Good," he said. "You get a car, you start in two weeks." I'm sure he more than half-suspected I was fudging. But if I could get it together, what was there to lose?

The problem now was to learn how to drive, pass the test on my first try and buy a car, all in two weeks. Considering that I had no driving experience and no money this posed a slight problem, but not an insurmountable one. My driving instructor was a friend, Jack Monet, who worked as a City College stringer at The Herald-Tribune. The Trib paid stringers 10 cents a word and Jack studied the paper carefully for a word-count of every tiny item he wrote to make sure he wasn't being cheated. He tossed the thumbed-over Tribs in the back of his ratty old Chevy so that they piled up, blocking the already narrow rear window. It was this vehicle in which my instruction was consummated.

We began at a stretch of empty trolley yards above 225th Street on the Bronx side of the bridge over Spuyten Duyvil hard by the Van Cortlandt elevated line. Monet was coming off a night shift at the Bergen Record, where he also worked, which made him sleepy, irritable, and in no mood to take guff from any motorist who had a problem with my driving skills. Despite his last name, Jack had the distinction of being tossed out of City College for failing French-2 three times. His mother was Irish, his father a Canuck and he had no great facility for language. This didn't stop him from going on to work in Paris for the brief-lived Paris edition of The Times and later the Paris Herald-Tribune—from which he got severance on three occasions over a period of 20 years before his final retirement. All the while, Jack took it is a matter of pride never to have progressed in French beyond his City College days—his wife and children were fluent and he traveled in expat circles. It wasn't till Monet's final days on The Trib that he condescended to try his hand at French.

Jack's free-spirited ways extended to his method of driving instruction. He sat me behind the wheel and advised with Zen-master aplomb: "Now just go forward; then aim it." He seemed to have total confidence and it was infectious. Strangely, I did what he said. The car lurched forward and we were on our way. Soon enough we were weaving under the Van Cortlandt elevated tracks with cars coming toward us from the opposite direction. I had sufficient but not complete control of the wheel, which seemed to upset the oncoming drivers who, for some reason, were blaring their horns at me simply because I was veering toward them with an occasional feint to keep them alert. Jack's response to this was to stick his head out the window, shake his fist and swear at them. I realized eventually that this was pretty much going to be the extent of his pedagogical technique. Perhaps it was as good as any. I must have had great reflexes because somehow we got back to the empty yards and started again. After a few forays, I seemed to get the hang of it. We did this for a week. Just before the exam I took the precaution of getting a few lessons from an auto school, which might have saved me.

My next hurdle was the car. A couple I knew had a friend. He owned a Studebaker that he no longer needed and was kind enough to let me take off his hands. The car was vintage Citrus Motors: a '55 Lemon. Our next door neighbor, Ben Pollack, brought it to his mechanic who said that it might have a little trouble starting but once activated, it would run. Which was more or less true. I dubbed the vehicle Rocinante and it proved equal to its name. The car cost $500, which I didn't have. I asked my father for the money. He had barely $500 in the bank. We weren't big savers. We weren't big spenders either, but there had never been that much to spend. My father didn't hesitate. It was his biggest withdrawal and his biggest investment. It was all he had and he understood that it would launch me. I paid him every penny in six months. A few days before I began at The Press, the Bergen Record hired me for $75 a week, but the Press had offered me $10 more and I went where the big bucks were.

You should understand that $85 a week, even then, was well below Guild scale for a starting reporter on a New York paper, which The Long Island Press—whatever its title—still was. The way The Press got around this, with a wink and a nod from The Guild, was that while its Queens staffers got union wages, the tyros who covered Nassau and Suffolk were officially employed by the ABC News Service, which rented us out to The Press. This also meant that on my day off, Friday, I had to drive in to Queens to get paid around the corner from The Press at the ABC News Service which was basically a payroll office. But why cavil? I was glad for the work.

I started at the Press on a Sunday night in late October. It was unusually cold for that time of year but the coldness was more inside the place than out. City rooms reminded me of airplane hangars with typewriter banks. This was the hangar at Gander. There is something transient and alienating about a city room at night. I don't think I ever got used to it although after several years I couldn't imagine another existence.

This being my debut, I arrived early at The Press and was the first one into the place except for Duffy, a wizened old bird who handed out assignments on Sunday evenings. Duffy must have had some kind of palsy because his hands shook; actually his entire frame trembled. He might not have seen me because his body was convulsed in sobs. Afterward, people told me this was simply a kinetic manifestation of whatever syndrome afflicted him, but in later years I came to the conclusion that he really was crying. I cleared my throat, gave him a moment to become aware of my presence, and introduced myself. Duffy pulled himself together and told me I'd be covering Rockville Centre, followed by a brief rundown of the various school districts and village boards for which I'd be responsible. I'd imagine he'd have liked to be described as avuncular, with a blue twinkle in his eye, as The Press might have written, but the best Duffy managed was a smile nailed to his jaw. My impulse was to get him a chair, except that he was already sitting.

Long Island at that moment was at the apogee of the suburban Fifties, derided and celebrated afterward by critics on various sides of the culture wars. At the time I was unaware that it was a proving ground for future social agendas and was simply trying to find my way around without getting killed. I generally attended at least three or four school, village or town board meetings a night, enough so that one had to juggle constantly to keep up—which I never really could. While the goal of spreading reporters thin and sending out tyros was to save money, a not inconsiderable side benefit was that it made them heralds rather than tribunes, unable to dig deep and long enough to do anything that would embarrass the municipalities whose legal ads and business interests helped keep The Press rolling.

Since these events dragged on interminably, the distances between them were daunting and one could never time the precise moments when any noteworthy matters might be discussed, reporters generally showed the flag and moved on. You learned to cultivate the appropriate town clerk, village mayor, school board trustee, community dissident, local activist or any other sentient source who actually attended the entire meeting, and get the story by phone on returning to the office. The trick was to get back early enough so that you didn't have to call them too late when they'd be tired and grumpy. Since most of them had an ax to grind and The Press was still a big deal, they were glad enough to talk; the better ones called you in any case. In effect, they functioned as unpaid stringers for their communities or voluntary publicists for their various causes, or both. As I was completely at their mercy for the accuracy of what happened, I had to learn quickly to size up whom I could and couldn't trust, and to what degree they were spinning events.

Occasionally, if there was a really feisty brouhaha, I might have to stick around for the color—it came in various shades of gray—and that's when I was thoroughly dependent on my informants at the other events I was putatively covering. Generally, the longer and more endless these meetings got, the more passionate people became about their various hobby horses. It was like going to a lot of Grade-B movies without the popcorn. My job was to appear sufficiently interested so that they let me spell their names correctly. Churchill's adage about all politics being local certainly held in these precincts. While covering my beat I never heard a word spoken in anger about the Russians marching into Hungary, but people became apoplectic about being unable to get a zoning change to widen their driveway. This gave everyone the opportunity to be Patrick Henry. The more particular and narrow the subject, the greater the conviction and level of rhetoric with which it was delivered. Give me a Variance or give me Death. (It was only in later years, when as a parent I became a participant, rather than an observer, at these events that I acquired the necessary lack of perspective to appreciate the choleric pulsations they can evoke.)

The zoning boards were the most onerous of these meetings. They would languish on about maps and sewers and boundary lines for hours, leaving everyone except those directly involved in a comatose state. I learned during this period to perfect a stare of feigned engagement masking advanced catatonia. This boredom was practiced by design since, by mesmerizing the public, the trustees were able to redistrict, rezone and reap the extant real-estate windfall to a fare-thee-well while a distracted commonweal and a complacent media gave them carte blanche. It was no accident that The Press dispatched to these precincts novices who had neither the time, the training nor the ability to read the not-so-invisible ink.

With the Republican lock on Long Island in those days—effectively a one-party system — a compliant press and the postwar land boom at its peak, it was a license to steal. Because they could act with impunity the local pols grew brazen and careless and within a few years left themselves open to a different kind of journalism practiced by my next paper, Newsday, which won its early Pulitzers by exposing some of these goings-on. The locals of course took umbrage at what they felt was a betrayal of a cozy relationship that benefited the deserving, harmed few and kept the economy humming. Many of them honestly believed they were innocent. What fueled their outrage was not that they were caught out but that the self-enriching rules they'd played by had become obsolescent. Many corruption scandals came not so much from outright sticking one's hand in the till—although this was not uncommon—but from ethical lag, mildly larcenous practices winked at by one generation and condemned by the next.

My first story of any appreciable size, a fire in an Atlantic Beach hotel, was instructive in what it taught me about myself. It was a three-alarm blaze that I actually never covered—there wasn't time—but pieced together over the phone from fire marshals, some hotel personnel and a little AP local copy. Although later on, I covered riots, demonstrations and other outdoor activities, I found that I could visualize something much

43

better in my head by not being there. Putting all the scraps together at a safe remove brought a clarity that allowed me to reflect on the event and tell it better, while being there, for me, was often a jumble of disparate events, a random hurly-burly. Happily, most reporters didn't share my inclinations, but it was clear to me that my proclivities were for indoor tasks: rewrite, editing, shaping the work of people who loved to go out and scramble, bang on doors and run with the pack. I did that for a few years because it was part of the craft, like mixing paints in a master's workshop, something I had to know to ply my trade. I've always mistrusted editors who've never been blooded in the street, but it was not where my heart was.

My second insight, equally important, came on a feature about a swimmer who was trying to set a record for staying underwater by holding his breath. He had almost drowned in what, you should forgive the expression, was a dry run. The guy was clearly no Houdini but game enough, and the hotel whose swimming pool he was using didn't mind the publicity. It was one of those typical stunts that the Long Island Press thought was cute—you must understand that this was only 20 years after flag-pole sitting—and that I had to work up into something light but not too frothy; it was, after all, ostensibly news. I sat there trying to come up with something clever, suitably disdainful, droll and entertaining all at once. I came up with nothing. The more I strained for something really brilliant, the less happened. After what seemed to me an inordinate amount of time, but probably wasn't more than a few minutes, the city editor, Dave Jacobs, looked up from his desk and, hearing the silence of my typewriter and noting my distress, glanced at the clock and growled at me: "Don't think about it kid. Just write it."

What Jacobs was telling me was that this was no big deal. It was ephemera. One of the most important services of newspapers is to wrap fish, a notable loss to digital consumers. The idea was just to keep it simple and I'd be doing myself and the reader a favor. I didn't absorb all this at the moment, but I got the essence of it and, spurred along by Jacobs, together with equal measures of fear and desperation, I pounded out something that satisfied him well enough. I progressed by fits and starts thereafter, but I learned to take writing the news seriously by not taking myself too seriously.

Virtually from the outset, my car haunted me and took effective control of my life. People who run things and can afford to have good cars, reliable maintenance and access to alternative forms of transportation when needed, have little appreciation of how hard and debilitating it is for those who lack their resources to simply get to and from work. Actually, I owe my old Studebaker a debt of gratitude because through its idiosyncrasies I learned a lot about automobile maintenance. My jalopy had considerable personality. It bore a cone-shaped nose like something in a Flash Gordon serial, and was painted charity-ward green, so that it managed to be jaunty and sickly at the same time. The car led a feverish existence, burning its candle at both ends and petering out intermittently. The problem was that it wouldn't start right away in warm weather and wouldn't start at all in cold weather. This had something to do with the choke, which was never feeding the right amount of fuel into the engine. If you floored it too much before starting, it would flood; if you floored it too little it would sputter, turn over repeatedly, but wouldn't turn on. I drove it—and it drove me—to a variety of mechanics, all of who fiddled around, made it a little better for a while, but in effect told me: "Nothin' ya can do; it's the choke."

In order to get from the East Bronx to the Press's Jamaica Avenue headquarters by 7 P.M. I had to be at my car by 4:30. It would generally take me about 40 minutes to get the Studebaker going. Sometimes, it took an hour. Occasionally, it would start right away and I arrived at work early. By about 5:15 I was rolling toward the Whitestone Bridge. At that time, they were doing massive construction around Zarega Avenue at what became the loop connecting what is now the Bruckner Expressway with the Hutchinson River Parkway. I got there at prime-time rush hour and enjoyed a traffic jam every night. I was terrified that the motor would give out in the stop-and-go. But it never died there, saving its swoons for the Queens side of the Whitestone.

Many were my stations of malfunction: Kissena Boulevard, Parsons Boulevard, Astoria Boulevard, Northern Boulevard. They would tow the car to a repair shop somewhere in the glutinous mews of what would one day be Shea Stadium and I would have to board the Flushing Line and make my way circuitously to the newspaper where, carless, I worked the phones. Finishing my labors at 2 A.M., I would then walk the several blocks to the IND on Hillside Avenue, change at Roosevelt Avenue, make my way back into Manhattan with the early cleaning people; change at Seventh Avenue for the connection to Columbus Circle, take the Seventh Avenue line back up to the Bronx with the late-night cleaning people and make one more change at 149th Street to pick up the Lexington Avenue. Since the trains weren't running too often at this time of night, I was lucky if I could get home by 4.

When the car was working, I had the additional problem of learning how to keep alive in heavy traffic since my driving lessons hardly qualified me to sit behind a wheel. Moreover, I had never even been to Long Island before. Tooling around darkened streets, many of them not even located on my tattered Hagstrom's Road Atlas, trying to read the map with one hand, steer with the other and keep an eye on street signs named after developers' children was a challenge. I arrived at school board hearings thoroughly disoriented and had to decompress before remembering what I was supposed to be doing. News people who've cut their teeth at metropolitan journals have a different primal experience than those who apprenticed at suburban or small-town dailies. Not only is their subject matter the stuff of general interest but they're usually familiar with the territory and can get there by public transit, if need be. The other world is more uncertain, akin to learning the terrain of a different planet.

What with my car troubles, I spent a lot of time in the office working the phones. This afforded me a chance to befriend two rewrite men who were older—but not a lot older—than I was. By happenstance, I sat between them: John Cashman and Dan Kahn. Both were to cast light shadows on my career. Cashman was the life of the party: a dark-haired handsome Irishman, funny, silver-tongued, mercurial, self-destructive. Danny was low-keyed, even-keeled, dependable. Together, they constituted a complete newspaperman. Both were perceptive, intelligent and sensitive individuals, but the gas in their lamps glowed with different intensity. Both would eventually move on, as I did, and die early, although not without leaving a mark.

Each manifested different attributes of the rewrite man: Danny's genuine interest in what was being said encouraged the speaker to keep talking. John was a bantam, who kept flicking right jabs at the subject's psyche, hoping to provoke him into something revealing. Both approaches work, but they have to be suited to the situation. Kahn knew how to get hold of sources, Cashman knew how to get at them. The Jell-O was still soft in the mold and it was a seminal experience. I myself have been told in later years how I said or did something with writers early in their careers that influenced them, and I have no idea what they're talking about. Kahn and Cashman might have felt the same way.

I don't remember the stories I covered for the Press as much as the predicaments I got into. One winter night, on leaving a story about a blood drive in Hewlett, I got back to my car to discover that it was perched on a patch of ice and everyone I'd just interviewed at the community center had decamped. I was in the middle of a wooded area with no help in sight. With my first earnings I had just bought a new salt-and-pepper coat, which turned out to provide my means of escape. Placing the garment under the rear wheels, I ran over my coat and rolled out of there. It offered good traction but there were large tread marks across the breast. The cleaners told me to forget about it.

I actually managed to cultivate some real sources who fed me a few nuggets and I got to spend some time in bars courting local gadflies. The best of this lot was Dr. Ralph Sorley who, a few years later, was to become the bane of Newsday's existence. Unaware that he loved to glom on to inexperienced reporters, I lent him my ears, which he bent in various saloons in Rockville Centre. According to Dr. Sorley—who in his non-whistle-blowing time maintained a practice—the better part of the Hempstead Town political machine was crooked and was manipulating the local urban renewal to line its own pockets, drive locals out, put friends in, and change nothing except their bank accounts. He would spend hours giving me chapter and verse.

When I went back to my editors, they dismissed him as a local nut. Newsday, where I later worked, did the same—although its editors, to their credit, insisted they'd checked out some of his stuff. Eventually, they wouldn't talk to him. As it turned out, some of his charges proved to be valid—several of the local politicos were a bunch of crooks—but not quite true in the way Sorley presented them. The lesson was that while we ought to be skeptical of crackpots, neither should we completely ignore them.

I covered a large swath of territory for The Press. It seems I shifted beats every few weeks. At one time or another, I touched down in Rockville Centre, Merrick, Lynbrook, Freeport, Bellmore, all the Five Towns and the three beaches: Atlantic, Lido and Long, plus occasional forays into the depths of Suffolk. I wrote about parking-meter scandals, school budget battles and local fires. When it wasn't snowing, it seemed to be raining a lot that winter. I remember driving in a downpour to a restaurant-bar on Long Beach Boulevard in Oceanside to ask then Republican Attorney General, Louis Lefkowitz, about a local GOP capo who'd just been embarrassed on graft charges. I came in dripping wet and

Lefkowitz and a few cronies were sitting around in the back plotting damage control. I introduced myself. Talk about a fool's errand. I felt I'd walked into the wrong pool room. Lefkowitz, who was then already silver-haired and on the downward slope but still commanded a certain dignity, particularly among the pugs he was sitting with, looked up and shook his head as if to say: "They sent you all the way down here to ask this?" He must have taken pity on me because he gave me a few noncommital quotes that might justify my gas mileage. I was grateful; I had the chance to get dry.

One night, my Studebaker died for good and the next day I gave notice. I had it towed to a junkyard where I got 50 bucks for it, minus 20 for towing. At that point, both the car and I had exhausted each other's possibilities. I had no sentiment about the car, which was pretty much the same way I felt about the paper when it folded several years later. The Press was a nondescript, exploitive and shabby affair that got stale and listless by always playing it safe and pandering. It was a pit-stop for young people on the way up and a backwater for hacks with nowhere else to go. It didn't so much fold, as implode.

I needed pavement, public transportation, daytime hours, New York, a real life. Since the big-time papers weren't hiring semi-formed morphs from the suburban press for reporting jobs the only route to go for a quick fix in Manhattan was the trade press. A few of my friends had already taken this path with such winners as Frozen Food Age (which lacked the imagination to call itself Ice Age). The fare these magazines covered was the stuff of bizarre anecdotes in the bars to which we repaired. We saw them as way-stations, providing a slight living, access to women and absurd fodder for the novels we were never going to write. They were tawdry, tacky and on the take, wanting only a Nathanael West.

The trades, of course, didn't really practice journalism since their subjects were also their only advertisers. The result was a promotional journalism, news of the rialto, trends, comings and goings, laudatory profiles, necrologies, bland editorials, backslapping and back-scratching, general genuflecting and an occasional brickbat tossed at a threat to the industry. Although most of us got out, those who remained in the trades joked less as they grew older. The reporters were generally steeped in their specialties but wanting on syntax. The editor's drill was to take a torrent of dull, unreadable copy and turn it into a stream of dull, readable copy: a minor craft requiring its own modest talents. Although they knew that none of their friends or neighbors would ever read, or want to see a word of what they'd labored over, this didn't stop them from getting involved in the process.

Had my older self been around to advise my younger self I would have counseled taking a step down and applying as a copy boy at The Times. I was young and life was long. But I often chose foolishly and, by the seat of the pants. I took the path of least resistance. My friend Ed Kosner's then wife, Alice, was working at a pop entertainment magazine called Music Vendor and they just happened to need a managing editor. (Any place that offers someone with less than three years experience a title anything higher than reporter or editor is suspect.) The job came with a 50 percent raise in salary. I took it.

Music Vendor was located at 157 West 57th Street, just a skip from Carnegie Hall but that was its only connection with high culture. My staff consisted of Alice and an ad salesman, Lester. I reported to a rapscallion named Max Gilman, the self-styled editor. The publisher was a jukebox distributor in New Jersey whom we called Big Bear. Our office had the somewhat seedy, faintly disreputable quality of Max Bialystock's lair in "The Producers," and indeed, Max Gilman was a kindred spirit to his namesake. He affected a rapid, staccato Broadway palaver perfectly tuned for the hard-sell. Confident, bristling, with an eye out for any target of opportunity, Max was a pocket buccaneer watchful for light craft on the outer reefs of Broadway. He was the inventor, driving force and reigning spirit of Music Vendor. Gilman loved to tell stories about his raffish experiences with work and women. It was only a little later I realized he was lifting from Henry Miller but, in retrospect, he embellished so well, that listening to Max was better than reading the original.

Gilman was one of those characters who applied boundless energy to small purpose. There was nothing too little that couldn't excite him. And once electrified, he would enlist our total effort in addressing whatever mote had just crossed his vision. One didn't so much take orders from Max as become infected by a virus. Bizarre behavior in bosses, like madness among the great, needs the attention of social psychology or, perhaps, a poet. All Max had was me. Working for him was like being in a Restoration farce. We should have worn wigs. Alarums, stratagems, quick changes, rapid entries and exits, Shturm here, Drang there. The phone would ring (Alice doubled as secretary and general amanuensis) and Max, after keeping the caller on hold while checking his stocks, would get on the phone with record executives as if he were holding court: "Mr. Preston Epps!" "Mr. Abbott Lutz!" "Sorry, I just had some people here from RCA." Blather, blather. But in an industry devoted to bluff and bluster, it worked.

Max managed to cobble together enough advertisements every week to keep the book afloat. He connived to get free ads to anchor the book from what was then the Big Four—RCA, Columbia, Decca and Capitol—by telling them that each of the other three were paying. And if they didn't believe it, so what? It wasn't costing them anything. Eventually, once the magazine got off the ventilator, they actually paid something because it had an audience. Then, with the big fish in tow, Max went after the lesser fry and reeled in enough to fill a 24-page book every week. It was still the early days of rock n' roll. He would dispense discounts and package deals like a Metternich carving up duchies. If there was a method to his madness no one understood it. Max lied to everyone and when confronted lied some more, so that there was such total confusion that no one knew quite how they were being conned. But he was such an engaging rascal people forgave him and there was enough free publicity in it for them that most came back. Max corralled everything from a full page from Atlantic to an ad from someone named Berry Gordy, nurturing a label in Detroit called Motown.

What these people would think up was beyond imagining. They were the progenitors of over-the-top; the only difference between them and what came later was technology and attitude. My role in all this was to chart the movements of various record honchos within and beyond their companies, cover trends—there was one about every three hours, do interviews with singers the labels were trying to promote—straight puff pieces, and write an occasional editorial denouncing record piracy. It was pleasant, mindless and occasionally libidinal work that allowed me to enjoy the pleasures of the city and the company of friends without having to devote any thought to the office once I'd left it— the equivalent of a post-graduate year abroad if you couldn't afford to go abroad. I tired of it soon enough— I am not built for the sybaritic existence—and I quit to write. This was a mistake since I had nothing to write about. Luckily, I was saved by the Army from inflicting any serious literary harm on either myself or others. I'd been at the typewriter for no more than two weeks when the Berlin crisis happened and my draft number was pushed up.

This remembrance is about newspapers so I'm not going to write about my military career. I've never cared for hearing Army stories and I'm skeptical about most. Suffice to say that I went in one day and I came out a couple of years later. I learned as much in orderly rooms as I ever did in city rooms. I can't say that I much enjoyed Army life and, if I had the choice, I wouldn't have gone. But aside from jury duty, it was probably the most democratic experience I'll ever have. Once I got through it and went on to real work, I emerged as an adult and put myself to serious purpose.

Except for a brief foray at The Paris Herald-Tribune, a detour at The Daily News and a couple of fellowships, I spent the next 41 years shuttling between Newsday and The New York Times. During my years on West 43rd Street if you told me I'd be going back to Newsday I'd have said you were crazy. And when I returned to Newsday I thought the tabloid would provide appropriate bookends for my career. But Yogi Berra's adage—"It ain't over till it's over"—proved truer than my expectations.

In early 1964, with my Army unemployment running low, the moment had come for a job. This time I was more focused. A City College friend, Bob Mayer, was already at Newsday and he put in a word for me with the Managing Editor, Al Marlens. Al was the most irascible, exasperating, demanding and by far the best newspaperman I ever worked for. If he had a short fuse and a long memory, he also lived by a rigorous code of honor. His anger was often fueled by a sense of moral outrage. Marlens could have inspired less fear and more enthusiasm in his staff and when he was wrong he dug in his heels, driving writers and editors to distraction. But he discerned talent and appreciated it. Newspapers are like a dreadnaught, not a democracy. There has to be a captain and the crew must have confidence in his decisions. Marlens acted decisively and acted out. He was driven and driving, explosive and charming, capable of great loyalty and grand retribution. Al turned all the disadvantages of working-class origins on their head. He flaunted his rough edges and made more polished staffers quake. His shirts and only tie gave new meaning to off-the-rack. But there was no mistaking the ire in his gravelly Brooklyn voice when he eviscerated a flawed story with concise, articulate, fierce logic.

Marlens didn't hire me for the newsroom off the bat but kept me waiting a few weeks. Then I got a call, not from him but William Woestendieck, a smooth gent running soft news who offered me a job in the Entertainment Department. This detour was a harbinger of my career. I would bounce back and forth between news and "culture" for the next four decades.

At Newsday, I led a charmed life from Day One. The Entertainment Department was cozy, the assignments were fun, and who could quarrel with show biz? The presiding spirit of our little clutch was the movie critic, Mike McGrady. Mike had tutored under the fabled publicity man Tex McCrary, best known to old-time radio listeners as co-host of The Tex & Jinx Show, a breakfast-club prototype of today's ubiquitous talk show. McCrary was a great showman, an audacious promoter, and Mike—who had more than a bit of the rogue in him—appropriated some of these traits to his advantage. McGrady could carry off with panache mildly larcenous behavior that would get the rest of us flogged. I envied his job: Going to the movies. McGrady brought a certain hip irreverence to the column. In the age of The Times's stuffy Bosley Crowther, it was just what a scrappy tabloid trying to cast off the suburban mold was looking for. Slowly, Newsday was recruiting a staff of young New Yorkers who overflowed the ranks of the city's shrinking dailies. They were going to alter the character of the paper, transforming it into a contentious enterprise provoking an adversarial relationship with many of its readers. This schizoid personality, half subversive, half suburban was to be the newspaper's great strength and ultimate weakness.

McGrady and I hit it off right away. We enjoyed banter, liked the movies, craved New York. I was now living on West 93rd Street, hard by a statue of Joan of Arc (a dead ringer for Charles de Gaulle) and commuting to Garden City in my reverse Nick Caraway phase, driving a six-month rental that was brand new and actually worked. Moreover, I didn't have to tool around that much and the weather was good. I must have been going to four movies a week in those days, plus a lot of catching up at revival houses like The New Yorker, the Regency and the Elgin. The New Wave was breaking, Fellini and De Sica were being imported from pre-ristorante Italy and the Grit-Brit films still had energy. Our staff went to lunch a lot—that I could actually eat lunch with newspaper colleagues provided one of those heady moments, like realizing you can swim. We'd invite other kindred spirits from different departments to join us. Thriving in the give-and-talk department was important in establishing a pecking order. You've got about ten minutes to get noticed at any place and one must seize the moment.

In every rise up the journalistic ladder, there's always an attention-getting piece, a story that alerts one's superiors that a newcomer is worth keeping an eye on. Mine came early and was perfectly idiotic. It was a feature on Pat Collins, a lady hypnotist working the room at Basin Street East in New York. I watched her act for a while and decided that the only way to make this mild scam interesting was to volunteer myself as one of the subjects. A flagrant intrusion into the story but, since this was the entertainment section, we didn't have to take ourselves too seriously, so I figured what the hell. I'm not the best candidate for hypnosis but I went along with the program and she had me do a pretty good imitation of the NBC peacock as well as a few other simulations. The crowd seemed to enjoy it. I phoned in a lead about how the mesmerist "who is literally knocking out the customers says that she hypnotized me into giving her a good write-up. But if she thinks I'm going to say her act is great . . . her act is great . . . her act is great . . ." The rest followed suit. I praised her with faint damnation. It was, of course, outrageous and I wince to think I ever wrote such nonsense but it worked. We did all the entertainment openings on deadline in those days so when I arrived at work the next morning, there was my piece in the paper. I got an O for Outlandish. As the managing editor Bill McIlwain told me, "Boy, you go ahead and stretch the bow; we'll let you know if it breaks." The fact that anybody liked such ripe stuff made me wonder just how sophisticated everyone out there was, but in retrospect what they may have appreciated was the story's exuberance and devilment.

I chronicled everything from Patti Page's "comeback" at the Plaza (silvery dress, piano to match) to the director Robert Rossen holding forth on his new movie, "The Hustler." I learned a good lesson here. I'd seen most of Rossen's films and came prepared so I had a solid interview. He seemed slight and frail —a lot of these larger-than-lifers are always smaller than you'd imagine—and was seated behind a desk the entire time. We were in the midst of an interesting exchange about "Body and Soul," when he went off on a different tangent. It wasn't until the end of the interview that I got back to asking him why he'd made Shorty, John Garfield's alter ego in "Body and Soul," and Sarah, Paul Newman's conscience in "The Hustler," both cripples. Just before I asked the question, Rossen got up to make a point and began limping around the room. After that I learned to do my homework more carefully and not to rush in so fast with questions until I had a better feel for the topography.

The best story I reported during my brief tenure in the Entertainment Section never appeared in Newsday. Richard Burton was opening on Broadway in "Hamlet" shortly after the media circus of "Cleopatra" and his celebrated affair with Liz Taylor, who was in town and in tow. The paparazzi were out in force. It was the Bard and the Beautiful with Shakespeare being upstaged by the salacious goings-on. There was a big crowd outside, mounted cops, a mild frenzy. The Times dispatched a reporter to see what all the fuss was about in its own back yard and the Post sent someone whom I knew from my college days. How our respective papers covered this was instructive. Burton performed brilliantly on stage and gamely off. The audience—a first-night crowd of claquers reinforced by gawkers— spent most of the evening metaphorically craning its neck. Lost in this spectacle was Hume Cronyn as Polonius. After the show, I spotted him being interviewed by a reporter from the BBC. The crowd, the cops and most of the press were elsewhere and after Cronyn left, the BBC man and I got chummy and compared notes, of which I didn't have too many and with which he was quite generous. It turns out that he knew Burton slightly from London and had arranged for a brief interview to which I was welcome, as we weren't really competing. I took it.

Sure enough, the theater cleared and there, from stage left, entered Richard Burton. He filled up the proscenium as if it were a vacuum and he a natural force. He had a voice like coffee grounds, slightly rasped after the evening's performance. He was doubly onstage and clearly enjoying it. Two other overseas types appeared, self-styled "journalists" who manage to insinuate themselves onto the fringes of such events. Burton used them as foils. The first one asked how Liz was faring in all this. Burton replied he didn't know Shakespeare had written her into the play. He made it clear that he wanted to talk about "Hamlet," not Taylor. He then went into a spirited exegesis of the play and, with little prodding, proceeded to critique the audience, observing that it had failed to respond to the jokes, the best lines, the silences. My tabloid heart was beating wildly. By the time Burton made his exit it was almost midnight. I raced for the theater phone with tab gold jingling in my brain.

I called our night man on the Culture desk, Bob Morris, and told him what I had. He was less than impressed. What I heard for the first time in his calculated silences was that unmistakable skepticism from the desk, a wariness that spells death to a reporter in the street. How could I verify it? I was there! Who else heard it? That's why I have it alone! Why would Burton have talked to you? It was an accident—I glommed on to someone else— but it's real. Could you get the tapes? They're not mine and it's midnight, and we don't have that much time! Well, Bob didn't know if it was worth remaking the page. Are you kidding? I was livid and frantic. But it was the editor's call and he would have none of it. Morris was not a bad deskman — he went on to have a decent career on The Times business desk. But I was a kid; he didn't know or trust me and he didn't want to take a chance. Also, he didn't want the bother. He had a nice quiet features page and he was going home in 40 minutes. If he bought this, it would be an all-nighter with calls to Marlens and McIlwain; he'd have to do the explaining; and he'd have to tear up the page, remake it, rewrite heads, get pictures. And if I was wrong, it was his head that would roll. I don't justify what he did but after serving my own lonely vigils on the late shift, I understand the feeling better. I was to see it happen on more than one occasion.

By the time I left the theater, the street was almost empty. Then I spotted my college pal from The Post, who was still hanging around, and told him what had happened. In those days, Newsday still wasn't a New York paper, so there wasn't direct competition and, perhaps imbued by the generosity of the BBC man, I figured my friend might as well run with the story since we weren't going to. The next day, The Times sniffed at the crowd scene with a short item, Newsday ran nothing and The Post played it up with the head: "Burton Pans Yanks." The Times didn't have to stoop, The Post had no problem stooping, and Newsday fell between stools. This was to be played out on a wider scale in years to come.

My life in show biz was brief. It was brought to a halt when William Woestendieck, the gentleman who had very nicely hired me, lost a power struggle not too long after my arrival and decamped to become managing editor of The Houston Post. His empire was promptly subsumed by the news side and in short order I found myself whisked into the city room where I was transformed back into a news reporter, which is what I had sought to be in the first place. I always thought McIlwain, a shrewdy, knew what was coming, but let me and the others get hired on Woestendiecks's budget, then appropriated us once we were in the door.

I was again a beat reporter but this time I was a little older, I knew the territory a lot better and I could get around easier. My domain was Lynbrook-Freeport-Merrick, which was only a skip from the Newsday office in Garden City. Compared to my labors at The Press it was a milk run. The main difference from my earlier experience was that Newsday sought out targets of opportunity and was actually interested in controversy. Most importantly, Newsday gave you a breather in New York.

I had only been there a short time when the '64 World's Fair began and the city editor, Tony Insolia, sent me aloft in a helicopter for a bird's-eye view of Opening Day. A coalition of activists, protesting minority hiring policies at the fair, was threatening to disrupt the ceremonies with a motorcade of cars, setting out from Harlem and Brooklyn. The plan was to block traffic on the roadways leading to Flushing Meadows and create a gridlock nightmare. We had reporters riding with the protesters as well as with the cops. Robert Moses, the iron-willed spirit behind the fair, was having none of this and the city had warned that any car that even hinted at slowing down would be towed and the passengers jailed. There was a large mechanized police presence. This was still a time when the people who ran things were unselfconsciously in control and the people who were protesting were still testing the waters.

It was a rainy morning, the kind where there are always a few breakdowns and people tend to go slow. McGrady, who had volunteered to ride in one of the protest cars, reported that the cops were out in force and whenever they pulled alongside, the driver hit the gas so hard he almost got a speeding ticket. The same was true everywhere. The drive-in was a dud. We didn't know this yet when Insolia approached me and said: "Hey, Jakey, you wanna go for a ride in a helicopter?" He spoke as if he were asking a kid whether he wanted to go on the bump cars at Coney Island. I told him sure, still not knowing what the assignment was, or if it was an assignment, but understanding that my only answer was "yes." Tony explained that, in effect, I was going to be a traffic reporter, but in this case, he was only interested in the traffic on the bridges and highways approaching the fair. The paper had thoughtfully provided a chopper on a nearby lot off Stewart Avenue. It was one of those little bubble jobs which is open on both sides and where you're strapped into the seat. My partner was Cliff DeBear, a Newsday photographer and amateur helicopter pilot whose Weltanschauung was not dissimilar to that of Slim Pickens in "Dr. Strangelove." Cliff loved playing the daredevil. Somehow or other he was planning to take pictures while we barnstormed over the target. I didn't want to imagine the logistics of any of this; I only hoped Cliff knew what he was doing.

We took off not far from Roosevelt Field, the same site that Lindbergh had flown from almost 40 years earlier, but we were heading west to Queens and I wasn't sure I was going to be as lucky as Lindy. I had been in dicier situations in the Army but I'd usually known the people I was with. DeBear was a blank. We soared aloft into a brooding drizzle and Cliff was having a grand time. "Great, huh?" he kept asking me, as he leaned into the wind and I dipped starboard. "Yeah, Cliff, great," I said. Cliff, was

57

euphoric. "Hot dog!" he was saying. "Hot dog!" He kept glancing at me for affirmation and I kept nodding, resisting the urge to tell him to look where he was going, because I didn't want to alter the chemistry.

After a little more dipping and doodling we straightened out and forked over The Grand Central Parkway. Our journey took only a few minutes. By the time we reached Forest Hills, the clouds broke and the sky started to bleach into a starched cotton. As we approached Flushing Meadows, the sun burst out like Apollo on an ancient map and rinsed the fair in a wash of pastel light: the pavilions glittering like melted crayons, the fanfare of futuristic shapes, the Unisphere glistening after the rain, the pointillist chaos of the crowds. For a moment, dazzled by the sheer beauty before me, I forgot why I was there. But I returned to reality, if not to earth, and scrutinized the roads leading to the fair. Traffic was zipping along. Cliff gave a thumbs-up sign, just like in the movies. We rolled down and made several passes over the area to confirm our findings. When I indicated I was satisfied, he veered east for home.

Cliff, as it turned out, was the Real McCoy and kept his cowboy enthusiasm at Newsday for another three decades. What I wrote that afternoon was just filler for a larger piece on the fizzled drive-in, which itself was a sidebar to the general coverage of the fair. But for a young person it was great to have a piece of a larger story. All those names on a group enterprise in a big news event are important for the lowliest participant, because for each, it's like having been to Troy, even as a cup bearer. At The Times, the legendary Peter Kihss was fierce about making sure that humbler sorts got credit for their leg-work on a group effort. It was the mark of an outstanding reporter or editor to see that this happened.

Newsday was then located in a low, boxy white stucco structure on Stewart Avenue about a five-minute cab ride from the Garden City stop on the Long Island Railroad. Inside, like one of those American cities of 600,000, it was small enough to be intimate, big enough to field a major-league team. It offered the only city room I've ever been in that could qualify for the proverbial clean, well-lighted place; not neat—it was, after all, a newspaper office—but scrubbed as well as scruffy. It was sunny in the daytime and not too fluorescent at night. The city desk and the copy desks anchored the middle with the reporters' posts rippling out from either side.

The news writers hunkered east, the style section west. The executive fishbowls were at the western wall, and there were relatively few of those. Sports, photography and the editorial pages were upstairs and the composing room was in the back feeding into the pressroom at the south end. I don't remember that there was a receptionist in the lobby—people sort of found their way inside— although we may have gotten some security after an irate reader came in one night waving a revolver. At The Times irate readers wrote letters; at Newsday they pulled guns. Tony Insolia grabbed a baseball bat and tried reasoning with him—Tony was sort of smiling all the time like he was the guy's best friend and wryly amused by his frippery. On reflection, a bat wasn't much of a defense against a pistol but it must have impressed the man because he put the weapon away and went into Tony's office and they talked for a while. I don't think we pressed charges—we couldn't afford to lose any subscribers. The guy did get to write a letter. I hope we spelled his name right.

The Garden City offices are long gone, succeeded by a facility for the ill-fated Long Island Lighting Company. The paper moved out to a plant in Melville. In subsequent years visitors were greeted by a security type in a glass booth who examined your ID card and gave you the fish eye if you fumbled too much with your wallet. He was checking you, not directing you. I guess they needed it, but I'd sooner take my chances with an occasional armed reader.

In those days, the reporters' desks were paired off in double-rows like grade school. The senior writers sat in the front rows and the rest of us were divided into a rough tracking system with the fast track in the right-hand rows facing the city desk and the rest fanning out toward the middle, left and rear. Occasionally, an arrival or departure might alter the arrangement, but generally, it held, and was maintained through the night shift. It made sense for senior writers, who got the lion's share of breaking stories, to be closest to the city desk, which was distributing the work, and the copy desk which was processing it; moreover it was understood that the top dogs got pride of place.

As a new beat reporter, I started out in the back with the scrubs, which is where I expected to be. My partner was Liz Trotta who went on to have a career as a correspondent for ABC in Vietnam and other foreign climes. My beat had been expanded further east along the South Shore to an area that included Massapequa and Massapequa Park. Its famous sons—Jerry Seinfeld and Alec Baldwin— were then in grade school. I inherited my beat book from a somewhat laconic colleague, Leo Seligsohn, who had been less than attentive in keeping it up to date. In that pre-computer age, a beat-book, handed on from one shifting reporter to another, was like a house key passed among merchant seaman as they went abroad. There was usually only one and to lose it meant despair. The book's upkeep was critical. If a town clerk, a school-board president, a helpful village police chief, a local political hack, was replaced, it was essential that the change be duly recorded in the beat book so that when the moment came late at night to run down a story, the right source was available.

While writers husbanded their own rolodexes, there was so much flux among beat reporters that the only way to survive when thrown in cold was to inherit a reasonably up-to-date beat file. Often, these books were only semi-legible, with names scratched out and others scrawled in journalistic hieroglyphics, the phone numbers confusing sevens and ones or threes and eights. Should these books ever fall into the wrong hands, little would be given away. Much of the time, you'd have to ask your predecessor to decipher what he'd scribbled and then reconfigure it in your own script, writing over what he'd already written over, resulting in a palimpsest of calligraphy that looked like the work of an inept Sung poet. If the reporter wasn't there, you had to call him at home and get him—often half asleep—to decipher from memory what he'd written down months before. If they'd left, God help you. Should a municipality be in turmoil it could mean countless scratch-outs as the book tried to reflect the vicissitudes of whatever was taking place.

The worst chroniclers were compulsives who tried to fit in everything at the end of a page. This meant increasingly minuscule chicken scrawls, like the bottom of an eye-chart designed for microbes. On the other hand, it showed diligence. More ominous was a beat book that was relatively unmarked, suggesting that it had not been kept up to date by one's predecessor and perhaps his precursors as well. Leo's was uncomfortably neat.

This led to a series of embarrassments, not the least of which was my phone call to the Mayor of Massapequa Park. I should note that although I may have wafted through Massapequa, I considered it a point of honor never to have set foot in adjacent Massapequa Park. This left me totally dependent on what was in the beat book. One night, responding to some alarum in that village, I dutifully called the Mayor. It was close to midnight and I had clearly woken the woman on the other end. I told her I was sorry to disturb her and asked if her husband the Mayor could come to the phone. She responded that he was unable to because he was dead and had been so for the last six months. She then proceeded, with some justice, to lace into me about how Newsday should have known this since we ran his obituary—although minutely— and this showed how little respect we gave to local coverage. For good measure she advised me that she only read the Long Island Press, that I was the third Newsday reporter who had phoned her in the last half year and if she got one more call she'd report us to the police for harassment.

I thanked her for her candor and promised she would never hear from us again. Then, trying to assuage her further, I observed that perhaps I'd mixed her municipality up with Massapequa. A mistake, since Massapequa Park had gone to the trouble of incorporating itself as distinct from Massapequa which was agglomerated in Hempstead Town. This set off a new diatribe about our general stupidity and ignorance. I let her ventilate a bit more—by now she was quite awake—and then I came clean and told her I'd blundered into this situation and threw myself on her mercy. She must have had a good catharsis because she gave me the number of the current mayor but told me not to phone him because he went to bed early. I called him immediately and got the story.

It is no accident that Evelyn Waugh's "Scoop" is such a favorite with newspaper people. While we like to think of ourselves as the likes of such larger-than-life correspondents as R.W. Apple, mingling with the great and dining lavishly, the deeper truth is that most of us find ourselves more often than not closer to Boot of the Beast: thoroughly disoriented in a situation we are not qualified to report about in the first place, coming in cold, playing catch-up ball and improvising feverishly both with those we're covering and those we're reporting to. It's only later on, for those who've developed a niche or a sinecure, that a certain confidence develops, but generally, the initial insecurity that infects most news people, stays with them in one form or another for the duration.

I would reflect on my misadventures to my desk-mate Liz Trotta, who found them vaguely amusing. Her response to my more ungainly mishaps was: "You nut!" We would compare notes—she was having problems of her own covering Glen Cove—and commiserate with other freshmen at Leo's, a bar near the train station and the only thing open in Garden City at 2 A.M. when we knocked off. Leo was a staunch Goldwaterite and, as the price of keeping his caravansary open until a bit past 3, we had to listen to his political harangues and eat his hamburgers—I'm not sure which went down harder. But like many conservatives, he was a genial host, generous with his drinks and his time, and willing to indulge us in our liberal foolishness. He also cashed pay checks for Newsday customers.

As fellow commuters— Liz lived in the Village—we occasionally car-pooled with some other New Yorkers who couldn't, wouldn't, or didn't have to use an auto. We would whiz back to the city airing complaints and anecdotes all the way and, with little urging, repair to an all-night eatery for breakfast. The sites varied—we were moveable feasters— but at that point the bars were already closing, so a round-the-clock place was required. The Brasserie in the East Fifties was a favorite, if for no other reason than that it served better hamburgers than Leo's. After a night of dealing with the flame-keepers of Muttontown, unwinding in New York gave us a sense of relief, and release.

I'm amazed at how young everyone was at our little bank of desks; I don't think anyone was much over 25. The Long Islanders were mostly married, the New Yorkers generally single. If there was a gestalt that distinguished the staff of Newsday from other tabloids, such as the one at the late Mirror, it was one of attitude. Not only were the Newsday reporters younger but most also believed that journalism could change things, as distinct from their counterparts at The Mirror a decade earlier who saw their roles as recording the foibles of a humanity that was basically irredeemable. Not that there wasn't a sufficiency of troglodytes at Newsday, nor a cheerful cynicism, anti-boosterism and gallows humor that is a prerequisite for any self-respecting city room. But the cynicism at Newsday focused on those in power; at The Mirror it was free-floating. The Mirror's credo was Get the Story; at Newsday it was Get the Bastards.

These two pulses—the Sensational and the Crusading were the systole/diastole of American journalism. It was only the emphasis that changed among papers and between eras. What was happening at Newsday, then a bellwether, when I came aboard was a tectonic shift to the crusading mode. It was driven by the vanguard of a newly affluent, better educated, younger, reformist rank-and-file who were kindred spirits with the muckrakers of the Progressive era. The quiescence of the 50's was about to be blown away by the very class that had profited from it. If the Civil Rights movement and the Kennedys had lit a fire, the journalistic fuel was already there. Newsday was a harbinger but it shortly had plenty of company.

The suburban Republicans got sloppy in the complacent 50's and became fat targets for a generation creating a new culture that saw them as Neanderthals ripe for extinction. On a national scale the same theme would be played out in the South of Governor Wallace and the North of Mayor Daley. By the time Vietnam happened, the infrastructure of dissidence was already well in place on American newspapers. That the Neanderthals had a lot more staying power than their young critics supposed, and that the insurgents' own idealistic wave would end in a tidal pool of cut-throat careerism, rationalization and expediency was something few could imagine at the time.

The shift among news staffs from aspiring-class origins to upper-class ones was probably the greatest cultural change to affect news reporting in the 20th century yet it has hardly been examined. As late as the 1950's, reporters on big-time papers earned roughly the same as most Americans they wrote about; often they lived in the same neighborhoods, shopped in the same stores and went to the same schools as their subjects. Once journalism—certainly post-Watergate—became respectable among the affluent, desirable among the elite, a source of cachet and access, it shed its raffish allure and became anthropology. The result was journalism with a whiff of Margaret Mead going among the Samoans. There is more than some truth to the charge of elitism that has driven the populist reaction against the mainstream media. And while the harangues from the demagogues of the Right are excessive and their nostrums woeful, they have been able to capitalize on a growing mistrust of what is popularly seen as a breed of mandarins reporting on the unwashed and ill-bred in varying guises of sympathy, dudgeon and detachment. The switch in city rooms from scotch to soda was decisive but its impact went unremarked, most notably by journalists themselves who were slow to acknowledge this shift. Who wants to admit that you're the oregano of the earth?

Over time, Newsday began to trust me with pieces of wider scope. Slowly, steadily, I evolved from beat reporting to general assignment and occasional night rewrite. This included a thorough grounding in the Death Department, which I refined over the years to figures of greater prominence, but the principles remained the same. Newsday was then very big on "local man" obits—"Local Man Dies in Florida Train Wreck." There are two ways to do a simple obit: Either they call you or you call them. The first is when the family wants to announce the death and take note of the departed, so they get in touch or are expecting your call or, in the case of the prominent, there are the advanced obituaries that await only the passing of the deceased. The second is when something gruesome or untoward has happened, often to a humbler sort. The last thing anyone wants then is to pick up the phone and start talking to a reporter. The trick is to hope some near relative answers the phone —an uncle who is close enough to provide pertinent details but not so close as to fall apart. Often, they are the ones who respond in any case; if not, you try to get them on the line or to call back. Failing these, you default to funeral-director mode where you exude empathy with the spouse/child/sibling and hold their hands while extracting the necessary data.

On more than one occasion, I was the first to break the news of someone's death; strangely, people were so shocked that they kept talking; they had to talk to somebody. Moreover, in those pre-internet days, you might be the only one with the information. Furthermore, by dint of being a stranger, you'd created a certain formality whereby it was inappropriate for people to unravel. And, in a bizarre way, no one wanted to look foolish in front of a newspaper reporter, or do anything that might appear embarrassing. That was for later. I remember calling a man whose daughter, a women in her 20's, had been killed when a train hit her car at a railroad crossing in California. The item had come over on a piece of UPI wire. For whatever unaccountable lapse of communication, it was clear, after a moment, that I was the one informing him. I told him he could have someone call back later if he liked but he said no, he wanted to stay on the phone. Once I'd given him whatever details I had, he went on in cool, distant, almost disinterested tones, as if he were reading from a phone book, to tell me about his daughter's life, more than I needed but less than he needed. He thanked me for the information like I was his stock broker, and hung up. I imagine that he succumbed afterwards but in the moment, perhaps a ten-minute phone call, it was as if he were disembodied and we were suspended in some otherworldly dimension where he was temporarily impervious to what had happened.

As noted, nothing of this sort obtains for the death of the great. At The Times, which has refined this to an art form, there are lengthy, prepared obits which, if things go well, need only a little update for filling and the cause of death for topping. Much of the work has already been done. The encomiums flood in and the only added effort may come in the form of an appreciation or chronology. It is more a matter of packaging than reporting. In those years, Newsday was not quite up to speed on this and little was done in advance. This afforded me the opportunity of writing everything from the obits of Sergeant Alvin York, the conscientious objector turned World War I hero, to Harpo Marx. I also developed a knack for writing historical pieces that ran as sidebars to larger events. For Churchill's 90th birthday, I knocked off a quick 900-word summary of his life and times, which opened: "When Winston Churchill began his career in 1895, a Havana Cigar was a good smoke, the Fourth Hussars were the ultimate weapon and the empire stretched magnificently over the globe. In the 69 years that transpired, the Fourth Hussars have been usurped by the thermonuclear cavalry of atomic missiles, the empire is a restive commonwealth and Winston Churchill, the not-too-bright son of Lord Randolph Churchill, has served his country in five wars and was twice her prime minister." It ended: "Now, at his 90th birthday, it is not so much the man, a frail shadow of his former self, but the idea of Churchill that has left such a profound impact on the language, the ideas and the moral lexicon of the English-speaking peoples." Ripe stuff, but I'd like to think Churchill, once a cheeky young journalist himself, might have given it a nod.

It was often a last-minute scramble but I liked writing history, even if it was on the fly. For the 50th anniversary of the outbreak of the Great War, I did a reprise of the Archduke Ferdinand's assassination at Sarajevo and, as the Tonkin Gulf crisis unraveled, I wrote histories of Vietnam, north and south. Strife then struck closer to home and I covered some of the racial violence of that era, reporting from Bedford-Stuyvesant and Harlem as well as covering the murder of Malcolm X, together with Tom Johnson, one of our two black reporters which, at the time, gave us a leg up on The Times. As the Gray Lady's John Hess observed, major-league baseball was integrated before The Times.

I covered a good bit of local politics though, more often than not, Jimmy Breslin's adage to "go to the loser ahead of the winner," applied in my case. For the mayoral election of 1965, I was sent not to John V. Lindsay's victorious camp, nor even to the redoubt of the vanquished Democrat Abe Beame, but to report on the Socialist Labor Party candidate, Eric Hass, whose headquarters happened to be in his living room. Together with his wife, Tillie, that made three of us. Tillie didn't seem too interested in the outcome of the voting on TV, averring as to how "if there was a good play on, I'd switch channels." It could have been worse. I might have been sent to cover Vito Battista of the United Taxpayers Party, clearly a man ahead of his time. Turning adversity to advantage, I got a nice piece out of Haas who, as it turned out, had been running unsuccessfully as his party's standard bearer in numerous elections for almost 30 years.

Newsday had a taste for such ridiculous stuff and I developed a deadpan knack for writing about it. Newsday was, after all, a tabloid and there was no cheap stunt or corny story too flagrant for it to resist. One Christmas they sent me to the Bowery—it snowed on cue—to see how the down-and-outers were doing. It was a page out of O. Henry in reverse: The Grift of the Magi. In those days the homeless (callously known in that harsher time as bums and vagrants) were concentrated on Skid Row as opposed to being dispersed throughout the city. Their precinct ran along the Bowery from Houston to Canal Streets. The vice of choice was drink although there was certainly a segment done in by drugs as well. Except for the habits of work and self-control, the denizens had internalized many of the values of the larger society and referred to themselves as bums and vagrants. They warned me about not being a soft touch for their colleagues who would only drink away whatever charity was offered.

They lived in rows of flophouses just north of what was the lighting and baby-furniture district and is today a redoubt of gentrification whose chic bars bear little resemblance to the saloons of yesteryear. To make their nut of a dollar-a-night for a flop, they panhandled the neighborhood or shook each other down. It would appear to be a zero-sum game since the area was desolate, but somehow, there were always enough slummers and predatory cruisers so that most managed to fork up for the rent. The "hotels" were bleak, bare-bulb affairs, night-clerks at caged windows, dormitories stinking of reek, booze and formaldehyde. It was clear why some preferred hanging out in the cold huddling around ashcan fires for as long as possible. On virtually every other block there was a bar that didn't even have neon but exuded a gangrenous light. The street was littered with Thunderbird wine and Manischewitz, both cheap and sweet.

I talked to a few hoteliers, a priest at a church where the more sober ones warmed up, a few bartenders and the citizens. Anyone would talk for a drink and if not they'd talk anyway. It was a time before victimization had become fashionable; people just had hard-luck stories. Most had been rehearsed—I wasn't the first down that way. None were true—everyone rolled their eyeballs at the other man's story—although you never know. None of them had a whit of sympathy for any of their peers and all believed that only they had landed there by mistake and somehow didn't belong. I was accompanied by a photographer and I realized that they were posing; dressing the part: primping in their ill-shaven, unkempt, ragged worst. They were putting on a bit of performance, acting out pre-assigned roles for some extra change. These were, after all, the lucky ones. The others went off the deep end and wound up on Ward's Island. When I came back from the Bowery, I wrote a piece that was half "Brother Can You Spare a Dime," half "Nobody Knows You When You're Down and Out." I didn't believe a word of it and neither would those who spoke to me. But as I wrote, I psyched myself up to spinning their stories into a tabloid morality tale. People liked it. Tabs sell for a reason.

The Civil Rights movement was then heating up and Long Island had its contingent of young college students who were going down to register voters in the Mississippi Summer Project of 1964. I covered a training session led by a young red-headed man, beaming good will and optimism. He was demonstrating the proper response toward police violence to his mostly white charges who'd shortly be heading south to register black voters. The instructor went through the rituals of going limp and assuming the fetal position if attacked by club-wielding goons. He spoke with the cheerful assurance of a scoutmaster showing boys how to tie knots. Everyone seemed to have the impression that rolling up in a ball would make them impervious to the blows of the benighted. These kids weren't Christian martyrs—they were in fact the first generation of postwar affluence, the vanguard of the baby boom; they had grown up on happy endings and seemed convinced that nothing really bad was going to happen to them. They were the good guys, right? I asked the instructor later "What if they keep hitting you, or do worse? They're pretty inventive." But he was absolutely confident that the principles of passive resistance would overcome brute force. I wished him well.

The turmoil of the Vietnam War reverberated within the paper where the publisher, Harry Guggenheim, who supported the war, felt himself increasingly isolated from a staff that opposed it. To balance the coverage Guggenheim sent his old friend John Steinbeck to Vietnam. No longer the dissident who'd written "The Grapes of Wrath," Steinbeck composed a series of dispatches in the form of missives to Newsday's late publisher and Guggenheim's wife, Alicia Patterson. If writing to a dead woman

67

was somewhat bizarre, the contents of the letters were stranger still: hawkish celebrations of the military enterprise and angry diatribes against the war protesters. Steinbeck's correspondence consisted of shrill polemics, unrelieved by nuance, wit or grace. He disparaged war protesters—whom he wrote about at a distance—as "Vietniks, dirty clothes, dirty minds, sour-smelling wastelings and their ill-favored and barren pad mates." Given the task of processing his copy, I felt I'd absorbed his style sufficiently to offer my own portrayal of a Steinbeck column and posted one on the office bulletin board. My version was a "Letter to Alicia" written by Steinbeck from Bakersfield, California, in 1935.

In this rendition the author covers a strike by Okies picking peaches in the Imperial Valley and comes down squarely on the side of the owners. He assures Alicia that he's been personally briefed by the Farmers Association and the State Police and he urges her not to believe the distorted tales of bleeding-heart New Dealers about the cops shooting strikers and the farmers exploiting workers who are simply too lazy to earn an honest day's wages. But happily, the strike has been broken "and for the next several days we hunted down the remnants of these troublemakers." However, the battle is not over. "Even now, there is trouble near Pixley. Someone named Tom Joad is trying to organize the Okies in the neighborhood. He was heard to say: 'Wherever they's beatin' up a guy, I'll be there.' Talk like this is positively communistic." Although never published, it was probably one of the best pieces I did at Newsday.

Whether it was because of my perceived affinity for the demi monde of the Bowery or merely a whim, Newsday sent me to spend a week in what was about to become the East Village. Like the proverbial Mr. Jones—who hadn't yet been written into myth—my editors knew something was happening out there but didn't know what. They sent me to scout. I had a pal who let me stay in his basement flat on East Sixth Street between C and D. I dressed in my old fatigues. I was the right age. It was an interesting time because the 60's, as we have come to know them—which is really 1966-71—were imminent, but only just starting to happen. The blocks of this venue were still slices on an ethnic layer cake: Poles on 10th and 11th Streets, Puerto Ricans (virtually the only Hispanics then) on 12th and 13th Streets; Ukrainians on 6th and 7th Streets; a sprinkling of Jewish holdouts huddled from Avenue A to Second. Tompkins Square Park was still a hangout for Polish oldies and only the vanguard of Hippiedom was dipping its toes into the waters of the neighborhood. The East Village Other was getting off its first issues, and what was to become New Age iconography was rare enough to be exotic. The streets were still clean and not affectedly grungy. The local public library had an impressive collection of books in Polish, Yiddish, Ukrainian and a variety of other languages. It served several generations of immigrants who insisted on keeping their own culture for themselves and their children. Assimilation in such precincts, as demonstrated by this library and so many others like it, was more gradual than ballyhooed by the popular myth of plucky European immigrants who magically embraced English, never looking back.

The East Village that I came upon was, on the surface, not too much different from what I'd remembered when I'd worked there at the print shop of my college newspaper in the late 50's. But the seeds were sprouting: the occasional head shop, drugs—which just a few years ago were "evil"—casually obtainable, bookstores and poetry readings, California bric-a-brac, juiced-up music, coffeehouses moving east from the gentrified Village (which now had to be identified with the pejorative prefix "West") and the unnerving and exciting notion that attractive middle-class girls were choosing to live in neighborhoods that their grandparents had fled. The sheer availability of forbidden fruit—women, drugs,— was enticing for a generation reared in the straight-laced 50's.

I chatted up people in bars, coffeehouses, stores: the new arrivals and the oldies who didn't yet feel threatened because the numbers hadn't tipped. Quite the opposite, the old neighbors were grudgingly impressed at having these nice young people around, if confused as to why they wanted to live there. "Why" was simple. It was cheap and unsupervised. No one cared what happened down there. It was like a big 10-block clubhouse for lost boys and girls, as the drug scene hadn't gotten ugly yet. For the first time, I saw young white people panhandling. I spoke to a few who were begging on the street who seemed to have suspended judgment of their actions.

I reported my undercover activities back to Newsday and told them I was onto something bigger, or at least better, than they had bargained for. I had stumbled onto the early rumblings of a counter-culture that was to cause so much social turmoil over the next 10 years. I needed a couple of more weeks to get people to trust me and open up. I got a flat no. They wanted to go with something quick and punchy and they needed me for something else. What they wanted was a Baedeker of The Lower Depths; a freak show where you could see the exotic types without getting too close. I gave them what they wanted but yeasted it with the warning that something was happening that was going to affect them, and probably wasn't going to be limited to The East Village.

Well before Newsday later specialized in subway coverage during its 10-year hiatus in New York, I had done a valedictory for the Myrtle Avenue El in Brooklyn. The route was a vestigial stump whose elevated scaffolding was getting in the way of progress. More importantly, as opposed to the equally rickety Flushing Line, it wasn't taking workers to and from Manhattan, but was simply an intra-borough affair, so who cared? Its fate was sealed. The last ride of the Myrtle Avenue El was supposed to debark a little before midnight and I had arranged to be on it. The station was skanky and in need of repair even by New York standards. The engineer and the conductor were not waxing sentimental. There weren't many passengers and although some made noises about being inconvenienced, most just wanted to get home. A few didn't know that the line was closing and it didn't seem to make a great deal of difference to them. Whenever I read about the great campaigns to save the facade at Grand Central or some such urban crusade, I think of the reaction to the Myrtle Avenue El: fatalistic, indifferent, sodden. I managed to put together a story in my notebook—the nice thing about journalism is that it doesn't take much to fill up 750 words. By now it was getting late and I attempted to call the desk but after trying three or four broken pay phones, I decided it would be quicker to just get in the car and drive to the office. It may be unfathomable to envision journalism in the days before cell phones or texting or tweets but such was the case.

When I got back to Garden City, the night editor, John Van Doorn, was livid. Where was I? Why hadn't I called? John was a man of some talent but with a raw edge and a quick temper. There were two ways to look at the situation. I was out there busting my chops after midnight in Brooklyn in what was not such a safe neighborhood and I'd brought home a nice little story. Or, I'd failed to call the desk and let them know where I was and what I had. Van Doorn was right, of course; I should have found a bar somewhere and phoned the desk to give them a heads-up. Van Doorn's ire had a tonic effect, and I didn't make that mistake again.

In those days, terrorizing people was a blood sport at Newsday and Van Doorn was one of its several adepts. Victims came in all shapes and sizes. Usually, the more compliant and diffident they were, the more they got knocked around. One of Van Doorn's favorite targets was Ken Brief who succeeded me on several beats, the last being Glen Cove. Diligent to a fault, Ken made himself vulnerable by his very earnestness. The more he strove to please, the more he became a quarry. Maybe it was his diminutive size that brought out the worst in Van Doorn but, whatever the reason, John ragged Brief mercilessly.

Al Marlens, of course, was a gold medalist in the intimidation marathon. The mitigating factor is that he could also be generous and you never knew which impulse was operative. Al's weakness, and strength, was that he had no patience for fools, or people he perceived to be such—a large swathe of humanity. Other mitigating factors: He never beat up on little people, which his lessors failed to observe in miming him. Instead, Marlens focused his ire on his superiors, meddlesome outsiders and, most particularly, his subalterns when he felt their standards were less exacting than his. Al didn't enjoy hitting people who couldn't fight back. Rather, he was enraged by the shenanigans of humanity and exasperated when his near-peers couldn't keep up with his demands. Until the end, he never lost his capacity for moral outrage. He wanted to do everything himself but couldn't, so he had to settle for lesser mortals and was constantly frustrated when they came up short. I probably respected him more than anyone I've met in journalism but I usually felt I was letting him down.

Like all originals Al was a closet borrower, appropriating selective mannerisms from Newsday's proto-editor, Alan Hathway, recruited by its founder, Alicia Patterson, from the Chicago Tribune of her uncle, Colonel McCormick. Hathway was a character out of The Front Page: a drinker, choleric, sclerotic, explosive, dictatorial; an outrageous practitioner of pugnacious journalism. Hathway gave me my first raise— $10 up from $125 a week By the time I came aboard he was already a toothless lion, half in the bag most of the time. He had pretty much left operative control in the hands of Bill McIlwain, the editor, and Marlens, the managing editor. And McIlwain, who himself liked the pleasures of the bottle and bed more than was good for him, delegated a good deal of responsibility to Marlens—who was only too happy to assume it. Al was de facto in charge, at least for the mundane realities of running our lives. If Hathway's growl was at this time closer to Bert Lahr, Al's roar shook the forest.

The editor who suffered most directly under Al was Stan Asimov. Azzy, as he was known, was then the night city editor working directly for Marlens. Whatever went wrong seemed to be Azzy's fault. Whatever went right was rarely credited to him. The result was a cruel game: Al demanding "how come?" and Azzy trying to explain. Azzy was a good newspaperman, but a softie. I was being groomed for the desk at the time—although I didn't quite know it or want to acknowledge it—so I sat next to Azzy during this period. After Al was through with him on these occasions his hands were shaking. Azzy was too much of a gent to try to lay off any blame so he absorbed all the body blows himself and never passed the pain along.

Years later, when Al was gone, Azzy, ever the sport, tried to make light of it, turning Marlens the Ogre into a legend-bearing Grendel with stories that were more outsized than oppressive, so that Al became a folk-hero, at worst a dispenser of rough justice. This was not the case at the time. Azzy was browbeaten; I think he hated every minute of it. Interestingly, Al did not treat his other subalterns—his right hand, Tony Insolia; the copy chief, Art Perfall; the Suffolk Editor, Mel Opotowsky, or the night editor, Dick Estrin—in quite the same way. Though they all came in for their share of upbraiding.

Azzy spent a good part of his life getting out from under the shadow of greater, albeit not better, men. His older brother was Isaac Asimov—God knows how much time he spent trying to carve his own identity out of that one. Then Azzy graduated to Al. But he emerged from this as well, a veritable Houdini of emotional escapes. Asimov's solution was brilliant. He segued into a job as assistant to the publisher in charge of newsroom budgeting, planning and technology, thereby leapfrogging over Marlens, or at least to one side, staying in the newspaper business while moving beyond Al's clutches. By the time Marlens left, Azzy found the job so much to his liking he kept it for the rest of his life.

What did I gain from all this? They say that a rabbinical student, to learn from his master, should not only heed his teaching but also observe the way he ties his shoelace—a man's behavior is also a lesson. From Azzy I learned to absorb abuse from above without inflicting it on those below. It wasn't simply a matter of "the buck stops here"—Al had that in spades—but of not passing along pain. I didn't learn that lesson right away, and I'm not sure if applying it was good for my stomach, although I never got an ulcer. From Al I learned to push people and not to settle; also anger. When I became City Editor of Newsday, I did a pretty good imitation of Marlens. I'm not proud of that but neither am I ashamed. It was not inappropriate to a time when acting out was acceptable managerial behavior. My secretary Cathy thought I was funny; my secretary Gertrude, less so. My secretary Shirley told me that I'd have to behave better at The Times where they were all gentlemen. I took her message to heart. A mistake. A bit more of Al and a little less of Azzy would've worked better there.

I was never really promoted from reporter to deskman. I was temporarily borrowed one night and never returned. All of my career advancement came in this manner. People recognized something they thought I could offer and they prodded me along. Usually, I was a reluctant dragon, cautious about my career moves and skeptical of my abilities. I was helped along by mentors who saw more in me than I did. When pushed, I came through, confirming them and surprising myself. But being advanced too fast, too soon—at least in my estimation—filled me with anxiety. I have since advised a succession of protégés that no enterprise of pith and moment is achieved without trepidation but I was not available to so counsel my younger self.

What happened at the time—the mid-60's —was that Marlens called me in and said that the night desk was short-handed and needed me for a brief stint, maybe a week. At that moment, I was just beginning to pull free of the beat system and expanding into general assignment with an accent on New York. I liked it, I was having fun and I enjoyed being outside. Also, I was just starting to get a feel for reporting, for its variety and richness. I was building my speed and confidence. I didn't want to go indoors, at least not yet. I said as much to Marlens. He told me he understood, but they had to feel they could count on me. If I volunteered, it would be good for my career; they'd remember me. Implicit in this was that if I didn't, they'd also remember me.

Al spoke gently, and fondly, like a parent who sees beyond the needs of a child. But he was firm and it was clearly not in my interest to turn him down. He promised me that they'd get me back on the street in a week or two. That was 50 years ago. After my appointed fortnight, I reminded the copy chief, Art Perfall, that my tour of duty should be over. Perfall, a genial and clubbable man, apparently wasn't aware that I had an Estimated Time of Separation. He was under the impression that I was his for keeps which, as it turned out, was true.

Although I was nominally working for Perfall I ultimately reported to the night editor, Dick Estrin, as we all did. Dick was arguably a minor genius at a modest craft. He was responsible for deciding what we could go with, and what would have to wait; putting the right spin on our best stories; playing traffic cop; acting as court of last resort and decreeing the fate of all late-breaking news. He also guarded the gates against anything libelous, scurrilous or troublesome. This often led to shooting matches with irate writers, but after 10 P.M. Dick called the shots. He also functioned as makeup editor, city editor, managing editor, chief copy editor and on occasion did a little rewrite— all of it flawless. It was like watching a ballplayer who could play center, shortstop and catcher with finesse and then come in and relieve for three shutout innings. I've seen people who could do any one of those jobs better, but not altogether at once.

Time passed and I reminded Marlens about my return to reporting. On each occasion, it was clear that he wasn't pleased by my importuning. But along with the stick went carrots. I got a raise. I was being praised for my deskwork. I seemed to be developing a knack for writing headlines under pressure, which was always at a premium at a tabloid. My "breakthrough" was a head announcing the ouster of Ghana's strongman Kwame Nkrumah. He was deposed in a palace coup while on a state visit to his ally Sekou Toure who was experimenting with socialism and third-world politics in nearby Guinea. Toure had graciously offered his guest asylum until the smoke cleared. I was expected to get the gist of this into a two line, one column head, in effect about four or five words, and make it sing. The problem was that Nkrumah had a lot more letters than a one-column head could accommodate. Also, the news had broken late and time was pressing. Still, it was easy enough. I gave them: "Black King / To Red Castle." Perfall bought it but Estrin thought it was too cheeky. The message, however, was delivered. After that I got a lot of juicy pieces and Estrin sometimes threw me Page One heads. They were called "wood" because, at a length of 72 points, they were too big for any metal type in the linotype machine, so they had to be placed with large wooden letters, hence the phrase "wood," which became synonymous with the front-page headline, and story, as in: "What's the wood tonight?"

The event that pushed me through the door was a story about a standoff between state troopers in Montana and a tribe of Indians who felt the authorities were encroaching on their fishing rights. When the cops came to confront the Indians they found themselves surrounded and had to call for help. I put a head on it but wasn't satisfied. That morning, at around 6:45, I was driving home on the

West Side Highway when the right head hit me: "Quick, Get All the Patrol Cars in a Circle." I pulled off in Washington Heights, found a phone booth, got Estrin and made the head fix just in time for the late press run. It wasn't so much the headline as the impulse.

As my patrons understood all along, I was becoming rooted in the copy desk culture. I had begun to enjoy my confinement and found it liberating. My friends and alliances shifted slightly, but noticeably. My perspective altered somewhat, and voila: I had gone from hunter to cave-dweller. I enjoyed watching Perfall operate. He handled the desk smoothly, was good with his people and resolute in a crisis. I also liked the fact that, although his job was copy chief, in a pinch, he could sit down and re-do a layout or anything else that was required to get the job done. I learned to admire the jack-of-all trades ability in seasoned editors and the pragmatism with which they applied it.

After the night shift, we'd sometimes adjourn to the Old Country Diner for breakfast. Or we'd just hang out at the desk shooting the breeze while the sun oozed in; no one much felt like going home. Occasionally, if we tarried too long, the promotions people would come in giving a tour of the Family Newspaper to a troop of Boy Scouts and there we'd be: half-in-the-bag, mettlesome, dissolute and generally disorderly. This usually led to warnings from the publisher's office to behave better, or at least to clear out and behave badly elsewhere, but in those easygoing days they were generally ignored. It was a time when the newsroom could with impunity tell corporate vice presidents to bugger off. The editorial side still dominated the paper, and a certain raffishness, even in the suburbs, was expected if you were to keep a staff worth its salt.

The publisher himself, Harry Guggenheim, seemed to have a grudging affinity for the bluff quality of the newsroom. Although he could have remained in his bank, where, according to McIlwain, he was fawned upon, Capt. Guggenheim chose to spend part of his last years at the paper. By then, gamely struggling against cancer, he'd often walk in after the early edition was put to bed and the night crew was still hanging around in the morning with their feet on the desk and a bottle as well. No one bothered to remove either as the Captain came through the city room, white-haired, blue-eyed, limping—an unnecessary trip but one he chose to make. "Hiya Harry," the boys would cry out. Or occasionally, "How's it goin' Captain?" When he got sicker, there'd be an occasional: "Hang in there old sport." To all of which he'd nod bemusedly and with a dignified wave of his hand. I don't think I ever heard him speak. But in his fading days, he seemed to prefer the give-and-take of this raucous bunch who treated him with democratic familiarity and a certain rough-hewn affection to the mausoleum of his bank.

By now I was permanently tethered to the night copy desk and immersed in its various operations. One of these involved a tour of duty in the composing room. This meant shifting from copy editing duties at around 4 A.M. to work with the makeup editor, Howard Halpern, till the edition closed at 6. I apprenticed under Howard for about a year. It was a valuable tutorial, and a humbling one. Halpern knew as much about the mysteries of type as anyone in the printer's union. The printers, who had little use for most editors, deferred to him. Howard was familiar with everything and everyone in those lower depths and loved to impart his arcane knowledge to willing acolytes. I wasn't going to make my career there—although I spent more time in such places than I cared to—but as things turned out, it came in handy. My familiarity with composing rooms and the ways of printers stood me in good stead later on at The Times. Just as today's reporters have to be skilled in a plethora of social and digital media, versatile editors of a bygone era were conversant with a spectrum of crafts within print. I came to appreciate the virtue of knowing all aspects of the business. Such experience brought respect for what others were doing, in what was an ensemble operation. At the time, many journalists would rather not have been bothered with such details and chose instead to focus on their own pursuits but I believed it was important to see the entire picture.

The printers were a tough bunch and one had to earn their respect. It took me almost a year until I really felt comfortable handling myself on the floor, much longer than any editorial pursuit. As it turned out I'd learned a dying craft but it served me long enough and I don't regret the exercise. Printing was then still done with linotype machines and the lead rows of type were warm to the touch. Editorial people weren't allowed to handle type, but I'd sneak in a brush-by just to feel the heat. The type was set in rectangular ice-cube-like trays called galleys, carried out by apprentices to large steel tables called stones, and placed by a makeup man in rectangular steel forms known as "chases." A stone usually held four chases and the white-collar makeup editor and his blue-collar opposite—the make-up man—would face each other from either side of the stone. They both followed a layout, or dummy, provided by a desk editor.

Ostensibly, the makeup editor was supposed to direct the printer, but a good makeup man needed little direction provided the layout was accurate. Halpern's rules were simple: Never help the printer unless he needs it. Always have an escape route. It was understood that things would usually go wrong and you were the last line of defense. Howard's job was to make sure that things fit and closed on time. At this stage there was no time for rewrite. If heads didn't fit, we'd call the desk or, if need be, fix them ourselves by pulling a word or a line out. Skilled editors would write a two-line head so that in a space crunch the second line could be dropped with the first one standing independently.

We kept a record of everything on a proof-sheet. Stories were often over-space and we trimmed them on the floor. Type that was held, or cut, was known as overset and was duly recorded. Too much overset was costly and sloppy and would lead to nasty notes from the higher-ups. Today, computers can measure space to micro perfection so that an editor can make a last-minute trim at his or her desk with a few strokes. In those days layout was an inexact science influenced as much by hope and human frailty as by calculation. The result was that things usually had to be readjusted on the composing-room floor. The swiftest way to do so was by slashing from the bottom up, which is why the pyramid form of news writing—information in descending order of importance— was as important to the harried printer as the hurried reader. "Framework" or O. Henry endings were the enemies of the makeup man. If cutting from the bottom wasn't possible we pulled whole paragraphs. The good writers would avoid transitions so that each paragraph was an independent bloc enabling the makeup editors to pull an unnecessary paragraph without breaking the logical flow of the piece.

The untrained eye never saw the difference but in the crush of deadline it meant life or death. Not everyone followed these rules and prima donnas would weave finely stitched tales that were hard to break up without resetting. They did so at their peril because the makeup editor would exact revenge by moving the story down the page or further back in the paper, or run it only in one edition "in order to save everything." Often, we'd cut "on stone," literally having the printer snip into the lead type with a cutter at the end of a clause, turning a comma into a period with his knife and lopping off the rest of the paragraph.. This shortcut was in defiance of union rules that required us to send the revised paragraph back to a linotype operator for resetting, but the good printers waived this rule, saving critical minutes of waiting.

I learned to look for widows, white space at the end of a line, to make a trim, or pullback, in the lines above. But we didn't want to blow all our widows because the page would look crowded. If a story was short, I learned to fill out with subheads, making sure that these "slugs" didn't bump in adjacent columns, or we spaced out with "leads" tossed in between lines. A good printer could disguise spacing so that no one would notice it was there. That was for us to judge. If we were really short, we'd throw in a box or a picture. Since photographs, or their photo-engraved wood-block likeness known as "cuts," couldn't be simulated at the last moment, we always had available two or three different sizes of the same picture, or a related picture, or a picture with an adjacent story so that if the "cut" appeared in the wrong size, as sometimes happened, we could throw in an alternate. Similarly, we had filler material of all sizes to toss into any hole that opened.

Newsday was a fat paper with a large news hole so there were many pages to be supervised. Halpern would march around from stone to stone dealing with the early pages in the back of the book first, then coming round to the late pages, and finally addressing the front page itself. He knew which printers needed watching, had an instinct for where trouble was brewing, a gift for putting out fires—always with an eye to the clock and, when necessary, a judicious way of prodding the desk to get the last pieces of copy on the front pages into the composing room.

Howard's final rule was Don't Lose Your Nerve, or should that fail, Don't Let 'Em See It. He was supremely assured that he could solve any crisis that arose. One morning, around 5:15, we had just finished a double-truck—a two-page extravaganza—on some special project that "the mucky-mucks cooked up," as Howard would say. It should have been ready days earlier, but there was the usual last-minute procrastinating, and there we were. Howard had managed to get the thing closed with about 40 minutes to spare. The printer locked it up, literally tightening the screws in the chase to keep the type in place. But he had gotten a little careless and, when the apprentice came to pick it up, both pages fell through, the lead literally raining on the floor, the kid, mortified, holding an empty frame. It was a case of pied type, a composing-room nightmare and, given the late hour, a disaster in the making. Howard was unflappable. Without missing a beat he called Estrin on the phone, got the dupes rushed to the composing room, had the copy cutter redistribute them in small takes, got the foreman to put his two best men into setting the new type in two separate chases and got it off to the pressroom within a few minutes of deadline.

What I got from Howard was the confidence that I could always close on time.

All of this has been superannuated by the computer and now one person can pretty much perform the multi-varied exercise described above. It was Howard Halpern himself, with probably very little sentimentality, who crafted the digital transition at Newsday. After I'd left the paper, Halpern set up Newsday's first computer system. Like Gutenberg modifying the wine press into a printing press, Howard simply adapted his knack for pica rules to software commands.

As for the rest of my duties, life on a night desk was a tour in the Twilight Zone. Anomie was built in to the very nature of the job. The hours, which began between 8 and 10 P.M. , were long, late and lousy. They wreaked havoc with personal life the way the sea absorbs the drowned, indifferently rather than by design. At its most manic, or depressive, it was an outpatient clinic for neurotics where the patients, mildly sedated, were allowed to leave the asylum, free to come and go provided that they reappeared when expected and remained as long as needed. There were, however, consolations. Since Newsday was then a lot smaller than its New York rivals, everything went through a single desk, which made for a degree of gruff conviviality and a certain grim esprit.

The work attracted a variety of misfits and the usual contingent of literary wannabes, some brilliant, some quirky, some cantankerous, occasionally, all three. At opposite poles of this curmudgeonly magnetic field were two prototypes, Murray Frymer and Bill Garrett. If Frymer was Mutt, Garrett was Jeff. Not that they were particular friends or hung out together, but their sheer juxtaposition on the desk bespoke the Laurel and Hardy quality of the place. Murray was loquacious, Bill was taciturn; Murray was excitable, Bill was phlegmatic; Murray was urban, Jewish and neurotic; Bill was rural, Gentile and repressed. What they both shared was a mistrust of authority, the difference being that Murray would make the speech, Bill would throw the bomb. During the first vain attempt to organize a union at Newsday, a list of salaries was purloined and posted, upsetting management. Bill got into hot water for doing the posting. I don't think his career suffered greatly because he didn't plan to have much of one. We both lived in the West 70's and occasionally, I'd give him a lift home. Often he'd choose to wait for a night train just to be ornery. Bill was a long drink of a fellow, stingy with words, which he clearly knew how to use when editing.

People mistook Garrett for a gawky mountaineer type although his tastes were more cultivated than most. Bill's only giveaway was a sporty cravat—generally viewed as an affectation—that he insisted on wearing over his open-necked shirts. It took Garrett months before he got to trust me enough to favor me with his asides, which were pretty good. One night, on the ride back to New York, Bill told me his story. He had been city editor of a paper in Charleston, West Virginia, when a rival stole his job and his wife, and a flood swept away his home. It was like listening to country music. Was this some wacky tale that he told to awed Easterners to gauge their wonderment? Making himself "believable" since this is what city slickers expected of country rubes in any case? Was it a fantasy that he believed to be true? Or was it, after all, the case? I chose to accept it, perhaps because it was the least implausible explanation.

Garrett was clearly miserable on the desk, not in the carping way that many affected but in a stone-silent suffering, an acceptance of earthly chastisement. He wore Newsday like a hair shirt. One night I asked him: "Bill, why don't you just disappear?" He fixed me with a baleful Ancient Mariner stare and replied: "Boy, I have disappeared." Bill stayed disappeared for more than 30 years. He was there toiling obscurely on the desk when I came back to Newsday two decades later.

In those days our lone woman on the desk was Alice Murray, which gave us one more woman than The Times had on most of its desks. Copy editing was a labor-intensive task for Alice. She worried a story the way ancient Japanese artists did brushwork: it was an intricate exercise, rich with filigree and finesse. When she lit onto a hole or a bump in a story she would subject the writer to a Jesuitical examination until the matter was clarified to her satisfaction. Since this would often take place at three in the morning with the reporter half asleep and Alice full of remorseless energy it was the equivalent of water torture until the poor devil at the other end of the phone surrendered.

Newsday was then an "editor's paper." Writers often talk about how a fabled editor pushed them to get a story they might not have otherwise obtained. They rarely mention those far more common instances where the desk drove them beyond endurance in a futile effort to satisfy someone's hobby horse. Ed Smith, a former rewrite man at Newsday, had two metal boxes of phone numbers on his desk, one labeled "Numbers where people cannot be reached for comment" and the other labeled "Numbers where people can be reached for 'No Comment.' " I was told of one copy editor in the Estrin days who boasted that before calling a reporter at home, he and his colleagues thought of the greatest number of questions they could ask on a single story. The other side of the coin was a "writers' paper" where the desk had been sufficiently neutered so that, once a senior editor had signed off, the copy was sacrosanct. Over time, the result was either a frustrated writing staff or a demoralized desk. Name your poison.

On Friday evenings with a smaller crew John Van Doorn filled in for Dick Estrin. Usually, things were a little more relaxed but on one such night, in dead winter, a snow-storm hit harder than expected and our already tiny band was reduced to a skeleton crew. I managed to make it in from New York in my black Beetle—the defrost was impaired and the frame of visibility kept narrowing so I had to use my hand to wipe the frost off the front window. I arrived at about 8 to find that, aside from Van Doorn and Alice Murray, there were only Leo Seligsohn, Ed Smith on rewrite and Ken Crowe who'd been recruited to work with us. Luckily, there was enough advance copy around and the wires were ticking away so we were in business. It only meant a bit of brisker rowing in the cut-and-paste department.

Ken Crowe was a big, gawky, well-meaning guy. A relative newcomer to the desk, he was a bit clumsy in his efforts, trying to feel his was around unfamiliar territory. As the night progressed, Van Doorn, who was trying to juggle a few different tasks, let the copy pile up a little more than usual. Since we were short on copy boys, he recruited Ken to help move the copy to the composing room. As Van Doorn cleared a piece of copy he'd hand it on, without looking up, to Crowe, whose job it was to stuff it into the pneumatic tubes and send it along to the printers through a pressurized air chute that went to the composing room. Ken dutifully logged each piece he launched. As it was pushing 5 A.M. Van Doorn increased the pace, tossing him batches of copy which Crowe sent aloft. The city room was a bell of silence, quiet as the snow wafting outside. Contrary to popular myth, newsrooms in crisis were not noisy places, even in the days before computers. The surface noise usually occurred with setting things up, but in the intensity of a close, everyone was focused and things got very still. In any case, we were pressing on when somewhere around 5:15, Van Doorn got a call from the composing room asking where all the copy was. He asked me to go see what was up. I went to the copy cutter in the composing room, to discover that virtually nothing had appeared. After poking around a bit the copy cutter found that some paper had been shredded in the air shaft. With a sinking feeling I went back downstairs. It was at that moment that I saw Crowe take a piece of copy and send it up the shaft. But he didn't put it in a pneumatic tube. In effect, he had shredded the edition.

I would have been horrified if I weren't petrified. I circled the city room to come in from the lee of Van Doorn and informed Alice. She had a soothing effect on John and was the only one who could break it to him. At first, Alice was aghast, but then she became very calm, rose, and conferred with John. I could see that while she was talking, very low and soft, his face was turning from red to white. It would have turned blue if we were genetically programmed for it. He turned slowly to Ken and, like a man trying to control his bladder, asked: "Ken, how were you sending the copy up the tubes." Ken, not quite understanding what was afoot, showed him. John, an adder about to spring, said through clenched teeth: "You're supposed to put it in the pneumatic tube first." Ken responded "Nobody told me." A mistake. John exploded "What kind of moron are you?" That was the nice part. What followed were a few choice expletives and comments about Ken's intelligence and career opportunities at Newsday. All the while, Alice held her hand on John's shoulder apparently to console and calm him, but just as likely to keep him from leaping at Ken and ruining his own future.

At this point, Leo managed to steer Ken into the men's room and John had to focus on recovering. The great virtue of a newspaper on deadline is that there is no time to carry on office grudges or personal vendettas. Van Doorn was probably at his best in this moment. We scrambled and got as many dupes as we could off the reporters' spikes, ripped off wire copy, tossed some heads on and sent it all to the composing room—this time using pneumatic tubes. The foreman pushed everything through—printers could always work faster but never showed it unless they had to. Howard Halpern appeared and was overseeing the action. We actually managed to close only twenty minutes late which, given the state of the roads, could be ascribed to the snow rather than production. It was a small miracle. Alice had saved Ken from John and John from himself. I believe Crowe wound up in Ronkonkoma or perhaps covering the Montauk Lighthouse for a while after that but it was all to the good, because from his Suffolk base he redeemed himself, going on to help win a Pulitzer in 1970 and later earn a reputation as a respected labor reporter.

After about two years of this, I was moved up to the night desk as an assistant Nassau night editor. I didn't realize it at the time but going from the rim to the assignment desk was migrating from the congressional to the executive. In space it was only moving 30 feet but in fact it was a world apart. On the copy desk—and certainly in the reporting ranks—you were one of many. You could dish off a piece if you became overloaded, and although you groused about being an interchangeable part, you worked together in a collegial enterprise. However, once someone moved to the other side of the aisle, they were on their own. What I hated most though were the mechanics of the job. I've always considered myself a closet dyslectic and drawing layouts for the paper's inside pages—one of the requirements of the work—was for me an onerous task. My talent, such as it was, lay in marshaling resources on breaking news, prodding reporters to follow their inherent instincts to get the story and then doing a creditable edit.

But when it came to packaging the results, I had to scramble. I couldn't draw a straight line at a time when sub-editors were expected to dummy their own layouts for the inside pages. It wasn't till I got to The Times that I encountered a system where makeup editors drew the layouts. At Newsday there was no such thing, pagination was light years away and art directors were strictly high concept. Consequently, my experience was somewhat schizophrenic. I spent an inordinate amount of time trying to translate words into inches, inches into picas, picas into columns. In the time remaining I tried to keep track of the beat reporters, pick out the few pieces that might develop into upfront stories and edit and move what came in. This process did not involve line editing which was left to the copy desk. Rather, it was one of substance: Did a piece make sense? Were there any holes? Was the lead right? Was the story in sequence? What went to the desk was still in a rough stage. The copy editors would make the trims, tighten things up and write the heads. Most importantly, they would pick holes in the stories that I was required to communicate back to the annoyed reporter.

There was an ongoing tension between the impulse to move the copy and the concern that the piece needed more work. The former usually won out because the worst thing one could be in that job was a bottleneck. There was a constant looking at the clock with an eye toward how much was left to do, what was late, what was still coming. The phones were ringing incessantly and the voices on the other end wanted immediate and total attention. Not all of them were reporters. Sometime they were irate readers or people seeking information. Since Newsday was a hometown paper, we were required to respond politely to all callers.

The real stomach churner, however, was when something major broke, not an infrequent occurrence, and indeed, our main purpose. This meant that the layouts had to be redone, stories juggled, squeezed or held. Should the new development involve a judgment call, the more timorous, cautious types would try, if possible, to deflate the importance of the story—knock it down— or fit it into the existing format. The former involved deceiving oneself and the latter made for an awkward juxtaposition. Neither were tolerated and anyone who pursued them was gone. Marlens was a bulldog about never letting the layout dictate the news. Ultimately, I grew to respect, if not welcome, the task of retooling as stories developed or died. But for years I had to overcome a surge of agita when breaking news overwhelmed the daily plan.

There is nothing like a crisis to test the mettle of a paper—its system, its leadership, its esprit. My first such challenge was the massive blackout of 1965 when power was knocked out over the Northeast and a swathe of Canada. The failure, caused by human error at a power station on the Canadian border, darkened New York City as well as its surrounding suburbs. It was about 5:30 on Nov. 9 and I was depositing a friend who lived on 12th Street before going on to work for my 7 o'clock start on the desk. I was driving down Seventh Avenue just above 13th Street when, passing a candy shop window, I noticed that its lights, which said "NUTS," began to flicker, and then went off. I thought perhaps they were closing early, though it seemed odd. Then, the building went dark and by the time we reached the corner the street lamp and indeed the whole street was out. I assumed it was a local outage and I dropped my pal off. But as I headed east toward the Midtown Tunnel, it was clear that, at the very least, a large chunk of the city was out. No one was panicking though. It was one of those events where New Yorkers could be proud of themselves— there was virtually no looting, a far cry from subsequent blackouts. Since the traffic lights were broken, volunteers with flashlights sprang up from nowhere to direct traffic. My only thought was to get to Newsday as quickly as possible. For whatever reason, the traffic in the tunnel was surprisingly light and the Long Island Expressway was also smooth enabling me to race out to Garden City. I arrived to an amazing sight.

The City Room was lit with candles, like a church with typewriters, and everyone was working at them. We had plenty of candle power and the phone system had not been affected, so the three essential elements—light, phones and typewriters—were all in place. The dayside people, who could have gone home, virtually all volunteered to remain. Everyone wanted to be part of the action and the prevalent cynicism and grousing had faded into a focused professionalism.

By the time I got there, everything was well in place. Reporters had called in from all over and we had them file from wherever they were. In Nassau County, our home base, we had the staff fan out to police headquarters, hospitals, schools and neighborhoods; our Suffolk office was doing the same. It was all very improvised and I got involved in some of the New York coverage. We had a large contingent in the city, some of whom had been stranded and we turned this to advantage. R.V. Denenberg, who wrote about the Supreme Court called in from an IRT platform and got some great color about riders being rescued from the subway. We sent reporters into high-rise buildings without elevator service where people were either trying to climb up to their apartments or get down into the street for whatever reasons. We had people in the streets, the hospitals, the precincts, the airports. We were all over Con Edison and LILCO on how the failure happened with charts of power grids from the art department and maps of the areas affected. And, of course, there was a great bar scene.

I took feeds from a disparate array of reporters and directed them to our rewrite bank. I also kept worrying that someone would knock over a candle and set fire to the place. The phones were literally jangling and the typewriters were clattering like runaway trains. But at the center of the storm, it was notably calm. Marlens, had commandeered a seat near the slot where he alternately conferred with Estrin, Insolia and McIlwain and eyeballed notes and copy that materialized before him. For all the amorphous quality of the evening, it was a controlled chaos harnessed to a single purpose: Get the paper out and tell the story. The daily drills that were second nature now all came into play. A news budget appeared. Assignments focused. Layouts materialized. Consideration was given to the secondary news and the rest of the paper, which would still have to come out with this edition. Steadily, a mosaic began to take shape. It is hard to convey the heady, almost delirious quality of an all-hands effort.

I don't remember all the details, not due to the passage of time but because it was an out-of-body experience. For a brief moment, we were in a time warp and what happened was something we couldn't quite take with us. What we were aware of was that the effort could not go for naught. The presses were knocked out and unless electricity returned by early morning, we wouldn't be able to get the edition out on time. But McIlwain had decided to push on, as if everything were normal, and hope that power would be restored by the early hours. I believe we had a generator that itself was having problems, and McIlwain, in touch with our production crews, would give us bulletins every hour or so on how the pressmen were doing at their end. But for those of us in the newsroom and in the street this seemed to be a mere technical problem that would correct itself at the right moment. It was unthinkable that Newsday wouldn't come out although I believe there were backup plans afoot to fly the paper out of the blackout area, produce a small edition, and truck it back to Long Island.

In any case, we pushed on under the assumption that if we kept at it, something would happen. By 2:30 A.M. the first edition was ready: copy in and edited, heads finished, layouts done, Page One signed off. All we needed was a little juice. No one was going home and we were already tinkering with the second edition and setting up follow coverage for the next day. A half hour went by; an hour. Time, which had been racing so quickly, now became plodding, heavy. Everyone huddled around candles, conjecturing, offering nervous banter, finding time at last for gallows humor. And then, a little after 3:30 A.M. the lights began flickering. "Gerries overhead," someone called. They flickered a bit more and, gaining in strength, went on to stay. A great cheer went up. Everyone congratulated each other, hugging, shaking hands. McIlwain made a little speech, thanking us for doing our jobs, and went off to make sure everything was right in the pressroom. Newsday was a few minutes late the next morning—but no worse than it might have been after a normal production glitch. It didn't affect delivery. The trucks were rolling and our readers got their news as usual. The morning man, Jimmy Jensen came in to clean up. Tomorrow there'd be another paper.

I hadn't been working as Nassau assistant night editor for too long— I was then at the ripe age of 27—when I got a new boss, Joseph Albright. Joe was the nephew of Newsday's founder, Alicia Patterson and, as a scion of the Medill-Patterson family, was newspaper royalty. After Alicia's death—shortly before I arrived in 1964—her husband, Harry Guggenheim, the paper's publisher, had left his editors in charge of the news side while he remained at the business end. This was all the more to his credit, as he'd allowed to Newsday's editor-in-chief Bill McIlwain that "there are only a dozen people here who aren't Bolsheviks, and you and I are two of them." The proviso was that a pedigreed overseer be brought in from the outside—the venerable Mark Ethridge of The Louisville Courier was one—to assure that things didn't get out of hand. But generally, these gents were so disarmed by McIlwain's southern charm that they kept out of the way, which permitted a certain amount of cognitive dissidence in the newsroom. Since Harry and Alicia were childless, Joe was a likely heir-apparent.

Newsday was tough on relatives. Dana Draper, a family member, had tried out earlier as a reporter and was expunged after a short trial, and perhaps not a fair one. The newspaper then maintained a fierce meritocracy, a reverse—some would call it perverse—social register where patricians were looked on askance. However, Joe, given his credentials and lineage, could have transcended this. Not only was he a legitimate heir but he had creative juice as well as blue blood and printer's ink in his veins. Joe also had good instincts, a willingness to learn and a certain humility about what he didn't know.

What would have been expected in Albright's case, was a grand tour of a few months in each of the various department's—news, circulation, production, business—to familiarize himself with the inner workings of the paper. All that was required was a Gentleman's C in a few subjects before going on to the real task of managing and directing. But Joe wanted to be a newspaperman before moving on to bigger game. Some people born to privilege need to reassure themselves that they merit their good fortune. A mistake, because once you're established, nobody really cares how you got there and, except for a few aging grumblers, everyone accedes to power. So, rather than just touching down for a while, Joe insisted on proving himself by becoming one of the natives. He took on the job of Nassau night news editor. Instead of scrutinizing he was held up to scrutiny. It isn't that Joe wasn't suited to the task—ultimately he proved to be an outstanding newspaperman. It was that he had chosen high-pressure duties that came with great responsibility and little thanks without having the experience to handle them.

I was his assistant during this period and it was painful to watch an intelligent, perceptive and dedicated man scramble in a job where he was out of his depth. Ironically, it would have been easier for Joe to have run the whole shebang under Harry's tutelage than to perform this onerous mundane duty. Here, he was on the spot. A failed publisher may at least assume the mantle of a

87

prophet scorned in his own land, but a flawed editor is simply someone who is no hero to a hundred butlers. Joe was a Gatsby in reverse. He insisted on a code of honor that no else much cared about and, in the end, it did him in. To exacerbate matters, Joe wanted to be one of the boys. Once, he had everyone over to his house in an attempt at down-home bonhomie that his guests saw as a gesture of noblesse oblige. As opposed to the raucous atmosphere that usually attended such parties, a mood of guarded decorum prevailed. Everyone was on good behavior as Joe's then-wife Madeleine—later to become Secretary of State—served canapés to the dutiful guests.

The nadir of Albright's journey occurred on a weekend tour of Nassau and Suffolk counties given by a few grizzled veterans to familiarize new editors with the farther reaches of Long Island. This was the brainstorm of the aforementioned Alan Hathway, the emeritus editor-in-chief of Newsday, who was then soaking away his retirement years in alcoholic splendor on Fire Island. There were about a dozen of us in a three-car caravan led by Tom Renner, the Suffolk police reporter, who could also down a few and was going to use the occasion—as were several of his colleagues—to spend the weekend imbibing on the company tab. Another car, a big, hearse-like job, was driven by the boxing writer Bob Waters, and Joe was holding up the rear in the third one. We gathered early in the morning at Brookhaven Town Hall and made our first stop at Hathway's Fire Island beach house where we repaired for the first of several roundelays of drinking. It wasn't much past 10 in the morning. Hathway greeted us wielding a cocktail shaker and sporting a Hawaiian shirt although there was already a chill in the autumn air. He was famous for his annual bacchanals where the staff disported itself in limbo dancing and other revelries. After much back-slapping, raillery, tale-telling and old-boy quaffing down the hatches, he waved us on, admonishing us to raise hell, and we left him befogged in his own rolling mist.

Although Tom Renner seemed unflappable, I knew the vodka was working when I noticed that we were heading east in the western lanes of the Southern State Parkway, with the other two cars in tow. Someone pointed this out to Tom. "Damn!'' he muttered, giving the impression that it was the road signs that were at fault. Luckily, it was still early on a fall weekend with whatever approaching traffic there was giving us a wide berth and we managed to swerve onto an exit before any damage was done. A cop stopped us but when he saw it was Renner he waved us on with a warning to be more careful. The rest of our expedition consisted of debarking to imbibe at various caravansaries along the South Shore. I remember a rather long, languid, mostly liquid lunch at something called the Shinnecock Inn. Things got only grimmer and hazier as the day regressed into a series of pit stops at Renner's favorite watering holes. Finally, we stopped at the East Hampton Inn where we were berthed two in a room. Luckily, I was paired with Jim Scovel, a quiet, level-headed guy who had managed to stay sober through this pilgrimage. Dinner still lay ahead. The meal, as it were, lasted till 11, and then Jim and I made our excuses—we were, after all, supposed to rise at 7 the next morning for the return journey. But the party wasn't over.

We learned the next day that a few of the bolder spirits decided to drive on to the fishing pier at Montauk owned by Perry Duryea, then the State Assembly Speaker and a friend of Newsday. Joe, trying to be a good sport and demonstrate that he could keep up with the boys, went along. They spent the early hours consuming pails of shellfish and fries washed down by beer and God knows what else. In the morning, the revelers, whose constitutions were used to this sort of thing, were all ready to roll. All except Joe, who was green to the gills. He managed to lie down and rest in the back seat of the large black van with someone else driving his car. We looked like a funeral cortege. We plodded on through the further reaches of the Hamptons traversing both forks in a wobbly processional. The ferry onto and off of Shelter Island—the fiefdom of Republican Supervisor Evans K. Griffing—was a nightmare. I thought if a cop stopped us this time we'd be arrested.

Joe, to his credit, seemed to rally by mid-day, just in time for a farewell repast at the Piping Rock Inn, before we headed back to our drop-off point. But I doubt he ever really recovered, not from the trek but from what it symbolized. I think Joe came to realize at a certain point that this Long Island duty wasn't a good fit. He went down to our D.C. office where he developed into a fine bureau chief and a crackerjack reporter. But his moment had passed. Eventually, he went on to work for the Cox News Service, first in Washington and then abroad, and had a distinguished career as a foreign correspondent. Albright never got to be a publisher but he achieved the well-earned respect that he'd always sought.

As it turned out, we might have been better off with Joe. He was "family" in a literal sense and basically he was trying to buy into the system. Instead, we got Bill Moyers who wanted to dismantle the system and remake Newsday in his own image of what a newspaper ought to be. At first glance Guggenheim's choice of

Bill as publisher and heir-apparent seemed inspired. Moyers had gained name recognition as Lyndon Johnson's press secretary, a post he left after they'd had a falling-out over Vietnam. He brought to Newsday a national reputation, connections with Washington, media skills, political experience and a heady mixture of gravitas and youth together with a certain heartland cachet, half Good Old Boy, half Shabbos Goy. Of course, he had never run a newspaper. But I think Guggenheim saw this as a plus. After all the incestuous dead-ends and insulated subversion that he'd endured, I suspect Harry wanted an outsider to shake things up. Moreover, he saw in Bill a reverse cactus—smooth on the outside, tough on the inside—who was just the man to rid him of the nettlesome rabble he'd inherited from his wife's tenure. A subtler influence on the publisher may have been the imperative of leaving a legacy. Guggenheim had no heirs and there was something almost apostolic in the manner of choosing Moyers.

To many Bill Moyers has become a secular saint in the last 30 years, a probing television personality and an unabashed advocate of liberalism. If any TV personality can be nominated for a communal halo, it is Bill Moyers. But Moyers had not served under Lyndon Johnson for nothing. He was a formidable political infighter and he had brought this talent, together with a sense of mission and a belief in the righteousness of his cause to the struggle for the soul of Newsday. Moyers wanted to mold the paper into something new. Not just a bully pulpit with a liberal agenda, but a newspaper that would experiment in all fields—with race, youth, format, technique, coverage, approach—a whole fresh agenda. He was determined to turn this suburban tabloid into a national newspaper and he was in a hurry to get there. Naturally, this brooked opposition.

The Old Guard—a nucleus of editors that had been reared under Marlens— was not about to see its arrangements turned upside-down by an amateur whom they saw less as an innovator than an interloper. To them, Moyers was a dilettante who may have been conversant with influencing newspapers but didn't know the first thing about running one. What they'd hoped for was a figurehead who'd operate the business side and stay out of their hair. At most, they could live with someone who was willing to be tutored. But Bill wanted to give lessons, not take them. One can only imagine Charles Foster Kane musing to himself on assuming control of the New York Enquirer that it would be fun to run a newspaper. But Kane owned the paper.

The morning Moyers walked into the city room, some of the bolder spirits greeted him with a chorus of "Bringing In the Sheep." Admittedly in bad taste but newsrooms, at least in those days, were never models of decorum, and Moyers seemed to take it with good humor. We could have our little jokes but Bill made it clear from the outset that he was in earnest. He threw the gauntlet down over control of the city room. The top editors, McIlwain, the editor-in-chief; Marlens, the managing editor; Estrin, the night news editor, were fiercely protective of their turf. Alicia Patterson had provided a protective umbrella for them and in the vacuum after her death they pretty much ran the paper as they wished. Newsday had always drawn a clear line between the business and editorial poles, which Harry Guggenheim had grudgingly respected. But from Bill's viewpoint, there weren't any no-go areas. If he was going to reinvigorate the paper, he was obligated to take control of the news and tread on a few toes if need be.

The Moyers era of the late 60's overlapped with a few different jobs I performed, from hard news to soft features. My first encounter—as day news editor—came indirectly. Our Washington Bureau chief at the time was the very capable Tom Collins. Moyers, however, felt we needed someone a little tonier for the position and replaced Tom with Nick Thimmesch of Time magazine. Thimmesch seemed like the perfect man for the job: tall, blond, Waspy, self-assured. Collins looked more like an Irish stevedore. Appearances can be deceiving. Thimmesch turned out to be a disaster—in the little things as well as the big ones. One of my tasks was to coordinate coverage with him—that is get the Washington report into the paper. Too often, Thimmesch was unavailable or late. And, when finally run to ground, he was vague on details, keeping us guessing as to what was actually available. It became apparent that the reason for all his smoke was that he himself was not on top of the stories he was pitching, which left things in a muddle and caused us to scramble, As a matter of necessity we wound up going around Nick, obtaining fill-ins from his staff, with whom we had prior relationships, in order to get a fix on what to expect when they filed. This caused understandable resentment on Nick's part because he thought he was doing such a bang-up job that the only plausible reason for our efforts was to undermine him rather than to get a reading on the day's events.

Thimmesch, meanwhile, had his hands full with his own staff, most notably Pete Hamill, who were in near mutiny because of his mishandling of the bureau. From Nick's point of view, this was all a conspiracy on the part of the troglodytes in both the capital and the home office to traduce the new man. Thimmesch had no allies because he commanded no respect. By the time he was deposed he was already finished. Moyers could not save him but provided a niche as a columnist for which Thimmesch seemed more suited.

My last stint under Moyers—there were a few others between— came when I was put in charge of the Specialist writers in a new section called Part II—an adaptation of the features that ran in the back of the book of a newsweekly magazine except that this appeared every day. Credit where it's due: Moyers was in good measure responsible for inspiring the idea but, once launched, he couldn't leave it to his editors to carry the ball. At the outset, he was friendly enough and chatted me up about my assignments and the strengths of my staff. I was flattered at first until I realized that this was a reconnaissance mission preparatory to a run on my writers. Part II was a three-legged stool: an Entertainment section, a Style section struggling to emerge from the women's pages, and my own department, which was made up of reporters who focused on various beats such as the Environment, Religion, Science, Health, Media, Consumerism, Behavior and Education. These subjects often got short shrift in the rest of the paper but Part II offered a showcase where they could make a splash. The section was a huge monster to feed on a daily basis In order to keep it going, I had to maintain a tight rein on the staff so that we had a steady flow of copy coming through the system. This is where the trouble started.

I'm sure Bill meant well but I found that he was making his own assignments to my writers on stories that might be appearing elsewhere in the paper, in the news pages or in our weekend section. The result was that my scheduling was disrupted and I had to scramble to fill the space. I'd ask our education editor, Martin Buskin, a reliable pro, where a story was and he'd tell me he was working on something else for Bill. When I inquired how that came about, he told me he'd run into Moyers in the hall and that Bill was very excited about an idea and wanted to bounce it off him. Perhaps Moyers didn't realize he was an 800-pound gorilla but if the publisher is interested in a story, it's generally a good idea to see that it gets done. When this began happening with some frequency, I had a friendly chat with Bill, the point of which was that I'd be glad to entertain any of his ideas but it was important that it go through the editorial loop since otherwise, there'd be chaos. He was perfectly amenable and said that the various incidents I'd cited were merely chance meetings where he was simply kicking around ideas with the staff. Within a short time, the pattern recurred.

I learned from other editors that they'd had similar experiences. Complaints followed. Our own top editors locked horns with Moyers. Friendly chats were followed by less friendly memos. The gist of our missives was that it was improper for a publisher to usurp the responsibilities of an assigning editor; that it disrupted the news flow, created conflicts among the staff and generally led to confusion and disorder. Bill's responses—by now increasingly in memos—was that it was perfectly appropriate to have conversations with the staff, to exchange ideas with them, and not to be quarantined from them in some editorial purdah. If news or feature stories came out of these talks it was all the better to fructify the soil. He clearly felt we could be doing more but, perhaps frustrated by the limits of mandating change through editors who did not always share his enthusiasms, he simply went around them. If this led to a certain amount of topsy-turvy in the city room, so be it.

The late 60's were upon us, change was in the air, the youth culture was in flower and Bill ran with it. There were a lot of young people on the staff who chafed under the old rules of objectivity and, inspired by the advent of the New Journalism, wanted to practice a more assertive, subjective mode of reporting the news. And there were those who were disaffected from a hierarchal system that they felt had excluded them. And there were others still who'd been alienated by an overbearing management style under Marlens & Co. They saw the whirlwind that Moyers had stirred as their chance to alter things. To be fair to Moyers, he was willing to experiment, sometimes successfully, sometimes not.

One of Bill's more controversial ventures was engendering "The Summer Journal of Morton Pennypacker," a magazine that ran inside Newsday's weekend section. It was a summer laboratory in experimental journalism, staffed and run by the young tigers in Bill's youth menagerie. It was supposed to be an adventure in free-form journalism, a voyage of discovery. Among the things that the Pennypackers discovered was that there were potato fields in Suffolk, clam diggers on the Eastern shores and rich people in the Hamptons. All of this was conveyed with a breathlessness and urgency as if it were the discovery of sunken treasure. To its critics on the paper, it was reinventing the wheel but without the spokes.

Risking such innovation inevitably attracted naysayers who were skeptical about some of these undertakings. Understandably, Moyers sought to recruit allies who were in tune with his ideas. He brought in David Laventhol of the Washington Post to run Newsday's feature sections but it was no secret that he had Laventhol waiting in the wings to replace McIlwain & Company given sufficient cause and opportunity. This didn't take long in coming. McIlwain, always a heavy drinker, developed a serious alcohol problem at this stage. Up till then, his managing editor, Al Marlens, had covered for him, and been glad to do so, because it meant that Al was the paper's de facto editor. But Moyers did not care for this arrangement, nor probably should he. A modest drinker himself, Moyers had no patience for his top editor's imbibing and, like McIlwain, a southerner, he was not taken in by the latter's good-old-boy charm. He certainly was not enamored of Marlens's management style or his direction of the paper. I wasn't there for the final bloodletting. I was on a Nieman fellowship at Harvard when the blades fell. When I returned a year later, the last man standing was Laventhol, the most unlikely survivor of the lot. During my hiatus, Moyers had eased out McIlwain and Marlens but, after a falling-out with Guggenheim, had himself departed. This left Dave Laventhol the last man standing. His recruitment was probably the best thing Moyers had ever done.

Like a lot of people, I underestimated Laventhol. Beneath his soft exterior, there was backbone. Also ambition and a formidable newspaper intelligence. These strengths would eventually get him to run the Los Angeles Times and its entire chain—The Times Mirror Corporation—which by then had incorporated Newsday. What Guggenheim had done was to turn Newsday over to his friend Norman Chandler who presided over Times-Mirror where, in Harry's eyes, it would remain in safe hands. For Guggenheim, Newsday, although a private enterprise, was still a public trust. What Harry couldn't foresee was that this gentlemen's agreement was ultimately going to take the paper out of gentlemen's hands. It was the start of a slippery slope that led Newsday from being a family-owned newspaper run by inspired autocrats and benevolent patrons to a cog in giant conglomerates where it would lose its independence to become a corporate pawn.

For a long time, I'd wanted out of Newsday. I could easily ascribe it to the bitter haze that loomed over the trench warfare in the newsroom. But in fact, I had served my apprenticeship and was getting the seven-year-itch. It had been a good ride. After a brief run as a beat reporter, I'd spent a few years on the night side, first as a copy editor and then assistant night Nassau editor, before emerging into the sunlight as day city editor. The title, of course, was an anomaly since Newsday was a suburban paper; I believe I was the last person to have that job description. In order to shore up my credentials, I was put in charge of Nassau, Queens and the World. One minute, I'd be monitoring a school board tiff in Locust Valley, the next a shooting in Queens and then staffing the coverage of the 1967 Glassboro summit conference between Lyndon Johnson and Soviet Premier Alexei Kosygin. I was very young for this, too young, but my betters seemed to have a belief in me that proved infectious. Although I had misgivings at the outset, I actually got to believe in their confidence.

It was an instructive time to be learning the business— the war in Vietnam and the war at home; the assassinations of Robert Kennedy and Martin Luther King, the riots in the cities—Detroit, Newark, Washington. A lot of stuff happened on Fridays. People seemed to get crazier at the end of the week when we were short-staffed and it was harder to recruit bodies. I recall being alone in the wire room when Detroit went up, and catching the first news over the UPI. Just after the initial few lines the machine jammed and my first thoughts about the Detroit riot was how I was going to get the damned printer unclogged. But given my superb training as wire-room copy boy at The Daily Mirror, I was up to the task. I got the printer fixed and we had people moving in good order.

Washington went up on another Friday afternoon. I got a frantic call from our Congressional correspondent, Mike Waldman, a terrific if tightly wound writer who had climbed to a vantage point in a gallery atop the Capitol. "We got a riot here," he told me, indicating where he was. I asked him what he could see. "There's smoke everywhere and everyone is leaving over the bridges. What should I do?" I told him to stay on the phone while I got a rewrite man, and then just to describe exactly what he was seeing. Waldman did a fine color piece and, since we had a bureau in place, it was simpler to cover than Newark, which was more accessible in distance but not in logistics. In the days that followed, once the adrenalin had settled, it was easy enough to joke about the frantic moments and the antics they engendered. But at the time, I was pumped because I didn't know in what direction things were going and one always imagines that the opposition has a million troops—which in this case may have been true. The lesson from this is that if you get enough trustworthy people in place, most of the time something good will happen.

Riots, like fires and other incendiary events, each have their own characteristics and peculiarities. In the late 60's you could have become a connoisseur of the phenomenon. But I had no wish to do so. I became weary of marshaling reporters for what seemed like an endless run of turbulence, and sending people into danger zones. I decided to call in my markers and this time, they deigned to listen. I wanted to go back to writing, and they gave me a column. I had a free hand that allowed me to write about everything from a war protester feeding his draft card to the seals in the Central Park Zoo to the detox center at Meadowbrook Hospital to the newly inaugurated whale hall celebrating the 100th anniversary of the Museum of Natural History.

Perhaps the most instructive event I covered during this period was the inauguration of Richard Nixon in 1969. As I huddled with a shivering cohort of print journalists before the grandstand on a cold January morning I couldn't help noticing that perched above us in heated glass booths were Huntley and Brinkley of NBC and their well turned-out peers from CBS and ABC, insulated from the elements, literally looking down on us. It was apparent even then that print had seen its best days and journalistic clout was gradually but inevitably moving toward the electronic media. Although the ascendancy of digital journalism was far in the future, it was already clear that print—whatever its ultimate nemesis—was beginning a downward trajectory.

After the inaugural ceremonies, I was assigned to cover the valedictory of the outgoing Vice President, Hubert Humphrey, the man Nixon had defeated. While "end of an era" is a much-abused term one can fairly observe that this was the last time a Democratic candidate could run as an unabashed New Deal liberal with a serious chance of winning the presidency, as Humphrey almost did. I learned that he was going to be hosted by the Democratic guru Clark Clifford at a farewell party in Bethesda so I high-tailed it there in a cab and joined a small pack of reporters on the death watch outside Clifford's house, hoping to pick up a few notes for whatever codas might go into the next day's news. After about an hour, Humphrey emerged leaning on the arm of his wife, Muriel. For whatever reason, ex-Vice Presidents didn't then get the security treatment of former Presidents and I was able to get up pretty close to the man who, with a little more luck, might have been sitting in the White House. Humphrey wasn't answering questions but wafted by with a fixed smile that politicians affect on such occasions. For a moment, he seemed to be looking around for an entourage but there was only a state trooper and Muriel who led him gently to a waiting limo. His visage was a death mask: blank, pallid, eyes staring straight ahead. But it couldn't hide the look of hurt surprise on the face of a man who realized that he had suddenly lost power.

After a while, I grew tired of hearing myself pontificate in a column and wanted to go back to straight reporting, but in a province that interested me—social behavior. At the time, it was a fairly innovative beat for a tabloid and a field that I had pretty much to myself, which meant a minimal amount of second-guessing from the desk. My timing couldn't have been better. I picked some pretty ripe grapes in a vineyard that was just becoming sexy, with stories on Stanley Milgram's pain experiments, Bruno Bettelheim's autism concepts, Alfred Bandera's work on social learning and William Shockley's controversial IQ theories. I could have gone on indefinitely but just at that time, Moyers came up with the aforementioned Specialists Section, which incorporated my beat, and Marlens figured that instead of writing for it, I might as well run it. So I went back to being an editor. Although the Specialists Section was a relief from the daily news grind, it was only a halfway house.

Restless, I applied for a Nieman fellowship at Harvard in the spring of 1970. I never thought I'd get it—not least because, as I was told, Capt. Guggenheim had nearly imposed a ban on such frippery after two incidents that left a bad taste in his mouth. The first involved a reporter who left shortly after returning from the Nieman year which gave Newsday little return on its investment. The second episode Capt. Guggenheim suffered in relation to the Nieman program involved Mike McGrady's fellowship year, which he spent editing the Jacqueline Suzanne spoof "Naked Came the Stranger." The novel's putative author, suburban housewife Penelope Ashe, was actually 17 Newsday writers who had each been enjoined to compose an erotic chapter about a fictional round-heels radio personality dubbed Gillian Blake who embarked on a roundelay of sexual adventures with a host of Long Island men. All good writing was to be blue-penciled out, an unnecessary admonition. After the hoax was exposed—or rather, self-exposed— the subsequent ballyhoo earned Newsday a week's worth of media fame in the dog days after Chappaquidick. Harry Guggenheim was not amused, not least because he was parodied in a chapter about a local newspaper mogul called the Baron; the offensive section was written by his own editor, Bill McIlwain. What most of us saw as a bit of city-room high jinks—I received the dubious distinction of "Best Writing Award" for my portrayal of Joshua Turnbull, a Long Island rabbi, as one of Gillian's admirers—the Captain considered an act of unwanted notoriety that besmirched the paper's reputation. It was only through the intercession of cooler heads that he relented and allowed Newsday staffers to apply for Niemans thereafter.

To make things even more difficult, I was competing against another Newsday colleague, the aforementioned Ken Brief, a nice enough fellow who was doubtless equally qualified. My supervisors gently tried to discourage me from entering a second Newsday candidate into the lists. But, in a lapse of self-preservation, I decided to forge ahead. Why not me? So I was pretty much at ease going into my interview figuring that the odds were so long that I had nothing to lose. What I had going for me was that I was editing this sexy new Specialists Section, which was still a fabulous beast in the journalistic forest and exuded certain transcendent qualities. Since I could hit to several fields, I lighted on my recent beat of social psychology as a possible region of interest at Harvard. This was pretty much baloney but, as I later found, so were many of the pitches that my competitors were giving, and the judges knew it. Nevertheless, I must have impressed them with the relative novelty of the beat and its potential for synergy in an academic setting. The clincher came when one of the admission committee's members, Warren Phillips of the Wall Street Journal, asked me why I really wanted a Nieman. I told him about a Times Op-Ed column in which Russell Baker said that he never got past page 80 of "The Magic Mountain," and that, in truth, neither had I, but if I obtained a Nieman, I'd at last get to finish the book. Phillips seemed amused by my faux candor and I knew I had a shot. Years later, after he retired from the Journal, Warren started a small press in Bridgehampton called Bridgeworks. By then, I was Newsday's book editor and was glad to give him a little break on his publications. Why not? He'd given me one.

But before the Nieman fellowship was realized, another adventure lay in store. I received an offer to work for the Paris Herald-Tribune as their news editor. The fellow who then held the job, Lowell Bonfeld, was heading back to the States and they needed someone to replace him. I told them I'd take it on a contingency basis: If I liked them and they liked me, it was a deal; but I wasn't ready for any commitments. The Trib was a pretty loosey-goosey place in that day and they accepted my proposal. I had a chunk of time coming from Newsday, so I took a de facto leave of absence and simply told them that I was going to Paris. They were probably aware of my destination since my Newsday boss, David Laventhol, and my Paris boss, Murray M. (Buddy) Weiss, had worked together at the New York Herald-Tribune before it folded, but Dave wisely let things play out, since he didn't have a lot to lose either way. My French connection was my old City College pal, Jack Monet, who had worked for the Paris edition of The New York Times and, when that vessel foundered, after a brief foray back to the mother ship in New York, returned to Paris and permanent expat status with a job on the copy desk of the Trib. Jack talked me up to Weiss but he didn't have to prime the pump too much because I had the right credentials. By then, as boy and man, I'd worked for four dailies, two in New York, Newsday was a hot paper on account of Moyers, and I had been its city editor and the editor of a Trib-like features section inspired by one of the refugees from its New York heyday.

The survivors of The New York Herald-Tribune's demise in 1966, like the Trojan exiles, became a band that would create its own legend and plant its seeds anew on fresh soil. Except in the updated version there would be several Romes: Clay Felker's New

York magazine and its clones, the Washington Post's Book World and its Style Section, the revitalized Los Angeles Times and later on, New York Newsday engendered by the self-same David Laventhol who would become the CEO of the Times-Mirror Company which came to own Newsday. And, of course, the Trib provided some of the best writers and reporters at The New York Times—Homer Bigart and Peter Kihss to name two—which took them aboard when the great ship went down. There have been whole books written about the glories of The New York Herald-Tribune; it needs no further elucidation here except to note that in terms of newspaper culture its diaspora formed a benevolent association whose influence went well beyond its numbers.

The old Paris Trib headquarters was at 21 Rue de Berri, off the Champs-Elysees, a few blocks down-slope of l'Etoile. The building was threaded with the bureaus of other news outlets—Newsweek magazine, for one, had an office there. The Trib city room had an improvised quality as if it were a stage set that would be removed during the day and used for other purposes—an off-track betting parlor or some-such. Only at night did it come to life—but a fitful life of shadows, a gloomy Brigadoon where the mist never lifts. There was a tentative quality about the office that reflected the transient lives of the editors it housed. As a group they seemed to be the last of the itinerant journalists who moved from one paper to the next in that quixotic odyssey fueled by romance, restiveness and rum.

The only anchored bodies were the French printers—virtually all Communists—who formed a permanent populace: stolid and disdainful but indulgent of the transiting Yanks. It didn't matter how long the Americans had lived there or what their commitment was to the expatriate life. They would always be foreigners. My friend Jack Monet tried to engage the printers in his taxicab Gallic, considering himself a latter-day communard, or at least an anarchist with the accent on anarchy. But they'd have none of it. They called him Monsier Marbre— printer slang for "Mr. Overset"—because of his compulsion to send the composing room far more copy on a story than could possibly fit, leaving whole trays of left-over type—words carved in marble— thereby his appellation. As far as they were concerned Jack's left-leaning affectations were belied by his American penchant for excess.

The city room of the Paris Trib carried a whiff of the seedy bars that used to dot the Bowery except that the denizens had upgraded the elixir of choice from Irish rotgut to French red. There was a pecking order to the staff. Pride of place was allotted to a venerable old sport mildewing in his virtue who was said to have fought for the Spanish Republic, already mythologized in these quarters. Another fellow planned to buy vineyards in Tuscany—I later heard that he'd actually done so. The Paris expat model for most, however, was not the outsized Hemingway, much less Henry James and his prissy aestheticism, but Henry Miller who offered a lifestyle that was improvised, anarchic and, ultimately, unaccountable. In the bars to which they frequently repaired, they were great spinners of disconnected stories that required the listener to fill in the dots. The ghosts of expatriates past hovered over the city room, smothering it with literary pretensions as evanescent as the smoke from the ubiquitous Gitane. Almost everyone affected to be writing a novel, or an article or something that justified their inglorious toil as copy editors at the Trib. And it was inglorious.

In those days, there was no reporting; simply cutting, splicing, reconfiguring what others had done and then slapping on a headline. In late afternoon, the news editor—me—who'd arrived an hour or two earlier, would cull the next day's news from the AP, UPI, AFP and Reuters wires and distribute them to the various copy editors who would transform them into a recombinant collage, with the "breaking" news updated periodically. This was done with scissors and paste-pots so that the copy desk looked like an adult version of a kindergarten table. Invariably, a shaky hand would spill a paste-pot, occasioning a messy cleanup with a telltale lump of glue spurting out from an edited piece of copy, creating an odd litmus effect by blurring the words so that the French printers couldn't read them. This caused the copy chief to glare and his peers to grumble at the offender. The glue fumes and the smoke ionized into a gaseous vapor that gave off a scent akin to a piney disinfectant, leaving the desk smelling like a hospital ward.

Later in the evening, the wires of The New York Times and the Washington Post would subsume the earlier news services. Along with the former-proprietor Jock Whitney, The Times and The Post were joint owners of the Paris Trib, tethered horses that pulled in different directions. The news-service wires were, in effect, a holding action, a second-banana serving to warm up the audience till the true protagonists appeared on stage. The drones in the Paris Trib office were simply facilitators who plucked and chose from the competing versions of the day's news that was now churning off the Times and Post wires emanating from stateside newsrooms just getting up to speed in cities where it was still early afternoon.

In effect, the editors at 21 Rue de Berri were little more than a brain-in-a-bottle, if you could call it that, while the arms and legs of the creature were elsewhere. If Paris was burning, let us say, the fire would be covered by The Times Paris Bureau across town, relayed to the home office in New York, edited on its foreign desk and then sent out on the Times News Service wire which, hopefully, would arrive at the Tribune's office in Paris in time to be incorporated into the newspaper's second edition that closed at 11 P.M. or, 5 P.M. New York time. The paper could be held for a late-edition re-plate should that be required, but often wasn't, as it raised costs. This was not crusading journalism. As I recall, the only material that originated out of Paris at the time was Art Buchwald and some food and fashion features. On the other hand, this left the staff plenty of time for leisure pursuits and other consolations, of which there were many.

The revels were presided over by the aforementioned Buddy Weiss, a charming soufflé of a man. After the New York Trib's demise Buddy had settled into his post as the editor of the Paris edition, performing his duties with an easy-going élan. He reminded me, as it were, of his erstwhile colleague David Laventhol, making me wonder whether all those guys from the old Trib had a deceptively placid exterior under which lurked their survivor's instincts and will to rule. Weiss had achieved an expat's dream, and used the Trib as an extension of that life, a calling card that gave him entrée to French society, a good table at restaurants and an aisle seat in the culture world. To keep it going he simply had to run a smooth ship, and placate his two masters. This was done by the expedient of allowing the Times and the Post virtually equal space or equal billing on all the big stories and seeing that visiting notables were treated royally.

So most of what we did was to make sure that the Times and Post copy got measure for measure in the daily report. Occasionally, we'd split the difference and opt for Reuters or AFP, or mix the whole shebang into a fine colloidal under the rubric of Combined News Services. It kept them happy, us employed and Buddy pleased. He appeared to be in perennial good humor, sliding in to the office before the first edition; reviewing the news list, eyeballing the galleys, checking the front page and then his wristwatch. He seemed always to be just arriving from somewhere or about to leave for somewhere else.

Buddy's enabler in all this was his managing editor, George Bates, a fellow Trib refugee who was as efficient, orderly and self-effacing as Weiss was outgoing. People like Buddy always need a factotum to execute their grand designs, someone who minds the store while they're out dazzling the public. I learned many years later that Weiss had moved back to the States where I believe, he wound up at Parade, the weekly magazine insert. Just his style: easy, low key, not too much intellectual heft but respectable. I ascribed his departure to one of the many contests between the Times and the Post that ended when The Times took full control of the paper. But during this middle period, as the dual monarchy evolved, what had once been a cozy sinecure became a contested chair where the two competing papers maneuvered to advance their own candidates. Before the Post's expulsion, those who took the job often received it as a consolation prize after losing internal battles in New York and Washington. It was also a convenient place to dump troublesome rivals who could console themselves as overseas eminences, the fate of such personalities as The Times's John Vinocur. Later, the Trib became a haven for lower-gauge personnel who'd hit a glass ceiling but had friends at court. During my tenure, however, we were still in the ink-stained wretch era.

I was staying in the flat of an old college buddy—yet another in a chain of City College newspaper alumni who had linked one another to the Paris Trib in our own version of the Old Boy system. The apartment was a nondescript barracks a few blocks from the Park Monceau, a favorite of Proust's, in the 8ᵗʰ arrondissement. All I remember of the place was that my mess somehow osmosed into that of my host; also the thin walls did little to insulate my digs from the noise of the love-making couple next door. In truth, I spent little time there, waking late, stopping at a corner café for the requisite baguette and, after a brief walk-about, turning up at my post and riffling through the filings. Since I was new to this particular aspect of the game, I wanted to make sure that I didn't miss anything and that I'd be a step ahead.

The result was that I spent most of this time in Paris—my blue period—not sparking the Audrey Hepburn of my dreams but snuffling through heaps of wire copy like a demented aardvark. When the others lolled in at 4 P.M., I'd already been there for a couple of hours. And when they left at 6 P.M. for their two-hour dinner break, I skulked over to the nearby Berri Bar where the burnt hamburgers gave a new meaning to French fried. (There's a reason MacDonald's succeeded in Paris.) Worse still, this was take-out, since I had to be back before the others returned to get the Times and Post copy prepped for the Second Edition. When my colleagues reappeared, they were so florid from their repast that it was dangerous to approach them before their blood had cooled. I performed these chores for a couple of weeks until I realized that the copy editors, who were ostensibly under me, actually had it much better than I did. At which point I declined the accolade and voluntarily demoted myself to the copy desk, leaving the laureate to a more driven soul.

For the remainder of my sojourn in Paris, my life improved considerably. I sipped my aperitif at the George V till shortly before 4, whereupon I strolled up the Champs-Elysees and took my place at the copy lathe. After two hours of what can only generously be described as work—I was being paid in American dollars mind you—I joined the others in what was the evening's main order of business: finding a place to eat that met the exacting culinary standards of this ménagerie. Each night, we rattled across Paris in two taxis, descending on someone's favorite eatery in a nondescript district. After a memorable meal and several bottles of wine, we'd whisk back across Paris and stumble into the city room, daring the unfortunate who'd replaced me to approach with anything like work for another half-hour. Eventually, we'd bend to our labors, and, at 11 P.M., voila! Fin. Then off to the Lipp Brothers, which was favored over the Deux Magots. Although both were by then well on their downward spiral towards Frommerland, the Lipp, nearing midnight, was still fairly tourist-free and good for a few hours of revelry. From there, on to some quieter venue on the Isle St. Louis, perhaps a morning steak at Les Halles, and finally to bed. It was truly a sybaritic existence and, though I'd like to think good sense would have prevailed and I'd have elected to return to Newsday, what woke me from my lotus-eating slumber was a telegram: I'd been accepted to the Nieman program. How could I say no to Harvard? Besides, it meant that I could remain at Newsday for a year without actually having to be there.

In subsequent forays to France, although I was only too glad to see the friends who'd stayed on, I felt like a resident of the Mother Country visiting cousins in the colonies who affected to keep up with life in the capital but were nonetheless several steps behind. Culture, by the time it had gotten to them, had somehow cooled—which didn't prevent them from being ardent in their cosmopolitan pursuits. Paris, at least for Americans, really was a backwater: charming, picturesque, but a museum; certainly not a place for serious work. My erstwhile Trib colleagues struck me as Brits who'd stayed on after the Raj, preserved in amber, calcified over time. And they'd completely lost touch with the energy of the very craft that had lured them abroad in the first place.

What distinguished me from my fellow Niemans at Harvard was that I was the rare soul who was an editor; most of the others were reporters. It made sense. Writers, after all, are the face that newspapers show the world. The judges usually relied on clips—the body of work a journalist had accumulated over his or her career. What could a deskman show? My later Times colleague John Corry, one of the few rank-and-file editors to win the fellowship, recalls asking the columnist Anthony Lewis, a former Nieman himself, for a recommendation and being turned down with the dismissive rebuke: "You're only a deskman." Which pretty much sums up the industry's attitude toward all but the most famous editors when it came to handing out prizes. Even Hollywood, for all its obsession with celebrity, has a place for its non-starring craftsmen at the Oscars. Those awards for Best Costumes or Lighting may elicit yawns from the TV audience but they still acknowledge an aspect of the trade. By contrast, The Pulitzers are all or nothing: Reporting and Writing. Occasionally, if a low-lying editor contributes to an investigative team, he or she might be acknowledged in a group roundup. But glory is not often their portion. Nor should it be. The midwife does not get the flowers when the mother bears the baby. What saved me was that I had clips with academic cachet from my recent social-psychology beat that dovetailed with my subsequent editorial functions, so I got a pass. I was a deskman tricked out in writer's drag.

The Nieman experience was a custom-built arrangement. Some people wrote books, some found their inner academic selves, others just let loose. One fellow, legend had it, plopped himself down in a single classroom and let the various lecturers spin by in an academic kaleidoscope. There were no requirements for the year except to take one class for credit which even the laziest of us could manage. I, for one, dispensed with my social psychology pretensions forthwith and embarked on an auto-didactic program of taking everything that I'd skipped during my misspent years at City College when I devoted virtually all my time to the school newspaper and the rest of it to night copy-boy stints at New York dailies. And I was being paid, no less. I even got a little bonus with the G.I. bill. I was aware that such an opportunity would never recur. I knew the clock was ticking and I had a year to become a Renaissance man. I still have my notes on the lectures of Daniel Bell in European intellectual history, Ed Reischauer in Japanese culture, and John H. Finley Jr. in Greek literature, and, perhaps best, the renowned Isadore Twersky in medieval Jewish philosophers. From Hellenes to Hebrews, I couldn't get enough.

Although the 70's had begun, culturally this was still the tail end of the 60's. It would remain so until we pulled out of Vietnam. The women's movement—which had evolved in step with the anti-war protests and was a beat behind the civil-rights movement—was in full gear at Harvard. The place reeked with virtue. It was also the heyday of such pied pipers as Kurt Vonnegut and other literary icons of the young. I sat in on a writing course which Vonnegut taught that year. The class didn't learn much about writing but he was an appealing raconteur.

The curator of the Nieman Foundation during my sojourn was Dwight Sargent, another alumnus of the New York Herald Tribune for whose editorial pages he'd written prior to bailing out well before the plane went down. In the rosy glow of nostalgia, people tend to forget that for all its trendy innovation, the Trib was a Republican paper, and Dwight, a Maine Yankee who prided himself on being able to talk on both sides of an issue at the drop of a publisher's whim, was temperamentally suited to the rock-ribbed Republicanism of his former owners. Which meant that he was on a collision course with many of that year's fellows, myself included, who had been energized by the radicalism that was then sweeping journalism—as well as everything else. In our case, it took the form of a general mistrust of authority, of which Dwight was an archetype. We took an instant dislike to one another, although I wasn't the only one. Sargent's real problem was that he was an anachronism. What was once an Old Boys' club had become a circus ring where he faced a threatening menagerie of proto-rebels who were having none of his by-the-numbers journalism.

The idea of asking uncomfortable questions that challenged our prestigious guests at the monthly Nieman dinners was awkward for Sargent. Consequently, after our invited speakers' address, when the Q & A began, Dwight chose a coterie of "safe" interrogators or the foreign fellows from the then protectorates: South Africa, South Korea, the Philippines, etc. When our class tried to invite some of our own guests to liven up the mausoleum, Dwight balked, not directly but through obfuscation, delay and subterfuge. From his point of view, we were just passing though and he was the permanent government. In response, by spring, we'd organized a committee that had a sit-down with Harvard's then-president, Derek Bok. Within the year, Dwight was discreetly superannuated.

Although we didn't benefit from this ourselves, it was the finest service we could have rendered to our successors.

My fellow Niemans that year constituted a varied field of newspaper types, from the ambitious to the ambivalent. Some were on the fast track, some were making a final lap before moving on to leaner pastures and some were content to graze temporarily in the fields of academe. At the center of our social hub were Dan Rapoport who'd covered Congress for the UPI and John Pekkanen who was Life magazine's Midwest bureau chief. The stars of the class were Jo Thomas of the Cincinnati Enquirer who'd go on to write for The Times, and Jim Squires, who'd made a name for himself as a city editor of the Nashville Tennessean. Squires was a protégé of the Tennessean's John Seigenthaler and would go on to a glorious career at the Tribune Company revitalizing the Orlando Sentinal and vaulting to the top of the heap at the Chicago Tribune itself where he reigned for eight years as editor-in-chief. Like all great story-tellers, Jim loved his own tales and had plenty to tell. He took an absolute delight in recounting the faux-pas of Tennessee's political and social elite. We would compete in a one-downsmanship of our corresponding high-flown malefactors, but Jim's cast of characters had everyone's beat.

Being a Nieman was like wearing a magic cloak that allowed me to move freely among all the elements of Harvard, both students and teachers. One of the faculty members I befriended during my stay was Prof. William Alfred who wrote "Hogan's Goat," the play about Irish ward politics that propelled Faye Dunaway to stardom. Alfred was an engaging lecturer and an equally delightful raconteur of life as a child of the Irish middling classes in Brooklyn. He could mimic to perfection his feuding aunts snubbing one-another at a funeral, using him as a go-between to bear back-and-forth messages of intensifying hostility, venom and spite. As a newspaperman, I had a few Brooklyn stories of my own, which Alfred savored. He appreciated the fascination I had with the scholarly life, coming from someone with a leg in the real world. When I evinced an interest in crossing over he said if I were serious, he'd speak to his friend Steven Marcus at Columbia. Alas, I was not. The tide of habit bore me back onto the shores of journalism. I simply lacked the will to break free from the gravitational force of the city room. The truth is that I didn't want a career of scholarship badly enough to make the sacrifices it required. So I settled for the next best thing, playing with the life of the mind while making a living in newspapers. As it turned out, I would wind up at Columbia, both as student and teacher, sooner than I thought, and the aforesaid Steven Marcus would one day write for me.

My academic career was not quite over when the Nieman year ended. In mid-June of 1971, I returned to my job at Newsday and my apartment in New York. While I was gone, I'd rented my digs, on the top floor of a rounded limestone at 44 Riverside, to a young fellow who was the editor of the Miami Herald's Tropic magazine. He had spent the year as an International Affairs Fellow in a program sponsored by Columbia's journalism department. He was in the last stages of packing when I arrived and, as I helped him carry his things to the car, he mentioned off-handedly that someone had just dropped out of the fall roster, leaving them one fellow shy. "Really?" I asked. "Really," he replied. "Why not me?" I asked? "Why not?" he replied. No sooner had we stuffed my benefactor's belongings into his car, then I was into mine, with his blessings. I raced uptown toward Columbia where I parked illegally and found my way to the Fellowship office. The program coordinator, John Luter, an ex-newsman who'd fed at the academic trough for several years, recognized a kindred spirit when he saw one. I applied for the fellowship and was accepted on the spot. It took a half hour.

The only catch was that to keep my job, I'd have to go back to work full-time while still fulfilling my obligations to Columbia. This meant a complete course load for a full academic year as well as attending all the dinners and seminars that the program offered. I agreed to everything. I explained that I could take all my classes from 9-1 and then get out to Newsday by 2, produce my section between 2 and 9 and cut out for the monthly seminars at the Columbia Club. This justification took another 20 minutes. Now I had to get Newsday to agree to it. Amazingly, they did. Not only had they kept my job while I was gone but they let me come back on my own crazy terms. Whether it was the fact that Laventhol was still feeling his way, or that he was simply dazzled by the sheer chutzpah of my proposal, or that I had friends at court who interceded on my behalf, he gave me the nod. Certainly, he thought I could carry it off and I proved him right. The entire negotiation was done in a day, including the paper work. To my knowledge, I became the only newspaperman to achieve back-to-back journalism fellowships at Harvard and Columbia. As the formal letter accepting me for the Ford Foundation Fellowship in Advanced International Reporting noted, making a grant to a Nieman was "an unprecedented step."

The following year was probably the most productive of my career. I literally led two lives. I took a full load of classes in the morning, raced over the Triborough Bridge to Garden City at 1, oversaw the Specialists Section and tooled back to Columbia where I read in the Butler Library till midnight and was up the next morning at 7:30 to repeat the process. Luckily, I was driving off hours both ways so the ride was quick. I seemed to have no trouble juggling my academic and journalistic lives. On the contrary, Columbia and Newsday seemed to energize one other. My campus responsibilities were easy enough. I was a grownup and was able to stay focused on the work and nothing else. It's not hard to go to college when all you do is go to college. The distractions and longueurs of student life had no appeal for me. The clock was ticking. As for papers, I treated them like news stories. I reported them, handed them in and never looked back. The writing was a pleasure. Of course, I had no social life—an important component of the Nieman—but it was worth the ticket.

I was more impressed with Columbia than Harvard. The undergraduates were as smart but I felt they worked harder. At Harvard, admission seemed to be all that was required for the next four years. At Columbia, you had to toe the line. Even the nature of my own program reflected the difference. The Nieman required one course for credit all year; the rest was very gentlemanly and clubbable. The Columbia program expected its fellows to take four classes a term, all for grades. I also thought the teaching was better with more top professors giving human-sized classes and making themselves available to the students—as opposed to the star-centered, set-piece auditorium lectures at Harvard.

In the midst of my academic endeavors, I managed to do some journalism as well. Through the International Affairs Reporting Program, I learned about a junket of U.S. business writers that was being organized by the Common Market. The European Economic Community was bankrolling this trip to make its case to the American public about the ongoing trade and monetary war with Washington, in anticipation of an upcoming Group of Ten meeting in Rome. To redress a trade deficit, the Nixon Administration had floated the dollar and imposed a surcharge on foreign imports which made European currency and products more expensive. Naturally, Europe wasn't delighted but it made a dozen American newspapermen very happy. I didn't know much about financial affairs but I figured what was there to lose? In fact, the trip offered an opportunity to fulfill an International Reporting Fellowship requirement for a research-writing project, so I'd be doing good by doing well. The trip fell for two weeks in November 1971, after midterms, so I was able to steal some time from school and I proposed a series for Newsday's Money pages. They bought it.

What followed was a gastronomic tour of the capitals of Europe: Amsterdam, the Hague, Brussels, Antwerp, Rome, Paris, Bonn and Cologne, with a stop-off in London where I got to dine in Parliament. What the Europeans spent on our tour could have restored the trade deficit right there. Being a scruffy news sort, I had no idea how some of my other journalistic peers lived, but watching these business reporters go to town was an eye-opener. We were wined and dined at luxury hotels, chi-chi restaurants and elegant ministries in every port-of-call, which didn't make my confreres shy about refilling their glasses and utilizing room service. I recall a particularly elegant and bibulous feed with white-gloved waiters at the Grand Hotel in Rome. But the other cities were equally up to the mark. I couldn't help noticing that my colleagues were spending more time taking in the sights than taking notes. I briefly considered making a career change when I got back to work. After I returned to Newsday I dutifully submitted a well-received two-part series on the situation.

My last days at Columbia coincided with Nixon's 1972 bombing of Cambodia. I remember walking across the near-empty lawn between the Butler Library and the statue of Alma Mater, the site of so many student protests through the 60's. A small knot of students surrounded a bearded young fellow with a bullhorn trying to attract a crowd to protest this latest atrocity, but there were no takers. The few passers-by hurried along, as oblivious to the speaker's appeal as they'd be to a panhandler on the subway. As I watched the tiny group's vain entreaties on this warm afternoon, I couldn't help thinking of reporting on the student strike at Hamilton Hall on this very same campus just four years earlier with large crowds flocking to the call of the student leaders who had seized the building. That class had by now moved on and its successors were hurrying by concerned with graduation or summer jobs, deaf to the blandishments from the huddled group of activist students whose plaints were as forlorn as their cause. How is it that the bombing of Haiphong and Hanoi could draw impassioned crowds but the equally horrific bombing of Cambodia could not? What had happened in the interim, of course, was the end of the draft. Once this crop of collegians no longer had to face conscription, the bottom dropped out of the protest movement. No shame in this, but less virtue than what had been affected earlier. As I left the isolated, ragtag lot on the Columbia campus and

110

crossed Broadway at 116th Street, I saw a burst of blue-and-white balloons at the entrance to Barnard celebrating a spring fete. I had just witnessed the end of the 60's.

*   *   *

Even before I left for Harvard, I had organized things at Newsday so that the Specialists Section was up-and-running by the time I returned. I don't remember drawing a strained breath during this entire period. I realized that I had created a perpetual motion machine. All I had to do was keep it humming. What doubtless helped was that by now, the principals in the drama that obtained before my departure had been carried off the stage. The intensity of Moyers, the animosity of Marlens, the unravelling of McIlwain were all gone, and with them went the current of volatility and Angst that mesmerized the place, a condition that we accepted as normality. All of the bullying and hazing inflicted by lesser editors that we took for granted also ended once they no longer had imprimatur from the top. You can save a lot of time if you don't have to keep looking over your shoulder.

I was fortunate in that we had no competition. No one was then doing Media, Education, Science, Health, Environment, Religion, Behavior, Consumer Affairs, etc., on a daily basis in a single package, in the metropolitan area or anywhere. The Suffolk Sun had folded and it would take The Times years to catch up with its fluff sections—the first of which I would later help start. Of necessity, I had gravitated toward the secret of executive success— the Tom Sawyer school of management: Let the other kids paint the fence and make them think you're doing them a favor. The drill was simple enough. On Fridays, we'd map out the following week's schedule. Every specialist would report on two or three stories they'd be doing and I'd figure out which one would lead the book, putting the others in their respective pages, already pre-slotted. There was always enough in the can so that if something broke I could toss it in to freshen the mix or parcel it out to the news pages. The trick was to get good people and let them do their jobs.

Newsday was very eclectic in its employment policies. Our religion writer, Ken Briggs, was literally hired off the street after being fired as the minister of a Lutheran church in Nassau when he refused to heed his board's warnings to stop speaking against the Vietnam War. Sans pulpit but cum car, Ken drove down Stewart Avenue and stopped off at Newsday. We were just starting up the religion page for the section. Why not a minister? We figured it was easier to teach a preacher how to write than to train a reporter in religion. Ken was a little wordy—the sermonizer in him—but he let us edit him and learned the craft well enough to go on to The Times in a few years where he worked the God beat.

My education writer was Martin Buskin who was the dean of metropolitan education reporters because The Times kept rotating its people and the tabloids had pretty much abandoned the field the way their readers had abandoned the schools. During my city editor stint I had already worked with Marty on stories like the Ocean-Hill Brownsville strike. We were light years ahead of the competition on the story because of Buskin's contacts—he had a lock on Albert Shanker, the Teachers Union leader—and because Newsday actually had some black reporters. Where the others were still playing catch-up, we had ready access to all sides.

It's hard to discuss Marty without speaking of my secretary or, rather, our secretary, Shirley Graham. I had commandeered her from Buskin when I became Specialists editor but she had been with him so long that it seemed cruel to deprive him of her altogether. When we rearranged the office to accommodate our section, I put Shirley at the apex of a triangle between Buskin's desk and mine so that we shared her. Actually, since Shirley worked in her own karmic universe, Marty and I went equally without her services. We also had to share space with Shirley's Great Dane, Esther, a gentle sort who curled up under Marty's desk and stayed there for the rest of the day.

Shirley, aging but ageless, still quite beautiful with her tall, tantric, dark-haired ways, Nefertiti eyes, and gravelly voice, materialized bangled and spangled with Esther every day in a flourish of psychedelic color After checking our vibes, she proceeded to phone her daughter or a variety of friends, or deal with a plethora of service personnel who were attending to her home in Levittown. Occasionally, she would seek our opinion on one topic or another, sometimes personal, sometimes metaphysical. More than once, I thought of letting Marty revert to his exclusive rights over her and depositing them elsewhere so that I could get a little work done but, such were Shirley's charms and Esther's gravitas that I subsumed them into my work week. Occasionally, even Marty would become exasperated and sputter that she had lost three of his phone calls or misplaced his Rolodex. To which she'd respond with great equanimity: "Buskeleh," as she called him—she was Roman Catholic but had spent a lot of time around Jews— "you didn't really want to talk to that dopey supervisor. Anyway, he'll call back. Let him want you."

Our media writer was Tom Collins. Like Ken Briggs, Tom had pretty much walked in off the street, although well before I'd ever arrived. After a few years in the Washington Bureau and then working with me on the day desk, Collins had had his fill of editor's work and teamed up with me again, this time as a media writer for the Specialists Section. Tom's great advantage was that he was a seasoned Washington reporter covering the media as if it were a daily competitive beat, one of the first to do so for a major American newspaper. One of the big running stories that he stayed atop of was the last stand of the newspaper unions as they fought their rear-guard action against the mechanization that was about to obliterate them. Collins was an intrepid reporter, once even getting mauled by some labor goons after straying into the wrong union huddle. Luckily, he only lost a pair of glasses and a little dignity.

I still kept my hand in at writing during this period, doing an occasional opinion piece for the Viewpoints pages. One of them involved the case of Hermine Braunsteiner Ryan, an SS guard at Ravensbruck and Majdanek who was facing extradition charges to West Germany on war-crimes charges. A writer, Nancy Ross, had written a previous piece in the Viewpoints section, suggesting that Braunsteiner was merely a Queens housewife being hounded by remorseless avengers. I demonstrated that she was a committed Nazi who volunteered for work at Ravensbruck and Majdanek and that she'd lied about her past to gain entry to the U.S. which constituted sufficient moral turpitude for deporting her to Germany where she'd face trial for her wartime conduct. I was told by the Immigration officer who prosecuted the case that my article had been "the best ever written on the Ryan case." Braunsteiner was deported to West Germany and convicted of murdering 80 people, abetting in the murder of 102 children and collaborating in the murder of 1,000. She was sentenced to life .

I stayed on at Newsday till mid-1973. Given the paper's generosity, I felt I owed it at least another year. Who knows, I might have remained forever, had it not been for a sequence of events over which I had no control. Al Marlens had left Newsday embittered after Bill Moyers' ascendancy. Although Moyers may have honorably protected Marlens from the wrath of Capt. Guggenheim, he had eviscerated Al's total control over the daily operation. When Al subsequently told Moyers, "It's your paper," he was, in effect, not only resigned but resigning.

Marlens spent a brief tenure at Time magazine but after it became apparent that the senior editor's job he'd been promised was not senior enough, he quit. For many men who've been at the top, sharing authority is a difficult and chastening experience, but for Marlens it was more than that. He absolutely had to have total control. The idea of kow-towing to anyone was unacceptable. There aren't that many jobs available offering such autonomy in big-time news organizations, certainly not for someone who'd been squeezed out of a post at a suburban daily. Fortunately, for Al —and me—he found the right fit. Max Frankel, fresh off a Pulitzer for his Nixon-to-China coverage as the Times's Washington bureau chief, had recently assumed the reins of the paper's Sunday Section. Sunday was still an independent entity, allowing Frankel a power base to continue his rivalry with A.M. Rosenthal who ran the daily paper. Max, a Washington power player, wanted to bring in his own people and breathe some life into a section that had grown moribund under the stewardship of his predecessor, Dan Schwarz.

The newsiest part of the Sunday Department, in which Frankel took a particular interest, was the Week in Review. And in choosing Marlens to run it Max had picked just the man who'd give it a competitive edge, not only with outside rivals but within the building as well. If Abe Rosenthal took no prisoners, neither did Al Marlens, and he'd be working under the protective umbrella of Max Frankel. Moreover, if Sunday was independent from the daily, the Week-in-Review was a doubly autonomous unit within the Sunday Department. All Marlens had to do was deliver, so Max was more than glad to give him his head. Frankel sought to remake the Week-in-Review in his own image. Instead of the scroll of news that unwound like a reel of film from first page to last, Max and Al broke the section up into units—Foreign, National, Metropolitan, Ideas & Trends—with an editor for each department. And Marlens, looking to bring in his own people, thought it would be a good idea to tap me for the job of metropolitan editor. Not only would I be his man but, in fairness, I was actually qualified for the job.

I'd also gotten other offers during this period. My old Nieman pal Jim Squires, who was then beginning his ascent at The Chicago Tribune, wanted me to come down to Washington and join the paper's bureau there but I didn't want to leave New York, although I recommended Jon Margolis, one of my Newsday protégés, for the job. Jon went on to have a stellar career at the Trib as a political writer and columnist. I also thought again of recidivating to academe. But for me, yearning for the academic life was like pining for an island haven where I'd vacationed, nostalgic but unreal. I was destined to stay in the newspaper game and if I was going to play baseball, it might as well be in Yankee Stadium. So when Marlens offered the brass ring, I grabbed it.

My interview at The Times was brief. On a mid-June morning in 1973, I arrived at the Eighth Floor offices of the Sunday Department. Al greeted me at the elevator and ushered me into Max Frankel's wood-paneled lair. Sitting next to Max was his sidekick and alter ego Jack Rosenthal. Sitting next to me was Marlens. It was like mixed doubles without a net. I have no idea what we talked about—politics, culture, world affairs—but I remember feeling completely self-assured and at ease. I don't think I was there for more than a half-hour. Very collegial. Max smoked a pipe, which I found oddly reassuring. We shook hands, I got up, left with Al, went into his office and he told me I'd been hired. I don't think they ever looked at my clips or checked another reference. And I never went through an orientation, then or when I returned almost 25 years later. Of course, what helped was that the fix was in. Al assured them that I was the man for the job and they took his word for it. If he was wrong, I'd be canned, as swiftly as I was hired. But it turns out he was right. I left Newsday at the end of June and on July 5, after Independence Day, I began my life at The New York Times.

Daily Mirror Copy Chief Sam Susskind in regalia as "Ibn Sam," 1957.
New York Daily Mirror

City College's Herb Stempel on the rigged quiz show
"Twenty One." The author's 1956 story in The Campus indicated
Stempel was not a struggling student.

The author, left, under the spell of hypnotist Pat Collins
at Basin Street East, for an entertainment story in Newsday, 1964.

The author covers the burgeoning beat scene for
Newsday in a 1964 series.

Al Marlens, Newsday managing editor and later editor of The Times Week in Review.
The New York Times

Mike McGrady, the guiding spirit behind "Naked Came the Stranger," 1969.
AP

Nieman Fellows on the steps of Harvard's Widener Library, 1970.
The author is in 2d row, far right. Next to him is James Squires. The
woman in the center is Jo Thomas.
    Nieman Foundation

Newsday
THE LONG ISLAND NEWSPAPER

10 CENTS
FRIDAY
JUNE 29, 1973

Jack Schwartz Reaches Journalistic Watershed

Departs Newsday For NY Times: Crisis Seen

'It may seem suspicious that he is leaving at the height of the Watergate scandal but ah understand he is fine boy despite the fact he has busy red hair and is of Jewish persuasion.'
—Sen. Same Ervin

'Schwartz doesn't cover up. Schwartz doesn't threaten or commit illegal acts. God only knows why he is leaving Newsday. Does Schirmer know?'
—Sen. Lowell Weicker

Who Is Greg Schirmer?

Page 3

Spoof front page of Newday on the author's leaving for The Times, 1973. Pictured are Sen. Sam Ervin (top) chairman of the Senate Watergate Committee and Sen. Lowell Weicker, a member of the panel, reflecting on the author's departure.

The author at The Times Week in Review, 1973.
The New York Times

Illustration of the author winging over the tri-state area as regional editor of The Times Week in Review, 1974.

The author demonstrates computer skills to the actress Helen Hayes.
At right is the critic Elliot Norton. Standing is Culture Czar Arthur Gelb.
Seated behind Gelb is the editor Ralph Behrens.
The New York Times

Tony Marro , editor of
Newsday

Illustration for the Fall Preview of Newsday's book pages, 1988. Front Row: Charles Dickens, John Lennon, T.S. Eliot, Billy the Kid, Langston Hughes, Golda Meir.
Rear Row: Margaret Thatcher, Leo Tolstoy, Barry Goldwater, Winston Churchill,
George Bernard Shaw, John F. Kennedy.
    Van Howell / Newsday

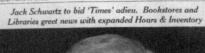

Spoof front page of The New York Times on the author's retirement, 2005.
    The New York Times

THE PAPER

I would imagine that most people who worked for The New York Times remember their first day at the place, not so much what they covered or wrote, but the simple impression of being there, a special sense of having arrived, the illusion that everything else they'd done was simply throat-clearing, rehearsal, preparation for the big time where they could show their mettle. Perhaps people who came in through the now defunct copy-boy system might have seen it differently, but I'm sure even the lowest scrub who ever trundled in for the first time couldn't help feeling just a surge of starry-eyed ambition and a tingle of hope at somehow making it through the doors.

I arrived at The Times in a series of ascensions. First I came up out of the subway at the 42d Street exit just west of Broadway. At the time, it was the Great Blight Way, at its nadir before the gentrification of the 90's set in. I emerged bat-like from the subway, blinking in the July sunlight. The first thing that hit me was the smell of rancid orange juice from the papaya stand on the corner mixed with the grease of sizzling meat and frying onions from a nearby souvlaki vendor. These vapors were tinctured with the funky odors of the various drugstore cowboys, white-booted ladies and purple-hatted gents who owned the street. The local theatrical fare was a plethora of porn houses advertising their wares on a recessional of marquees along a street sprinkled with dirty-book stores. Around the corner was a penny arcade that catered to chicken hawks and the predators with a taste for them. Across the street was the carapace of the Allied Chemical Building, an ugly sarcophagus that entombed the structure of the original Times Building. The ribbon of news that sputtered around it seemed anomalous, flashing superfluous information to the indifferent eyes of passers-by hurrying to get out of there.

Amid all this were flocks of picture-snapping Japanese tourists who didn't seem to mind the ambience, treating it as if it were simply an inverted Disneyland, a proto-Ginza that had failed, a quaint harbinger of American decline that would lead to the ascendancy of Toyota. Beyond this was an obstacle course of cheap camera shops, luggage stores and souvenir emporia, all of which were forever going out of business and advertising last-minute fire sales. Along the way were a string of buskers, beggars and grifters, giving pride of place to the three-card monte sharks at the corner who seemed to draw a cluster of marks amid the shills that worked for them. Presiding over all this was The Republic of

China, a second-floor restaurant reached by a narrow stairway and advertised by a red-and-blue neon sign that flickered day and night in its windows which looked down, physically and socially, on the agora below. The Republic was one of the favorite hangouts of mid-level Times staffers plus stray tourists and actors in-between-jobs. The stone-faced help seemed oblivious to what was going on outside. No matter how bad the neighborhood, a Chinese restaurant serves as an oasis, a fortress impregnable to the disarray of the street. Although there was a menu, they seemed to have a set fare: Combination No. 1—Wonton or Egg Drop, Chicken Chow Mein or Chop Suey, Egg Roll, Fried Rice, Tea in a porcelain pot, Pineapple with toothpicks and Fortune Cookies with real fortunes rather than maxims. I don't think I ever spent more at a sitting than six bucks, tip included.

If you made it to the corner, there was a coffee wagon with a line-up of regulars, and beyond that, farther along 43rd Street, Al's Deli getting its own crowd of coffee-and-bagel customers. There were invariably colleagues on these lines, some of whom you wanted to see, others whom you didn't and, depending on whom you were stuck with, the wait could be interminable. On the other hand, the coffee lines were a good source of gossip, but not too good because only a fool would divulge anything serious at this venue.

By now, I was in sight of the building; a few stray rectangular-rigged trucks parked outside the delivery bays down the block toward Eighth Avenue, the digital clock hovering overhead, the flags more like bunting than banners, the revolving doors and finally, I was in. I remember feeling a bit of a letdown because, it being the day after a summer holiday, the building was half-empty, manned by skeleton crews rather than the full complement of staff. The street seemed to have been abandoned to its denizens. But once inside the air-conditioned lobby, a sense of order and purpose reasserted itself. I took the elevator to the Eighth Floor, and there I was, in the Sunday Department. It was as calm and orderly as a hospital ward.

The Sunday Section of The Times was designed like a giant hand. With Max Frankel's office serving as the palm, it stretched its fingers into the five branches of the department. Once past Frankel's sanctum sanctorum, the room opened up into a gym-sized, high-ceilinged expanse of gray flat-topped desks arranged in squads of double-rows. Each cordon contained a distinct section of the Sunday Department. Facing east, along the far left wall was the bastion of the Magazine Section under the redoubtable Lewis Bergman. In the center was a phalanx split down the middle between the Travel Section overseen by the less-redoubtable Bill Honan and the Drama Department which was still more Arts than Leisure under the aegis of Seymour Peck. Off at the back towards Eighth Avenue was the Book Department in the heyday of the boy wonder John Leonard and, along the 43rd Street wall with streams of light coming in through the double-windows, was the newly refurbished Week-in-Review where I was to work. The symmetry was somewhat marred by Sy Peck's charges who floated out behind the Week-in-Review. This meant I was sitting catty-corner from Abe Rosenthal's sister, Rose Newman, who worshipped Sy and bore an uncanny resemblance to Abe with a wig.

The first person I met on my maiden voyage to the Eighth Floor was the Week-in-Review secretary, Joyce Jensen, who was the apotheosis of her calling: discreet, loyal, self-effacing, permanently 45 and brimming with understanding for her difficult boss as well as sympathy for his harried underlings. Joyce, who got in even earlier than I did, showed me to my to desk, which was Seat 1, Row 3 from the windows in our little classroom. My mate in seat 2 would be Carolyn Herron, also newly minted, but from a more cerebral provenance. Carolyn had been recruited for the Ideas & Trends section. I'd have preferred that beat myself, given my own background and inclinations, but I was glad for what I could get.

Our desks were convertibles that folded out into typewriters which took up considerable space leaving scant room for books, papers, and the ubiquitous copy spikes that littered the place like a field of Kaiser's helmets. Coffee was balanced precariously on ledges and sandwiches were stuffed into desk drawers, often getting tangled up with headphones hooked to the desk rims. But, given my previous venues, the office seemed spacious. Some chroniclers talk of the frenzy and chaos of first encountering The Times. For me, it was the opposite. I felt as if I were aboard the Queen Mary after sailing on freighters and banana boats. Coming from a smaller vessel, one is struck by the tremendous infrastructure of The Times. At the Paper of Record, there's a net beneath the net. The world was there to accommodate you, your staff was name-brand, your supervisors were as confident as Conquistadors and everything from the morgue to the library to the mail room functioned serenely. Even the pressure appeared to be ordered. I don't remember much of what I did that first week but I do recall shutting off the lights in the office—the other

118

departments by then had gone home and only the Week-in-Review worked late. After I snapped the last switch I paused in the darkened office to look out the window at the nightscape. Even the Hotel Carter, with its ugly façade and rough trade, seemed to glow as I essayed the possibilities of a new life. It was probably the last moment I was unreservedly happy at The Times.

The newspaper was an aircraft carrier whose confines I traversed over the next 15 years. During this voyage I worked in supervisory and subordinate capacities, had a hand in or touched down in a goodly number of quarters, some of which didn't yet exist when I arrived and others that disappeared before I left. To cite only a few: The Week-in-Review where I started, the old Family-Style department, the Metropolitan Desk, the Magazine, the Science Section, the Suburban Regionals, and all three of the Culture Departments: Weekend, the Daily pages and Arts & Leisure. Some of these had subdivisions and all had layers of top editors, sub-editors and copy editors refracting one another's efforts. If one considers this a climb, looking back down can be vertiginous. I will try to bring the terrain into focus and turn a light on some who sojourned there.

Max Frankel's goal was to renovate the Sunday Department thoroughly. He planned to reorganize each section along more rational, hierarchal, centralized lines. Those sections chief who signed aboard for the new era were welcomed, at least temporarily; those who didn't would be replaced with more malleable personalities. This policy earned Frankel the sobriquet Max the Ax, although I felt it unfair because any new boss is going to reshape a section in his image. In general, I found the pipe-smoking, avuncular Frankel to be determined but reasonable. Certainly, the old Sunday Department needed some shaking up and Max wasn't above breaking a few eggs in order to make his omelet. On the plus side, Frankel revitalized the Week-in-Review, replacing the genteel Robert Clurman with the hard-driving Al Marlens, and gave John Leonard his head in books. On the minus side, he marginalized Lewis Bergman, whom some consider the finest editor of The Times magazine in its glory days. Presumably, they had different visions for the Magazine and Lewis was probably too much the dissident to get on board Max's train. Bergman was reputed to have an impish nature that belied his rigorous standards. Marlens told me he once saw him tap-dancing along one of the desks in the early morning.

A different limb that Max sawed off was Seymour Peck at Arts
& Leisure. Peck, one of the survivors of PM, Marshall Fields's
noble experiment in a public-service tabloid that eschewed
advertising, was a walking repository of theater lore. You didn't
need clips if Sy was around. But Frankel sought a more rounded
Arts section, and he bridled at the soft celebrity features that were
a talisman of Peck's tenure. Max wanted interpretive reporting—
why things happened; the politics of entertainment, the business of
show business. His goal was to put more oomph in an Arts Section
that had changed little since the days its front page was festooned
with Lewis Funke's "News of the Rialto"—a tout-sheet for
Broadway publicists. Sy felt this was so much posturing; that all
people wanted to know was what was the next hot show, who was
starring in it and what the critics thought. For Max, this was knee-
jerk, predictable, business-as-usual. Ironically, Sy, who knew
something of politics and more than something about the dynamics
of Broadway, could have been a real asset in this enterprise but
their personalities never meshed. Peck was certain that Frankel
was out to get him and he was right. He had become mildly
paranoid in the process and, being an obsessive, he probably took a
few measures that he might not have done under other
circumstances. A clash was inevitable and Peck was shortly
demoted to a theater writer on The Magazine. Presumably, Max
hoped that a humiliated Sy would fall on his sword but Peck
merely swallowed it and lived to fight another day.

While Frankel's strategic impulse may have been correct, his
choice of personnel to carry out his agenda, was sometimes less so.
He anointed Bill Honan to be the new Arts & Leisure editor, a
decision that was later to have a significant impact on my life.
Honan was not Mr. Popularity with his staff who were resistant to
his "ideas" agenda, which they considered superficial. Moreover,
the martyred Peck, adulated by his staff, knew his subject cold
while Bill, fairly or not, was considered an apparatchik, a
reputation that stayed with him throughout his employment at The
Times. This did not prevent him from having a luminous career
culminating in being named the first editor to have dominion over
all three of The Times's entertainment Sections: Arts & Leisure,
Weekend and Daily Culture. The immediate impact of Honan's
Sunday appointment was the departure of Guy Flatley, Peck's
respected assistant, and the rise of Bob Berkvist who used his
steady skills to forge a bond with Honan that carried him along as
Bill's star ascended, and would ultimately transcend Honan's
demise.

None of this affected me at the moment, except as an observer. I was sufficiently distracted by my duties at the Week-in-Review. In addition to staff-written essays on various local topics, the section's metropolitan report also boasted a regional roundup. This consisted of short takes on news of the suburbs, all of which had to reflect trends. And, if they were indeed trends, they perforce had to be ubiquitous in all the suburbs. Consequently, if there were a crabgrass epidemic on Long Island, I would be required to find a similar malaise in Westchester, Connecticut and New Jersey. This made some sense with pieces on taxpayer rebellions against school levies or car-pooling during a gas crisis, but most stories are sufficiently distinct so that their particulars cannot be generally applied. But to come up bare was to confound the reigning assumptions. And Marlens was a remorseless enforcer of the ideology. My guess is that Frankel's intent was more flexible but Al played hardball.

Under these circumstances, I undertook prodigious efforts to squeeze square pegs into the round holes of Al's preconceptions. In the three years we'd been separated, I'd forgotten what a martinet Marlens could be. And since an enterprising reporter can get people to say a lot and to dig up almost anything, I managed to sew the crazy-quilt reality of the disparate local venues into what appeared to be a pattern of regional unity. However, this took an inordinate amount of time so that the tail of reporting these items wagged the dog of assigning the essays to staff reporters, which was the most interesting and challenging aspect of the job. In truth, I'm not sure if very many people read the briefs, which were a sop to my supervisors, but they were my price of admission. That more than half of our readers were New Yorkers who were hardly interested in the suburbs at all, only added to the absurdity of my task. When I made this point, the solution was to incorporate city stories into my suburban motif. Nevertheless, I plodded on, driven by Al's insatiable will to be proved right and my own fear of failure.

When the essays came in, after I had edited them, Marlens applied his old Newsday tactics, asking—or rather, having me relay to the reporters—a battery of questions, a few of which were good, many of which were not, but all of which had to be answered. But whereas at Newsday, no one dared to question the Marlens style of editing, at The Times, most writers had no intention of being treated like the hired help by the likes of a

Johnny-come-lately from Long Island. Moreover, none of them actually worked for the Week-in-Review but rather reported to the news operation. For them, appearing in the section was a free-lance option which some did for the money, some for the prestige, and some to refurbish "string"—material that had been held out earlier—with an interpretive flourish so that it would see the light of day. But none of them were required to labor for the Week-in-Review and more than a few grew to refuse assignments. My job then became one of mediating between ruffled writers and a driven boss. I fell back on a common ploy of diplomacy telling each of the contending parties only as much as they absolutely had to know and implying that they were a lot closer to agreement than was actually the case. Although Marlens was absolutely obdurate when sending me into battle, he usually backed off a little when dealing with the writers themselves so that the outcome was very close to what I had originally proposed.

After a while, Marlens conceded, without admitting anything, that not every item required a clone in the Tri-state area; things eased up a bit provided that I threw him a regional bone from time to time. His table of organization also gave way to the reality of news—a busy Foreign week, a light Ideas and Trends week, vacation, sickness, the flux of personnel— so that most of us, myself included, took turns in overlapping jurisdictions. This gave me the chance of roaming as far afield as Economics, Education and Science. The great opportunity of working for the Week-in-Review was getting to know writers over a cross-section of the paper without ever leaving one's desk. It allowed me to cross-pollinate and I took advantage. I formed long-term friendships with writers such as Gerry Gold—then a consumer reporter in a hiatus from his duties on the Foreign desk; Dick Shepard, an all-purpose Metro Maven and the Saint of the City Room, and Richard Eder who, at the time, was our man in Madrid. I cultivated a brace of Metro reporters ranging from the political pundit Mickey Carroll who talked as fast as he wrote, to the deft wordsmith Frank Clines to John Darnton, an up-and-coming young reporter then cutting his teeth in Connecticut, who would eventually become Metropolitan Editor. Almost 25 years later, as Culture Editor, Darnton would re-hire me for my last go-round at The Times.

The unraveling of the Nixon regime in the summer and fall of 1973 was the dominant event of my blooding at the paper. It was on Max Frankel's watch as The Times's D.C. bureau chief that The Washington Post had gotten its scoop on the Watergate scandal and Max was determined that we were not going to be beaten again—even in the Sunday Department. In those days, the Week-in-Review closed late on Saturday afternoon, at virtually the same time as the early edition of the Sunday paper. So, in effect, we were competing not only with Time and Newsweek but also with Woodward and Bernstein at the Washington Post and, most importantly, with our own daily newspaper. We obviously couldn't scoop the Daily, but the 20-year rivalry between the Sunday Editor Max Frankel and the managing editor Abe Rosenthal played itself out in Week-in-Review news analyses that were as much news as analysis. Equally important was the competition for resources. While The Times, in playing catch-up ball with the Washington Post, had by then thrown considerable forces into the chase, there were only a few available writers at the top who had cultivated the necessary sources, could write quickly and think on their feet. Naturally, both the Daily and the Week-in-Review wanted maximum use of their time, particularly as the week wound down. By right, the Daily should have been able to exercise droit du seigneur, but in fact, Frankel used his clout and contacts as recent Washington bureau chief, as well as the prestige of the Week-in-Review, to cultivate a network of reporters that managed to serve two masters.

Our mainstays were John Crewdson and James Naughton. They were a dazzling high-wire act, alternately feeding the daily beast with regular updates and, without seeming to break stride, turning in more than a thousand words of lucid prose to the Week-in-Review that covered the same material but somehow seemed fresh. This included fielding with good grace the fusillade of questions that came from our squad of editors. All by 4 on Saturday afternoon. We'd then rush the copy to the composing room. This was still in the days of hot type, so that copy had to be set by a printer at a linotype machine and arranged on the stone by a make-up man directed by an editor who'd be reading the metal letters upside down and backwards. I'd be there to see to my own pages but, since the front page of our section was the last to close, I'd invariably sidle over.

Not every editor cared to be on the composing room floor but I enjoyed the dynamics of the close. And Marlens liked having me around for the finale, along with whoever else was working their pages. It was one of those all-hands-on-deck phenomena, when everyone huddles around the chase as the last pieces of the puzzle are put in place. The makeup-man— at this point a top-of-the-line practitioner— with his blue-collar suspicion of the shirts opposite him, methodically placed the segments of lead like chips on a roulette table. With late copy on breaking stories or the Watergate rush there was often no page proof and one cut on the stone with an inward eye on the clock. We simply had to make do as best we could and have it out with the writer later.

Miraculously, we always managed to finish by 5 P.M. The Week-in-Review rolled off the presses with the rest of the paper, was in the trucks by 7 and out on the news stands by 8. This was at the high tide of the break-in scandal, when Richard Nixon, in a lather to caulk the leaks of his sinking ship, ordered the Saturday Night Massacre, firing the special Watergate prosecutor, Archie Cox, and precipitating a mass exodus from his foundering vessel. It seemed that almost every major bump during that roller-coaster season occurred on a Friday or Saturday, so that the section had to be torn up constantly and reinvented at the end of the week—in effect virtually becoming a daily. I was convinced that Nixon's late-week ploys were his revenge on the liberal press. On most Watergate stories we simply had the reporters write B-Matter—background material that fleshed out the body of the story—and waited for the inevitable shoe to drop as the weekend approached. But this worked only up to a point because the unfolding details were so complicated and protean that the stories usually needed a complete rewrite to make any sense.

It was fascinating to watch writers like Naughton and Crewdson file 1,500 flawless words on the ongoing drama in under two hours, a tour-de-force of journalistic prowess. Truth be told, all I had to do was enjoy the show from a ringside seat unless I was drafted into service when one of the Nation editors needed help. To be sure, there was some residual impact. Although our sections were theoretically compartmentalized, when we shared space on the front page, if a Watergate event—or for that matter any other piece of news—bumped or reduced my Metro space, it would create a domino effect in which I'd have to juggle stories with last-minute rewrites and trims to make everything fit. It was like manipulating a giant Rubik's cube. But it afforded good training and better bonding. When it was over, we'd repair to Al's office in the southeast corner of the Sunday department, and Marlens, an Ahab moments earlier, would transmogrify to Starbuck mode, plucking a bottle of Johnnie Walker from his desk and offering its contents in paper cups to his house carls. In a moment, what had been traumatic an hour before was now hilarious; yesterday's Angst folded into tomorrow's lore.

My comrades were as quirky as they were talented which, I guess, came with the territory. Our dean was Anthony Austin, who was responsible for foreign affairs. Impeccably dressed and well-tailored on even the hottest days, Austin would have considered dress-down Fridays an abomination. Tony had the cultivated, disengaged air of a rootless cosmopolitan, exuding equal measures of worldliness and world-weariness as the occasion required. He prefaced a few lectures to me with "My dear Jack," this itself preceded by a muted sigh hinting at the hopelessness of enlightening me on anything involving the nuances of diplomacy.

When the Yom Kippur War broke out, we were gearing up for our Saturday close, Marlens was away and out of pocket, so Tony, as the senior man and foreign maven, got to make the call about coverage. It was still early in the day in New York with plenty of time to remake the cover—at least by Al's standards. It meant, of course, tearing up the front page, running down reporters and stringers in the Middle East, reassigning pieces, killing stories, trimming others and running the risk of closing late. Which, of course, is what we were in the business of doing. Had Marlens been around, there'd have been no question of what to do. But Austin took a more judicious approach and decided that this is what the Daily was for. We would reflect on the fighting the following week when the fog of war had lifted. There was a brief discussion in which some of us urged that we press on, even with a single over-all piece, just to be in the game. But Tony, who'd wavered earlier, was resolute now that his mind was made up. And, being politically attuned, he convinced Max to sign off on this—which perhaps Frankel did because he felt that Tony wasn't up to it— so our coverage consisted of a box on the cover saying the Yom Kippur war had happened and, for further developments, read the Daily. Next Week in Jerusalem!

When Marlens came back the following week he called Tony into his office and closed the door. You could hear the shouting throughout the Sunday Department. Forty-five minutes later, Tony emerged. I never knew what the color of "ashen" was till then. Pallid, shaken, Tony looked as if he'd been impaled on a copy spike. After that, Marlens made sure that when he was gone, Austin would no longer make any decisions, which was just as well with Tony who was a thoughtful man but not an aggressive one. The rough-and-tumble of a daily paper, which is what Al sought at every opportunity, was not for him. I worked with Austin several years later when I was copy chief of The Times magazine where he had by then moved. Tony was back to his old urbane self.

I think that after the trauma of Marlens, nothing was ever able to shake him again.

Bob Stock, while nominally in charge of our National pages, was in essence our Mr. Fix-it, a Swiss Army Knife of an editor who could rewrite anything on any topic in short order. Virtually every section needs a Bob Stock, someone who can absolutely get the job done, swiftly, deftly, with unerring reliability. You never had to explain anything to Bob. He intuited what was needed. Stock, who bore the burden of our Watergate coverage, was the only staffer whom Al treated as a virtual equal, and well he should. Bob, a Travel Editor who'd been bumped for a more malleable sort, was clearly overqualified for his job. Al—who had taken his own lumps at the hands of what he felt were lesser men—respected Bob for both his skill and for accepting a somewhat diminished role with grace.

Stock was the first in a long line of by-passed talent I was to meet at The Times and, in a way, he served as a model, a harbinger and a warning. There were no more than a score of plum editorial jobs at the paper and an equal number of reporting assignments. With hundreds of staffers vying for them this meant that the overwhelming majority —which included some very talented, ambitious and frustrated people—would fail to reach the top of the greasy pole. More likely, some of them would get halfway up before being pushed back down into the scrum. To the outside world you were still a gentleman from The Times, an exotic creature with access to all the excitement at the pinnacle of journalism. But in your heart you knew you'd fallen short. People respond in many different ways to this. The most reasonable— perhaps the majority—carve out their little plot and take whatever pleasure, consolation or benefice they can from laboring in the paper's vineyards. There are, after all, the rewards of craft, the gratifications of gate-keeping, the compensations of minor status, the consolations of perks, the realities of security and salary, the advantages of access and the occasional satisfactions of impact. But for some restive spirits this is not enough and they simply light out for the territories. A seat-of-the-pants survey of the defectors I knew shows that most did well. There was not just life after The Times, but a very good one for those with the pluck to break out.

The Week-in-Review, like the Arts & Leisure Section, did not have a copy desk but relied on its own staff, reading back on one another, to serve as copy editors. The pace on these sections was presumed to be sufficiently glacial so that the assignment editors would have the time to perform the duties of monitoring copy for accuracy, sense and style, normally the province of copy editors. Of course it never worked out that way and the reality probably would have been a risky business except that the editors were so good, they kept gaffes to a minimum. What actually happened was that de facto copy editing chores fell to two people, John Van Doorn, Al's deputy, and Tom Butson, a swing-man who toggled between Foreign and National as the situation warranted. Van Doorn had worked for Al as his Night City Editor at Newsday and Marlens brought him to the Week-in-Review as a major domo.

Tom Butson, confident and self-assured, tended toward making pronouncements ring with such authority that you were convinced he was right, which he often was. Once a controversial question had his imprimatur, it was settled. When the Marlens era came to an end, Butson found a nest in a triad on "the bullpen." This was a city room job where the News Editor and his minions read back on the entire newspaper and challenged any copy that might appear inaccurate, offensive, libelous or simply troublesome. It was the equivalent of being one of the three judges of the Underworld and Tom was a perfect fit.

Among the afflictions that befell the country in 1973 was the Arab oil boycott which led to the energy crisis that turned stagflation into a full-blown recession and threw tens of thousands out of work. One of the anomalies of stagflation was that the price of things was going up as consumers were less able to afford them. I commissioned a graphics piece, which I reported, tracing the cost of a chicken from the farm to the supermarket, showing how everything from the price of eggs to the cost of crating and freighting, to store rents had increased over a given period—with energy needs driving the upward spiral—to make the consumer pay more or force the producers and providers along the way to retrench with losses or layoffs. It was an appealing idea, a little superficial in retrospect but illustratable, and it made a point. And if journalism is history on the fly, this was journalism off the cuff. But it took some work and Marlens liked it. More important, Frankel liked it. It was just sufficiently out of the box to get noticed. The result was my first publisher's award, which was actually my last publisher's award. This accolade consists of a monthly cash prize given in a variety of categories, ostensibly for the best piece of writing or reporting during that period. Mine was for enterprise. Actually, the prize is a fever chart of most-favored status in the company. Writers who are on the way up or editors who need a pat on the back will serendipitously find they've gotten

127

the laureate. Not that their work isn't good. But it's not that much better than a lot of what their less fortunate colleagues are producing at the same time. Being a new boy and still sufficiently naïve, I assumed that my prize was based solely on merit.

I plodded along for another year at the Week-in-Review with Marlens becoming ever more demanding. I don't know how much longer I would have lasted when down came a deus ex machina in the guise of a job as Deputy Style Editor. Charlotte Curtis, the Style Editor, was moving up to the Op-Ed pages and her successor, Joan McCracken Whitman, needed a deputy. I had already indicated my concerns to my friend Peter Millones, who was making personnel picks for Rosenthal on the third floor, and Abe was only too glad to steal an up-and-comer from Frankel. It worked out well since it looked like they'd sought me out, which indeed they had, and the job was so good that no one would fault me for accepting it. So I was able to bid adieu to Al with no hard feelings. For all the tumult, I'd had the privilege of working with a great editor. It was not to be the case in my next go-round. In mid-1974 I moved down to the third floor, for the first time, as Deputy Style Editor. There is a little squib in the paper of about an inch attesting to this. It is virtually the only instance that my name has ever appeared in The Times except for a Nieman award and an earlier article on the "Naked Came the Stranger" hoax. Whatever the lack of heralding, my career in the newsroom was about to begin.

My tenure as Deputy Style Editor was rough sailing. Charlotte Curtis had briefed me at a lunch in the Times cafeteria that I was about to enter troubled waters but her metaphor was insufficient. The essential problem was that I'd been sent to shore up Joan Whitman, who'd served as Charlotte's deputy and succeeded her more by default than choice. Joan, who'd been a perfectly serviceable deputy in the shadow of the charismatic Charlotte, was perceived by management, correctly, as a weak sister who pretty much deferred to her charges, which was fine with them, but not with the higher-ups who wanted to bring them to heel. Charlotte had cracked the whip but her real interests were in projecting her image as an arbiter of fashion and a re-inventor of style writing, so she left a lot of the detail to Joan who in turn delegated it to the staffers, some of whom were understandably protective of their prerogatives and their turf. To be sure, most of the women on the staff—the Style reporters were then virtually all female—were solidly professional but too often the tone was set by a cluster who were less so.

Basically, I'd been brought down from the Week-in-Review to apply newsroom standards to a department that the top editors feared would revert to fluffball recidivism once Charlotte was no longer at the helm. I think they already had an eye toward the Living and Home Sections that would be invented just a few years later and they wanted to streamline the Style Section and bring it into line with the criteria of the city room.

A particular challenge came in the person of Judy Klemesrud, a star who had made a reputation for herself as a priestess of the celebrity interview. Judy seemed to view the Style Section as a base of operations from which she could roam freely over the breadth of the paper, materializing in her own pages when convenient. One of my mandates was to curb Judy's appetite for outside adventures and get a full week's work out of her in the section for which she was ostensibly working.

I had hardly been on the job a day when, in her sweet sing-song, Judy told me: "Don't get in my way. We have our own way of doing things around here." It sounded like something out of a Western. What took me aback was that she managed to carry off this clunky cliché with a straight face. I told her that I didn't plan to get in anyone's way provided that they did their work.

Klemesrud didn't wait long to test me. I picked up the Daily News one morning to see that she had a feature interview in its Sunday Section. Judy had upped the ante, not only writing for another section without permission but for another newspaper. I called her in the next day. "Judy," I told her, "You know you can't write for a competing paper." She didn't understand what the big deal was. I reminded her that she was being paid by The New York Times, but if she wanted to write for the Daily News she was free to go there. "You can be fired for that," I told her. This seemed to get her attention. She claimed she didn't know there was anything wrong with doing a little work outside the paper. Since this wasn't simply a local infraction but went beyond the department, I had to raise it with Peter Millones, the Assistant Managing Editor who handled personnel problems for Abe Rosenthal. Millones wrote Judy a formal note reminding her of the paper's free-lancing guidelines which, had she adhered to them, would have spared her, and The Times, "the embarrassment of seeing your byline over an article in our chief competitor, the Daily News." Millones was concerned that she could do this "without at least wondering whether it was in conflict with the paper's free-lance policy," most particularly since she'd recently been admonished for a similar infraction. Earlier, Klemesrud had submitted an article rejected by The Times to another publication, although it was done on the paper's time and was Times property. Judy pleaded ignorance, shed a few tears and affected contrition. It didn't take her a week to recidivate.

Judy's big moment came with the fall of Richard Nixon. The President's demise brought Gerald Ford to power. The Times geared up for the inauguration. The Washington Bureau was going to cover it to a fare-thee-well with additional firepower supplied from New York. The Style Section's contribution was to send our star reporter, Judy Klemesrud, down to Washington to cover Betty Ford's day as her husband was being inaugurated. This is what's known as a piece of cake. No Watergate. No Deep Throat. No hostile interviews. Instead, a new First Lady who was all-too-willing to be profiled by The New York Times. Our reporter, Ms. Klemesrud, would have complete access to Mrs. Ford and, with luck, perhaps a story on Page One below the fold. Not a bad deal.

I called Judy the evening before the big day to apprise her of what, for anyone else would have been a plum assignment. I thought, in fact, that this might be a helpful step in her rehabilitation. But when I gave Judy the news she began crying. She informed me that her parakeet was ailing and she didn't know if she could leave it. Did she own a parakeet? I assumed for the moment that she did. "Judy," I told her. "This is the best story of the year for us, and you are a newspaper reporter. This is not overseas duty. It will take a day. Cover the cage with a cloth, get a neighbor to bird-sit, put the vet on alert and get yourself down to Washington." She reluctantly agreed.

The next morning, I got a call from Klemesrud. She was still in New York. "My parakeet is worse," she said and burst into tears. "Judy," I told her, "you'll have a lot more to cry about if you blow off this assignment. You're already late. Parakeets have long lives. Abe Rosenthal is going to be very unhappy to hear that you blew this. Now get yourself on a plane and get down to the capital." The threat of Abe's wrath seemed to wrest Judy from her despond.

Meanwhile, I was getting a call from Bill Kovach, the Washington Bureau Chief, who wanted to know where Judy was. I was caught between covering for her or telling the truth. I opted for the latter. When I told him what had happened he went ballistic. What he told me, in terms that are printable, was that we were covering a new presidency and he didn't have time to put up with a prima donna. If she didn't show up he was giving the story to one of his own people. Judy is now unheard from for the next three hours. This is in the days before cell phones. What this also means, among other things, is that during the noon story meeting, when all the editors are pitching their pieces on the Washington coverage, I'm drawing a blank, just indicating that Klemesrud is down there, presumably somewhere with Betty Ford.

Around two o'clock, I got a call from Judy. She missed getting hold of Betty Ford who was no longer where she was going to be when Judy was originally supposed to meet her. But Klemesrud is bird-dogging the First Lady and hopes to catch her later in the afternoon. "Judy, where are you?" I ask her. "I'm in the Washington Bureau of the Chicago Sun-Times." "But Judy, you work for The New York Times. Why are you in the office of a competing newspaper?" It turns out that she has good friends at the Sun-Times and she'd be a lot more comfortable doing the story there than at the New York Times Bureau. "Judy," I tell her. "I don't think it would be a good idea to tell anyone what you've just done. I want you to pick yourself up, get in a cab and get over to The Times Bureau where you will have support, back-up, a direct line to home, and a chance to run down Betty Ford and file a story before the day ends."

"Do I have to?" This, in a whine. "Yes, you have to, right now." Click. About an hour later, I get another call, this time from Bill Kovach. Leaving out the expletives, what he tells me is that in the midst of all the frenzy of trying to coordinate 20 stories on the inauguration—news analyses, what this means for the Democrats, the GOP, the republic, the direction in which Ford will take the country; sidebars on ascendant vice presidents, the fate of Richard Nixon, foreign reaction, the impact on Vietnam, Russia, China, the new cabinet, etc., in walks Judy complaining that she can't find a desk, she can't find a phone and she can't find Betty Ford. The unflappable, immaculate, silver-haired Times legend Clifton Daniel, loses his patience and publicly upbraids her for exhibiting one of the most unprofessional performances he has ever encountered in a newsroom. Klemesrud again sheds tears blaming it on her moribund parakeet and the cruel editor who forced her to leave the bird on its perch. Judy has now succeeded in doing what she does best—steal the spotlight. Kovach tells me that he's assigning Diane Henry, a bureau news assistant, to the story. Diane will, in short order, make contact with Betty Ford, now eagerly awaiting anyone from The Times, and file, on time, a perfectly serviceable piece that runs somewhere inside the paper. Judy is pulled from the story, receives a second tongue-lashing from Kovach and is sent home in disgrace.

Shortly thereupon, I get a call from a hysterical Klemesrud. She is in a Washington hotel room that is being used by visiting Times staff. "I quit!' she screams and hangs up the phone. I tell Alex Palmer, the Style secretary, to send a telegram saying "Resignation accepted." But I've got to check with Joan, who procrastinates despite my admonitions that Judy has done enough to be fired several times over, and now has done us the favor of resigning. Alex meanwhile has deferred sending any telegrams. Judy, thinking better of her resignation, is now carefully calling Al Roberts, the Style copy chief, and other allies, whom she allows to talk her out of quitting. The next day, Judy returns.

Peter Millones sends her a blistering memo, the substance of which is that she muffed "an assignment that virtually all reporters would consider a welcome opportunity to report on an historical event," yet she resisted going without offering a reasonable explanation. Millones goes on to recount Klemesrud's behavior: "Your subsequent conduct in the Washington Bureau . . . forced both the Washington news editor [Bill Kovach] and the Washington bureau chief [Clifton Daniel] to reprimand you for unprofessional conduct. Your response was to abandon your assignment. . . . The editors re-assigned the story to one of the least experienced people in the Washington Bureau and she completed it without incident. Indeed, the assignment required no particular skills that any reporter of The New York Times did not possess. . . Your conduct and performance were sorry and unprofessional. Such conduct, if repeated in any form, will leave the editor to take whatever disciplinary action necessary to maintain the journalistic standards of The New York Times." Abe is already furious at Judy for pushing the limits of his patience. She's hauled before Millones and might have been canned. But Judy, no fool she, arrives flanked by two union stalwarts who claim that she was emotionally distraught by the events of the day, both personal and professional, and said and did things that she regrets, but this is insufficient cause to fire her. Management relents and Judy gets another life. The parakeet meanwhile makes a miraculous recovery.

Whatever such distractions, I was able to liven up the pages, sharpen the copy and stimulate some of the more enterprising staffers to do some good journalism. I slowly began to cultivate a cluster of allies. Our ace was Georgia Dullea who had a wry and biting sense of humor and refined antennae for the tiny detail that could make a story. I also encouraged Enid Nemy who had a wicked eye for the pretensions and inveterate faux pas of the ladies who lunch, and an artful way of skewering her subjects without angering them. Enid would later become keeper of The Times's Metropolitan Diary—a perfect fit because in this guise she didn't so much have to garrote her quarry as let them hang themselves.

As Deputy Style Editor I felt obligated to learn a little more about the fashion business and enjoyed a crash course under the auspices of Bernadine Morris, The Times's fashion writer. Despite her up-scale name she was a Hunter College graduate who was more Morris than Bernadine and we hit it off right away. She spoke in a raspy outer-borough slang and brought a down-to-earth approach to the rag trade that I found refreshing. Bernadine's ministry consisted of letting me accompany her to a spate of fashion shows. She enjoyed feeding me tidbits on the misadventures of her subjects. But whatever her many opportunities for Schadenfreude, Morris was a no-nonsense operator when it came to reporting her beat. She covered fashion like a police reporter and was never blinded by the glitz it gave off. It was here that I first met the ladies of the fashion press, not the least of whom was Carrie Donovan, someone I'd grow to know better when I came to edit her at The Times magazine.

Operating on a different wavelength altogether was a young Jane Brody, still not transfigured into the tribune of fitness that she became in subsequent years. The Science Section, from which she was later to hold forth, was yet in the offing, and Women's Health was still under the auspices of the Women's Section which, disclaimers aside, the Style Department remained. Later on Jane would drop the female aspect and dispense her prescriptions and proscriptions to all of humanity. But, during my tenure, she was still mostly limited to patrolling the ramparts of womanly well-being. What I liked about Jane was that, although a bit of an advocate, she was a bulldog when she got her teeth into something and wouldn't let go until she'd obtained the story she was after.

I came to conclude that progress in this section would be a matter of small victories. What I wanted was good writing and responsible reporting, whatever the provenance. In this regard I was also able to introduce a little counter-programming to the Style pages. One of my projects was a twin-out involving seltzer and pastrami. Al Siegal, a news editor who had taken leave of his desk chores to become a reporter in the Bronx where he'd grown up, was the son of a seltzer man. Siegal and I had gone to the same public schools. He was a year behind me in high school where he became the pet of the journalism teacher, Dr. McCadden, who predicted that I would never have a career in journalism. On Al's new beat—which he imagined as a way station for his fanciful pursuit of an assignment in Southeast Asia— he stumbled upon what appeared to be the last seltzer man in the Bronx. This was in the days before bottled seltzer took on a retro cachet with the gentrifying classes. When I heard of Siegal's discovery, I thought it would make a bright piece for the Style pages. At about this time, I had assigned a writer to search out the best pastrami in the city. This took my sleuth to four of the five boroughs with the winner in Brooklyn. I married the two stories as a twin-out, starting with pastrami in Brooklyn followed by a chaser of seltzer in the Bronx.

I was still on the rise at this stage and, as such, experienced the paper's equivalent of a laying on of hands. As the Style Section's representative, I attended the morning front-page meetings where the day's news budget starts to take shape from various section editors pitching their candidates for Page One. I often didn't have much to do except kibbitz but Rosenthal would occasionally seek me out on some front that wasn't always within my province and I would respond with something that sounded good although I just as often had no idea what I was talking about. Abe was delighted and, guess what, so was everyone else. I was anointed, a boy wonder, an up-and-comer. I knew better than to affect any hubris but it was a good lesson in power dynamics. If the boss loves you, you can do no wrong; if not, whatever you do, no one will care.

I soldiered on at Style for about a year but ultimately I concluded that I was a resistible force. The powers that be didn't like Joan but they weren't going to cut her loose. Working at odds with her, I found that improvement was hard to come by. I vowed that before I took another management job, I'd make sure to have the power to go with the responsibility. For now, it was better that I left on my own steam. Two weeks later I moved over to the rim of the Metropolitan Desk as a copy editor. At the time I saw it as a holding action until something better came along. Actually, it was a turning point.

I spent the next dozen years in and around The Times newsroom. It was an era in which Abe Rosenthal, as Executive Editor, and Arthur Gelb, as Metropolitan Editor and culture czar, bestrode the newspaper. If I write about them at some length it is because it is impossible to avoid the profound impact they had on the paper. I was more directly involved with Gelb so, for better or worse, often both, he will keep turning up in these pages. Under his aegis, I fared well and less well. I climbed several rungs up the ladder but not nearly to the top. My story was no different than many in its general outlines although the particulars may differ. I had some important mid-level jobs that came with a few perks and I managed to be engaged if not always embraced. Rosenthal was known for his temper but I never got any of it; on those rare occasions when we worked directly, he was professional and generous. Gelb was another matter. I didn't always march to his tune and took some heat for it. He was an overpowering presence who could be inspiring and intimidating; brilliant and flawed. But I managed to roll with the punches and, over-all, had a pretty good run during their tenure. I was to return two decades later to a far different paper. In what follows, I've tried to dispense with the inevitable grousing about one's superiors. Rather, I hope to invoke a few choice examples suggesting that during Arthur Gelb's tenure, The Times Entertainment Section, undoubtedly pre-eminent in its heyday, was not only a ship of state cruising majestically on cultural waters but, from where I sat, just as often a floating soap opera. In so doing, I've chosen to limit myself to my own precincts. Abe and Arthur had a considerable impact on the rest of the paper but what transpired in the Sports or Foreign sections was beyond my purview and is something for others to more ably address.

It became clear from the outset that my sojourn on the Metropolitan Desk was not going to be an easy ride. The week I started, my father turned 80 and I asked for the weekend off to make a quick flight down to Florida and back so that I could be there for his party. I was told by the copy chief, Joe Herrington, that he absolutely could not afford to let me go. This, of course, was nonsense. The point is that he made clear who was in charge. As copy chief, Joe was at the center of an arc-shaped desk with the editors forming a hemisphere around him so that he could toss copy their way and confer or cavil without leaving his seat or raising his voice. The pivot within the arc from which the chief dispensed news stories was called the slot and the copy chief was known as the slot man. The semi-circle that the copy editors formed around the chief was known as the rim. Although the introduction of computers, cubicles and a far-flung ensemble of desks has done away with such archaic arrangements, copy chiefs, whatever their gender, are still referred to as "the slot" and their subordinates as "the rim."

At 8 P.M., Herrington signed off on the final headline for the last piece of copy in the first edition. At which point, he'd give the slightest hint of relaxation, fold his fingers together prayer-like and intone: "You're up." The "you" in this case was plural, addressed to the entire copy desk. Until we received this benefice, nobody moved. Then, and only then, we'd rise, sometimes unintentionally in unison, and disperse for a half-hour's dinner. This drill-sergeant mentality was then a hallmark of many a copy chief, who worked on the assumption that they couldn't control the flow unless they controlled the men. Occasionally, when Joe was pleased with our performance, he'd alter his pronouncement to: "Gentlemen, you're up." In those days, there was only one woman on the desk, Sharon Fujiyoka, who was also the only Asian on the rim, a two-fer.

Should Herrington be in a wildly expansive mood, he might allow two or three of us to repair with him to Gough's, the workingman's Sardi's. A couple of greenish photos of baseball players and boxing pugs provided the décor, with a long bar in the front, wooden booths on the side and tables in the back. Herrington liked sitting away from the bustle in the front which was a mix of off-duty pressmen, reporters, editors and various characters from the sales and advertising departments. Joe was very particular about his dining companions and it took me almost a year before he allowed me to accompany him on one of these forays. Herrington ate sparingly—given the quality of the hamburgers at Gough's this was a wise culinary choice—but he'd order a small martini pitcher that he poured judiciously at intervals into a juice glass. He was so meticulous—taking the same care with the libation that he did with the copy—that you hardly noticed that by the time dinner was over, the pitcher was near empty, with always a little left. Then, back to work. At precisely 11, when the second edition was put to bed, Herrington would look up from his work, survey the desk as if he were doing a head count and then say: "Goodnight gentlemen."

My new hours were nights and weekends, 4-11, with Mondays and Tuesdays off. Because of the union rules, which were geared toward seniority, I could work weekends in perpetuity unless someone above me moved on. No one was ready to give up an iota of their prerogatives or consider an occasional trade. As new man on the roster I could look forward to taking vacation for two weeks in January.

These were the years of New York at its nadir, the city in receivership, the bailout under Felix Rohatyn, Fort Apache, the

South Bronx a basket case and swaths of Brooklyn not far behind, the racial tensions of Bed-Sty still simmering, the public schools on their long downhill slide, the white exodus in high gear with gentrification barely a gleam in the distant future. The atmosphere on the copy desk seemed to reflect the news. Along the rim copy editors sat cheek by jowl with just enough elbow room to work. In front of each editor was a copy spike where dupes—duplicates of that night's edited copy—were impaled, together with a paste-pot to re-glue stories for inserts, material added after an article had been submitted. Not infrequently, a story needed significant altering. If a reporter objected to the fixes and won the tussle, the copy would have to be reconfigured yet again. The worst thing a copy editor could do was spill a paste-pot, causing a flood of goo that might not only destroy his copy but spill over onto the work of his colleagues. The reporters wrote on "books, " or sheets of paper sandwiching several carbon dupes. The writer kept one, the backfield editor kept one, the copy chief kept one, the copy editor kept one. The original, now pretty marked up, bumped along this assembly line until the copy chief signed off on it and gave it to a copy boy who placed it in a plastic cylinder and shot it through a pneumatic tube to the composing room on the floor above.

The headlines were usually written separately with the name—or slug— of the story attached so that it could be retrofitted onto the piece in the makeup process. I had a knack for writing heads and some of my efforts would appear under "Trophies of a head-hunter" in Winners & Sinners, a bulletin of bouquets and brickbats emanating from the Times's bullpen. Among these offerings: On a droll piece by the redoubtable Israel Shenker: "Groucho Marx Uses Room Service to Press Suit"; on a love story that John Galsworthy had written about his younger self: "Publishing: A Hindsight Saga" and, in a story about a gunman who regularly seemed to rob Penn Central's Credit Union in Buffalo at a certain time: "Station Robber Right on Schedule." My personal favorite was about a graduating class of farriers at Cornell: "They Shoe Horses, Don't They?" Writing a bright head could ease the burden of heavier duties.

As for the body of the story, after going through a linotype machine, it came back in galley form for a final read to check for errors, typos, glitches and occasional last-minute tinkering. There was usually a difference of opinion between the reporter and the desk as to whether an adjustment was necessary and the time was sufficient. Reporters with weight or who had cultivated the desk, could lean on the editors to buy a little more time, but God help the editor who stuck his neck out for a writer and caused the section to be late.

Directly beside the Metro Copy Desk was the roomier Metro Backfield Desk—the operation's nerve center where, during the day, the Metropolitan Editor Arthur Gelb presided, along with a brace of sub-editors who assigned stories and plotted the day's news budget. The National and Foreign desks, to our left toward the 43rd Street side of the building, were set up similarly. At night, the backfield served as a first line of defense, making sure that the stories were generally accurate, the major holes filled and the wishes of their daytime bosses met. Most importantly, as stories broke, the backfield editors were responsible for being on top of them. And at night's end, they were charged with responding in writing to the criticisms of the dayside about why they'd failed to carry out everything required of them during the previous evening.

In the months after The Times got beaten by the Washington Post on Watergate, the Washington desk had to leave a note for the still-livid Abe Rosenthal listing every front-page story running in the first edition of the Post and what the Bureau had done to match it. The responsible reporter was then required to confirm and advance the Post's article (a challenge), or knock it down (preferable). At minimum, this involved sorting through a complex, story late at night with one's sources unavailable. Should no news appear, an explanatory memo from the writer, embellished by the deskman, was then passed up the line for further backfield enhancement until it landed on Rosenthal's desk for perusal the following morning. The Washington Bureau's reparation was experienced by virtually every backfield at one time or another. In terms of keeping one's job, the craft of the defensive memo—explaining why something was or wasn't done, shifting responsibility, defusing accusations without offending the heavy-hitting accuser—was an art form of its own. Those who learned its mysteries did well; those who didn't found themselves on the Large Type Weekly. There was one other wretch, the late man, whose burdens were those of the night-desk compounded.

Behind the Metro Backfield were two double banks of reporter's desks extending north and widening into an apse near the 44th Street windows so that the entire ensemble formed a T-Square. Pride of place went to the rewrite men and senior writers who sat in front, with the more junior staffers falling in behind. At the time the legendary Peter Khiss anchored the front desk in the daytime and Bob McFadden, already earning his chops on night rewrite, did the same in the evening. As the night regressed the reporter's section of the city room emptied out so that only a few rewrite men and a stray reporter were left. By 10 P.M., the newsroom tableau was one of a great emptiness.

The desk at night was a quiet place; the busier it got, the quieter. Commands were given in a shorthand of gutturals and responded to in a lexicon of grunts interspersed with a growl when the occasion required. Hand signals were not infrequent. The communications style was curt, laconic and precise. Fun was a shot of gallows humor laced with frustration about the copy. One of the virtuosos in this department was our deputy copy chief, Richie Roberts, who wore a green eyeshade when it suited him— among the last I recall seeing on a copy desk. Richie was a master of repartee and he was very good at his job. He had no patience for the incompetents on the reporting staff of which there were several. A diva of exasperation, Roberts would glower at one of their articles, wave it in the air and exclaim: "This is gibberish." When really vexed he would cry: "This is utter gibberish." And, on rare occasions, for an Oscar of incoherence: "This is utter, fucking gibberish." Then he would toss it at one of us and say in disgust: "Here, you go fix this. I can't look at it."

The Times, let's face it, made some bad hires who were there too long to be expunged and, since the paper would never admit its mistakes, the desk had to compensate for them. I never minded the bad writers who knew they needed help. It was the bad writers who thought they were good ones that were maddening. One of their longer pieces was known as "The Accolade." Joe Herrington would look at the designated victim with the only trace of sympathy I can remember. Then he would sigh, stare at the luckless copy editor, intone, "The Accolade," and, holding it at the corners like a long-dead fish, flick the offensive article at the recipient. The only virtue of receiving an accolade was that you got the better part of the night to wrestle with it, so you were exempt from the run of the rest of the paper. But this was small compensation for the psychic turmoil of having to turn an incompetent's leaden prose into serviceable dross, followed by the real stress: the pain of struggling over the changes with the perpetrator. Even Joe was careful to distribute the accolades equitably—at least among the younger editors; the seniors were generally exempt. One wag suggested that for the less offensive pieces we be allowed to trade on advance articles: two, or even three stories by good writers for a bomb. For instance, two Mickey Carrolls for Reporter X or an Albin Krebs and an Eric Pace for

Reporter Y. Much as I dreaded these moments, I owe my later skill of dealing with problem pieces and difficult writers in part to the training I got handling the accolades on the Metro Copy Desk.

And then there was Al Davis whom I'd labored for as a lowly copy boy at The New York Post in the late 50's when he was the night managing editor, one of the most powerful newsmen in the city. The Davis I worked with at The Times was not the martinet I endured at the Post almost 20 years before. The current Davis had a host of illnesses. Life had afflicted him but he seemed more resigned to its blows than any of the petty alarums that would have upset him in the past. The new Davis was reflective, easygoing and generous. He had a fund of patience for people's frailties and a fatalistic wisdom about expecting much from any situation. His advice was sage, he counseled forbearance, he was a source of equanimity. The Davis that I recall was meaner, a flinty glare behind the glasses, a tensile hardness in his bulk. It wasn't that Davis had been reborn but different aspects of his character had come to the fore, and others had gone offstage. My earlier judgment was right, but limited.

During the 8 o'clock lunch break Davis usually hung back and trundled to the rear of the near-empty city room. Al rarely went out, preferring to carry food from home. Sometimes he brought no lunch but would just sit there, staring. If he went out at all it wasn't to Gough's, but to a down-at-heels diner frequented by the flotsam of Times Square halfway between the fleabag hotel in mid-block and the cheap valise store on the corner of Eighth Avenue. And this was Al's haunt on the evenings when he felt good enough to venture out. On the other nights, when he sat in the back I'd join him occasionally. Davis was perfectly polite when charmed from his reverie, and engaging in an avuncular way. In laconic, Nestorian style, he'd tell stories about all-night drinking and raucous confrontations after-hours in bars favored by The Post in its glory days. When stirred, Davis was an amusing raconteur. He was also a good editor. Al's death went generally unremarked. And yet he had been a contender. Had he worked for the right newspaper at the right time, he might have made the reputation that at one point he so very much wanted.

It was about this time that I got my big break, in a manner of speaking, my ticket off the Metro Desk. Be careful what you wish for. Arthur Gelb called me at home and asked me to come down and meet him in his office. Arthur was not only Metropolitan Editor but the First Friend of the Executive Editor, Abe Rosenthal.

As such he served as Abe's alter ego and de facto No. 2 man on the paper. Gelb patrolled his position assiduously, rationing access to whatever degree he could, confident that ultimately he'd have final whispering privileges on most decisions. The key to success, Arthur understood, was Location, Location, Location. He planted himself right next to power and made sure no one else got close.

To illustrate how this worked I cite a story related by the veteran reporter Frank Prial, later to become a wine columnist. Before leaving for France to write for the Paris Bureau, Prial stopped off at Rosenthal's office to pay obeisance. On Frank's way in, Gelb accosted him and gave him some avuncular advice on how to start out in Paris. In effect, Arthur told Frank to hit the ground running, write first impressions, go with his instincts, get in the paper right away. Prial then entered Abe's sanctum with Gelb positioning himself at Rosenthal's side. After a few preliminaries Abe got to the heart of the matter. "I don't want you to write anything off the bat," he told Prial. "Take your time, get the feel of the town, and only when you're ready and have a good sense of the place should you write your first piece." As Frank was leaving, Arthur chimed in: "And you heard it from the horse's mouth."

Arthur Gelb was a brilliant showman. He had a knack for stunts, for calling attention to himself, for carrying out what was simultaneously promotion and self-promotion. As a boss, one of his favorite sayings to goad on his minions was: "This story is going to be noticed." At times, Arthur couldn't distinguish between what was news and what would be noticed. He was also a great enthusiast. And his enthusiasm was infectious, so that Gelb actually motivated his writers to action with his own manic energy. One of the marks of an exceptional editor is the ability to invigorate the troops and Arthur, whatever his flaws, had the gift. The worst thing you could do to Gelb was fail to show enthusiasm for one of his ideas because it not only demonstrated a failure of imagination on your part but it deflated his balloon as well.

Which is where I came in. Arthur had tabbed me as the editor-apparent of the first of the regional weeklies, the Long Island Section. Unaware of my good fortune, I walked into Gelb's office and got a big hello and a hug. Arthur was not only charming but warm and friendly when he liked you. But he could switch from backslapping to backstabbing without skipping a beat. It's also important to remember that Arthur was tall. He towered over most people and used his physical presence either to impress or intimidate, depending on which was necessary. He had a fine mane of hair, already graying, a big, full-boned face, almost chiseled, a gravelly baritone and large hands that fluttered all over the place as he talked. When Arthur spoke, he had the persuader's trick of making you believe that you were the only one in the room; that what he was asking of you was of the greatest import and, that if you didn't do it, you would not only be letting him and the paper down but, most important, you'd be letting yourself down.

What Arthur wanted was to consult me about a prototype for a proposed Long Island weekly. Until then, we produced something called the Brooklyn-Queens-Long Island edition known as the BQLI. It had been run into the ground by Marty Gansberg, a genial old-school plodder churning out pedestrian features more suited to a country weekly than a metropolitan daily. The section was little more than an agglomeration of retread stories usually done by news clerks out to make a buck or third-string free-lancers who wanted to get their names in the paper and maybe do a service for a client. The Times had decided to end this embarrassment. More important, it wanted to end the embarrassment of being beaten by my alma mater Newsday, not only on stories and features, but on all those juicy Long Island ads on which Newsday battened while The Times turned up its nose at suburban coverage and looked the other way. Which is how I got the call.

After much flailing and bluster, Gelb came to the point. He wanted to do away with the BQLI and, out of its ashes, would rise the phoenix of the Long Island edition, a weekly that would run as one of the many appendages to the Sunday Section. It would cover news, features, events, local sports and entertainment, offer columns, opinion and advice, range far and wide over the breadth of Long Island and dig deep into its heart. Controversy would not be avoided and no expense would be spared in getting this bird off the ground. Over the next week, our conversations—not word for word, but in tone, tenor and substance—went something like this: "What we need Jack," said Arthur, "is someone with your smarts and experience to run this." I was flattered. With my background running the news and Specialists sections at Long Island Newsday as well as editing the regional department for the Week-in-Review, and a few years at The Times under my belt, I may well have been the best qualified candidate for the job. "What do you say?" Arthur asked, which meant, "I assume you're on board." I said that I would prepare a prospectus of what I thought the job would entail and present it to him within a week. He took that for a yes. "We know you had that trouble in the Style Section, but don't worry about that," Arthur assured me. "They're a bunch of nuts anyway.

You do this and you'll be golden again.'' Translation: You let us down on your first try so we're giving you another chance. You better do this right.

I spent the weekend writing an eight-page outline of what I thought should go into a new Long Island Section. First of all, I'd need a staff, at minimum three reporters covering politics, features, entertainment; an art director, a good photographer, a clerk, a listings person and an expanded Long Island office to accommodate this staff, which would only grow. I'd also need a serious free-lance budget to get good writers instead of the hacks who'd been filling space in the BQLI. I would also have to borrow from the younger staffers and more ambitious clerks from time to time, and, for the launch, I'd need to appropriate someone of columnist stature for a short period to give the section some pizzazz. I presented a list of story ideas, beats, features and gimmicks that would keep the staff busy for several weeks, the concept being that in due time, they'd be off and running and my job would be more to manage and inspire than feed. I'd been able to do this at Newsday and I saw no reason why I couldn't do it at the far more powerful New York Times.

I actually became intrigued by the challenge and made it clear that I'd give it a full-court press. I asked only that they find a nice way to put their current Long Island bureau chief, Roy Silver, out to pasture. Silver had been grazing in the Mineola office from time immemorial. It was a cozy sinecure and it worked perfectly because The Times wasn't interested in Long Island news and Roy didn't have to provide any. Roy's philosophy seemed to be a get-along, go-along version of "don't ask, don't tell.'' Of course, an ambitious politician trying to make a name for himself was out of luck. Eugene Nickerson, the Democratic Nassau County Executive who at the time wanted to make a run for Governor, grumbled about not getting serious coverage in The Times, which he attributed to Silver's laissez faire attitude. On those occasions when I had to call Roy, he was invariably friendly and invariably unable to provide much help.

I submitted my memo early the following week and shortly thereupon I got a call from Gelb's secretary to come see him. I arrived in his office to find a somewhat subdued Arthur. He embraced me in one of those intimate hugs with just a hint of distance. "Hey, Jack, this is great. This is one of the best memos I've ever read. How d'you know so much about Long Island? This is terrific. Just what we wanted. The only thing is we're not ready to go with something so ambitious yet." What they were ready to go with was Roy Silver. There was no room in the budget for reporters, it would be hard to borrow a columnist, did I really need a clerk, I could put in photo requests for a photographer along with everyone else, they might be able to give me a little extra in the free-lance budget but not too much. And of course, I could share an art-director for the cover. A makeup editor could do the rest. Oh, and there was an extra desk in the Mineola office but Roy would like to keep his.

"So what you're telling me Arthur," I said, "is that you are virtually ignoring my memo and you'd like me to put out this new section with no support." A shadow crossed his face, but he persisted. "Listen, if this works, you'll be able to build your staff, but it'll take time." By my reckoning, it would take years, if ever, before they spent any money on this backwater operation. What they wanted was a tricked-up BQLI with an attractive cover layout, a couple of pleasant features, a few nice pictures and no trouble or extra expense. Their total added investment in all this was me and, since I was an add-on in the Metro Section, it wasn't costing them anything. The most they'd have to pay me was a little overtime and, if they promoted me to management, they could dispense with that.

I told Arthur I'd think about it. "What's there to think?" His face clouded over. "It's a big responsibility," I said. "I need a day." He seemed surprised. "Well I hope you make the right decision, Jack. This is an important job. We need you on this one." I had already thought it over. What they wanted was for me to fill the breach on a hopeless assignment and, if I played ball, I might get another hopeless assignment. There was no way they were going to commit the resources needed to produce a serious section in an area that held no interest for them. They just wanted me to take responsibility for a problem and make it go away. Though I should have known better I was rankled that I could have done something really good with this section and there was no way they were going to let me.

The next day I dropped a decorous note to Arthur saying that although I was flattered by his offer, under the circumstances I didn't think I'd be the best person for the job. I thanked him for his confidence and wished him well in finding a suitable editor. I even suggested some candidates who might be up for the task. I never heard back from Gelb but suddenly, it was as if a switch had been turned off. You could hear the generator thrum to a stop. I could sense a chill in the air. Of course, they had no trouble filling the slot. And I could see where many of my suggestions eventually were incorporated, albeit piecemeal, into the section. Ultimately, it did get the support, or at least some of it, that I'd asked for. Had I shown more prudence my fortunes might have augured differently. I would have done their bidding and in time perhaps entered the circle of dependable enablers whom they rewarded accordingly. But then I wouldn't be who I am or, at least, who I was.

I continued on the Metro Desk for several months longer. During this period, I handled everyone from veterans like the redoubtable Dick Shepard to newcomers like Ari Goldman whom I provided with a little hand-holding since they weren't getting much help from the Metro Desk. Ari went on to become a religion writer at The Times, an author and a venerated professor at the Columbia Journalism School. During downtime I could shmooze with newcomers passing through like John Burns who'd just arrived from the Washington Post where he'd been covering Johannesburg.

As for the Sulzbergers, they will be absent from this chronicle for the simple reason that our paths rarely crossed. My first go-round at The Times coincided with the tenure of Punch Sulzberger whom I recall simply as a benign presence. The reigning personality during this era was most definitely the editor, Abe Rosenthal. From my distant perch, the publisher seemed content to maintain a discreet distance from the city room and bestride the larger operation from his aerie high above. Sulzberger was unfailingly polite when sighted and affected a genuine noblesse oblige if encountered in the lobby or an elevator. The only time I remember hearing from him was when he observed, through my supervisors, that the desks in the Culture Department were in disarray—the detritus of reporting piled high on them—which made a poor impression on visitors. Couldn't we do something about tidying them up? Apparently, we couldn't because we received such requests on several occasions, which suggested frequent recidivism. Punch's son was a more active presence in the city room, first as an editor on the Metro backfield during a brief immersion into the various satrapies of the paper, and then when he succeeded his father as publisher. I attribute this perhaps to a greater need to show the flag in a more adverse time as well as the fact that no editor—whatever their considerable talents— dominated the newsroom like Rosenthal, thus allowing the spotlight to shift a bit more to the publisher.

Meanwhile, during my Metro Desk sojourn in the mid-70's, I was called from time to time to work on the Second Front—the first page of what was then the second section of the Daily, which consisted of the best features or topical news pieces in Metro, usually by its premier writers. The stories were longer, more thoughtful and better crafted. And the hours were daytime. This was like a rest cure and probably what I should have been doing in the first place. The atmosphere on the Second Front desk was more congenial and relaxed. It was there that I first got to meet Marvin Siegel, one of the Second-Front editors who would figure prominently in my future. Among the luxuries the Second Front afforded was the time to work on a piece of copy without feeling that I had to railroad it. This is what I imagined editing at The Times would be like before I got there.

My tasks ranged from the challenging to the absurd. In the latter category, on a piece by Lucinda Franks, a careful reporter, involving a West Side protest over a proposed hamburger-chain intrusion in the neighborhood, I had to correct "McDonald's" which was misspelled—with an "a" as in "Mac"—more than a dozen times, albeit consistently. I guess she never ate there but we shared a laugh.

On the other hand, I was tapped for a stint handling the volatile and irascible John Hess in his prize-winning pursuit of Dr. Bernard Bergman, the notorious nursing-home operator whose name became a byword for warehousing the old under the most shameful conditions. Hess, rightly outraged by the charnel-house conditions he'd discovered, saw himself as an avenging angel. And while Hess was correct about Bergman in general, his impulse to snare his quarry and bring him in by the neck sometimes got him out ahead of the story. A tale, perhaps apocryphal, told by Marvin Siegel, is that Hess, a white-bearded bantam with a holier-than-thou approach to his bosses and a big chip on his narrow shoulders, badgered a reluctant Arthur Gelb into having lunch with him to talk about his prospects. Arthur—who had avoided this meeting since Hess had returned from France loaded for bear in the belief that he'd been passed over as Paris bureau chief—was finally cornered but contrived a defensive plan. Just before the fateful lunch, Gelb commandeered Siegel and told him to cancel his own dining plans; "You're eating with me," he said. The strategy was for both of them to talk non-stop to prevent Hess from venting. Early in the conversation, Gelb began relating a recent baleful experience visiting his mother in a nursing home, hoping this would distract Hess well into dessert. The conversation, however, inspired Hess to consider investigating the possibilities of nursing-home abuses. The rest is history.

Before Hess was through with the nursing-home scandals he had wrung Bergman, as well as several editors, through the ringer. John peppered his editors with verbal buckshot when he thought they were trying to curb his efforts to bring the miscreant Bergman and his minions to justice. For whatever reason, with me John was appropriate. In the end, Bergman got his comeuppance and Hess got his kudos, but it happened gradually, with the story developing as the facts warranted. By then I was back to my night duties.

One of the benefits of my copy desk chores was to be around late Saturday afternoons when things were fairly quiet and there wasn't much to do except advances for Monday. I'd wander back along the aisles and banter with the reporters. My favorites were two old-timers, Irving (Paddy) Spiegel and Manny Perlmutter. They would tipple from a bottle of plum brandy that Manny had tucked away in his desk and reflect on how the paper was not what it once had been. They told wacky stories about the doings at the old Police Headquarters on Centre Street, now a condominium, and the characters who presided at the cop shack across the street. One of their favorites was a police reporter named Willy Kane, a one-armed maverick who had a special knob attached to his steering wheel allowing him to drive with his good arm. Willy was distinguished from Jew Kane, no relation, by his penchant for packing a pistol and dragging neophyte reporters to a nearby nameless hell-hole generally known as the Dago bar. The police shack was not a redoubt of political correctness.

Perlmutter, paunchy and balding, played Sancho to Paddy's Quixote. They must have been doing this act for years. By that point Irving wasn't doing much more than the Alternate-Side-of-the-Street-Parking briefs for the Jewish holidays. Occasionally, Manny got a homicide but they came fewer and farther between as the Times became less gritty and more yuppified. Once in a while, the silver-haired Edith Evans Asbury, a grand dame of the paper, who was then still working, would come by and engage in a back-and-forth of anecdotes with her two old comrades. Who knows what truth there was in any of it but the atmospherics were good.

On occasion, I'd have to stick around and clean up some advances into the early part of Saturday night. When I emerged, on winter evenings, I'd stop off in the street as the Sunday paper was rolling off the presses and the handlers were bundling them into the Times trucks. There was always a cluster of pressmen huddled around an ashcan fire, smoke coming out of their breath, some wearing ear flaps, others still in white caps made from newspaper stock, shooting the breeze, taking a nip, shivering in the frost. Then, with a snap, they'd close a filled-up truck which would pull away, making room for the next one. I enjoyed the coziness of loitering in this truck-bay area with the presses thrumming above, the hoarse shouts of the pressmen and the wind causing just a slight chill as I stood under the doorway globe lamps.

I knew this situation couldn't last much longer. Something was going to pop and sure enough it did. As noted, the absolutely worst job on the paper was being the Late Man, also known as working the Lobster Shift. The hours were horrendous—8 P.M. to 3 A.M.—guaranteeing that you had neither a day life nor a night life. There are various interpretations about the origins of the term. One school has it that its operatives never got home till the lobstermen came out. Other enthusiasts trace it to the idea that lobsters swim backwards and that by working nights and sleeping days, those consigned to this shift did everything backwards. Still others maintain that "lobster" was 19th-century slang for "fool" and only fools would work such hours. Whatever the etymological sources, there was little argument among those who had to work the shift that it was indeed a fool's errand. Your job was to clean up after everyone left and to be responsible for getting late-breaking stories into the final edition, or at least updating with wires, since you didn't have a staff. If you failed to re-plate you were upbraided; if you did so, you were wasting money. You spent the better part of your night answering notes from the dayside about what you'd neglected to do the night before and leaving notes to the dayside covering yourself on what you were about to neglect to do that evening, or rather, that morning.

Each of the major sections—Foreign, National and Metro—had a late person. We commiserated with one another like abandoned explorers on a tundra since there was nobody else in the building to talk to. As it turned out, the Metro Late Man actually liked his job or, rather, he put up with it because he had a handicapped boy at home and the hours enabled him to spend extra time with his son during the day. Gelb, however, was convinced that he needed a replacement—me. Far be it from me to suggest that a retributive thought would ever cross Arthur's mind. But a little exemplary chastening could have a tonic effect on a refractory soul. Naturally, I declined the opportunity. The Late Man, for his part, was content with his lot and didn't want to move. But his domestic problems or

148

my existential ones were not Gelb's concern. After all, Arthur had to think about the big picture and mayhap I was just the man for the job. I didn't have a leg to stand on, except quitting. Hmmm.

The Late Man, who could have played Job in the musical, had recourse to the union, claiming that removing him from the Lobster Shift caused a personal hardship, surely a first of its kind. Nevertheless, while the Guild and management thrashed this out, the grievance bought me a little time. I did, of course, have to fill in for him on weekends as a taste of my future penance but this was still tolerable. During these forays I became friendly with my fellow late editor on the Foreign desk, Barbara Crossette, who eventually escaped to cover India and later the U.N. She'd written for me in Style and we hit it off—we shared gallows-humor and helped each other out as best we could.

The union case wasn't going to last much longer and I was desperate for an out when along came salvation in the form of a new section, Weekend. This was the first—and probably the best—of the special daily sections that were to turn around The Times's financial fortunes from the mid-70's to the late 80's. The idea was simple and elegant: Tell people what's coming up in the entertainment world on Fridays, when they're about to start their weekends. Arts & Leisure would be the home for more reflective essays on the various component parts of culture, but for the bread-and-butter stuff—the big movie openings, the jazz and music festivals, the art exhibitions, Weekend would be the showcase. Marvin Siegel, the editor whom I'd worked with on the Second Front, was named editor under Arthur's imprimatur. Siegel went about cherry-picking the best people for his sub editors. I was one of them. Weekend was going to be an autonomous unit, working alongside, but not within, the orbit of the Culture desk. I suspect that Gelb might have balked over my nomination at first, but this undertaking superseded any previous agendas. There was real money and prestige on the line. Marvin wanted me and Gelb acceded. Magically, shortly after I escaped, it was no longer deemed necessary to move the Late Man from his duties. I imagine that a little push from my friend Peter Millones, who was overseeing personnel affairs, also helped me along. In April 1976 I moved over to the new Weekend Section, just in time to gear up for the Bicentennial. I'd been sprung.

The first issue of the Weekend Section, April 20, 1976, features a large photo of Peter Martins and Suzanne Farrell about to perform George Ballanchine's "Jewels" that evening at the City Ballet; a

149

lead story by the theater writer Mel Gussow headlined "New Faces / Lighting Up / The Season / On Broadway"; a Critic's Choice by the dance critic Anna Kisselgoff on the Swiss mime troupe Mummenschanz, and a flourish of teaser headlines on opera, art galleries and jazz clubs referring to stories appearing on the inside pages. All of this is anchored by a Going Out Guide offering a listing of Friday-to-Sunday events in the metropolitan area from photography shows to gamelan concerts. While the names have changed, features have come and gone, color has been added, the technology has altered, the pictures have gotten bigger and the section has grown, the format has remained basically the same. From the beginning we knew we had something good and were privileged in the sense that we were protected from the vagaries of the rest of the paper. We also had some of the best writers on The Times in the Culture staff and its critics so that the editing chores were relatively light. And the hours were daytime.

Although essentially part of the Culture section the Weekend Desk was an autonomous unit of four editors that drew on the Culture writers for its substance. The autonomy was critical because it created a wall between us and a Culture copy desk that had become a dumping ground whose denizens could only do harm to the Weekend copy. But if we were insulated from the copy desk we were still in the grip of our ultimate leader Arthur Gelb whose Metropolitan reach extended to Culture. Our cluster, mostly recruited from the Metro Desk, consisted of myself, a copy chief, a third editor, and Marvin Siegel, the section head. There were actually two Marvins: The first was cultivated, charming and funny. The second could be irritable, testy and overbearing. You never knew which you were going to find or when the first would suddenly morph into the second. Like a lot of complicated people, Marvin was a font of contradictions. He prodded us and protected us. What he was actually guarding was his own turf, maintaining an insular fiefdom within the Culture Department. Of course, Marvin had good reason to be wary of the Culture copy desk. It was only many years after his departure that a much-improved desk took responsibility for copy editing the Friday section, allowing the Weekend editors to revert to the normal backfield duties of assigning, overseeing and reading back. In Siegel's day nothing was normal.

Marvin was one of the best cultural editors The Times ever had: intelligent, knowledgeable, creative; had he been more prudent he might have had a longer run in Culture the first time around. Marvin had a complicated relationship with Gelb that framed him as both defiant and acquiescent. He had a wicked sense of humor, a streak of orneriness and considerable intellectual heft, which made dealing with him harder than with many straight company types. At the time, I thought of him as a throwback to those old-country shoemakers who were attentive to their well-heeled customers and scolded their shoeless children. He was a Cerberus at guarding the section's expense accounts—at least from the lower orders. On one occasion, Anne Mancuso, a hard-working news assistant got permission to take a departing staffer to lunch—a modest gesture after years of service. When she returned, Marvin growled, "Where did you go, Lutece?" She answered in the affirmative. "What are you, crazy?" Marvin exploded. It didn't help that Anne explained it was a prix fixe lunch. The idea of staffers stepping out on the company dime, whatever the discount, was insupportable. But the rancor could vanish like dew and behold, there was an engaging companion and a brilliant editor. Both were true and this was the ambiguity that made Siegel such a paradox.

Despite all this, I couldn't help liking Marvin. When he toggled out of grumpy mode he could be amusing and entertaining. And to give Siegel his due, he was right to be a little paranoid about some of his staff. If he'd cherry-picked his editors, there was still enough bruised fruit on the copy desks so that he'd gotten a mixed bag. For instance, our copy chief, an unremarkable version of Colonel Blimp, was no world-beater. But at least he did no harm since the copy was relatively clean and pretty much pre-edited before it ever got to him.

The fourth member of our quartet was an agglomeration of minor Dickensian caricatures, half Pecksniff, half Gladgrind. A master of "gotcha," he was forever catching little errors and letting you know about it. He was politically correct before political correctness. I once wrote a headline about a female vocalist who was leading a tribute to Billie Holiday. My head was "Lady Sings the Blues." Pecksniff— then temporarily in the slot—bounced the head, observing that "Lady" was frowned on in the Stylebook in reference to human females. He corrected it to "Woman Sings the Blues." Luckily, Marvin intervened and reason was restored.

After we had passed the test of coming out—no big deal because Gelb always threw in a brigade of troops for a new enterprise before withdrawing them again—our first real challenge as a unit was Op Sail '76, the Bicentennial celebration scheduled for that July 4. Weekend would include a special supplement on the hundreds of vessels that would converge from around the world on New York's waterways and I was put in charge of keeping track of the armada. Pride of place was to be given to the tall ships, majestic three- and four-masted vessels that were a throwback to an earlier seafaring age but were still used as training ships and showpieces for the navies of various nations. A flotilla of these would be moored in the harbor and then sail up the Hudson in a grand naval parade. In addition, hundreds of war vessels from the U.S. and other countries would be berthed at piers along the East and Hudson rivers as well as at docks on the Jersey and Brooklyn waterfronts, before joining the flotilla. Each one of these was designated by a name and numbered pier.

It was one of my jobs to oversee a map that located all of them. Another one of my tasks was to supervise a page in which all of the tall ships were silhouetted, with a description of the name, nationality and type that each vessel represented. Since I didn't know a brig from a barkentine, this presented a vertiginous problem. Moreover, the vessels kept changing berths as more of them wanted to get into the act, and competition for premier moorings led to adjustments that exacerbated the inherent confusion. What saved me was Dick Shepard—he'd once reported on shipping news and was himself a former Merchant Marine— who held my hand. And what saved Dick saving me was the man in charge of the entire Op-Sail enterprise, Frank Brainerd. Frank, an old source from Dick's shipping-news days, proved a patient, tireless and invaluable resource.

I was also handling the copy for the tall-ships supplement as well as my regular complement from the normal Weekend Section. The map and silhouette stuff was something I was supposed to be doing with my left hand, the proverbial piece of cake, as I was told. It was then that I first came to appreciate the immortal dictum of the venerable Culture sage Abe Weiler: "Nothing is too hard for the man who doesn't have to do it." This was still in the days before cold type, so that in lieu of computer graphics, which radically simplifies things, the procedure, had to be done by hand. I would journey to the 11th floor and present the locations of the war vessels to the chief mapmaker, Andy Sabbatini. Andy had before him, a large map of the New York waterfront on which was superimposed the berths of all the visiting vessels shaded in black. On each one he placed a small white button just large enough to contain two black numbers that he applied to the tablets with tweezers. Eventually, this would be photographed and reproduced into a giant map. The catch was that every time a ship changed its berth, the tabs and the numbers altered, out came the tweezers and the map changed and had to be re-engraved. Miraculously, the last number on the last tab on the last map after the last re-berthing went through engraving and the section came out. I don't know whether we got it all right or how we possibly could have. But we received no complaints and had to run no corrections. My guess is that in all the confusion no one could quite figure out the difference anyway. After this I never worried about doing a map.

The next day, for my efforts, I was permitted aboard a Times motor launch that chugged out into the harbor toward the Verrazano Bridge amid the tall ships. From flotsam level they were indeed awesome but not as intimidating as their silhouettes. And I still didn't know a sloop from a schooner. I shared the ride with Syd Schanberg, then the Metropolitan editor who'd won a Pulitzer for his coverage of the war in Cambodia, and Marty Arnold with whom I'd work alongside in several incarnations at The Times. On the return trip, we were just passing the Battery when the crowd broke out into great cheers. I thought for a moment they might have been applauding my exceptional efforts in producing the special section until I realized we were being trailed by an Israeli warship and the cheering was for the news of the successful Entebbe raid. I thought about what Dick Shepard had told me the previous day, as he nonchalantly lit his cigar amid the tumult: "Remember, Jack," he said, pointing at the paper, "tomorrow they're going to wrap fish in this."

The Bicentennial issue was a great success, as was our special section on the Democratic convention which ran at about the same time. Both blockbusters sold out, the first time the newspaper had done this since the initial moon walk. No one seemed to mind that in undertaking such initiatives the paper had become both a celebrant of, as well as a catalyst for, these events. While service journalism was a staple of the business, The Times had now given its imprimatur to the genre and was going all out, a phenomenon soon to be followed by newspapers throughout the country with its inevitable tilt toward boosterism.

The Culture Editor, who then presided over the daily entertainment pages, was Bill Luce. At The Times there was a period where Luce was thought to be in the running for high office. Bill was the real thing. He had the experience, the intelligence, the judgment. But he lacked a crucial ingredient for success: allies. Bill's supporters, such as they were, had receded or been shunted off under Rosenthal's aegis, leaving him in the exposed position of a venerable court official from a previous dynasty.

It was at about this time that Rosenthal staged his signal coup and took control of the Sunday Section, sending Max Frankel temporarily into exile as editor of the Editorial Pages, the last autonomous redoubt on the paper. Rosenthal's seizure meant that all of the Sunday departments were now consolidated under the control of the newsroom. This had the most dramatic effect on the Arts & Leisure Section which was brought downstairs to the newsroom on the third floor and incorporated into the Culture Department, although its operation remained autonomous—a headache for many future Culture editors.

The Culture Section was divided into three parts: The Daily pages, Friday Weekend and Sunday Arts & Leisure, all under the suzerainty of Abe's vizier, Arthur Gelb, who presided as culture czar, giving him immense power in the entertainment world. The first thing Arthur did was set up his chess pieces. The accommodating Bill Honan was reaffirmed as Arts & Leisure Editor. Ever-eager-to-please, Honan was a reed through whom Arthur could play whatever tune he wanted. Marvin Siegel had already been chosen for Weekend. The last piece in the puzzle was Seymour Peck.

As mentioned earlier, Peck had been languishing at the Sunday magazine after being demoted by Frankel. But, as a favorite of Abe Rosenthal's sister, Rose, he would fester no more. Instead, Sy was tapped as the new daily Culture Editor. It took no more than a short time to pry Bill Luce from the job. Gelb became increasingly dissatisfied with everything Luce did and undertook a campaign of harassment and subversion that, in short order, drove him out. Luce withdrew to the Bullpen, an honorable retreat, where he labored till he retired. Once Luce was neutered, there was no need to humiliate him further and he was allowed to continue shuffling around, a dignified shade. One of the myths about Gelb is that he had an eye for talent. This may have been true in the writing department but it did not always apply elsewhere. When it came to editors, Arthur feared talent—at least among potential rivals.

Not that Seymour Peck didn't have talent to spare. As already mentioned, he was a walking repository of theater and movie lore, and intimately acquainted with the intricacies of the entertainment world. But Peck's strength was in weekly rather than daily journalism, features rather than news — which he'd never done at The Times. In fact, Sy would have made a wonderful Arts & Leisure editor. Which, of course, was a job he'd already done brilliantly before Max banished him. So instead of restoring Sy to his true calling, dumping Honan and keeping Bill Luce in place on the Daily report, Arthur installed the wrong people in the wrong jobs. His goal was not to have the most effective helmsman at the tiller but the most pliable. In this, he achieved his end. Still, Peck posed a slight problem in that he was an acknowledged authority in cultural matters and would, on occasion, balk at some of Gelb's more bizarre mandates. Sy had a droll way of rolling his eyeballs without appearing to move his facial muscles. But ultimately, Arthur wore him down. One eye-witness recalls a scene in which Gelb insisted that Sy send a reporter on a hare-brained assignment that actually got in the paper. The next day Abe hit the roof and called Peck on the carpet. After Abe finished his tongue-lashing, Arthur chimed in that Sy had to be more careful before making such assignments. Peck bit his lip and took it.

At Arts & Leisure Peck had been a one-man band, a habit that he maintained on the Daily to ill effect. While a weekly afforded the time for a compulsive practitioner to be chief-cook-and-bottle-washer, the Daily did not. It was a collaborative undertaking and Sy's compulsion to micro-manage drove his subordinates to distraction. At one point, he inherited as a deputy Gerry Gold, a one-time assistant Foreign Editor, who had virtually run the Foreign desk during the Vietnam era. Gold, whose crusty ways and Brooklyn accent precluded him from ascending to the top tiers of management, possessed a steel-trap mind, prodigious analytic powers and formidable organizational ability that put him front and center when the paper faced a ticklish problem. One such occasion was the Pentagon Papers. Although Neil Sheehan deservedly won credit for getting the story, Gold played an unsung but critical role. What The Times had on its hands in June 1971 were thousands of pages of the secret Government study of the Vietnam War that it had obtained from the RAND Corporation analyst Daniel Ellsberg who had worked on the report.

While the larger battle of publishing the papers was being fought in the Supreme Court, a different struggle was being waged to glean the nuggets from the sludge of undifferentiated Xeroxed pages that were going to make the story. Sifting through these massive files was a daunting task for Sheehan. Enter Gold. Amid the hue and cry, Gerry gathered up the boxes of documents and, hidden in plain sight, sequestered himself in a room at the New York Hilton. While Neil waded through the papers—it took the meticulous Sheehan 17 years to subsequently write his Vietnam saga "The Bright and Shining Lie"—Gerry burrowed through his copies, entrusting them to a safe at night. Together, Gold and Sheehan presented their findings to Abe Rosenthal and a battle plan emerged for publishing the report. When the Supreme Court ultimately supported the paper's right to publish the study in a landmark First Amendment decision the Times was ready to go. Although others got the bylines, Gerry's Herculean feat in initially siphoning the essence from the mass of documents, was a legend inside the paper but unknown to the rest of the world. What appeared on the front page was often the tip of the iceberg, beneath which was an ensemble effort of myriad hidden talents.

While the saga of the Pentagon Papers is often approached with reverence by an awed posterity, it actually provided a plum assignment for the lucky staffers recruited to help Gold—five weeks at the Hilton, free. As Gold's task force grew, more reporters began showing up taking additional rooms, all of them identifying themselves as Gerald Gold. For weeks a series of Gerry Golds appeared to a bemused hotel staff prompting some of them to wonder if he weren't running a bordello—which in the Times Square precincts of that day wouldn't have been a stretch. Finally, when the last article was finished, the real Gold emerged to settle up at the front desk. When the clerk asked who he was, Gerry naturally replied: "Gerald Gold," to which the clerk apocryphally replied: "Yea, right."

For Gerry Gold, Rabelaisian, gruff, impatient, the Culture desk was a notions counter. He had no intention of being taken for a novice and let Peck know as much in loud, angry recrimination. It was a contentious marriage of an Odd Couple, two distinct talents with utterly different perspectives. Gold was a free-wheeling pro who needed no instruction and Peck was a control freak. Ultimately, they had to be separated—Gerry moved on, eventually becoming Music Editor of Arts & Leisure. But Gold's experience was typical of the way that Peck treated his staff. It exposed Sy's weakness as a Daily editor. Peck's strength lay in handling writers with finesse, particularly younger ones whom he could bring along. But in doing so he bypassed the backfield and copy-desk system. It may have been just as well since the copy chief, Artie Neuhauser, had all he could do to maintain damage control with the walking wounded he had for a desk. Peck and Neuhauser came to a tacit understanding: Sy would handle the big stuff and

Neuhauser would push everything else. It was a Rube Goldberg arrangement that demoralized an already dispirited copy desk.

Among the things that Bill Luce was never credited with during his short tenure was bringing order to a chaotic Culture report. Prior to his arrival the Culture section was pretty much an appendage of the Metro desk, an outlying territory aptly known as Culture Gulch. It had been overseen by a series of provincial satraps of varying talents and temperaments. The revolving door rivaled the turnover of Italian prime ministers with no one able or willing to satisfy Gelb's caprices. At one point, he took cognizance of this reality and, turning adversity to advantage, instituted a rotating series of editors, dragooned from the reportorial ranks. Most of Arthur's choices were eminently unsuited for the job. They ranged from the sainted Dick Shepard to the sassy Grace Glueck.

Dick, one of the great chroniclers of New York life and a mentor to generations of younger reporters, was simply too good-hearted for some of the kick-ass duties that came with the territory. He could do the hand-holding but not the arm-twisting. As a reporter, Shepard had the knack of literally carrying out the worst of Arthur's crazy ideas and presenting the results, deadpan, at which point Gelb would be horrified and kill the story wondering what ever had gotten into Dick's head to pursue such madness. Appearing chagrined, Dick would shake his head, mumble, "I guess you're right chief," and sidle off, having dodged another bullet. With his ever-present cigar in hand, Shepard literally blew smoke in the editors' faces. A natural linguist Dick conversed easily with the owners of the various ethnic restaurants in the neighborhood and was always getting us perks at their establishments. He was a welcome regular at such eateries as the China Peace and Cabana Carioca, an upstairs Brazilian joint better known as "1-2-3-4-5" from its address, 123 West 45th Street, where he amiably chatted up the owners in whatever lingo suitable to the occasion.

One of his favorite haunts was the Edison Café, a déclassé eatery in the Edison Hotel on 46th Street that had seen better days. He befriended the proprietors, Harry and Frances, a Jewish refugee couple form Poland who served up pastrami sandwiches and matzoh-ball soup for the regulars while offering blander fare to the out-of-town hotel guests. Dick always had an eclectic assortment of editors, reporters and clerks in tow—he was ever looking out for the strays. The watchword on these outings was strict democracy where the brass had to sit humbly with the help. The place was known informally as The Polish Tea Room—a nose-thumb at the snootier Russian Tea Room where the upper echelons sometimes lunched. After Shepard's death, the tradition continued, the fondest tribute the paper could pay him.

Such was the power of the press or the image of the Times in its halcyon days, that even the dumber ideas got a free ride, since most readers assumed that the people in charge must know what they were doing. One sweltering July day someone observed that it was hot enough to fry an egg on the street. Before you could say "cliché" Arthur had a reporter out the door, frying an egg on the hood of a car.

At his best, Gelb was an idiot-savant, but the savant was at times lacking. He was not so much an idea man as a foundry of ideas, quite a few of which were awful. His talent was to allow himself to be pulled back from the brink and take credit for the good ones. And he had good ones. To cite only one among innumerable instances, when The Challenger space vehicle went down, amid all the technical focus, Gelb made sure that the religion writer Joe Berger interviewed a cluster of deep thinkers about the cosmic significance of the event. Under Arthur's all-encompassing watch, The Times sought to cover every aspect of a major event. And, to those that produced for him, Arthur was a patron who generously fostered their careers. Even the reporters whom Gelb drove to distraction evinced grudging admiration for him; editors less so. This was in part the legacy of Rosenthal's ambition to make The Times more of a writers' paper at the expense of the desks that had once dominated it. But serving as Abe's enforcer also afforded Gelb the opportunity to bring the desks to heel and stifle any potential competition which, in those days, would most likely rise from the editors' ranks. As for Dick Shepard, when he began to develop stomach pains during his season as Culture Editor, his wife Trudy told him it was time to go back to reporting.

Grace Glueck was another matter. Glueck was a whiz on the art beat with a writing style that was sophisticated and droll. Whatever Grace's many strengths, organization was not one of them. Stories were lost, assignments forgotten, schedules were misplaced, vacations conflicted and overlapped, memos went down a rabbit hole. Grace weathered her trials with remarkable insouciance peppered with just the right dizzy-dame, who-me affectation that provided the perfect madcap touch to the screwball comedy of her tenure. As a memento of her leave-taking Grace left behind a drawer-full of notes from both supervisors and staff which were marked "Urgent," "For your immediate attention," "Please respond promptly" and "The show is closing."

It was during Grace's brief tenure that the upscale skin-flick "Deep Throat" achieved notorious prominence and The Great Gray Lady, after a few harrumphs, lifted up her skirts and marched boldly into the future. To distinguish itself from its racier competitors, The Times decided to treat the movie as a cultural phenomenon. This was the first porn movie with pretensions. By giving its imprimatur to this film as sociology The Times was reassuring readers that it was permissible to sample such forbidden fruit without fear of being considered perverted. Nevertheless, the fact remained that much of the audience for the movie still consisted of voyeurs who covered their laps with newspapers—thus gaining the sobriquet "newspapermen." What to do? Arthur Gelb wanted to sneak a peek at the steamy goings-on as much as anyone, but certainly didn't want to get caught emerging furtively from the Times Square porno house where the movie was playing. And so, Arthur hit on the novel stratagem of safety in numbers. He organized an expedition of the Times cultural staff, led by him in person, to explore this phenomenon and write about it for the benefit of Times readers. It was nothing more than the Paper of Record's fulfilling its responsibility to report on all aspects of culture without fear or favor. So one afternoon, Arthur led his troops pornward into the funky precincts of Time Square. In tow was Grace Glueck who, as putative Culture Editor, had been dragooned onto the boarding party.

Not invited was the TV writer, Fred Ferretti, who was a bit of a tummler and not one of Arthur's favorites. But Fred had gotten wind of the expedition and, somewhat of a practical joker, decided to play one on the Truth Seekers. He called the porno house, got hold of the manager and told him that he was from The New York Times and that Grace Glueck, the paper's Culture Editor, was at that moment in the audience and that an emergency had arisen and she was needed back at the office immediately. He told the manager it was urgent and asked him to page Grace over the loudspeaker and repeat her name because she was somewhat hard of hearing. The manager dutifully complied and Grace's name was blurted all over the porno house, interrupting what happened to be a climactic moment in the on-screen drama. Grace sheepishly scurried out of the theater leaving Gelb holding the bag so to speak. Arthur came back furious, accusing Ferretti, rightly, of perpetrating the hoax and threatening to fire him but Fred denied it and Arthur, lacking evidence, backed off.

Coda. Thirty years later, Fred, by then forgiven and retired, gets a call from Arthur, who wants to use the incident for his memoir since it's become part of Times legend. As Fred tells it, Arthur says: "Fred, when you made the call, you asked the manager to announce my name, didn't you?" Fred, politely replies: "No Arthur, I asked the manager to call for Grace." Arthur, more insistent: "No, the way I remember, it was me, they called for." Fred points out that the whole point of the joke was that the manager of a porn house was making a public announcement calling for the Cultural Editor of The New York Times who happened to be a woman. Arthur, still more insistent. "That's not the way I remember it, Fred. I'm sure it was me." Fred, seeing where this is heading, complies and says: "You know, Arthur, it probably was you." Arthur thanks Fred for confirming his recollection because that's the way it was going into his book.

What Fred didn't know was that at the very same time Grace Glueck was getting a similar call from Arthur. And, as Glueck relates it, the conversation was virtually the same. Grace maintained that it was she whose name was called out by the theater manager. But Arthur wouldn't back off. After a while, Grace got the point. Why bother fighting over something so silly? And she acceded saying: "You know Arthur, perhaps you're right after all." Arthur replied: "Yeah, I'm sure I am."

I don't know if Grace or Fred ever got together on this, but each of them told me this story separately, and their accounts, of both the first incident, and its sequel 30 years later, match. Arthur, of course, recounted the story in his memoir as he "remembered" it in his own inimitable way. Not content with telling a good story, he had to be at the center of it and push the real protagonists to the periphery, if possible, eclipsing them. Though he well knew what had actually transpired, he cajoled the witnesses into accepting his version of events. He not only altered the story to his advantage but he got the two chief participants—Ferretti, who had played the joke, and Grace who had been its victim—to acquiesce to his mythmaking and used their names as sources to verify his accuracy.

As it turns out, Grace Glueck—who knew where more than a few bodies were buried—was there at the onset of quite another phenomenon. During her tenure, Arthur's son, Peter, was

160

embarking on his career as a publicist and artist manager. Grace herself was newly ensconced as Culture Editor, and feeling her way into the job. As Grace recalls, one day, not too long into her stewardship, Arthur came by with an interest in a concert that, on the face of it, Grace felt didn't warrant coverage. Arthur disagreed and insisted that Glueck do a piece. So she assigned it to the music critic Don Henahan. The review, together with an accompanying article, ran prominently. Over the next two weeks Arthur kept coming to Grace with assignments for music reviews that grew ever stranger. Finally, Henahan approached Grace and gingerly asked whether there could possibly be a connection between these bizarre non-events that Arthur was pressing on the Culture department and the fact that they featured clients of Peter's who were getting an inordinate amount of ink in The Times.

Grace, as she recalls, was outraged and decided to have it out with Gelb. Lewis Funke, the longtime writer of A&L's "News of the Rialto " and a Culture desk functionary, advised her not to go ahead. Henahan said he didn't want his name mentioned. So great was the fear of Gelb that his minions were more concerned about offending him than blowing the whistle. Undeterred, Grace stormed into Arthur's office and confronted him, angry, but also half-concerned that she might lose her job for doing the right thing. After listening to her, Gelb hesitated for a moment and then said: "You're right." Then he added: "From now on, I'll let Peter talk to you directly himself.'' While it was not uncommon for agents to call and pitch an act, it was highly unusual for a publicist to have the kind of access Peter did. And indeed he had some worthy clients. The question is not Peter Gelb legitimately promoting them but to what degree they were privileged in The Times –a gray area to be sure but one that left the paper vulnerable to growing charges of nepotism.

Over time, Arthur's patronage became the target of open mockery from the paper's critics. One of Peter Gelb's most important clients was the pianist Vladimir Horowitz. Here is the Village Voice's media column, a frequent Times gadfly, in an item titled, "Enough Already": "Three more front-page columns on Vladimir Horowitz? As The Times would say, 'Mr. Horowitz is managed by Peter Gelb, son of the Times's Deputy Managing Editor Arthur Gelb. The senior Mr. Gelb, among the luminaries who attended the concert, was reportedly seen in animated conversation with the Times's music critic at the conclusion of the event.' '' There were many such barbs in the opposition press in the Gelb era but The Times was impervious to the drumroll of ridicule.

This pattern repeated itself over the ensuing years enabling the rise of Peter Gelb to the top ranks of New York's entertainment publicists, to a lucrative career as an executive at Sony Classical Records and, finally, General Manager of the Metropolitan Opera. What is at issue is not Peter Gelb's progress—he has amply demonstrated his talent—but, to what degree Arthur compromised The Times to foster it at crucial junctures. It is these turning points that make or break a career, or are the difference between a good run and a great one. When the Boston Symphony—another of Peter Gelb's clients—went to China in 1979, it was front-page news in The Times—which meant it was a big story in all the other entertainment media that followed in the paper's wake. It was certainly a valid story—a cultural aspect of the opening to China— but was it front-page news or rather the lead of the Culture Section or simply a front-page reefer to an inside story? And did it deserve the intense coverage it got as the Boston Symphony wended its way through China? And did the Boston Symphony's other forays deserve the trumpets and fanfare they received from The Times during Peter Gelb's tenure? (The joke at the paper was "Boston Symphony Goes to … Ulan Bator, Tierra del Fuego, Baffin Bay.'') The question is not whether the Boston Symphony's travels deserved coverage but how The Times handled it and, in so doing, contributed to a luminous career for the scion of its Culture czar.

Gelb's forte was to entangle his own interests and those of his friends with genuine news, so interweaving them that nobody could tell the difference. If Arthur thought it was news then it was news. Gelb was a genius at putting short-term memory to effective use. He reordered reality so that whatever came out suited his fancy. The Arthur who was flogging the aforementioned Boston Symphony in the belief that it was a great story forgot about the Arthur who was advancing his son's career as the orchestra's publicist. But after all, wasn't the Boston Symphony a big story? Look at all the space it got in The Times. It was a tour de force of circular reasoning. After salting a dig with his own relics Arthur then declared the site to be a find, in fact Troy itself. The importance of his discovery was self-validated in The New York Times which justified ever expanded and continuing coverage. Well into the process, Gelb's hobby-horse indeed became a story since it was impossible to extricate private interests from public ones. Arthur had triumphed because the story didn't need him anymore. A whole new cadre of editors would cover it not because Gelb wanted it but because a previous set had done so. All they had to do was check the clips. This was truly a brilliant innovation and Gelb was without doubt the unsurpassed master of the craft.

162

For all this, I was fascinated by Arthur. He had the roguish ability to make you like him as he was picking your pocket. Despite his faults, I couldn't help thinking of him affectionately. I hesitate to recall his excesses because they were mitigated by his virtues. As Metropolitan editor he was instrumental in supporting reporters such as David Burnham covering police corruption and overseeing the Serpico and Bernard Bergman investigations into crooked cops and abusive nursing homes. In the final analysis I found Gelb to be an exceptional editor but a flawed man. His enthusiasm stirred many to do their finest work. There are those who swear by him. Others swear at him. In Culture, I saw both. Arthur's talents enhanced the paper. His faults compromised it. To be fair, whatever Gelb's flaws, he was a man of considerable talent and he could be inspired and inspiring, just as he could be arbitrary and self-serving. He was a complex creature: a force of nature that lived by his own rules. In the end, this is not about Arthur Gelb. It is about a capricious system that afforded men with his ambitions and appetites the opportunity to take advantage of its failings.

Whatever its defects, the Culture Section was blessed with an impressive array of critical talent in virtually all of the arts. In movies there was Vincent Canby, perhaps the finest film reviewer of his day although he'd blush to hear himself described as such. In theater and dance there was a still lucid Clive Barnes before his appetites, both professional and otherwise, whirled him out the door to purgatory at the New York Post. Barnes thought that his name would take his readership along with him but he soon learned that, whatever his manifest enthusiasms, his audience cared for his opinions only when they were wrapped inside The New York Times. He would have fared better in the free-wheeling digital age. Into the breach stepped Anna Kisselgoff in Dance and Walter Kerr writing on Sundays. Both Kerr and his predecessor, Brooks Atkinson, had theaters named after them which indicates the prestige that The Times carried on Broadway in those days. With all due respect, it is unlikely that the Shuberts are going to name one of their stages the Ben Brantley Theater. The main reason is the paper's diluted impact on Broadway. In the brave new world of the internet, television, Disneyfication, Facebook, Twitter, downloading, streaming, blogorrhea, road tours and critic-proof promotion, the clout of The Times and its reviewers is greatly diminished. In the words of W.S. Gilbert: "When everyone is somebody / Then no one's anybody."

In those days, however, there were still quite a few somebody's on the staff. The chief Art Critic, Hilton Kramer, was a formidable presence in his world. Although Kramer subsequently became mocked as a stick-in-the-mud neo-con, it may be forgotten that he was a champion of modernism when modernism still counted for something. He was also a knowledgeable and erudite critic whose reviews were crisp and fair. And he was fiercely protective of his staff from the attacks of artists with overweening egos who had friends at the paper. On one occasion, Vivien Raynor, a staff critic, took out after a prominent artist's widow whose gallery show she skewered. The widow complained to Rosenthal who wanted to fire Vivien for being gratuitously cruel, but actually for simply doing her job which, in this case, meant being tough on someone he knew. Kramer, to his credit, intervened, made a speech about the integrity of the critic and Vivien's right to be harsh, if she thought it necessary, without fear of what management might say. Hilton held Rosenthal up to his own standards and Abe backed off, although Raynor had to lay low for a while. Kramer was followed by the elegant Englishman John Russell who looked and sounded as if he'd stepped out of a Joshua Reynolds portrait and whose lofty prose, British erudition and refined tastes set a tone of elegance that charmed the new class of collectors and arrivistes who were forming a significant part of The Times's art readership and its advertising base.

And then there was the legendary Harold Schoenberg, the critical embodiment of Aaron Copeland's "Fanfare for the Common Man." This may seem strange since Schoenberg was such a voice for the Romantic tradition and some of the great classical interpretations of symphonic music. But it was in his lucid style and straightforward, no-nonsense approach that Schoenberg revealed his democratic belief that anyone could appreciate a good review. Not only was Harold's criticism accessible but so was Harold. A polymath and a chess whiz, Schoenberg would come in from a late concert, bat out 1,200 words on a Verdi opera in machine-gun-like staccato and stop for a few chess moves with one of the night staff. Harold never went back over his copy. When he sat down at the typewriter, the magazine was loaded; all he had to do was pull the trigger. Schoenberg's successor, Donal Henahan, was cut from a different cloth. Don wrote with a spare prose that belied his wide-gauge knowledge of music and his intense dedication to craft. He brought a dignity and sense of purpose to his work that could rarely be matched.

The most rambunctious group to handle were the book critics: literary lions who would roar, and occasionally claw, at their keepers and one another. Foremost was Christopher Lehmann-Haupt, who held the job for more than 25 years and did it with a consistency that was amazing for its sheer fortitude. If he rarely soared to Trillingesque heights, neither did he disappoint.

At the opposite end of the emotive spectrum was John Leonard. About the time of Rosenthal's seizure of the Sunday Department, John ceased to be the Book Editor. His consolation prize was to be the second of the daily reviewers. Leonard, who'd been a fair-haired boy at the Book Review, was a little too hip for Rosenthal's taste. As far as John was concerned, Abe was a narrow-minded troglodyte and Arthur was his hit man, intent on bowdlerizing Leonard's copy now that they'd muscled him out of his Sunday post. He made it a point of honor to challenge them with double-entendre and risqué puns that he thought would get past their notice, which created a cat-and-mouse game that grew in intensity. John was a Man of the Left heading into the buzz saw of a boss in the early stages of a drift to the Right. Rosenthal saw his own conservatism in Burkean terms—a traditionalism that would protect the paper from the inroads of the New Journalism. Leonard saw it as a thin disguise for a reactionary agenda. He kept testing Abe by slipping his political opinions into reviews—he was after all a critic and, as such, had leeway to range wide in the realm of opinion. Rosenthal thought not.

As a line editor of many of the book reviews, I was often caught in the middle of this. I tried to mediate before John's more provocative passages got through but, in the end, it was his copy, and the end came soon enough. What did in Leonard was not his politics—Abe was too wise to confront him on that—but, as Rosenthal would have it, his smart-aleck attitude. After sufficient hammering on Abe and Arthur's part, John had enough of what he felt was their tampering with his copy, and left. He went on to become a venerated book editor at The Nation, where his politics was welcomed, as well as a sought-after critic on the pages of many publications, not the least of which was The New York Times Book Review in the years after the Rosenthal era.

The third member of the literary triumvirate was Anatole Broyard, the maddest and baddest of the lot. Anatole has written his own celebrated memoir of Bohemian life in the Village of the 50's. By the time I got to know him, 20 years had elapsed and he was a domestic creature commuting in from Connecticut. But at heart, Broyard was still the Bohemian with an eye for the ladies—at least in terms of palaver, a natural irreverence, and an attitude of not taking anything too seriously, most particularly his job. Anatole was noted for reviewing short books—under 250 pages if possible—with wide margins and preferably lots of illustrations if they were nonfiction, although he preferred fiction. A consummate elitist, Broyard looked down his genteel snub nose at most everything, loved to tweak his bosses and twit the straight arrows. And, to my dismay, he saw it as a gentleman's creed never to hand in a review until the absolute last moment. He understood that the later he submitted his piece the less opportunity the copy desk would have to meddle with it.

A great raconteur with a lively imagination, Anatole was particularly innovative at making up an infinite variety of excuses for why his copy was tardy. Since I was his editor and charged, ostensibly, with riding herd on him, I wound up playing straight man for some of his creative fancies. We had developed a sort-of dog-and-pony act: Broyard's role was to spin a tale of woe and misfortune built around the basic theme of "the cat ate my homework." Mine was to evince sympathy, shock, awe, chagrin and, finally, disbelief. On one occasion, he affected sympathy pangs for his wife's period as the reason for his writer's block. Although one might conjecture that she was well beyond this phase, I congratulated him on her regularity and his chivalry. Then, I insisted that he must bear up and turn his attention to producing a review. Once his piece was in, I had to monitor it for naughty words that he tried to slip by just for the fun of it. He was a scamp to the end, trying to put one over on the uptown crowd. The problem was not in catching Anatole —his ploys were almost boyish—but in convincing him that his little jokes would embarrass not only the paper, but himself.

One of the perks of working on Weekend was editing our restaurant writer, Mimi Sheraton. The bonus of this task was that I got to work on Mimi's copy Wednesday night and the section didn't come out till Friday. Which meant that I had a page proof of the review in my pocket on Thursday evening after the paper closed. This was gold for a bachelor dating in New York. Every Thursday, I was dining at the hottest restaurant in the city, about to be anointed on the morrow by The New York Times. I had already studied Mimi's review for the best courses and might only surreptitiously glance at it in a pinch. The next day, of course, my date was much impressed by my taste.

One of my other food pals was Patricia Raymer, whom I'd befriended when she arrived on the Culture copy desk, Pat, who was interested in cooking, had managed to move to the Living Section as a food writer, where she also did occasional reviews. One of her many functions was to work in The Times's kitchen on the sixth floor where she tested the recipes that went into our cooking articles. On occasion, Pat would invite me up and I'd sample the leftovers of whatever was going into the paper that week. Pat exuded a rosy-cheeked, middle-American cheerfulness straight out of a Saturday Evening Post cover. She was an ideal younger associate: a good team player, outgoing and diligent. But, in Mimi Sheraton, she was not in the good grace of a powerful presence and concluded that her ambitions at The Times wouldn't be fulfilled. At the time, Pat happened to be dating Walter Wells, a courtly editor on the Foreign desk. Walter had also hit a ceiling. Since he'd never been a foreign correspondent, whatever his talent, he could climb only so far up the ladder. When he got an opportunity for a horizontal move to The Paris Herald-Tribune, of which the Times was part-owner, Walter grabbed it. And Pat went with him. The rest is history. Walter went on to become editor-in-chief of the Paris Trib and Pat became Patricia Wells, the doyenne of French-food critics, the author of numerous cook books, a Gallic successor to Julia Child and the entrepreneur of a cooking school in the French countryside with a waiting list that is years long.

The younger set among the reviewers included a cluster of supporting players, most of whom went on to achieve top billing, and others who simply went on: The three Johns: Rockwell, Pareles and Wilson, who covered rock, pop and jazz along with Bob Palmer on blues and country; Mel Gussow in theater, Janet Maslin in movies; Jennifer Dunning in dance, Gene Thornton and Andy Grundberg in photography, Paul Goldberger in architecture and John O'Connor providing television commentary. For all its critical strength, The Times in those days did not have reporters assigned to all arts beats so that coverage was often an adventure. The usual suspects, rounded up when news broke, started with a few catch-all Culture reporters and radiated out to critics— particularly the younger ones—dragooned to cover developments in their specialties. For bigger stories general assignment types were recruited from the newsroom.

There were also "niches" designed to absorb the detritus of press releases and gossip that passed for "news" in areas like theater— the Broadway column— as well as equivalents in the film, art and publishing worlds. The presumption was that Culture was still a critic's game and that Reviews were News—or at least the basic news that Times readers cared most about. As this assumption changed radically in the ensuing years, management ordained a more ambitious news strategy without committing the necessary resources. There was an institutional lag of decades before the section's reportorial forces caught up with its news needs. The intervening years provided a painful interregnum for the Culture editors who were responsible for an expanding front of reportage with a thin line of troops.

At that moment The Times was easing out something called "punk." This was local argot for "filler" items of two or three lines that would appear at the bottom of an inside page literally to fill out empty space beneath a story, a hole that was too small for a house ad but big enough to be noticed. The material for punk usually came from wire-service shorts that nobody else wanted. Punk was the news equivalent of a Chinese fortune cookie and, if snipped out and rolled up, could have fit into one. Selecting punk was literally the bottom of the editorial barrel, usually assigned to dead-enders who couldn't be fired. Improved technology, a more sophisticated readership and embarrassment at some of the howlers that ran under the rubric of punk finally led to its demise, but a place had to be found for its attendants. The Culture copy desk was one.

Yet such cast-offs were far from the Culture desk's worst problem because, if left alone, they wouldn't bother you. This could not be said for some of their colleagues, the most notable of whom was the Shop Steward who had appointed himself tribune of the copy desk. Whatever the comradely principles of the Guild, he acted as commissar for any infractions of union privileges. He treated backfield editors with considered disdain, projecting an unspoken reproach that by seeking advancement they had sold out to management. As for his peers, he made sure that they did no more than required, else they were being exploited. The effect was that the poor wretches on the desk were harassed by their bosses and harried by their own.

The atmosphere on the Culture copy desk was so corrosive that anyone with a modicum of skill, ambition or self-preservation, got out as soon as they could. Women found it particularly hard on that desk. Talented ones like Nora Kerr and Pat Raymer went on to work in the Regional and Living Sections respectively. But women did make some headway as critics, as Anna Kisselgoff had done. It was at this point that I began developing long-term friendships at The Times. One of them was with Jennifer Dunning, who became

Anna's second banana in the Dance Department. Jennifer had been Hilton Kramer's secretary and was one of the few who ever vaulted from the ranks of clerk to critic. Hilton promoted her cause, another generous deed from a conservative that many of his more liberal critics could learn from.

Like Jennifer, many of my friends were the secretaries and news assistants in Culture. Probably the most colorful of them was the drama secretary, Clara Rotter. Clara had no men in her life except the ones she served at The Times. She was fiercely devoted to them—Brooks Atkinson, Clive Barnes, Walter Kerr, Richard Eder, Mel Gussow. There is the legendary story of Atkinson having second thoughts about a letter he'd sent and Clara badgering the New York postmaster until he retrieved the missive and returned it, unopened, to sender. During her heyday, the last question on the test for newly minted theatrical agents was: "Who is Clara Rotter." Anyone who didn't know the answer would find out soon enough. She eventually ceded the job to Carol Coburn—who kept it for another 30 years.

It was at about this period that The Times underwent one of its periodic renovations—this in preparation for the transition to computers—and we adjourned for several months to a rear chamber in the old Annex toward Broadway which put us virtually in the Paramount Building. Actually, it was possible to enter our new quarters directly through the Paramount Building on Broadway and avoid the 43rd Street entrance with its security guards altogether. This was achieved by taking the elevators in the Paramount's Broadway lobby to the third floor where an iron door led through a dark tunnel to another iron door that opened into our temporary home. In those days, before the era of security alerts, there were many such paths of entry to The Times building. Another route was through the China Peace restaurant—now Carmine's—on 44th Street. This was particularly convenient because, after eating a Chinese meal, a few of us could sneak through the rear of the restaurant and emerge via a back-stairs route into the third floor newsroom. Such alternatives did not count coming up through the 44th Street truck bay via the freight lift—if the operators liked you—or going out the back door next to Sardi's which was a ploy known to many. The China Peace and Paramount entries were somewhat more recondite. All of these charming little portals were sealed after the terrorist threats.

The Culture section, which was shunted to the back of the bus during this sojourn, looked like a work in progress: Wires hung down ominously from the ceiling threatening to electrocute anyone who touched them. This, of course, was a false scare which I proved one day by standing up on my desk, grabbing a fistful of cables, and holding forth with a rendition of "High Anxiety." The fact that we were stashed away from everyone else gave the place an antic quality with people literally disappearing into the woodwork and popping back out again. Poor Sy Peck, a stickler for order, was driven nearly crazy by the chaos. His staff was dispersed at desks plopped helter-skelter throughout a discordant space that looked like an abandoned warehouse.

The reign-of-misrule atmosphere during our Paramount days was nowhere more palpable than in the late Friday afternoon salon presided over by a coterie of prominent dissidents who were under house arrest in the provinces. For whatever reasons of temporary expediency, the moving mavens had plumped Syd Schanberg's office next to the Culture Corner. It was either a logistical accident or a deliberate attempt to put as much distance as possible between Schanberg and Abe Rosenthal, who were already on the outs. Schanberg had come back from Cambodia and its killing fields in the mid-70's where his work had earned him a Pulitzer and the coveted job of Metropolitan Editor, which put him on a fast track for mast-head status. But in a not-uncommon scenario, he was soon enough demoted from fair-haired boy to prodigal son. Rosenthal was a veritable Kronos in devouring a series of adopted heirs for whatever perceived betrayals, and then anointing a successor who would soon enough be doomed to a similar destiny. This fate fell most heavily on the Metropolitan editors. Their cause was not helped by the fact that both Rosenthal and Gelb once held the job themselves and had definite ideas about how it should be done. Moreover, Arthur was always nervous about any potential competitors and the Metro Editor was definitely a stepping stone toward Managing Editor, a post that Gelb coveted and eventually attained.

Schanberg, a celebrated foreign correspondent whose credentials for higher office were superior to Arthur's, was a definite threat. Gelb had worked the paradigm of compromising competitors down to a science. First a brief honeymoon period where Abe played the proud papa and Arthur the doting uncle to the prodigy. Then doubts would set in about wrongheaded assignments, missed stories, poor coverage; all the while Arthur played Iago to Abe's Othello, egging him on, undermining his rival privately while genuflecting publicly. Finally, when Rosenthal was primed with sufficient accusations—incompetence, lack of leadership,

170

unsuitability for the job, failure to fulfill the confidence The Times had invested in the wretch—Arthur would supply the coup de grace: insubordination. The miscreant was a loose cannon, an ingrate who had broken trust. Off with his head. Someone once suggested that instead of the flags outside The Times building, a more accurate reflection of the paper would be an array of pikes bearing the visages of all the losers in the power struggles at court. Schanberg was certainly one of them. His head hadn't quite been lopped off yet—he was still being held in the Tower—but his fate was sealed.

On Friday afternoons, Schanberg conducted an open bar in his cubicle. The guests included other notorious dissenters like Seymour Hersh—whose growingly leftish investigative slant was starting to irk the growingly rightish Rosenthal— and Roger Wilkins, a thorn in Abe's side given his longtime alliance with Rosenthal's nemesis Harrison Salisbury on the Op-Ed page. In my case proximity helped— my desk was nearby; also, I had gotten to know Schanberg a bit during his tenure as Metropolitan Editor. The atmosphere was convivial, amusing and sardonic. The participants would play a Can-You-Top-This of horror stories about Abe & Arthur (they were always referred to as a single entity, like Horn & Hardart). There were, of course, other topics— it was a democratic process and after a few nips, tongues were loosened and spontaneity ruled—but sooner or later the subject generally drifted back to the Dynamic Duo.

One of my tasks during this period was to edit the Broadway column, then being written by John Corry. This was a considerable improvement over his predecessor Tom Buckley who affected a drill sergeant's voice and a manner to boot. The desk had to bear the brunt of Tom's disdain made more painful by the fact that he sometimes had a point. Buckley gave the distinct impression that the Broadway column was far beneath his talents. And he took it out on whatever editor came his way which, as often as not, was me. I didn't take it personally. Tom was just mad at the paper. Eventually, his whipping arm may have withered from overuse, or he finally flogged himself out of a job. John Corry was a relief.

Like all good things, our idyll in the Paramount Building came to an end and we were back in the same old digs, but they were not the same at all. Our typewriters had been removed and in their place were screens and keyboards. We had entered the computer age. Weekend was one of the first sections to go over to the new system and I remember the trepidation at the first piece of live copy we set in cold type—the digital process that did away with the need for casting type in hot lead. If any moment in my career was the beginning of the end of the Print Age, this was it. Everyone stood around my computer and we hummed Richard Strauss's opener to "Thus Spoke Zarathustra" from "2001" where the apes hover around the spaceship on the verge of a millennial moment. Little did we know that we would be the monkeys. Then, bingo, I hit the button, and nothing was ever the same again.

The new machines took some getting used to. It was clear that the editors were now going to become printers. The thing I hated most was kerning. This was a process necessitated by the art director who would order an illustration that required the type to bend around the border of the sketch. In order to achieve this, an editor had to instruct the computer to take the numerical equivalent of the capital letter of the first word of the story, and then, subtracting from the width of each line, write out a complicated formula so that the cold type would digitally curve around the drawing. And if the lead paragraph of the story changed you'd have to do the whole thing over again—and again. Those Hirschfeld cartoons were a great delight to the reader but a digital challenge to the harried editor who was still trying to get the hang of this new-fangled buggy.

The Times, in its wisdom, had chosen to enter the digital world with the unwieldy Harris System that became virtually obsolete not long after it had been purchased. Newsday had better researched the process and acquired Atex computers that were far superior and easier to handle. Along with the Harris System, The Times had also acquired a computer supervisor, Howard Angione, who used his knowledge of the machines to browbeat the digitally challenged mortals in his charge. Howard seemed to think that the process—which he controlled—took precedence over the subject matter. He was right, just a little ahead of his time. Angione was a first hint that we were falling into the grip of technology. Not surprisingly, he was roundly disliked and, eventually, dispensed with. But not before inadvertently helping me make a few friendships for which I am grateful. Given my duties I simply had to learn certain basics or I couldn't function. But others— particularly certain writers—could for a time actually avoid, or at least postpone, the unwelcome prospect of entering the computer age. It was only a later generation that arrived at newspapers digitally fluent. At this stage, the transition could be painful to some, who were thereby needful of assistance.

One of them was John Gross, certainly the most erudite person I ever worked with. Gross, who'd been air-freighted from England originally to bring some badly needed stature to a flagging Sunday Book Section, had wound up as a daily book reviewer. John had been the editor of the Times of London's Sunday literary supplement, probably the most prestigious book editor's job in journalism. A person of refined sensibilities, the author of "The Rise and Fall of the Man of Letters," as well as several cultural studies for Oxford University Press, Gross was simply unused to the crass behavior of the Gelb functionary who ran the Book Section. After a short, painful sojourn in Sunday Books, John was allowed to retreat to the Daily which he enhanced with beautifully crafted literary reviews. But he was leery of signing in to his computer which he approached as a bomb-defuser might a ticking device. So I did it for him under a generic code and once John was launched it was simply a matter of typing.

This mild deception drove Angione crazy because it meant that someone was working on a terminal without actually signing in under his true code. As Howard saw things, it defied the basic strategy of getting everyone aboard on computer usage. Technically, he was right but in human terms he was wrong. The important thing was for Gross to get to frame his thoughts rather than fool with the new gadgetry. Our bonding experience came one afternoon when I was signing John in as he sat next to me and Howard just happened to swoop by and catch us in the act. It was like being arrested in the men's room at Hyde Park with a subaltern of the Coldstream Guards. Angione gave us what for. I'd had enough and returned the favor, disabusing Howard of the belief that the tale should wag the dog. He threatened to report me and I told him to do his worst and buzz off. Poor John meanwhile was trying to slip inside the monitor screen as the bullets whistled overhead. I got called into Gelb's office but when he heard the way Angione had treated Gross, if not me, he mellowed. In the end, Arthur was still a newspaperman and ready to close ranks against an outsider. Also, at the time, although the lower orders had to learn the ropes of computer language the top brass was absolved of the obligation, so perhaps Arthur felt a twinge of sympathy for John's plight. In any case, since I'd taken the whipping for what was essentially Gross's sin, John was ever grateful and we developed a friendship. Editing him was a pleasure since I hardly had to lift a pencil although he always affected to appreciate the occasional suggestion I offered.

I later thought that Gross's digital reticence was something limited to the early days of computers. But even later on I never ceased to be surprised about how much some of my older colleagues didn't know, didn't want to know and felt they didn't need to know about the brave new world of computers.

The real resistance to the digital age, however, came not from the white-collars in editorial but from the blue-collars in the composing room whose days were numbered by the new technology. They made their last stand with the strike of 1978, a siege of almost two months duration. The Guild—me included —walked out with them, a compliment that was not returned when management played hardball with a give-back contract several years later. Although the printers managed to find plenty of work to tide them over in the non-union shops throughout the city, their white-collar co-workers had to scramble a bit more. Strike papers were started up but the pay was bad and the stability shaky. For me, the strike was a mixed blessing. Because my wife was making a good salary as a surgeon and we'd saved a little, I was able to finally get around to doing some projects I'd always talked about and never found time for. Eventually, the strike ended, as it had to, and we marched back to work in October, refreshed or depleted, take your choice. The printers had won a Pyrrhic victory buying them a little time with the understanding that their days were numbered. The rest of us had less leverage, as we were to learn.

We had hardly returned when I got a call from Marvin Siegel one morning. It was November 1978 and The Times was about to launch its Science Section, the last piece in the puzzle that would complete its weekday lineup of special sections: SportsMonday, Science on Tuesday, Living on Wednesday, Home on Thursday and Weekend on Friday. Having indulged the paper with moneymakers in the last three, Rosenthal wanted to do something uplifting and, to his credit, fought for the Science Section against an advertising department that feared it would be a sales disaster. As it turned out, they failed to anticipate the computer explosion that carried Science in its early going, so Abe wound up doing well by doing good. No editor today would have the sheer clout and charisma to carry through such a project. Nor could The Times now afford such an indulgence.

My role in this was a footnote, albeit a telling one. As indicated above, the new Science Section was to appear on Tuesday, the 14th, and it was Monday when I got a call from Siegel asking if I wanted to make a little overtime. I suspected by his ingratiating tone that something was up. Cautiously, I said yes. The strike had left me a little short and I could have used the money. "What do I have to do?" I asked. "Just report to Arthur," Marvin replied. "He'll tell you." Whoops! It was clear that whatever Arthur wanted Siegel was too smart to get himself into so he'd volunteered me. It was about noon when Marvin called and I high-tailed it down to the building and got to Gelb's office a little before one. He was just going out to lunch. "What's up?" I asked. His answer went something like: "We're putting out this Science Section and Bill Connolly, whose running it, is gonna need a little help with the heads and things. Should be a breeze for you." Sure Arthur.

I hurried over to a make-shift desk that was the new Science Section and there encountered Connolly, a good soldier, who was totally frazzled. It turns out that he hadn't yet learned how to work the new computers and copy was piling up on his desk, none of which had been edited because, in fact, he had no editors. Abe and Arthur had decided to launch this project without a functioning infrastructure, assuming that The Times's resources were such that a desk could be tossed together at the last minute and produce a section. It was clear that I was being thrown into the breach because the Science Section formats were similar to the ones Weekend used, also maybe because I could write heads, captions and process copy. Our deadline was six o'clock and nothing was set. We had five hours.

I sized up the situation and, without hesitating, I raced back to Gelb's office. Luckily, a phone call had delayed his lunch and he was heading for the lobby. I caught him at the elevators. "Arthur, this is going to take more than me and Bill." "Really, Jack?" he asked. "Yes, really, Arthur." The elevator was opening. I rode down with him. "I need carte blanche from you to bring in anyone I can to set up a desk, or else this won't come out." Arthur: "You think it's gonna need all that?" Me: "Absolutely." We're now downstairs in the lobby. Arthur looks at his watch. He's late for his lunch. "All right, do what you have to," he says, somewhat grumpily, and disappears through the revolving door. I go back upstairs and turn to Connolly. "Help is on the way," I tell him. I call up two Weekend desk colleagues and tell them that Gelb insists that they show up immediately to move copy on the paper's new Science Section which is closing in less than five hours. I appropriate a picture editor and cajole a make-up editor. By two we've set up a desk and we're off and running. Bill Connolly is backfielding, I'm trouble-shooting and everyone is railroading. An improvised arrangement, but a workable one.

Amazingly, layout, copy, pictures, captions, all fall into place and we're done by two minutes to six. Except for one headline, a toughie because it had to explain a daunting story—when will the human race die out—in a narrow space. At which point I get a call from Gelb. He tells me that Chick Butsikares, the composing room honcho, is upset because our last page hasn't closed. I tell him that it's waiting on one head. "You gotta work faster Jack," he tells me, and hangs up. That was the last word I ever heard from Arthur about my efforts. A minute later we sent the head—"Doomsday / Debate: / How Near / Is The End?" and the section closed within range enough of its deadline. A miracle. And that is how Issue One, Volume One of Science Times came out. Bill Connolly thanked me profusely. The next day, when the dust had settled, Connolly insisted they'd better establish a real Science desk immediately. Sure enough, a desk was created. Having always been interested in science and tiring of my chores on Weekend, I volunteered for the Science Section. But it was not to be. I suspect Marvin wanted to retain my services on Weekend and may have put the kibosh on it, but I could never prove it nor, in the end, did it matter. Bill Connolly went on to a reputable career at The Times, eventually became one of the paper's wiser heads and was instrumental in revising its Style Book. Our paths crossed only infrequently but, when they did, I'd say: "Science Section, Issue One, Volume One," and he'd give me a rueful laugh.

By now I'd been on The Weekend Section for three years and, as indicated, was growing restless. The work was comfortable enough, perhaps too easy, and I had to resist feelings of complacency. For distraction, I taught a class in copy editing at NYU in 1977 and in interpretive writing at the Columbia Journalism School the following year which, while stimulating, did not provide an answer. After a little more time had elapsed, I was finally able to move on. As luck would have it, an opportunity afforded itself back in the Sunday Department. Ed Klein, the editor of The Times magazine needed a copy chief and I was tapped for the job.

I was called up to the Times Magazine by Klein in 1979 to replace its copy chief, Sherwin Smith. Sherwin would stay on as my No. 2. The reason for my ascension was that Smith, a gifted editor in the morning, was not the same after lunch. On his good days Sherwin would take a lone luncheon at the Pantheon, a Greek joint on Eighth Avenue, where he'd fortify himself with their egg-lemon soup and a single martini while whizzing through The Times Crossword Puzzle in pen. On his bad days he'd come back a little later and a little wobbly. But on the following morning, he always managed to get himself together and somehow show up, shaved, mint-breathed, tie straightened, coffee mug in hand and ready for a day's work, or a half day's. Certainly, Sherwin's half-day was better than the full-time efforts of many others. He was a magician with copy, a master of style and grammar and could tweak elegance out of the most labored prose. My task was to get the best out of him before the worst took over.

I had no doubt I could do the job. By then, I'd been in the business for 20 years, and at the Times for six where I'd already worked four different sections including one in the Sunday Department. Moreover, my knock-about career had also earned me friends in a lot of different places. As it turned out, I'd worked next to Klein on the Newsday copy desk after he came back from a sojourn in Japan before becoming the Foreign Editor of Newsweek during its heyday in the Vietnam era. He had caught the eye of Abe Rosenthal during a mutual junket to the Far East and been tapped to run the Magazine when Abe took control of the Sunday Section. At our first meeting Klein held aloft an embarrassing "Jimmy Conor" headline of recent vintage, in which the Magazine misspelled the tennis star's name on its cover. He told me that he was so confident in my abilities that he would make me personally responsible for any error that appeared in the section. In those bullish days, the Magazine was a much heftier product, going up to 212 pages containing 10 or more stories, in the pre-Christmas issues, dwarfing its output of later years. Our tiny summer sections never went below 96 pages. I was responsible for between 60,000 and 70,000 words a week, and all of them had to be right.

The Magazine, as it turned out, was even more Byzantine than the Daily. For a writer to get a story through involved running an ascending gantlet of editors that allowed each one up the line to question the author at every step as well as challenge the work of their subalterns down the line. A writer who'd been given one set of marching orders by an articles editor could have that mandate reversed by a senior editor and altered yet again by the Magazine deputy or the top editor himself. Moreover, each of these strata was encouraged to second-guess their lesser colleagues as a sign of their perspicacity, so Monday morning quarterbacking was built into the system. At the start of each week the staff would assemble for a story conference. This exercise had the air of a legal proceeding with the articles editors making a brief for the defense, senior editors playing the prosecutor and the top editor acting as presiding judge and grand inquisitor. On top of this, the other articles editors were free to add their comments to the discourse.

And this was only for the proposal. Keep in mind that the articles editor who offered his lamb up on this altar had accepted his author's original proposal with some enthusiasm, so he or she acted as its advocate while the others proceeded to give it the fish eye. Armed with these revised marching orders, the articles editor would relay them to the writer who would either have a fit or swallow the new mandate because this was, after all, The New York Times magazine. The author would then dutifully re-report the story and complete what he or she hoped would be a finished product but was, in fact, a first draft. The articles editor would give the piece a light dusting and make copies for all of his colleagues who would read it in advance of a second story conference on the following Monday.

The putative finished copy now inspired further suggestions and alterations with the articles editor vainly trying to hold the revisions to a minimum. Back the piece would go to the beleaguered writer for more tailoring. At this point, the author wasn't so much writing a piece as fielding a fusillade of questions fired by a squad of unseen editors so that what had once been a smooth tale often became a ragged affair. This second draft was submitted to yet another story conference where, should it pass muster, it rarely managed to escape without a few final emendations. But sometimes there was even a third go-round when the piece, now unrecognizable in its original form, was sent back to the author for yet further re-upholstering. This usually happened when the top editors, weary of nibbling the story to death, opted for a mercy killing but the articles editor, determined that it should see the light of day, got a reprieve for a final go.

Those articles that managed to run the gantlet eventually found their way to the copy desk and it was our job to make the rough places smooth, extract the errors that had been introduced during the editing process and, when possible, disinter the corpse of what had been the writer's original concept. Since it was impossible for all of this to occur in orderly fashion, the process often led to gridlock with the copy desk and researchers harrying the poor writer simultaneously as the piece closed. The result could be a grand snafu. The production chief, Anne Hollander, whom Klein had brought over with him from Newsweek, would be beside herself, the writer was on the verge of collapse and the articles editor was frantic. It was a formula for fraught nerves and frayed tempers. Rarely did a Friday closing go by without an outburst from one quarter or another. I can recall the sainted Dorothy Seiberling, a grand dame of the magazine world brought in by Klein to steady the ship, confronting Anne Hollander on one of these occasions. Anne—who was herself under pressure from the production honchos in the composing room—was screaming at Dorothy: "You've got to close this RIGHT NOW." To which Seiberling austerely responded, "I'll close this piece when it's finished," and continued working, ignoring Anne's entreaties.

It could also happen that at the end of the hazing period, Klein, in his wisdom, decided to reject a piece. He had brought to the tortuous process a further top-heavy layer from his high-flying Newsweek days in which the senior editor exercised a droit de seigneur in dismembering and ultimately killing a piece. "It doesn't cut the mustard," he'd say. The articles editor would protest that the writer had done everything we asked and Ed would respond that we had given the author repeated chances to make the story work and he had failed to do so. If the articles editor reminded Klein of all the work the writer had put into the story, Ed would reply: "That's what a kill fee is for." Should the articles editor suggest that the irate writer had done an inordinate amount of work and might not want to write for the Magazine again, Klein would say, "Give 'em the full fee." Of course, the fee, while appreciated, was not why most writers put themselves through this torture. The reason was to appear in the pages of The New York Times magazine. Many writers swore never to work for the Magazine again and a few kept their vow but most eventually succumbed to the cajoling of the articles editors, the temptations of prestige, the dimming of memory and the illusion that lightning couldn't strike twice.

If Klein could be brusque with his staff, he was in mortal fear of Abe Rosenthal and shaped his decisions around pleasing his patron. Ed was Abe's man in every sense. He was an outsider who had been brought in by Rosenthal to energize the Magazine with some of the adrenalin that had pulsed through Newsweek in its glory days. Rosenthal felt that the Magazine had grown tired, complacent and predictable and he wanted to infuse it with a new dynamism. Klein certainly brought energy to the enterprise, but it was a nervous energy, driven by Ed's constantly looking over his shoulder to make sure that Abe approved of his actions. The watchword under the Klein regime was "would Abe like it?"

Consequently, Klein managed to be overbearing but not feared by his staff because he himself was apparently so concerned about what Abe would think. To his credit, Ed left me alone, perhaps because my efforts involved processing rather than promulgating. Whatever his issues with the rest of the staff— which I regarded with bemused detachment— Klein treated me decently and I never had a problem with him.

The Magazine's fashion director was Carrie Donovan, a doyenne of the industry, hired to pump in some needed street cachet to the section's dowdy style pages. She oversaw its content and wrote a weekly column. Although Carrie was a tough lady she was putty in Ed's hands. Carrie understood that while she knew fashion she needed help in the word department, which is how I came to be her editor. Carrie knew her onions and whipping the prose into shape wasn't hard because she let me do whatever I wanted. Occasionally, I'd take her around the corner to Joe Allen's, treating her uxoriously and making flattering small talk. Eventually, we'd get to the point of her wanting to can one of her entourage or get more space for her section, or push a favorite, but this was done casually, a cordial savored at meal's end.

Carrie sported outsized eye-glasses, flamboyant frocks and tons of jewelry that jangled as she approached. It was said that she never bought a thing on her back. Rather, her attire consisted of gifts from the various design houses she was writing about. This did not pose a moral dilemma for Donovan. Although such behavior presented a conflict and was strictly verboten in later days, at the time, it was a rule more honored in the breach. Years later, Carrie wound up promoting Col. Sanders' Kentucky Fried Chicken on television. When you think about it, how much difference is there between hawking haute shmatas and flogging fast food?

The Times magazine had an impressive array of articles editors. The two most senior practitioners were my former colleagues at The Week-in-Review, Bob Stock and Anthony Austin who had moved over to the Magazine following the death of Al Marlens. Tony flourished as a magazine editor which, for him, was gentleman's work. He was responsible for most of the foreign stories that he handled as if he were the legate at an imperial satrapy. Stock was consummately unflappable and a master at shaping a piece to a smooth finish. On one occasion, Klein had commissioned a cover about international communist subversion by Claire Sterling, a specialist on spooks who was esteemed by the conservative classes. Sterling—a current favorite of Rosenthal then in Cold Warrior mode—was about to publish "The Terror Network," a tome that the Right was promoting on how a worldwide web of Soviet-sponsored intrigue was undermining U.S. global interests through force and violence. We were to offer our readers a foretaste of her efforts.

Klein, in his enthusiasm, lit on the idea that we condense her entire book into one article. Sterling made a futile run at it but as the deadline neared she was thrown into a panic. We had already committed ourselves to a cover and the planes were flying. So it came to pass that on a Friday morning—closing day— Stock and I met an anxious Sterling at 8 A.M. at my desk and we proceeded to crunch her book, chapter by chapter, into a single narrative. We finished moments before the 6 P.M. deadline. The result was "Terrorism: Tracing the International Network," a screed that politically fulfilled the paranoid fantasies of the Right, but professionally was a tour de force of condensation and relative clarity. Sterling noted that it took her publisher a year to do what we'd accomplished in a day, and our edit was better. For Sterling it was an amazing experience. For Stock it was all in a day's work.

Our staff was enhanced by such stalwarts as Gerald Walker, Holcolm Noble and Glenn Collins, all talented articles editors who responded to the exigencies of the Magazine in their own idiosyncratic ways. Walker was our Culture maven. With his dark hair, movie-star good looks, and seductive baritone, he looked the part. The Magazine was a sideline for Walker. His real trade was books. He was the author of "Cruising," a popular novel about the risky culture of gay men seeking sex written well before coming out became fashionable. It was made into a movie starring Al Pacino during my tenure which turned Gerry into a bit of a celebrity, but one who still needed the weekly paycheck. Walker fought for his writers, giving Klein as hard a time as possible without getting himself fired. They took turns exasperating one another.

Hoc Noble was a feisty character who confronted Klein head on. Among his many tasks, Noble handled the science pieces and he bristled over what he felt was Ed's dumbing down of the articles with his "Arrows to Toyland" approach intended to guide the reader through the story. Klein maintained that this was simply an audience-friendly tactic meant to clarify abstruse science pieces. Hoc considered this simplistic, arguing that any Times reader sufficiently interested in the article would be intelligent enough to understand it. Had the issue simply been about an honest disagreement over magazine writing they might have reached an accord, but in essence, it was a Manichean struggle. Noble would stage 15-round bouts that he'd invariably lose—Ed was the referee as well as the opponent—but Hoc was big on moral victories.

Glenn Collins handled the lighter stuff and had an easygoing way of disarming Klein. Collins possessed a wry sense of humor that was able to defuse a lot of tension. Just as Hoc's demons would turn the heat up, Glenn's better angels would lower the temperature. But many years later Collins acknowledged that even after three decades, the memory of Ed Klein made his blood boil. Like almost everyone, Glenn escaped from the Magazine as well, winding up in the newsroom where his deft touch made him one of the master practitioners of the light feature.

Most memorably, there was Ed Klein's deputy, Martin Arnold, who was, to put it mildly, a big-picture man. That is, Arnold had neither the temperament nor the inclination to deal with the minutia that went with his post. Marty, who was bluntly honest about his own abilities, would have been the first to acknowledge this. Or as he might have more characteristically declared: "I don't have time for chicken shit." Arnold's strength was to spot big holes in stories, apply the brakes on a major project that was going nowhere, confront a fractious writer or rambunctious editor and serve as both straw boss and enforcer for Klein. Marty also served as a conduit from the Magazine to his friend Abe Rosenthal. Arnold had in good part been placed there by Rosenthal to shore up Klein's newsroom bona fides as well as keep an eye on him for Abe. Most importantly, Marty served as an alter ego for Klein, allowing Ed to bounce his concerns and anxieties off an elder statesman in whom he could confide. All of this was absolutely necessary for the effective running of the section but it nevertheless left a gap at the top in the line-editing department since Arnold, who offered a sharp news sense when focused, had a limited attention span at other times and was not always to be found as he made his social rounds through the building. For all this, Marty could supply a necessary dose of horse sense whenever the more fluttery Magazine types went off on a tangent. Arnold's job was to bring everyone down to earth. Nor was he shy about invoking Rosenthal's name in doing so. When pressed, Klein could rely on Marty's imprecations and Abe's imprimatur.

Marty Arnold fulfilled a newspaper role that is not listed on the syllabus of any journalism school but is a sine qua non in most city rooms: Professional Pal. He played it to the hilt for his entire career, first as a reporter and then as an editor. I don't mean to diminish the importance of this calling. It is more than being a mere hanger-on. A Pal must have done his time in the trenches with the powers that be, presumably when they were all coming up together, so that there is a sense of camaraderie in the mix. It's critical that the Pal would have made his bones together with his betters. Next, a Pal has to have a solid set of street smarts, hard-earned wisdom, a reserve of talent and a good store of anecdotes that can cover most occasions. Most importantly, a Pal, while a social equal of the boss, can never be a professional rival; rather, he would have ceded all such ambition well before his Palship. When effective, he serves as jongleur, court fool (but not too foolish), institutional memory and willing hit-man, someone in whom the boss can confide. The Pal's reward for this is to be sent to pivotal outposts where he serves as legate, enforcer and listening post. As the Pal ages, the Boss sees to it that he is taken care of in a declension of sinecures appropriate to his throttled-down needs. Marty was a virtuoso at the game and deserved an Oscar for Lifetime Achievement in this endeavor. Bellying up to the bar at Sardi's with Sidney Zion, Abe Rosenthal, Arthur Gelb & Company, Arnold played the part to a fare-thee-well.

While most of the copy at the Magazine went through the grist mill described above, there were a few articles that passed unscathed. The writer of one such piece was Barbara Gelb, Arthur's wife. There was nothing Klein wouldn't do to placate Gelb and what would please Arthur most at the moment was to have his wife, Barbara, whip up a frothy tribute to the author Jerzy Kosinski, a house favorite not only of Gelb but of Rosenthal. Abe and Arthur had come under the sway of Kosinski, whose novel, "The Painted Bird," rendered the Holocaust as Grand Guignol. In his various guises and emotional quick-change performances Kosinski cultivated a gaggle of the great and near-great and enchanted them into guileless geese who swallowed whole his tales of survival under the Germans, picaresque adventures in his adopted homeland and kinky night-crawling in the demi-monde playground of contemporary New York. Kosinski was the whoopee-cushion for the media elite in its glory years, everyone's favorite bad-boy with the moral admixture of Holocaust survivor.

Barbara Gelb's encomium to Kosinski was more than 6,500 words at a time, in early 1982, when the Magazine was on a campaign to keep stories to no more than 5,000 words. When I attempted to make a few minor trims, I was informed that the author chose to keep her prose in its virginal state. Klein was only too glad to acquiesce. Under the rubric "Being Jerzy Kosinski," the panegyric appeared in pristine condition. Barbara's prose could have used some editing.

There were rules for Abe and Arthur's friends, and rules for everyone else. A stellar example of the Gelb machine in action was the treatment given to Arthur's compadre and Apthorp neighbor Joseph Heller. Although Heller's creative juices seem to have ebbed since his best-selling "Catch-22," each new book of his was treated by The Times as a major literary event—which, it inevitably became. Heller's novel, "Good as Gold" was anointed with a hefty interview in the Magazine by none other than Barbara Gelb in another 6,500-word-plus extravaganza. "Good as Gold" also received stories in Arts & Leisure and Daily Culture plus a front-page review in the Sunday book section as well as a Daily notice. Needless to say, Heller's earlier novel, "Something Happened," got a front-page article in the Times Book Review as well.

When in full throttle, the Gelb Express was something to behold. It could transcend coded warnings by reviewers because it encapsulated Arthur's anointed in a bubble of hype that made the book a cultural phenomenon rather than a work subject to critical appraisal. And with such advance notice, the bookstores would give pride of place to this consecrated volume, adding to the bonanza. It could hardly be surprising that with this sort of a launch the book leaped onto the Times Best-Seller list closing the circle on a Gelb-generated promotion. A look at some of the most important books issued at this time makes it apparent that few had the clout that Heller enjoyed for a decidedly mediocre outing.

To be fair to Rosenthal, he was much better at being edited than Barbara Gelb—perhaps because, for all his flaws, Abe was a great editor and respected the craft. After a trip to China, Rosenthal wrote a lengthy piece for the Magazine and Klein handed it to me as if Moses had just brought the Tablets down from Sinai. Ed didn't want anyone else to touch the article and admonished me to approach it like the High Priest entering the Temple sanctuary. I proceeded to ignore Klein and treated the article as I would any other piece. It was well written but needed massaging and was sprinkled with the usual grammatical and spelling errors as well as the transitional glitches that any professional would make in the normal course of a long piece. What Klein didn't understand was that I was there to protect Abe, not anoint him. When I finished, I bypassed Klein—who I knew would have a fit—and went directly to Rosenthal with my fixes. He went along with virtually all of them, told me how much he appreciated my help and, as I'd hoped, called Ed to tell him so, which insulated me from any retribution for my end-run. After that, Rosenthal and I always got along pretty well. We were never close. I wasn't going to be one of his boys after turning Gelb down for the Long Island job. But I seem to have earned his grudging respect which, under the circumstances, was the most I could expect.

In addition to its brace of articles, the Magazine also ran regular features, not the least of which was William Safire's column on words. Safire, who had made his bones as a publicist for Richard Nixon, jumped ship during Watergate and found a safe haven as a conservative columnist on the Times's Op-Ed page. And in a wily move he positioned himself as a weekly word maven on the Magazine. At the time, Safire owed his maven-ness in part to the copy-editing skills of our Sherwin Smith who roamed through the savannah of his writing every week to pick out the errors— grammatical, syntactical and etymological— that the wordsmith scattered so that the page proof was red with the markings of Smith's pen. To be sure, Bill was at least appreciative that Sherwin was saving his bacon.

Safire, who was a quick study, may have finally gotten it right over the years—or maybe glommed on to a competent researcher. In either case, he flourished long after Sherwin had left the scene and came to be considered one of our great authorities on words. My only encounter with him occurred late one Friday afternoon. Sherwin was away and, earlier in the day, among the gaffes Safire had made that I quietly corrected was one in which he confused the Yiddish term for someone's mother-in-law-to-be—"machatenista" with "meshpucha," the word for family. I sent along the fixes. Then, later in the day, just before closing I noticed a more serious problem that had cropped up in Safire's lead and, as time was pressing and we were about to close, I figured out a way to resolve the difficulty that would keep his point, maintain the tone and stay within space. I called Bill, apprised him of the complication and started to volunteer my solution. Without hearing me out, he intoned: "I need no help in altering my lead." He might as well have added " . . . from the likes of you." I looked at the phone and was about to respond: "Bill, anyone who doesn't know the difference between 'meshpucha' and 'machatenista' needs all the help he can get." But by training and disposition I let discretion prevail and simply said: "I await your fixes. You've got five

185

minutes.'' I could never think of Safire afterward as anything other than a self-inflated phony.

If Bill had a talent it was for stepping aside just as the lead started flying. He bailed out for the finale of Watergate but by the repeated use of phrases like "Korea-gate" and other "gates" he subsequently tried to make it appear as if there was some similarity between the run-of-the-mill Washington scandal and his former boss's efforts to suborn the Republic. It was a smarmy use of equivalence to get Nixon off the hook and tar everyone else with the same brush. One of his targets in this endeavor was Bert Lance, Jimmy Carter's director of the Office of Management and the Budget, who was forced to resign and stand trial after questions arose over his conduct as a bank executive in Georgia. Safire led the attack and won a Pulitzer for his column "Carter's Broken Lance." What people forget is that the charges didn't stick. Lance was subsequently acquitted and made a political comeback but the publicity embarrassed Carter and allowed Republican detractors to imply that the Democrats were no better than Nixon. That the Watergate scandal was of a different order of magnitude—and that Lance emerged guiltless—got lost in the hue and cry. While Safire was carrying water for his old boss he was not endearing himself to the National Desk that was being pressed by Rosenthal to chase Safire's leads, which some in the Washington Bureau considered oversold. The story goes that a redoubtable Timesman who had been ordered to follow Safire's tips confronted him and said: "I'd like to switch jobs with you for about two weeks. I'll write the fucking column and you try to prove it.''

Typically, Safire's last hurrah came with his incessant columns purporting to demonstrate that Saddam Hussein had tons of chemical and biological weapons and nuclear material all set to go off at a nod from the tyrant— a critical aspect of the propaganda campaign beating the drums for the Iraq War. This turned out to be as accurate as his original word columns but when time came to pay the piper, Safire had slithered away. It was Judy Miller — The Times reporter who'd swallowed some of the disinformation from the Iraqi émigrés for whom Bill was shilling—who took the fall.

After two years, I was once more growing restless and yet again an opportunity arose without my seeking it. I got a call from William Honan in Culture. For services rendered, Bill was promoted from Arts & Leisure chief to Culture Editor which meant that he was in charge of all three Entertainment sections— Weekend, Arts & Leisure and the Daily. Honan's main job was to run the daily pages, but also to supervise the other two and coordinate the entire operation. Bill looked the part of a Culture editor: tall, distinguished, mustached, convivial, well-spoken. He called me in congenial mode, speaking sotto voce, like a conspirator in opera buffa. Could he see me in the lunchroom right away? He had something of great import to discuss with me. I was cautious but I thought I'd hear him out. Bill's pitch was simple; it went something like this: "Jack, we've heard what a great job you're doing for Ed Klein and I'd like you to be my deputy." He told me I was the right man for Culture and the right man for the job. I told him I'd think about it. The Magazine was a known evil. The Culture Section had its own headaches and the last time I'd left the Sunday Section for the Daily, I'd regretted it.

When I failed to leap at Bill's offer, he seemed taken aback. These people are always surprised, even somewhat wounded, when anyone doesn't jump at the chance of working for them. Nevertheless, I was firm. I'd become suspect of all pitches made by The Times and wanted to chew this one over. Then came Bill's trump: "Arthur really wants you back down here, too." Translation: "All (or most) is forgiven. You're back in Gelb's good graces, sort of. But don't turn him down again." An offer I couldn't refuse. I told Bill I was flattered but that I was happy where I was (a lie) and I didn't want to let Ed down (a greater lie). It was a big decision and I wanted to sleep on it. Honan acceded to my request and we agreed to talk the next day. In truth, I'd already made up my mind. The Magazine was a cul-de-sac and I probably belonged back in the newsroom anyway. Gelb had given me the green light and Klein certainly couldn't oppose it.

The next day I met Honan back in the lunch room. We talked about the job, my responsibilities, about salary—I'd get a raise, etc., and, after a little back-and-forth, I agreed to take it. "Great," Bill said. "I'll tell Arthur and post it now." Having learned caution in these precincts, I insisted that Honan wait through the weekend to allow me to confide the news to a few friends and talk to Klein on Monday before any formal announcements. After some hesitation—Bill wanted the problem behind him—he acceded to my wish. Of course, I spoke to no one, but simply waited.

On Monday morning, I got a call from Honan, who seemed agitated. "Jack, you haven't talked to anyone have you?" I reminded him it was my idea to keep the lid on. "Well, it's a good thing," he said, "because Arthur thinks we need a woman on the team and he's just offered the job to someone from The Daily

News." Nice. "Bill," I responded, "if Arthur thought we needed a woman he would have known that wasn't me when he told you to offer me the job on Friday."

Bill: "Well that was my own idea."

Me: "You didn't check with Arthur?"

Bill: "Well, sort of." Translation: "You were so far down the pole that I didn't have to bother" or, more likely, Arthur said: "Line him up, and if we do better, we can always dump him."

Me: "Bill, do you usually go around offering people jobs that you can't make good on."

Bill: "I'm awfully sorry, Jack"

Me: "You know this would have been very embarrassing for you as well as compromising for me, if I'd followed your advice and let you announce it last week."

Bill: "Yes, I know." A little more pro forma contrition. Then: "Look, I've got to take a phone call. Let's talk some time." Click.

As it turned out, the woman from The Daily News didn't take the job with Bill—at least not that one. Marvin Siegel eventually wound up with it. My relations with Honan pretty much followed this pattern for the next six years. You'd think I would have learned a lesson but you'd think wrong.

In May 1982, shortly after my 44th birthday, I got a call from Bob Berkvist, the Arts & Leisure editor, who reported to Honan as Culture Editor and ultimately to Gelb as Culture Czar. Berkvist wanted me for his deputy. I had almost 10 years of experience on The Times and had served on five different desks, one of them as deputy and one as copy chief; all of them were rough going. I had the respect of the staff and knew my way around the building. I'd acquitted myself well enough on the Weekend Section during my previous stint in Culture and was generally considered someone who could pull his weight. It was the right job for me. I told Bob I'd take it. We shook hands. He indicated that the deal was all but done. I went over to Honan who congratulated me and told me he was glad to have me back on the team. The announcement was forthcoming. That was also on a Friday.

The following Monday, I was on my way to the subway at Broadway and 79th Street when whom should I run in to but Eva

Hoffman, a fellow West Sider, who was the Deputy Book Editor. She was looking strangely frazzled that morning and we agreed to share a cab to work. Once inside she turned to me and said: "Jack, they've just asked me to be the Deputy Arts & Leisure Editor. You worked down there. Do I want to do this?" I was absolutely deadpan and proceeded to question her as to how this came about. She said it was quite sudden. Honan had approached her and told her how much he'd heard about her and how her intellectual qualities were exactly what the department needed. When she protested to him that she knew nothing about working for Arts & Leisure, he assured her that it was her mind, her ideas and her fresh approach that he wanted. He asked her to meet Gelb who was very enthusiastic, told her it would be a great career move and hinted that it was an offer she couldn't refuse.

But Eva had heard enough horror stories about Honan and the Culture Desk to give her pause. It was clear that she had misgivings about the job and was seeking, if not a way out, at least some reassurance about its pitfalls. I played dumb—a professional role I'd grown adept at. I advised Eva that she might as well take the job because if she turned it down they'd eventually find something even more onerous for her to do. As for her being unschooled, they were interested in seeing her succeed so they'd look out for her, and she was certainly capable enough to catch on, so she'd do quite well. Also, Honan wasn't that bad, provided she was careful not to trust him. Eva was grateful for my counsel. I never let on. When we arrived at The Times I insisted on paying.

Later that morning, Honan called and asked me to come down to his office. I told him not to bother. I related that I'd just taken a cab to work with Eva and I recommended that she take the job he'd offered her. For once, Honan's WASP impassiveness came unglued. He began to stammer an excuse. "Don't bother, Bill," I told him. "It's only business." He insisted on floundering on a bit, like a fighter trying to find his feet after absorbing a blow to the head. This time, I was the one who hung up. Berkvist, at least, had the decency to drop me a note:

"Dear Jack, I really must apologize for the second-hand way you learned about Eva Hoffman's appointment to the deputy's post in A&L. I have been absolutely swamped down here and in any case had planned to hold off on any announcements pending a final go-ahead up front. I should have moved faster, knowing what a small shop this can be when something of significance is taking place. Please believe me when I say I was rooting for you, but that certain imperatives proved irresistible. ---Bob Berkvist.'' The imperatives were that they wanted a woman and I was expendable—backup should they not succeed. That I was more experienced, better qualified and probably Berkvist's choice, was irrelevant.

For me, their decision was a fateful one. Because eventually, I did return to Culture, although not in Arts & Leisure. Rather, I wound up working for the Daily. That September, in 1982, my mother died and Marvin Siegel showed up for the shivah at our West Side apartment. After a few brief preliminaries, Marvin observed that with my parents gone and my family growing it was time for new beginnings and, since the Culture backfield needed a strong No. 3, they wanted me. "Am I going to get any more surprises?'' I asked. "That was Honan, not me,'' Siegel said. That much at least was true. I had to go back down and see Honan, who was effusive about my return, as if nothing had happened. He seemed to have forgotten about our recent encounters and was lavish in my praise, promising me a promotion and the raise that went with it, which he'd arrange after I came aboard. And that is how I returned to the Culture Desk.

In the fall of 1982 the Culture Section of The New York Times was located on the third floor, separated from the News Department by a thick wall containing interior staircases, a ladies room, a coat closet and sundry other logistical pockets. This barrier opened at either end into aisles that connected the two realms. If someone were suspended from the ceiling—which occurred metaphorically from time to time—the observer would have looked down on a corridor of desks that extended in gray ranks toward the 44th Street windows and a view of Shubert Alley. This was the venue of the Culture Section at whose midpoint sat the backfield editors—the deputy Marvin Siegel, and myself, the assistant editor, or No. 3. The third man in this triumvirate was actually a pivotal assignment since, on a small desk, it meant doing virtually everything in terms of assigning and being the first reader in the editing process, thereby shaping the nature of the news. In sections with a larger backfield— the control center between the reporters and the copy desk —the workload was more widely distributed; in Culture it was concentrated. Facing us was the copy chief and his deputy. Strung out behind them were the rest of the copy editors, one on each side of the desk, in a line that ended at the office of James Greenfield, the assistant managing editor who was one of the inner circle that ruled the paper's roost. If there was a fire pole available in Greenfield's office, he could have shinnied down and landed just outside Sardi's.

Behind Siegel and myself, heading south toward the lobby, the elevators and 43d Street, were our secretaries, Carol Coburn and Ruth Strauss; beyond them a few seats for our general assignment reporters and, further along, the Weekend Section, from which Marvin and I had graduated, then run by Annette Grant. At the south terminus of the desk, the Culture Department made a sharp right turn and opened into the vast expanse of Arts & Leisure. The hinge of this angle was a stone slab on which A & L was laid out, so to speak, and where it's page proofs were examined on Monday nights when the section closed. This allowed Arthur Gelb, on his way to the elevators and a dinner party, to halt briefly in sufficient time to tear up the section so that they could start all over again at the 11th hour. Hugging the wall along the inner aisle of the Culture Desk were the critics' offices, cork-lined cubby holes, open to the desk, but still sufficiently sheltered to afford some privacy. Presiding over all this was the Culture Editor, William Honan, whose office was opposite Marvin's desk. Honan and Siegel took a dim view of one another. Marvin felt, with some cause, that he'd been pushed out of his Weekend duties and forced to serve under a man whom he considered to be a cultural lightweight. Bill felt that Siegel was insubordinate and out for his job. Both were correct.

I was caught in the middle of all this, literally and figuratively. My desk was on the outside aisle, just before the corner of the corridor, so that anyone heading back toward the copy desk or the management enclave, had to pass me. Consequently, people were always walking by, chatting me up about one thing or another as I tried to concentrate on my work while maintaining an affable facade. Gelb, who would often bring celebrities through to thrill them with a frisson of the City Room would stop by my desk and have me give them a lesson on how the new computers worked. On one occasion, he brought a photographer along and I got snapped giving a digital tutorial to Helen Hayes. Arthur was apparently under the impression that I was an adept, which shows you how little he knew about his staff's abilities. What saved me was that my high-flown students knew less than I did.

Directly to my right across the aisle was a vestibule that housed one of the low-speed printers, incessantly clucking and invariably running out of paper. Beyond the printer, this alcove led to a stairwell which, taken downstairs, led out the back toward 44th Street and Sardi's. Taken a flight up, the staircase afforded ready access to the composing room where I was to spend a considerable amount of time closing the section. Being the No. 3 on a three-man backfield meant that I was not only chief cook and bottle-washer but also head-waiter. Honan was the proprietor, greeting the guests and setting the tone; Siegel was the restaurant manager supervising the personnel and the food operation. The problem was that they were at loggerheads over the menu, which kept changing daily.

It didn't take long to realize that the desk was in disarray. The minimum requirements of organization, communication and lines of responsibility were absent. Instead the process was flaccid, a jerry-built operation whose modus vivendi was a free-for-all. About a month after I arrived, I wrote a polite note to Honan suggesting that we tighten our procedures. Among my recommendations: That we have a brief meeting in the morning to set the day's priorities; that specific editing responsibilities be given for all pieces except minor reviews; that each backfield editor should initial every story that he's handled so the copy desk knows who did what; that the Daily must take priority over long-term projects, and that we talk to each other, as well as to those with a need to know. None of these measures, which are ABC's of any desk, were carried out. I have saved a postcard of the Three Stooges affixed to the bulletin board during Christmas of that year. It shows Larry and Moe in frock coats and top hats, squeezing Curley's head in a vise. The salutation reads: "Season's Greetings to the Culture Staff, from Bill, Marvin and Jack." I'm the one in the middle.

There are further memorandums throughout 1983, the burden of which is that there is no delineation of function, no distinct chain of authority, no systematic apparatus for ordering and monitoring stories and virtually no time for preparation or planning. Each memo, on these and similar procedures, takes on a greater sense of urgency and each is ignored. In popular lore, newspaper desks are portrayed as frenzied. Actually, they are orderly, else they couldn't function. We were hardly that. It would take a new regime before any of these elemental procedures were introduced.

Meanwhile, they kept me hopping. I got in around 9:30 and made straight for the advertising department where I'd pick up the flimsies that indicate the ad layout for the day around which the editorial content would be built. This gave me a sense of not only how much space we had but where the copy could be slotted. The ads invariably changed —they'd sell till the last minute—but at least this offered a general heads-up on story placement. While we were allotted a pre-ordained amount of space every week, this could vary depending on the exigencies of the news section or our own needs for extra space. Ideally, this was a problem for the makeup editors. In theory, we were supposed to give them our story lineup, tell them where the major pieces were to go, and they were supposed to make things fit. But since our makeup editor was graphically challenged, I often had to keep an eye out on this. In the days before makeup became digitalized, everything was done in pencil with layouts drawn on paper in mid-afternoon and sent on to the composing room. It was not an exact science and the price was often paid on the composing-room floor with improvised last-minute trims.

After returning from the ad department, I'd go over our story list and see what was on schedule for the display page that led the section, and what our lead reviews were. Then I'd check the lesser pieces and the held-over reviews trying to salvage as many as possible by running them before they became stale and died. Today, with the internet, space is not a problem, and reviews that don't make it into print can still have a digital life on the web. In that earlier time there was no such fallback. This was still in the days when The Times was the only game in town and a young artist's career or a fresh theater voice could be hung up on a kill spike. I spent a good deal of time trying to find a home for these orphans before they perished. I'd then place a few quick calls to our writers to make sure that those who were down for the next day were aware of their deadlines (they sometimes feigned surprise) and their space requirements (they often asked for more). The ensuing negotiations were akin to buying a rug in the Levant.

I printed out a rough schedule for Marvin, Honan, the copy desk and the assorted need-to-know honchos. I saw this early story list as a fragile piñata that various top editors, writers, publicists and the fates took alternate turns beating so that by day's end it was no longer recognizable. What passed for a daily meeting was Marvin and I off-handedly batting things back and forth for a few minutes between 10 and 11 in the morning—there was still no formal staff meeting. Honan was rarely present for these sessions. He would waltz in at some point and sequester himself in his office where he busied himself with important affairs that transcended the mundane doings of the daily report. About mid-day he'd come out to check on us and usually tinker with the story list based on further bulletins from his bosses or occasionally a whim of his own which would set off Marvin and they'd repair to Bill's office to hash it out while I kept my head down. This was a doorless cubby-hole so the confrontations weren't very private. Marvin started out in fourth-gear pointing out why Bill's suggestions were unsuitable. Honan persisted in a dogged, self-assured way, as if he were a cop persuading a crazy man not to jump from a ledge. And indeed, Siegel was courting Nemesis.

Not that Marvin was heedless—he acquiesced to Gelb like everyone else—but he was convinced that Honan was so befuddled that he could badger Bill into submission and thereby become the de facto Culture editor, rectifying an administrative error. A mistake. Honan may not have been playing with a full deck but he held all the aces. Since he was carrying out the wishes of the higher-ups he could simply stand pat. Siegel often mocked Honan's obsequiousness, picturing him as an amoral servitor. What he really objected to was not Honan's penchant for following orders but his inability to execute them properly. What Marvin failed to appreciate was that while he responded better to Gelb, Honan anticipated his chief, a trait that gave him the edge.

The atmosphere varied from tense to volatile. Once the schedule was hashed out I spent the next hour or so trying to move early copy and push the critics to get in as many reviews as possible and to move on whatever new assignments or directives came playing out of the various pipes of our superiors. In what passed for my spare time I tried to gin up advances for the next few days—we were invariably scrambling for features. Although this was probably the most visible part of my job, it is not the one sealed in my memory. My most vivid impression was simply that of feeding the maws of the beast with its insatiable daily demands and assuming peripheral burdens, not the least of which was handling corrections. Writing them was a process worthy of kabuki theater with a back-and-forth that could last all day until the sages in the bullpen were satisfied that the exacting requirements of the art form had been met.

There was also a declension of notes from on high: top editors clamoring to know why this or that was missed or not properly executed. And there was an ascension of notes from down below: writers demanding to ascertain why their pieces were butchered, held or killed; publicists upset that their hobby-horse had been ignored and readers irate at just about anything. We tried to delay responding to these for as long as possible because to get caught up with them early would destroy any semblance of managing the day. But this would not protect us from outside phone calls. In those days, although Honan had his own secretary, Ruth Strauss,

194

screening his calls—her Brooklynese greeting of "CULTCHAH!" was a memorable if discordant greeting to a generation of callers— the rest of us were on our own. And since few outsiders called the copy desk, the bulk of their calls came to the backfield. We were then on orders to be unfailingly polite—easy enough for the order-givers who didn't have to answer the phones. On many an occasion I'd settle a bar bet on the order of whether it was Gale Sondergaard or Anna May Wong who played Bette Davis's nemesis in "The Letter."

Lunch was usually something gobbled down at my desk from Al's Deli across the street. By early afternoon our makeup editor materialized—often a few minutes late which added to the nervous-making quality of the day. Occasionally Marvin and—less occasionally, but devastatingly—Honan would weigh in and we'd have to start from scratch, doubtless why the layouts were ominously called scratches. This was often after we'd already assigned trims and headlines based on the original layout, which meant that they had to be redone. Yet another brick in the copy desk's edifice of resentment. Alas, our copy desk was not up to mundane labors much less demanding ones. The problem extended from the peripheries of the rim to the slot-man himself, a hold-over from Weekend who had gravitated into the Daily slot, an economy of motion in which he hardly had to move his chair.

The copy chief is a section's last line of defense against error. He or she should have intimate knowledge of the subject matter at hand. Copy chiefs have to be sensitive to the strengths and weaknesses of their staffs in terms of how much, what sort of, and who's copy each editor can best handle as the day wears on. They have to be cognizant of the demands that will be placed on the copy desk by the backfield. They must be ready to improvise at a moment's notice and have a reserve available for last-minute crises. A chief must wield an adroit pencil and be skillful at rewriting headlines so that they are catchy and appealing. And copy chiefs must earn the respect of their staff and the confidence of the top editors. Most critically, they must show grace under pressure as the section closes and things often threaten to unravel. Many a decent editor may lack this delicate balance of skills and temperament. One of them was our copy chief. The result was that Marvin and I had to intervene and read back on the major stories after they had left the copy desk, as well as rewrite the main headlines, a situation that would be unacceptable on any desk except the dysfunctional one that we operated. At the time, it was easier to live with a problem than to solve it.

The only way we survived was through the good offices of one seasoned professional and two exceptional young copy editors. The old pro was Ralph Behrens, a linchpin of the Foreign desk who chose just that moment to move over to Culture where his interests as a music lover lay. Ostensibly, Behrens worked for Weekend but during its many lulls we could borrow his services and we took full advantage of him. Ralph served as a swing man, deputy copy chief and occasional backfield. He could pitch in and do everything, and he often did. In a situation that could border on chaos Ralph was an anchor of stability and sanity.

The newcomers were Andrea Stevens, a gifted and tireless mainstay, and Tom Wallace, a talented editor out of Harvard who performed gracefully under fire. As the situation grew more strained, Wallace became the de facto slot man, a task he disliked but performed dutifully until Martha Wilson, who had the right temperament for the job, came to the rescue. Wallace later became Deputy Culture Editor and eventually went on to bigger and better things as editorial director of Conde Nast.

Fortunately, The Times had sufficient reserves of talent to throw into the breach so that even a poor desk was saved from the consequences of its weakness. The paper gave us just enough reinforcements to survive and fight another day. For many, Gelb's tenure epitomized the glory days of the Entertainment section, but as far as the Culture desk was concerned, it took many years after his departure before it functioned properly.

After the layouts were completed and photos chosen, the rest of the day was spent prodding reporters to relinquish their copy and hand-holding writers who were having the usual innumerable problems with the copy desk, their sources, various editors or life. The job was one-third therapist, one-third traffic cop and one-third editor—the last being perhaps the least important. I had to take the writers seriously as colleagues and fellow human beings while spurring them to the corporate goal of submitting their copy on time and subjecting themselves to the editing process. With a pro it was easy enough but there was always an abundance of others— prima donnas of both sexes, assorted neurotics, nervous wrecks— to compensate for the normal ones. It was in working with them that I earned my salary.

The crunch of the day came between 3 and 5 P.M. by which time everything had to be off the desk. We were invariably late and tried to make up the difference in the composing room which is where I finished my day. Prior to this, however, there was a race to process all the copy. The drill was first to move the reviews and decide which should run and which should hold. Then we dealt with the feature writers, stray columnists and anything that was coming in from Washington, national or occasionally the foreign bureaus although with the time difference the overseas copy was usually in by then. Marvin and I divided the stories and rammed them through.

By now, it was time for the early Page One meeting—in those days it was in mid-afternoon. The purpose of this was to bring all the sections together to get a sense of what was going to be on the front of the next day's paper. The news departments, of course, got pride of place which left only a little room for the other sections to compete for the remaining Page One real-estate. The early meetings were usually attended by the deputy backfield editors, each of whom would pitch their best stories to the managing editor who'd preside. Marvin generally represented us at these events, although if things were really dull he'd send me in his stead so that I'd have to spin gold out of that day's straw or account for why we failed to come up with anything worthy of Page One. I found that candor and brevity were best on such occasions. Generally, my presence itself was sufficient to indicate that there was nothing worthy emanating that day from our domain.

Honan himself liked to appear for the later meeting at 5:15. The matador taking his bows at five in the afternoon. Usually, most of our proposals were ignored, but occasionally one of our burnt offerings found favor in Abe's nostrils. This meant we had to re-dummy the section, often tearing up our main display page or, at the least, throwing out some reviews to account for the jump from Page One. It also meant a whole passel of questions from Rosenthal, Gelb and the bullpen, some of which the crazed reporter couldn't answer, resulting in desperate last-minute phone calls, railroaded copy and the probability of error the next day leading to a new round of corrections.

After the last piece cleared the desk, I got a coffee from the traveling lunch wagon manned by the incomparable Fernando, a white-uniformed lunchroom attendant who looked like a cross between Groucho Marx and Cantinflas. Nowhere in any chronicle of The New York Times have I read mention of Fernando. But for many years at 5 P.M. he was one of the most important figures in the building. There were no food runs at The Times, only Fernando. The Times cafeteria was located on the 11th floor and for people trying to meet deadlines, otherwise harried or simply too depressed to face the maddening elevators and the company lunchroom or too depleted to run to the deli that was then across the street, Fernando came to the rescue. You could sense the herd pawing in the sage as the hour approached. Some people casually positioned themselves near his resting station after Fernando emerged from the third-floor elevators with his tea trolley and his cry of "kah-fee." People who could make whole industries quake and P.R. men tremble scrambled to beat the rush caused by his emanation. The reward was unremarkable coffee, unexceptionable tuna fish sandwiches or unimaginative pastry. But it was nectar and ambrosia to people, some of whom four hours earlier were nonchalantly lunching at Orso's.

Refreshed through Fernando's good offices, I exited via the staircase to the right of my desk and trekked up one flight to the production department. Although a composing room is supposed to be chaotic, I found it to be a rest cure. First of all, there were virtually no editors around. Since the news pages didn't close till later, my peers had yet to arrive in force. The only connection with the third floor was the telephone and sometimes I'd just let it ring. Second, the pages lined up neatly in front of me seemed to wrest order from the chaos of the close. Third, I felt the working-class camaraderie and horseplay of the printers-turned-makeup men far more congenial than the neurotic hostility of some of my editorial colleagues. And, not least important, this was the era of cold-type, a transitional moment when hot type and lead were left behind but editors still worked with make-up men— not with lead on stone but with strips of laminated paper on paste-boards. You weren't looking down at a chase but straight ahead. And it was quiet. The clackety-clack of the old mechanical composing rooms had been replaced by silence.

There were four boards to a station and four or five stations to our department depending on how big the section was that day. On each board was affixed a layout with the corresponding page and next to the board was a hook with strips of type that fit onto the page. As new type came in, it was shot from one or two central bins, picked up by a printer and moved to the appropriate page. The make-up men then pasted up the page following the layout, with me having only to keep an eye on them. Most of these guys were pros so they needed little help. Where I fit in was catching glitches, finding lost copy and making last-minute switches, additions and trims which the printer did with a razor. The boss was Stanley whose good side you had to keep on for favors, but the ace was Artie who was a whiz on the boards and particularly valuable during a late close. There were many talented craftsmen among the printers whose skill I admired. One of the fastest shuffled around sporting his old blue apron—now redundant—like the defiant escutcheon of a defeated clan. We hardly exchanged a word except for nods, grunts and a pointed finger. One of the big advantages to cold type, besides not getting ink on your clothes, was that you could work four or five boards at the same time so that it made for a quicker close, particularly when there was a rush at the end.

The only down side of the composing room was that, sooner or later, I had to answer the phone and it was invariably some hare-brained request to fix this or get that which involved a scramble until the gods were appeased. The other negative was that since we were often late, Chick Butsikares, the editorial composing-room enforcer who looked like Mr. Clean, would come bearing down on me, berate Culture for holding up production and order me to close the page immediately. I'd respond that Rosenthal wouldn't like it if we came out with half the display page missing. Chick, whose bite was worse than his bark, threatened to have me court-martialed or whatever they do to insubordinate editors. Then he'd stalk off but somehow manage not to come back until after we'd finished. My colleagues upstairs were less generous. Marvin would grumble that Gelb was on his case. The reason that management knew about our pages running behind was that there was a big board over the bullpen lit by red electric bulbs. When a page closed, the bulb went off. Ostensibly, the only bulbs still permitted to be lit after 7 P.M. were Page One and the last open news pages. But if a bulb still flickered on an inside features page it was literally a red flag that would bring down the wrath of the bullpen on the offending section and the recalcitrant editor who was closing it. I would then get a call from Honan himself who demanded to know why I was lollygagging. It was pointless to tell him that the reason we were late was due to his procrastinating, since that only got him more upset. Invariably, we closed and the crisis passed.

Having finished in the composing room I would take a final swig of my now-cold coffee and trundle back downstairs where, together with Marvin—Honan had by then left or was leaving—we'd assign some advances as well as get up a ghost schedule for the next day. Finally, Siegel would leave but I'd stick around and, together with the late man, I'd read the proofs, which were by then arriving, for fixes to the second edition. If we'd made changes in trimming a review, I never left before apprising the critic of the editing so there were no surprises or hurt feelings the next morning. Usually, the critics went along—they just wanted to be told. By then it was 8 o'clock. Time to leave. I arrived home drained but not too tired to engage my 3-year-old son, Max, in a duel of light-sabers—I was Darth Vader—which reminded me why I was doing this. I continued these labors for another three years.

The reader may well wonder how the entire ship sailed so grandly while numbering such an odd crew. The fact is that many, if not most, of the editors and writers throughout the paper were superb and, by achieving critical mass, they set the tone. Every desk had a concentration of centurions who made sure that nothing too egregious got through. The Culture desk was particularly dysfunctional during my tenure but it had an outstanding group of critics and enough goalies so that the ineptitude of a few was checked and the whims of the mighty were filtered.

Although the reigning administrative motif of the Culture desk under Bill Honan was serendipity, the one venue where responsibility was assigned was television. I drew the short straw. Marvin's passions lay in the more venerable dramatic arts of theater and movies. As for Honan, he boasted that he rarely watched TV. Working for a Culture editor with an aversion to television had its compensations. It was one province in which Honan left me alone.

My idyll came to an end in December 1983. Arthur, doubtless prompted by the advertising department, decided that we were giving short shrift to television with only three columns a day; our readers needed more coverage. We were only thirty years behind the curve but, better late than never. Our television critics were the two Johns, O'Connor and Corry, the first of whom reviewed everything but favored the high-brow fare of WNET, the second who did both news commentary and, when needed, doubled as the reporter he had once been. Our news writers were led by the redoubtable Sally Bedell-Smith—daughter of General Eisenhower's Chief of Staff and a one-woman army of reportage who managed to vacuum-clean her beat despite having two children and a third on the way.

The burden of Gelb's ukase was that the Culture Section was to extend its television coverage by 20 percent which would result in having a quarter of the daily Culture report devoted to television. Moreover, the TV pages were to be anchored by a major review every day as well as a second one. We were making up for lost time.

Not surprisingly, the job eventually devolved to me. I provided Honan a detailed schedule with room for adjustment but one that had to be adhered to if we were to fill the space expeditiously. I stressed that this would only work if Gelb got the heads of other desks—Washington, Business, Foreign, etc.—to commit to filling a weekly amount of space. Needless to say, help never came. Instead, our staff was cut. Sally Bedell-Smith, our mainstay and workhorse, was due to begin maternity leave shortly after the new section was launched. I wrote repeatedly to Bill warning him of the disaster that loomed if we didn't replace her, stressing that whoever did so would need at least a week of working with Sally to insure some transition.

Nobody replaced Sally, which solved the transition problem. She left to have her baby and I was left with her No. 2, Peter Kerr, who himself departed not too long afterward to be replaced later on by a general-assignment reporter. Box score: In order to meet the amplified new TV section, the television staff had been reduced in quantity and quality.

Fortunately, by then I knew a lot of people in the building and I must have called in every chit I had. In the first three weeks of our expanded television coverage we had the requisite number of pieces from our TV staff, Hollywood, Washington, Business and the rest. The section was well received with a few innovations, some bright graphics (courtesy of the art director Roger Black) and a dexterous smattering of picture boxes. Bill was glad enough to take the bows and stay out of the way. And, by giving Gelb more than what he wanted, I was saved. Lo, one Monday, we ran not five but six columns of television fare to fill a hole on the daily pages. Arthur had a fit, declaring we were running too much TV news which was throwing the balance of our cultural coverage out of whack. Gelb demanded that we cut back to three columns a day. He was by now in full "Why do I have to think of everything myself" mode. It was not uncommon that Arthur would do a volte face and Honan would be caught short like Wiley Coyote skidding to a full stop as Road Runner zagged in the opposite direction.

Sid Caesar once did a television takeoff on the Arthurian legend of the Sword in the Stone. In the skit, to win lordship of Camelot, various knights try to pull Excalibur out of the stone, but in vain. After each contestant fails, when no one is looking, Caesar, playing the slop boy, marches over, removes the sword, polishes it off, inserts it back into the stone, and then resumes his menial tasks. It was a pretty good metaphor for my efforts. To Honan's credit, he did recognize them, albeit not directly, in a candid memo to Gelb on the TV mandate wondering "how shall we deal with the editorial requirements of handling 20 percent more copy every day?" and acknowledging: "Our backfield is stretched extremely thin. I don't believe that any other desks in the building process as much copy per editor as does Culture."

If the backfield was short-handed, it wasn't helped by Bill's management style which left something to be desired. He stumbled into unnecessary imbroglios with the most unlikely targets. Among them was Sam Freedman who was then one of our best young writers and most prolific reporters. Honan told Sam that he was writing too much for other sections like Arts & Leisure—which Bill happened to supervise—and not enough for the Daily. Presumably, Arthur must have mentioned something off the top of his head to Honan who interpreted it in the worst possible way. In fact, Freedman appeared in the daily Culture report more than any other staffer and, when accosted by Bill, he'd just had a story in the paper with two appearing the previous week and two on hold. Without checking the clips, Honan asked Sam to furnish a list of everything he'd done for the Daily in the past month. The list showed that he appeared with impressive regularity. Instead of acknowledging his error, Honan cited a week that Freedman hadn't appeared to which Sam responded it was because Bill was sitting on two of his pieces.

Of course, a fair-minded person could argue that Honan, while perhaps not the most accomplished staff manager, was a fecund source of story ideas. Here is one of them. From a memo he wrote to Gelb: "Arthur, 'Sophie's Choice' is the greatest movie I have ever seen. If ever there was a case to put a movie review on the front page of The New York Times, this is it! If Don Henahan [the chief music critic] discovered a new Caruso, we would put it on Page One. This movie is a new Caruso. Or better yet, a new Dante!" Doubtless the late Alan J. Pakula would have been flattered to have his movie compared to "The Divine Comedy," but even the accommodating Leonard Maltin in his Movie Guide allows that Meryl Streep's Oscar-winning performance can't carry "the deadeningly slow-moving adaptation of William Styron's book." Fortunately, Gelb consigned Bill's proposal to oblivion.

Yet, wherein does the responsibility lie for Bill's long tenure? In truth, the blame is not Honan's because who can be faulted for being ambitious? Rather, the onus lay with Gelb and Rosenthal, who knew better but preferred to have a straw man to a strong one. What counted was to install their creature at a critical chokepoint to carry out their mandates. Where this model could not obtain, in areas like the National or Business pages—in which Abe and Arthur's competence was limited and the competition keen—they allowed cooler heads to prevail. But in venues where their interests and appetites held sway, such as Culture or Metro, they insisted on malleable operatives and made short work of any independent spirits. Honan's longevity during their regime was a sign not of his competence but of his pliability.

All these high-jinks did not go unnoticed by the outside world. The dissident press, The Village Voice and Spy magazine among others, had a field day with the Culture section's faux pas. I should note that although Spy had many insiders contributing to its pages, I was not among them. I believed that, as deserving as my leaders were of exposure, as long as I was taking The Times's dollar it was unseemly to be telling tales out of school. I would save what I knew for a later reckoning. Moreover, while I appreciated Spy's mandate to dispense rough justice to The Times's sacred cows, I felt its broadsides were often over the top, rants that skewered their targets rather than illuminating them. While some of these people got their comeuppance they were not stage villains but rather flawed human beings in an imperfect system. So I've attempted to see them whole, their strengths along with their weaknesses.

If pressed, I'd allow that Bill was a good company man—in the best sense. He really believed in the institution, was proud of his role in it and, like a loyal officer, would dutifully execute any orders issued by the high command—the brisker, the better. He might have made a great master of ceremonies. I can picture Bill, jovial, clubbable, introducing the monthly speaker at the Century Association or toasting Wassail at the Harvard Club's Christmas shindig. He was indeed, an accomplished presenter at The Times's annual Book and Author lunches. But as a Culture editor, to my mind, he was miscast.

At this juncture I was, by default, responsible for the TV report as well as all my other duties on the Daily, not the least of which were obituaries. Riding herd on the advanced obits—often 2,000-words plus appreciations and reacts—was a job in itself but not having them was worse. In those days, each desk was responsible for providing the obituaries in its own field. I recruited the Times's two full-time obit writers, the redoubtable Albin Krebs, an acerbic Mississippian who had once been Newsweek's press editor, and Eric Pace, a consummate professional who had come in from the cold after serving as a foreign correspondent in the Middle East and Europe. I also cultivated a coterie of staffers whom I discovered were interested in the lives of various cultural figures whose age, health and status made them candidates for advance obits. For millions of readers, these final salutes were the last word on the lives of the great, near-great and not-so-great. For me, they were a minor aspect of a much bigger job, but one that required attention, and time—which I didn't have.

In my spare moments, along with assorted other backfield editors in the city room, I was asked to do evaluations of job applicants trying out on other desks. We were informed in writing by Marie Davitt, the Abbess who supervised the news clerks and assorted underlings, that Bill Stockton, who was in charge of personnel, had "become inundated with applications for reporters positions." So the usual suspects on various backfields were recruited to screen them regarding whether they merited an interview by Stockton or Jim Greenfield. I noticed that the inundated Stockton was arriving later and leaving earlier than I was. And I certainly didn't want to interfere with Greenfield's lunch plans. So I added screening job applicants to my other duties, which I did as homework since I couldn't do it on the job. The "quick assessment" to which Marie Davitt referred was belied by the two-page, single-spaced set of instructions that accompanied her note requiring us to rate the applicants from 1 to 5 and "comment extensively" on their qualifications.

I look back on all the names of the many applicants I evaluated—few made the cut—and wonder what happened to them? I did, however, give a strong endorsement to one young candidate who had just graduated from the Columbia School of Journalism that May: "Based on the work I've seen, I would say that he demonstrates genuine potential as a writer and reporter . . . I understand that he has limited experience but I would take a chance on him." Stockton, in his wisdom, ignored my recommendation. The writer turned out to be Ron Suskind who went on to win a Pulitzer Prize for the Wall Street Journal and to write some groundbreaking books including two major reports on the inner workings of the Bush administration. The Times finally did get around to having Suskind in its pages. In 2004, he wrote an important piece for The Magazine on the Bush presidency. Fortunately for him, 20 years earlier the Times didn't listen to me.

My life in those years on the Culture desk makes no sense unless one appreciates the gravitational force exerted then by the mainstream media, The Times, and its Culture section, which orbited one another in concentric circles of influence. We didn't realize it at the moment but it was a wrinkle in time that is unlikely to be replicated. During that three-year period, from the fall of '82 to the fall of '85, the press was still basking in the glow of Watergate and the Pentagon Papers, network news had a lock on people's attention, the big papers and TV stations generally commanded public respect and their authority was little challenged. Their humbling retreat under the onslaught of cable, the internet and the Right was more than a decade away. Newspaper competition in New York had virtually disappeared with both The Post and the News floundering before their rescue by trophy owners. The new consumer sections—Weekend, Living, Home— caught the wave of 80's hedonism, proving a bonanza for the paper. And Abe and Arthur could take direct credit for managing the turnabout in the paper's financial fortunes while enhancing its editorial prestige. The stock was up. The publisher was happy. The readers were faithful. Rosenthal and Gelb were on a roll. Whatever they touched—Science Times, SportsMonday— glistened.

Arthur Gelb may have been a gifted newspaperman but his real talent was as a producer. He developed a stock company of devoted players, a vaudeville of consumer sections, innumerable stunts and high-wire acts; he was a master at inspiring his cast, and he stage-managed the Culture department as the truly longest-running hit on Broadway. Like all supreme manipulators the mark Arthur conned best was himself. He'd convinced himself that he never crossed the line by simply extending it. When I got there it was, in the words of his favorite playwright, beyond the horizon.

Arthur in full-throttle was a sight to behold. To appreciate his legerdemain let us consider the death of Tennessee Williams, the Pulitzer Prize-winning author of two dozen plays, not least among them "A Streetcar Named Desire." The Times obituary, while paying due respect to the shade of a man considered by many to be the foremost American dramatist of his age, provides a somewhat reserved take. To the innocent observer, this would seem no more than a laudable effort by the editors to make sure that its reporting was not effusive in taking the measure of the man and that opinion was left to an appreciation that ran inside by a young Frank Rich. Except, in this case, the obit writer was Mel Gussow, himself a seasoned drama critic and an acknowledged theater authority whose valuation was well earned. But in the name of separating news from opinion, Arthur was keeping a tight rein on Gussow's ability to make any judgments.

Most of the obituary had been prepared in advance by Mel himself so there was little to do but dust off the piece, wrap in the cause of death, update it and refine the first three paragraphs which would serve as an epitaph and summing up, in effect, the paper's last word for many readers who wouldn't go beyond the front page where the lead would doubtless appear. But what looked at first to be a straightforward exercise became a laborious one with Gussow rewriting his lead several times before it passed muster with Gelb. The problem lay with Arthur's concern that Mel might suggest that Williams had been arguably America's greatest playwright rather than, let us say, Eugene O'Neill. And while one can make a case for O'Neill as our pre-eminent dramatist, the place to do so is not in an obituary of Williams.

While ostensibly playing the card of objectivity Gelb feared that Gussow might so enhance Williams that he'd come to overshadow O'Neill, the subject of a biography by Arthur and his wife Barbara who had invested a good part of their private lives in the O'Neill industry. Through his control of the paper's Culture pages Gelb had engendered his wife's— and his own —bona fides as O'Neill's definitive biographers. They had anointed themselves high priests of the O'Neill legacy. Keeping the flame was not just an intellectual passion but a lucrative pursuit since their book sales were fostered by elevating O'Neill's prominence among American playwrights. Ergo, Arthur's obsession with making sure that the tone of Mel's obituary would be respectful but subdued. To the untutored eye, the obit appears generous enough but that is only because the reader doesn't see what was altered or omitted. Gelb would insist that he had every right, as Culture czar and a veteran theater man, to supervise the obit of a leading playwright. On the other hand, discretion might require that in this instance, he recuse himself.

I worked directly with Mel on the obit and witnessed what transpired. On three occasions Gussow offered honest leads based on his own assessment, putting Williams at the pinnacle of American playwrights, a claim that Mel had the critical authority to express. And on each occasion Arthur hurried over with undue interest, and bounced the leads, expressing concern that we were giving Williams more than his due. Translation: O'Neill's glory could be dimmed if posterity might infer that Williams's star shone as brightly. This was all carried out through dissimulation — dissatisfaction with language, concern about fairness, debate over special pleading. While struggling with his fourth try, Mel concocted a lead that began: "Tennessee Williams, who was simply not as good as Eugene O'Neill, immortalized by Arthur and Barbara Gelb . . . " Eventually, Arthur wore Mel down—as he did with everyone—and we came up with a lead that acceded to the Word According to Gelb.

Arthur would argue that he was only making it better, which just happened to dovetail with his own personal agenda. To Mel's credit, he resisted Arthur's ultimate blandishment which Gelb had tried to inject from the outset—that O'Neill be acknowledged within the opening three paragraphs as first among equals. So Arthur came up with a solution. In the third paragraph of the story, a reefer (a bracketed line referring to an accompanying piece inside the paper) reads as follows: ["Tennessee Williams was the most important American playwright after Eugene O'Neill. An appreciation by Frank Rich, P. 10"] In it's sheer brazen self-interest, this is pure Arthur. Mel didn't have to sacrifice his integrity and Gelb got his way. This was Arthur's idea of being magnanimous.

The Williams obit was only the tip of the iceberg in Arthur's flogging of the O'Neill doctrine. In 1974, Louis B. Sheaffer won the Pulitzer Prize for "O'Neill: Son and Artist,'' the second half of his magisterial two-volume biography of Eugene O'Neill, which took him 16 years to complete and was praised as "commanding" by Diana Trilling in a front-page review in the Times Book Section the previous November. The earlier volume, "O'Neill: Son and Playwright'' was lauded by no less than the critic Harold Clurman who wrote in a 1968 Sunday book review that Sheaffer "appears to have unearthed every document, interviewed every relative, friend and acquaintance, read every letter ... by or concerning his subject.'' Clurman concluded that Sheaffer's book "should take its place in every library of those seriously interested in American theater, literature and consciousness.'' Trilling's laudatory review ran just prior to Rosenthal and Gelb's takeover of the Sunday Section, and with it the Book Review.

A check of the Times clips subsequent to Arthur's ascendancy as Culture czar shows the faucets abruptly turned off in terms of

Sheaffer. His book is mentioned on the occasion of its winning the Pulitzer for Biography in which it is lumped in among the winners, a list that The Times was virtually required to publish. It gets seven lines buried in the roundup. But wait. After I left the paper The Times covered a controversy over demolishing a New London boarding house where O'Neill had lived, in which it quoted Shaeffer as an authority on the playwright, citing his Pulitzer-winning biography. Surely a gracious nod by Gelb, who was then managing editor, which should deflate any charge of favoritism. Yes? Not quite. It turns out that Arthur had got wind of a book called "Fit to Print," by Joseph Goulden, a critical look at the Rosenthal-Gelb years which cited Arthur's treatment of his rival biographer. As Shaeffer wryly observed in a letter to me, quoting him prominently in The Times served to pre-empt any talk that the newspaper had sought to eclipse him.

One might consider strange indeed the virtual disappearance from the Paper of Record of a Pulitzer Prize-winning man of letters, particularly one who received acclaim for a subject as dear to The Times's heart as Eugene O'Neill. On the other hand, a check of The Times clips during Arthur's tenure showed 13 hits for the Gelbs' book, usually referred to as "the definitive" biography of Eugene O'Neill. Presumably, if a work can't be the Pulitzer Prize-winning biography, "definitive" is the next best thing. Of course, one might wonder, why "definitive"? The Gelbs were relentless at insinuating themselves into the O'Neill ascendancy. Whenever an event occurred celebrating the playwright—dutifully mentioned in The Times after a phone call from Arthur to one of his minions— they were always on the podium with an invariable line in the paper noting that among those attending were Arthur and Barbara Gelb, authors of the definitive biography of Eugene O'Neill. When I was book editor of New York Newsday, I had Louis Sheaffer do an incisive review of a collection of O'Neill's letters. I made sure in the italics that he was identified as having won the Pulitzer Prize for his two-volume biography of the playwright.

Arthur's reach extended everywhere. One of his favorite feeding grounds was the publishing column where he drove the beat writer, Ed McDowell, to distraction with the various contracts for his friends. The most dangerous time was between 2:30 and 3 when he came back from lunch at Orso's, the Four Seasons, Sardi's or some other celebrity restaurant with what he called "an exclusive." Typical of this phenomenon was one post-lunch foray when he returned with his friend Phyllis Grann in his wake. Grann was the savvy and successful editor-in-chief and publisher of G.P. Putnam & Sons. She was a smart executive who had an impressive batting average in getting a high percentage of her mid-cult authors on to the Times Best Seller List. Gelb was instrumental in keeping the public apprised of Putnam's progress. Not that we didn't attend to other friends in the publishing industry as well, but some publishers were better attended than others.

We learn in bulletins from McDowell in March of 1983 that G.P. Putnam had four books simultaneously on the Times hard-cover best-seller list—fair enough. Then, two weeks later, we are told in a lead item from Ed that G.P. Putnam has signed Donald Barthelme to a three-book contract, this in keeping with the house going upscale and onward. But in the same breath, McDowell also slips in that Putnam has contracted to do a book by none other than Arthur's buddy and Apthorp neighbor Joseph Heller, along with his adherent Speed Vogel, chronicling Heller's recovery from Guillain-Barre Syndrome. Despite Arthur's enhancement of Heller's career, as noted earlier, the writer's ship had been listing. And here was Putnam offering a convenient lifeline after Knopf and Simon & Shuster had parted company with Heller. And there was The Times, promoting Putnam's agenda. If Heller's book never sold a copy, the publicity Putnam gained in the overall picture was priceless. To be sure, Phyllis Grann's behavior was perfectly appropriate. Why shouldn't she publish a best-selling author who'd been through a crisis. Amid the hoopla, it's very hard to hear the sound of one hand washing the other.

Moderation not being Arthur's strong suit, this phenomenon sometimes got out of hand. On the afternoon that Gelb sailed back from lunch with Grann in tow, he bore down on me like the proverbial dreadnaught. Sure enough, Arthur announced he had an important item that we had to get into the next day's paper. His breathless news was that the somewhat embarrassed Phyllis Grann, who was standing next to him, had added "president" to her titles of "publisher" and "editor-in-chief." It was clear that Arthur was doing this as much to impress Grann as to intimidate me. I wasn't cowed. I pointed out that Ed McDowell's publishing column was already done, that he'd have to cut to get this item in and, with all due respect, the news wasn't sufficiently earth-shattering to warrant a rewrite. I could see Arthur's face darken. I was not only defying him but doing so in front of company, the very outsider that he wanted to flatter. Gelb insisted that this was significant news in the publishing industry and we had to get it first before word got out. I held my ground, pointing out that we had a lock on this and it could wait a day. Grann, by now aware of the ruckus that was being stirred on her behalf, tentatively interjected that she could hold the release for a day but Arthur, upset that he was being thwarted, avowed that this was breaking news. I decided to tick him off a notch more by asking if this was an order. He growled that it was and stalked off with a chagrined Grann behind him.

I ran down McDowell, an ex-Marine who had learned to follow Arthur's commands, and gave him the lay of the land. Basically a decent sort, McDowell rolled his eyeballs and asked if there was any way we could get a reprieve. He had just finished a complicated item, was on to something else and, having to deal with Grann and trim his piece to accommodate Gelb, was something he didn't relish. But I told Ed the fix was in and he acquiesced. He proceeded to "interview" Phyllis in a cubicle, and inserted the brief into his column, which he cut to make the Grann announcement fit. In condensing his main item in a rush before deadline, Ed made a mistake. The next day, we had to run a correction. I got a call from Arthur demanding to know how the error had happened and why Ed couldn't keep such gaffes out of his copy.

A footnote. Shortly after Abe Rosenthal was pushed out of his job as Executive Editor he landed a position as editor-at-large at a prominent publishing company. The post, in which he would acquire and edit books on foreign affairs, would at the least offer Abe a consoling piece of change. The publishing house was G.P. Putnam whose chief executive officer, Phyllis Grann, took the occasion to note what a great honor it was to welcome Rosenthal aboard.

Just a few years ago, after Gelb and I retired, I ran into him at the gates of Columbia University where he was emerging with—guess who?—Phyllis Grann. They were on the Pulitzer Committee— The Times won three that year—and Arthur was only too glad to see me. Now my buddy, he introduced me to Phyllis. Her son had married the daughter of my recent Culture editor, the estimable John Darnton. I made small talk about the marriage and then observed that Arthur had introduced me to her more than 30 years ago. She, of course, had no recollection of our meeting. Nor did Arthur.

I wrote a headline for a local Steuben Day festival in New Jersey that went: "Things Go From Brat to Wurst,'' and it was definitely the way things were headed. Marvin and Honan were continually at each other's throats and their acrimonious relations infected the department. It wasn't so much that people chose sides as that they ducked for cover like movie extras in a bar when the shooting starts. Honan, for his part, didn't so much respond to Marvin as wrap himself in a cloak of impassive scorn. This drove Marvin to distraction and he took it out on some of the rest of the staff, particularly its lower echelons.

One of his handiest targets was Ed Rothstein, then a young classical-music critic. A card-carrying intellectual, Ed had a habit of expounding on the performance he was reviewing with apercus, allusions and occasional opinions as to what the artist should have been playing. The result was that a 350-word review of a small concert at Judson Hall often turned into a 700-word appreciation of the composer, the musician, the provenance of the piece and its historical context. "I just want a review, Rothstein, not a dissertation," Marvin would bark, throwing the piece, literally, back at the miscreant. Ed, unadvisedly, would try to explain to Marvin why he couldn't do justice to the performance in any less space. This would only provoke Marvin into apoplexy. That's how I became Rothstein's editor. I had a calming effect on Ed and, since I was the only thing between him and Siegel, he acquiesced to my pencil. Not that Marvin wasn't right in substance, but his style was wanting. He felt Rothstein had been imposed on us and he made his frustration known. It was noticed.

Siegel seemed to be unaware or unconcerned that Honan was quietly keeping a log on him and submitting it to Gelb at regular intervals. Marvin was supposed to underpin Bill, not undermine him. There was an inevitable blow-up, or two, or three; the particulars didn't matter. The pair were incompatible; Arthur grew tired of playing referee and listening to their mutual recriminations. He opted for Honan. Marvin was given time off to think things over and wound up in the Book section where he would become a valued deputy to Rebecca Sinkler.

Once the smoke had cleared, you could hear the audible sigh of relief—except from me. At first, I was relieved because the tension had lifted and Marvin's upsets had ceased. Bill left me pretty much to myself which I counted as a blessing. Until I realized that he was leaving me completely to myself. I looked around and saw that I was alone on the tundra. Marvin may have been irritable at times, but he pulled his weight. Also, he could run interference with Arthur who now descended on me when Bill wasn't around. As luck would have it, that spring and summer saw a spate of major stories, any one of which would have required an editor's exclusive attention to pay them full justice. On my watch, it didn't happen. Bill, of course, relished marching in and taking command of the big stories, but this only made things worse and I'd often have to work around him. There were lots of things breaking at the time but the two big stories that season both involved media personalities.

In March 1985, Sy Newhouse acquired the New Yorker for his Conde Nast empire heralding the demise of its venerable editor, the sainted William Shawn, and causing much hand-wringing among the chattering classes. And in July, another magazine mogul, the real-estate wheeler-dealer Mort Zuckerman, who owned the Atlantic Monthly and U.S. News & World Report, gobbled up the New York Coliseum at Columbus Circle for his Boston Properties. Jane Perlez wrote a lengthy profile for the Metro Section of Zuckerman, a realtor who was on the make to become a player in the celebrity circuit of New York, Washington and Boston. If you composed a to-do list of what the out-of-town arriviste must do to climb the power-player social ladder, Zuckerman— a naturalized Canadian who made his first windfall in Boston with shrewd real-estate dealings—checked off every one.

Zuckerman had bought a de rigueur house in the Hamptons and was a regular at the media softball game in Sag Harbor which was a club for the high-flying journalist types who summered there. And he was squiring around the feminist icon and Ms. editor Gloria Steinem. Not bad for a somewhat new boy in town. Acquiring the Coliseum—for a nifty $455.1 million—made Zuckerman a natural story and Jane Perlez was assigned to do the piece; in essence to explain who this guy was, where he came from, what he wanted and how he operated.

Jane was a superb reporter whose story was a thorough, warts-and-all portrait of a talented, restless, ambitious man with acquisitive appetites, a desire to be a big fish in a big pond, and in a hurry to get there. The piece went through the usual editing process and no one seemed to have a problem with it. Except the subject. Apparently, what Zuckerman had been expecting was a wet kiss. He was outraged and sought satisfaction. And he got it. Rosenthal bought his story and weighed in on Perlez. Retribution followed swiftly in terms of an Editor's Note that could have been written by Zuckerman himself. The Editor's Note is a major nostra culpa that goes well beyond a Correction and is used only when the paper feels it has not simply erred but broken its own rules.

The main rap on Jane Perlez in her Zuckerman piece was that it "violated The Times's standards" by using "pejorative phrases and anonymous quotes" that created an unbalanced portrait. In retrospect, a close reading of the Editor's Note compared with what Perlez actually wrote shows that it was 'lawyered,'' the sentences abridged, the quotes elided, the words taken out of context so that it looked like the subject of the profile had a genuine grievance and The Times deserved to be contrite. In fact, while the Editor's Note huffs and puffs about blind quotes, Perlez interviewed half-a-dozen people by name including Zuckerman himself. But there is one media friend who is not named in all of this: A.M. Rosenthal, a detail that The Times failed to take cognizance of, nor that Rosenthal and Zuckerman had dined together just prior to the paper's apology, as Fortune magazine subsequently reported.

Let's see how these standards were applied elsewhere at the time. The other big story of the season, as mentioned earlier, was the Conde Nast takeover of the New Yorker earlier that spring. We sent Doug McGill out to cover the story. Here's what he wrote:

"William Shawn, the editor of The New Yorker for 32 years, told his staff members yesterday that 'we were not asked for our approval and we did not give our approval.' . . . The tone of regret in his statement was widely shared by many in the corridor and underscored a general belief that the sale was a betrayal of the 77-year-old Mr. Shawn, a legendary figure in the literary world, by the magazine's board of directors."

Just who was in the corridor widely sharing these feelings we don't learn. But the message that the board members are a bunch of traitors is loud and clear.

McGill: "In a word, the magazine has been sold right out from under us,'' said one New Yorker writer." The writer is unnamed. McGill goes on: "But on 43d Street, Mr. Newhouse's assurances did not alleviate worries among the editorial staff." What worries? Which staff? Unknown. Unnamed. And on: "Others...expressed skepticism or worry about the continued editorial independence of the magazine." What others? The New Yorker, of course, went on to thrive and, under David Remnick, it has achieved an acme of readability, authority and independence.

This was only a few months before the Zuckerman story. McGill's piece went through unscathed and no one said boo. Shortly before Jane Perlez's article ran, The Times did a story on another media figure in the Newhouse empire, Robert Bernstein, the chairman of Random House. The reporter was our publishing writer, Ed McDowell. Like the Zuckerman piece, it was a profile, but in this instance, of a luminary who presided over the most prestigious publishing house in America, albeit one that may have been resting on its laurels. Here are excerpts from McDowell's story: "There has been widespread industry perception, based in part on the management style set by the low-key and gentlemanly Mr. Bernstein, that Random House has become complacent and smug, that it lost its competitive edge." Pejorative statement. No attribution.

More. "There is also a perception that certain Random House editors are, in the words of one industry critic, 'pseudo-intellectual snobs' who shun overtly commercial books and feel superior to many authors and agents who come calling." Critic unnamed.

More. "Mr. Bernstein's laid-back management style has led some rival publishers to suggest that he is largely a figurehead manager." Rival publishers unnamed.

What occurred here was a professional hit by unattributed sources. Robert Bernstein was characterized as a wimp who presides over a cluster of eggheads who eschew commercial— i.e. moneymaking—books; rather than a hands-on leader, he is little more than a figurehead with a laissez-faire attitude. No wonder his house has become complacent and lost its edge. Imagine how Bernstein felt knowing that his new boss, Sy Newhouse, who was very interested in the bottom-line, was going to read this.

The accusations here—all un-sourced—are far more pejorative, and damning, than anything that appeared in the Perlez piece. Moreover, this was doubtless carefully read by our higher-ups, as were all the major publishing stories. No one objected. The vaunted Times standards did not seem to be in play when it came to Bob Bernstein or, for that matter, the New Yorker. These are only two out of numerous examples of un-sourced quotes that were rife in the pages of The Times. The editors knew about them. They turned a blind eye or occasionally rapped a knuckle. It was when a friend's ox was gored that they were sure to take umbrage. By all means Perlez should not have used un-sourced quotes without prior consent. Yet the burden of Rosenthal's ire was prompted not by the lack of sourcing but an affront to the subject who sustained it. His misplaced show of rectitude almost marred the career of a fine reporter to salve the ego of a privileged crony. Jane Perlez, to her credit, managed to weather this and go on to have a glorious career as a foreign correspondent doing a magnificent job covering the Afghan war and the unraveling of Pakistan which won her a Pulitzer.

One area where Rosenthal literally kept the paper straight was in the province of gays. He actively sought to cleanse the city room of the taint of homosexuality. It is a matter of conjecture whether this was because he thought gays could be held up to blackmail and thereby compromise their integrity or that exposure would leave The Times vulnerable to conservative critics or because of a visceral aversion to homosexuals, or a combination of all three. Consequently, Rosenthal was obsessed with keeping the city room free of gays. A telling instance is his treatment of Jeff Schmalz who rose from clerk to metropolitan reporter. When Rosenthal learned of Schmalz's sexual preference, he pressed to have him fired. Other editors, who respected Jeff's talents and were horrified by Abe's strictures, fought a rear-guard action, distracting Rosenthal and putting him off with various excuses every time he inquired why Schmalz had not yet been sent packing. Eventually, through this game of newsroom Scheherazade, Jeff outlasted Rosenthal who was succeeded by Max Frankel and a far more enlightened attitude at The Times.

A short while thereafter, as the cultural climate changed, Jeff contracted AIDS and wrote a moving piece in The Times magazine about his struggle with the disease. The article was widely praised and Schmalz accepted accolades with typical modesty, but one call surprised him. It came from Rosenthal. Abe told Jeff that he had always been one of his biggest fans and insisted that they have lunch at his table at the Four Seasons. Jeff was trotted out center-stage with Abe publicly hugging him and telling everyone within earshot how he had always fought for gay rights at The Times. Jeff, a mild, easy-going and forgiving soul, accepted it all with rueful good humor. I have no doubt that Rosenthal sincerely believed everything he said.

In the summer of 1985 and well into the fall, everything seemed to break at once but in terms of relief nothing was happening. Honan, in a burst of magnanimity, had allowed a substantial segment of the staff to take simultaneous summer vacations so that our forces were further depleted at the very

215

moment that we needed all hands aboard. The only staffers seemingly around were the brass, full of ambitious and ever-changing ideas about how to handle the stories that were inundating us. Honan, for his part, seemed strangely even-keeled in these waters, which might have been assuring until you realized that he was not so much calm as becalmed. When I apprised Bill of our situation he reassured me that we'd muddle through.

Late that summer Honan moved his family from their East Side digs to a new home in West Redding, Conn. Like many such moves, this one was burdened with a concurrence of travails that required Bill's presence on premises. Instead of setting aside a week to deal with the movers, he chose to handle the problem by taking the mornings off, and part of the afternoons. Presumably, he felt he couldn't give himself a holiday after dispensing with Marvin and releasing the staff. Bill would stroll into the office sometime between 1 and 2 whereupon I'd give him a quick reprise of the day's schedule. Then, he'd go huddle with Arthur and, if he deemed it worthy, he'd attend the preliminary Page 1 meeting; if not, he'd send me in his stead. He was full of cockamamie ideas that I couldn't always talk him out of so he'd toss me to the early Page 1 conference as his lightning rod. If his proposal was shot down—and me along with it—he'd withdraw it, and wait for further marching orders from Gelb before materializing at the 5 o'clock conference. I dreaded these events because I had the choice of either trying to explain a proposal that couldn't be defended or confess that the idea had been foisted on me by my boss. Since decorum prevented the latter option, I had no other recourse but the first one, which meant that after a few questions from the top editors, I was impaled on the illogic of Bill's conceit.

There were afternoons when Honan didn't show up till even later in the day, which didn't prevent him from requiring a rundown by phone and offering me his suggestions on what I might raise at the early meeting. Whether to show that he wasn't malingering or because he simply enjoyed taking me into his confidence Bill would apprise me of the difficulty he was enduring supervising his move to Connecticut. He continued to fight it out with the movers for what seemed like the rest of the summer. I was no happier than Bill when his last piece of furniture was delivered. The only virtue of this was that in Honan's absence I occasionally prevailed on Gelb for reinforcements. The ploy was to impress on him that something important was up and it would be to his credit if he got "the best people" on it. Whereupon he'd dragoon a writer from another desk, which is how I was able to survive.

Except for the tendency of celebrities to die on late Thursday nights without an advance obit, Fridays allowed for the one breather in the week. The downside was that we were putting out three days worth of Culture report, broken into pieces: Saturday's section—which then included a book review, the Sunday pages, and setting things up for Monday. This involved making sure that the features were completed, the advances assigned, held-over reviews slotted and new ones prioritized; also leaving pictures, caption material and schedules, as well as issuing notes warning of any potential difficulties. By the time I got home Friday night I was drained, although my children managed to revive me. The copy chief usually handled things on Sunday but, for a few weeks that summer when he was out, I worked that shift as well. This had one consolation. I knew where everything was on Sunday because I'd left it there Friday.

In the days before the digital wonders of the internet, photos were left in folders and copy came in through a variety of different modes. If a folder was misplaced you could waste an inordinate amount of time that you didn't have looking for it, or for the individual who'd misplaced it. This meant coming in early, just to cover yourself. The office was a moonscape on Sundays. The debris of the weekend spilled over on the desks. If there was no one to bother you, neither was there anyone to help. I would occasionally wander over to Metro or National to commiserate with whoever was my equivalent on the other desks. Eventually, a skeleton crew would scuttle in to Culture. Even with people around, Sundays were quiet; everyone performed as if underwater.

There were some pluses to all this as well. One of them was the opportunity to cultivate relationships with some of the outriders among the writers. I developed friendships with the photography critics, the amiable southerner Gene Thornton and the super-hip Andy Grundberg, both of whom were to write for me at Newsday. I enjoyed the company of John Wilson, the long-time jazz critic who filed dutifully for years without benefit of benefits. I also got to know the pop critic Bob Palmer, a pale wraith who was an authority on the Blues. He later went back home to Memphis where he and the blues hailed from, eventually migrating to the University of Mississippi at Oxford where he taught till his death.

Another young writer whom I inherited was the art critic Michael Brenson, brought over from Paris by our chief art critic John Russell who shepherded his career here. Unfortunately, Russell could not insulate his protégé from life in a rough neighborhood.

217

Brenson was subject to a boot camp in which he was blooded with reporting tasks. Michael, who was burdened with a fatal sense of honor, felt duty-bound to prove he could operate in an alien venue. Although he did some fine work, down the road, he'd run afoul of a section editor whereupon the supremely politic John Russell adroitly detached himself from his erstwhile protégé, leaving Brenson little choice but to bow out. Michael announced his resignation to a group of well-to-do admirers over lunch. As he later recalled, there was a notable silence followed by someone asking to pass the coffee. His tenure as gatekeeper was over, as was his utility in those precincts. But there is life after The Times and Brenson went on to have an honorable career as a teacher, biographer and critic.

At about this time, Honan had to take a few days off and, as a temporary gambit, Arthur brought in Bill's right-hand man, the Arts & Leisure editor Bob Berkvist, to replace him. Ostensibly, Berkvist was supposed to serve in Honan's spot as the ranking Culture editor after Bill. Actually, he was put there to act as a ready conduit for Arthur's orders; also, to make sure I didn't do anything to subvert them. Warm and fuzzy was not Berkvist's strong suit but he was a capable editor. Observing what was no more than a typical day on the desk was an eye-opener for the normally phlegmatic Berkvist . Arts & Leisure, after all, came out once a week; the Daily came out once a day, actually more, with several editions. In a later morphology, Berkvist would gravitate to the very job I had—although by then there were three editors aboard, a number that would only grow through the years. Over time, Bob became a venerable figure in the Culture backfield. When he retired they erected a green street sign on the wall opposite his desk labeled Berkvist Blvd.

If I made Gelb uncomfortable it was mutual. Whenever he came flailing down the aisle toward me waving a note from some client, I went on Red Alert. Arthur picked up on this and didn't like it. When he sought to have a contract filled for one of his kith or kin, he expected his minions to snap to attention and say: "Right you are, chief." I wouldn't, or couldn't, do this. Even when I executed without protest Gelb picked up on the reservations I had for his projects. He knew deep down I was judging him and found it unsettling. His solution was to use me but always put a buffer between us for carrying out his fiats. This didn't always work and occasionally our gears locked.

By then, since I was de facto running the desk I thought at least I should get the newspaper to acknowledge my efforts with the appropriate title and the raise that went with it. I said so to Bill. He praised me lavishly and told me what an outstanding job he thought I was doing. I told him that this wasn't going to make me any richer. He said he'd work on it. I told him that wasn't good enough. I was coming through for him in the here and now and I expected him to do as much for me. Honan said he'd do his best but I'd have to let him handle it. I told him I'd give him a little time but I expected a progress report. Not that I had any leverage except leaving the paper, which both he and I knew was unlikely.

That summer, I spoke with Norman Pearlstein of the Wall Street Journal about a job there. I had lunch at the Café des Artistes with one of his editors but nothing came of it. The fact is, in those days The Times was the only game in town and I couldn't do much more than inflict guilt. Nevertheless, I kept pressing Honan to name me as his deputy, which, in effect, I was. He kept putting me off, but always in his friendly, avuncular style. One night, later that summer, after a particularly grueling day, he slipped into an air of camaraderie and I reminded him that things could not go on this way. I couldn't continue being responsible for the desk without having the nominal authority to do so. Bill told me he understood and he was going to broach the matter with Arthur and support my cause. I observed that the last time he assured me of his support, I got blind-sided. Bill gave me one of his little chuckles. "I doubt lightning is going to strike twice," he laughed. He told me he understood how hard I'd been laboring and suggested that I take off Friday. He'd fill in for me.

The following Monday, as was my habit, I got into the office early, but Honan arrived not too much after me, unusually ahead of time for him. I could see he was flustered. "Jack, I've got to talk to you," he said, calling me into his office. I walked into his cubicle and he said: "Jack,"—whenever they call you by your first name you know you're about to get screwed—"I'm afraid I don't have good news." The not-good-news was that they had still deferred on a decision but in the interim they were going to bring my old friend Eva Hoffman over from Arts & Leisure where she was deputy to serve as Bill's deputy on the Culture desk. And since he was going on a much-needed vacation in a little while, she would start immediately and I would report to her. Makes sense, n'est-ce pas? Who could object to having the Deputy Arts & Leisure editor fill in as the Deputy Culture editor? On paper, it was perfectly appropriate. Except for the minor fact that Eva hadn't spent an hour on the Daily. When I pointed this out to Honan, he said, "Well, you'll keep an eye on Eva. I know I can count on you to help her over the rough spots." Of course, Eva was being brought in to keep an eye on me, one of the several "minders" that Gelb recruited to make sure that I'd never have effective control of the desk.

Shortly thereupon, Eva showed up, completely lost as to how the operation of a daily desk should function. She was intelligent enough to realize that she was in over her head. I helped her as best I could. None of this was her doing. I kept my distance from Honan, speaking to him only when necessary. Bill brought Eva into his cubicle for long confabs. Arthur tried to avoid going by my desk. Virtually everyone on the staff knew what was up. By now, they'd beefed up the Culture Desk with the first-rate Martha Wilson becoming copy chief, and Tom Wallace moving up to the Culture backfield. I have never seen the unflappable Wallace ruffled—that is, except when the name Arthur Gelb is mentioned. Tom's experience under Honan and Gelb was so awful that one day he simply left without the prospect of another job. In retrospect, things worked out infinitely better for Wallace who, as mentioned, would rise to prominence at Conde Nast. As for myself, I asked out and they found me a job around the corner working for Bob Berkvist in Arts & Leisure. For Honan, it must have been a relief. For me it was a vacation.

I spent the next three years at Arts & Leisure—the easiest gig I ever had at The Times. The first thing you have to understand about the department is that in those days it was around the corner from the Daily Culture section so that we were hidden in plain sight. Bob Berkvist, my erstwhile almost chief, was responsible for A&L. As solid as he was stolid, Berkvist was the prototype of a good company man—a compliment, since these are the people who actually make the place run. He served as Honan's conduit just as Bill channeled Gelb, which allowed Bob a certain initiative with the proviso that he fulfilled his marching orders. Although Berkvist was usually summoned to Honan's lair, Bill rarely came around to Bob's office. Generally even-keeled, Berkvist could become peevish if he thought an underling wasn't rowing fast enough. But, by-and-large, he laid off if you did your job and we got on.

The Section was then in the process of dumping its Leisure aspects, such as coins, stamps and attendant pursuits, ceding space to the more lucrative genres of movies and galleries. The

"Leisure" moniker hung on vestigially, a gray ghost on the section's logo. Nevertheless, a leisurely aura permeated the department. Stories were planned weeks ahead of time, staffers wandered in at 11 A.M. and worked at their own pace. Some finished early. Some dallied and ended with a rush. There was often a scramble at the finale but this was a small price to pay for the relative autonomy of working on a weekly. Monday nights, when the section putatively closed, and Tuesday afternoons, when it really closed, could be hectic, but a late night was water off the proverbial duck's back compared with the relentless beating one took on the Daily.

My duties consisted of handling the Arts, Architecture, Theater and TV pages. This meant editing John Russell, the Chief Art Critic; Paul Goldberger, writing on Architecture; Gene Thornton in Photography, and our Man of Letters, John Gross, as well as assigning assorted art, architecture, theater and television pieces. Since the two Johns needed virtually no editing, Goldberger, hardly more than a light dusting, and Thornton a little tweaking, I only had to worry about four or five assignments a week, far less than I did in a day on the Daily. Admittedly, the articles were longer—1,200-1,500 words—but not that much bigger than a main feature on the Daily, less the second-guessing and attendant burdens. Although we did our own heads, captions and copy-editing I didn't consider this a chore.

The core of our staff consisted of Larry Van Gelder who edited the movie pages, Gerry Gold in music and Gene Lambinus who handled Dance. Lambinus was an old Army buddy of Honan's whose fealty to his benefactor did not prevent him, when provoked, from casting a critical eye on his boss. He was forever in a tizzy up until his last day, which turned out to be not his last day. Gene had taken a buyout and was given a going-away party only to learn that the deal was premature and so was the party. Lambinus had to work several months more before the real buyout materialized.

Gerry Gold had bounced around from the Consumer beat to the Magazine to the Daily Culture backfield— I had worked with him in all three morphologies. He seemed to have found a niche as the music editor—or as much of a haven as his restive spirit could ever countenance. The fact is Gold was never really happy after leaving the Foreign Desk where he functioned as the de facto Foreign Editor. The nominal chief, James Greenfield, was more than glad to let Gerry pull the wagon up the hill as long as Jimmy could receive the plaudits. To Greenfield's credit, he knew he owed Gerry a debt and looked out for him whenever Gold stormed out of whatever job he'd been saddled with. Invariably, Greenfield would find yet another square hole to try to fit the very round peg that Gerry presented. Because of Gold's long years of service and his formidable talent, Gerry's supervisors gave him the wide berth he needed, but it was only postponing the inevitable. Eventually, he'd roil himself out the door in a fit of umbrage. For the moment, he was content to hibernate in a section where he could cultivate his love of music.

Gerry would usually choose his writers but if one of Gelb's protégés was palmed off on him, he'd rise up at his desk like Moby-Dick emerging in wrathful anger from the sea, wave the offending copy about like a chicken sacrificed at Rosh Hashanah, and shout in his booming bass: "Who the hell writes this shit?" Followed by: "And what shit-head got him here?" This was followed by a general reading of the miscreant's scribbling—"The Emperor's New Prose"—as Gerry called it, followed by more invective, climaxing in "I can't take this crap anymore!" Then, a fluttering of both hands above his head in a shimmy of despair, capped with a throaty "Aaaargh!" and finally a declension, receding into heavy breathing. It was a bravura performance. Gold had no patience for pretense, folly or cant, which made him persona non grata with Honan and Co. Nevertheless, he still had friends at court, so Bill had to put up with him.

Larry Van Gelder anchored the section, in part because movies had replaced theater as the dominant art form and chief money-maker of Arts & Leisure, and in part because he brought not only sagacity but sanity to the department. Larry was a veteran rewrite man who could do anything quickly, smoothly and efficiently at the last minute. He had labored at the World-Telegram and the hybrid World-Journal-Tribune, so that between the two of us, we had worked at all seven New York dailies with a little left over. We had both started as copy boys at The Daily Mirror and our careers had maintained a cracked mirror parallel of toiling for a choice assortment of madmen.

One of Larry's duties as Movie Editor was to serve as impresario for the previews to which The Times cultural staff was invited. These events, held at various midtown screening rooms, ostensibly gave the Times editors, film writers and other personnel with a need to know, a heads-up on forthcoming films so that the paper could plan its cultural coverage accordingly. In fact, it was a perk that allowed the paper's bigwigs, along with their kith, kit and assorted caboodle, to see all the hot new movies without having to wait on line or pay for them. It also enabled them to hold forth at cocktail parties on films that most other guests had yet to see. While other big media players had similar deals, The Times, because of the clout it enjoyed, was usually first among equals.

These arrangements, while ostensibly keyed to the paper's production schedule, were actually geared to Gelb's social calendar. If Arthur was busy the preview had to be rescheduled and everybody who planned to see the movie had to adjust accordingly. This meant that Van Gelder had to notify everyone who'd signed up for the screening that there had been a change of plan. Not least among the notified were the production companies which bristled at being jerked around but endured the affront as part of doing business rather than antagonize The Times. It was Larry who bore the brunt of their wrath while Arthur remained blissfully unaware of the tangle he'd caused.

After his job as movie traffic cop, Van Gelder found the task of editing the film page a breeze. Larry had gotten his training as a rewrite man, which meant that he took the often discordant telegraphy of leg-men, police reporters, beat correspondents and stringers, and turned it into a cohesive narrative. The skills of night rewrite were highly adaptable to handling high-strung cultural writers and Larry was a master practitioner. Writing for a newspaper is not the same as writing for a learned journal and many personalities, specialists in their fields, couldn't get the hang of it. They were more than glad for Larry's services. "I'm gonna massage your story a little," he'd tell them, and then proceed to eviscerate the piece and reconstitute it in sparkling prose. The beauty part was that, when he'd finished, his writers were convinced that the result was their own. This entailed a combination of faux consultation, therapeutic smoke and mirrors and judicious flattery that disarmed the recipient of any authorial misgivings. After all, it was under their byline that all this prose glistened.

I had my own menagerie of freelancers on the theater pages. The last traditional Sunday drama columnist we had was the aforementioned Walter Kerr, who was pretty much at the end of his run as I came aboard. There was no touching Kerr. Walter's idea of editing was to dictate his Sunday piece into the recording room and then have an editor read it back to him to make sure there were no typos. Presumably, this is a homage due to divas.

223

How often do you edit someone who's going to apotheosize into a theater? I half expected a pillar of cloud to emerge from the phone when his copy was transcribed. I once suggested to Walter that he might have gotten a fact wrong and the sneer was audible from his silence. When I mentioned this to Gerry Gold, he observed: "He always was a pompous ass."

Whatever Kerr's flaws, he was a passionate theater man and a genuine presence on The Times's drama pages. His departure created a vacuum that was never filled. It was decided that Frank Rich would concentrate on the Daily. There was sufficient justification for the decision. It was reasoned that Rich had enough to do attending to Broadway without worrying about a column, that he should devote his full energies to daily reviewing rather than be distracted with Sunday criticism, and that commenting on the same shows he'd just reviewed would be redundant. Fair enough, but on the other hand Frank's predecessors wrote for the Daily as well as maintaining a Sunday presence. And his peers in the other performing-arts continued to do so. Harold Schoenburg and then Donal Henahan in Music and Vincent Canby in Film, did both their daily reviewing as well as regularly writing thoughtful Sunday pieces.

There was certainly opportunity back then for a critical Sunday voice, if not Rich's. In Mel Gussow, The Times had a consummate theater critic who was admirably suited to write reflectively about the stage world. Gussow, a winner of the George Jean Nathan award for dramatic criticism, was an authority on Beckett, Williams, Pinter, Albee and the champion of a host of young playwrights who later achieved fame. He would have offered a fine complement for Frank's daily reviewing. But since Mel had been passed over as chief drama critic in favor of Rich there was little chance that Gelb was going to allow him this forum. Gussow was shunted to internal exile where he soldiered on nobly until his death. At his funeral, many years later, a Who's Who of playwrights and theater nobility turned out to pay him tribute.

Lacking a Sunday voice on its native grounds, The Times reached out to London. It recruited the estimable Benedict Nightingale who wrote with elegance and panache but lacked the authority that went with the franchise. Despite the good grace Nightingale affected, one could sense an audible sigh of relief on his part when his tour of duty came to an end. There was subsequently a half-hearted attempt to fill the bill with David

Richards but the effort foundered and nothing further was heard about a complementary Sunday drama voice. This was the beginning of a decline from which Arts & Leisure never recovered. Its stage venue was not simply another column. It had a pedigree going back to Brooks Atkinson and beyond. Arts & Leisure, in fact, was informally known in its day as the Drama Department. To lose its theater presence was to diminish the authority of the entire section. It thereafter trafficked in tricked-up-features and reportorial free-lance pieces that, except for length, could have been found in the Daily.

For me, the problem was coming up with a brace of theater writers who would try to fill the vacuum. In the end, it hardly mattered because the stories were, in effect, pre-writes— advances that were little more than puff pieces designed to turn readers into ticket-buyers. Nevertheless, I had a good relationship with Nightingale— part of my British trio that included John Gross and John Russell, all of whom added a touch of luster to a fading section. They were also delightful gossips whose outsider takes offered a droll perspective on the bizarre tribal rituals of The Times. Gross referred to Abe and Arthur as "Potash and Perlmutter," two bumblers from early Yiddish films. Whenever I called John Russell at home, his wife, Rosamund Bernier, would answer and we'd make polite chit-chat before John came to the phone to make fixes. After a few years she began referring to me in the third person as "Dear Jack"—"John, Dear Jack is calling"—making me feel like an old retainer. After I left The Times, I used the family ties to recruit Rosamund's son, Olivier— an author and connoisseur of French culture— as one of my writers at Newsday's Book Section.

The television pages, while a much easier lift at A & L than on the Daily, presented their own challenges. One of them was recruiting a cohort of dependable freelancers for the grunt work of TV features. These were the quaint days when the networks still ruled and Cable Television was in its infancy, a sideshow that fell under my aegis in the form of Cable TV Notes. The stories about this new medium were often left to relative striplings which involved my conducting a tutorial in Elementary Feature Writing.

There were also problems with our regular staffers though not always of their own making. Peter Kaplan, who came aboard as an enterprising young television reporter, was caught in a buzz saw at the 1984 Democratic convention and had been scrambling ever since. Certainly, the fault was not Kaplan's. Although Peter was said to have attended prior conventions back to 1972 as a young political junky, appearing as an observer and reporting for The New York Times were two different things. He'd been dispatched with little preparation, to cover a story that would challenge a veteran. But rather than taking responsibility for their own mishandling of a newcomer, Kaplan's supervisors turned up the heat. The next two years were often harrowing with Gelb and his minions finding fault with much of Peter's efforts. Try as he may, he was unable to satisfy their whims.

Kaplan's experience at The Times provides a cautionary tale of how not to treat a talented young reporter. Peter would operate quite differently when he became the storied editor of the New York Observer, a mentor to innumerable young writers who went on to media stardom. Unwittingly, his tormenters had done him a favor. Had Kaplan stayed, with luck, he might have had a career as a department head or a specialty writer, but it is unlikely that he could have spread his wings within The Times's rigid contours.

During this purgatory, I got to handle Peter from time to time and provided a sympathetic ear for his anxieties. I dubbed him "Mr. Television," an ironic allusion to his mercurial beat as well as to the outlandish Milton Berle, the slapstick star of the first popular show on TV. Peter a connoisseur of the old media, ruefully appreciated the sobriquet. Later, I simply called him "Jedidiah," a reference to the luckless critic Jed Leland in "Citizen Kane" whose integrity leads him to run afoul of his former pal, the newspaper mogul Charles Foster Kane. When Peter left, we stayed friends for a while. It was not a good time for him. After a sojourn at the Museum of Radio and Television, he wound up working for Clay Felker, another demanding celebrity boss, on a start-up business magazine, Manhattan,inc., located in the Graybar Building at Grand Central. We'd meet nearby at the erstwhile Cadillac Deli on Third Avenue where Peter would unburden himself over matzoh-ball soup. In the eulogies at Kaplan's funeral last year, attended by an outpouring of New York's meda elite, Felker's name was briefly invoked linking Peter to an apostolic succession of legendary editors. But, as I recall, whatever the laying on of hands, Kaplan was despairing at once again being in thrall to yet another driven martinet. Eventually, Peter would go on to work as executive producer for Charlie Rose at PBS and finally find his métier as editor of The Observer before going on to become editorial director of Conde Nast's Fairchild Fashion Group. In the interim, he created a legend as one of the great editors in New York journalism. He had left The Times well behind him.

If Peter Kaplan represented a wave of the future, Hans Fantel epitomized a ripple of the past. I had supervised his work during my sojourn on the Culture desk where he wrote a weekly feature about electronic equipment for music lovers, a column that eventually migrated to Arts & Leisure. I was fond of Hans who was a remarkable character. An elfin, white-maned refugee from Vienna, he had spent time in a concentration camp after Anschluss before fleeing to America. Fantel made a reputation as an audio authority writing for specialty magazines, which is how he got to The Times. Hans was a genuine expert on recording equipment, a sub-genre that had a small but avid following in the music world. It was also a throwback to the extinct hobby departments of Leisure and as such was a threatened species. Fantel's days were as numbered as the Hapsburg Empire. A man of great charm and dignity, he faded as gently as the final strains of a Strauss Waltz.

As time wore on, I became restive. The work had a sameness and, as I complained to my wife, Nella, I seemed to be working with five percent of my brain. We'd also moved from the West Side to Chappaqua and the late duty on Monday became an added burden because missing a train—which I usually did—meant an hour's wait at that time of night. As work became more onerous my family life became more meaningful and I found it maddening to spend an extra hour in the still-grungy Grand Central Terminal instead of being home with my children, owing to some top editor's whim that could have been addressed the next morning. Invariably, as I was preparing to leave, Berkvist would find some nit to pick at 9:25 which would keep me at my desk till 9:35 so that I would just miss the 9:48 and have to hang around the station with derelicts until the 10:48 which wouldn't get me home till 11:40 when my kids would be sleeping.

At about this time, the recurring game of musical chairs in Culture temporarily left Berkvist without a deputy. Larry and I filled in de facto while the brass scrounged around for a designated victim. After a while, I thought, why not me, since I was doing a goodly share of the work anyway. At least I'd get a raise. I imagined that enough time had gone by and I'd paid my dues several times over for Gelb to get past whatever grudge he may have held for my spurning his offer to be the first of the regional editors. I failed to appreciate that a short attention span for detail does not gainsay a long memory for grievance. In any case, I volunteered myself for the position. To my surprise Berkvist was receptive. I was a known quantity, he wouldn't have to go on a long search or break in a new body. Moreover, he was aware that I was a good editor, popular with the troops and a seasoned hand who knew the ropes and could sail the ship in his absence. He told me not to go to Gelb—why raise old hackles?—but that he'd make my case with Honan. A mistake. But I felt it was a Hobson's choice. In any event, once we got down to the nub of it, I'd have to make a command performance before Honan and Gelb.

The process wore on for several weeks. From time to time, I'd ask Berkvist for a reading and he'd respond that he was working on it; we'd have to be patient. This continued for a while longer, me being careful not to press too much but neither to let things drift. Finally, one Friday afternoon, I told Bob that I wanted to go to Honan and Gelb to plead my case. He relented and we agreed that I'd see them the following week. When I arrived Monday morning, Berkvist called me into his office. He seemed upset. "They gave the job to Connie Rosenblum," Bob said. He swore he knew nothing about it, that they'd gone over his head and behind his back. I chose to believe him; what else was I going to do? Constance Rosenblum was working for Mike Leahy in Travel. She'd been in Philadelphia and at the Daily News before then. I should note she wasn't aware of any of this. It was just in the cards.

Berkvist affected to be unhappy by the decision. The only reason his story made sense is that I was no threat to Bob—I'd never be allowed to go higher than his deputy—and Connie was. She was ambitious, a candidate for a slot that could be given to a woman in the aftermath of the feminist suit, and Bob was expendable. I wasn't altogether surprised although this was the third time in a few short years that they'd managed to compromise me in the most inventive way.

As for Connie, she would face a rough passage. Gerry Gold remarked that whenever he went up to Travel to shoot the breeze with his old Foreign Desk buddy Larry Shannon, Rosenblum bristled at the distraction. "I don't like her already," he said, "and I haven't even met her." Connie was due to land the following week when Berkvist had already planned a vacation. Under such circumstances, the Section Chief would usually put off his leave-taking by a few days just to assure an orderly transition, but Bob simply went ahead with his plans, leaving Connie to swing in the breeze. She arrived on a Monday morning, when the section was ostensibly on the cusp of closing, without a clue as to what was going on. As the day progressed, things only got worse—stories missing, writers unavailable, nothing in place. The composing room began calling for copy and there was no copy. The art director's layout didn't dovetail with what was on the page proofs. The situation threatened to spin out of control. I entertained the thought that Berkvist may have hoped it might work out this way. Technically, he had left Rosenblum everything she needed, so he was off the hook. But practically, unless she knew where to look and whom to ask, what he'd left her was virtually useless. At best, Connie would be forced to throw herself on Honan's mercy and have him call for help to bail her out, which would be humiliating.

At about 9 P.M., I had finished my work and sent it up to the composing room. Except for Larry, most of the others were gone. The Culture department was virtually empty. Connie was alone at her desk. She had just come back from the composing room where the printers, resentful of a woman boss and a newcomer at that, were not about to give her the time of day. Larry and I looked at each other. "Well, do we go home?" I asked. "Or do we help her out?" It was a rhetorical question. We could have left and she couldn't have stopped us, even if she knew better, which she didn't. "You're cutting your own throat," Larry said. "You can let her swing. She took your job." I observed that I could, but I wouldn't. The fact was that Connie never meant me harm. I don't do retribution well. I walked over to her. "Could you use a little help?" I asked. She could. "Let me make a few suggestions," I said. We got things organized and went up to the composing room where I used my good will with the printers to get them to hunt down and paste up the stray Arts & Leisure copy that was hanging on hooks and buried in bins all over the place. My pal, Arty, the assistant foreman, was there along with Stanley the foreman, who grumbled at the disruption—we were now throwing them off schedule by our lateness and disarray—but he went along with it. We found some more copy downstairs, wrote a few heads and, before midnight had things pretty well in hand. The next day, we got everyone to do a full-court press, rounded up some usual suspects and the section closed, almost on time.

Connie weathered this storm and eventually became Arts & Leisure editor, a job she held for many years. After a hiatus to write a book she went on to run the City Section where she did an outstanding job. It was one of the best departments in the paper and she deserves full credit for making it so. She was a talented editor. They'd bet on the right horse. Almost 20 years later, shortly before my second and final retirement—by then I'd left The Times, returned, and had several other lives— Connie approached me. She said: "I know you saved my neck that first night; I don't know what I would've done. I'll never forget it." "You would have managed," I told her.

As it turned out, Berkvist's misgivings were correct. It wasn't long before he was out, replaced by Mike Leahy, Connie's old boss in Travel, whom she would eventually succeed at Arts & Leisure, but by then I was gone. Leahy was the first temperate, equitable and decent editor I'd worked directly for since starting at The Times almost 15 years earlier. This took some getting used to. If my ambitions were limited so were my responsibilities and I could devote more time to my young family. The section produced its usual quota of turmoil but I didn't have a dog in these fights.

During my years as a deskman at The Times I had developed an unlooked for reputation for dealing with problematic writers. It became a chore that followed me from the Daily to Arts & Leisure so, although I enjoyed the best of the lot with John Gross and John Russell, I also got the other end of it. Of the latter group, a special place belongs to John Durniak, The Times's erstwhile photo editor. As the story goes, Durniak's claim to fame was that during his brief tenure in Photo he'd supervised the paper's picture coverage of the release of the American hostages from Iran. Durniak, who had come from Life magazine, must have thought he was assigning something on the order of "A Day in the Life of America." In his enthusiasm, he posted a small brigade of free-lance photographers to virtually every state where the scores of freed hostages touched down. The fact that The Times could run no more than five or six photos selected from a few sites failed to deter him. At a stroke, Durniak exhausted the paper's free-lance photography budget for a considerable period. We had thousands of contacts depicting the homecomings of each of the hostages in various states of euphoria and most of the states of the Union. When the horrified editors learned what Durniak had done they were in a state of shock and Durniak, never quite appreciating the havoc he'd wrought, was in a state of denial. That was the f-stop on John's career as the paper's picture editor but The Times, never willing to admit a mistake, eventually "promoted" Durniak to a photography column in Arts & Leisure. Enter me. It was the beginning of a dutiful friendship.

I learned quickly that the problem was not with Durniak's ability to write but with his capacity to think. The hostage fiasco was only a manifestation of this failure. Since I knew nothing about photography and John knew nothing about writing, we were perfectly matched. Every week he would faithfully submit a story that was a celebration of mind disorder. I would try to parse John's copy as best I could, whereupon I'd interview him on the phone about what he meant to say. Sometimes I could disentangle the thicket of his intent. More often, I'd have to call up Gene Thornton or Andy Grundberg, our photo writers, and have them try to unearth his meaning. Then I'd bring John in, show him what I'd done to avoid error and, after another go-round, he'd agree that this was what he'd meant to say.

What saved my sanity was that Durniak was a Teddy Bear when it came to editing. Sometimes, rendering him into English could take the better part of my week. So fearsome was Durniak's reputation that, when I went on vacation, my colleagues trembled at the thought of having to deal with him. The solution was that since Durniak and I were attached at the lip, if I took time off he'd write a column in advance. This meant I could edit him twice or more in a single week. To be fair, I owe John the debt of a memorable lead which has remained a fond memento in my family. In a summer column warning vacationers not to leave their film in a hot place lest it spoil, he started out with the words: "Film is like a tomato . . . " It was one of his most memorable lines. Clearly proud of this, Durniak wanted to know if I liked it. I told him it was exceptional but it might need a little work. I related this to my children and subsequently we never went on a vacation without them reminding me, as we loaded our camera: "Film is like a tomato."

I continued in this manner, in cruise control, for two more years. Then, on my 50th birthday, a deus ex machina materialized in the form of an old friend from Newsday. Out of the blue, my phone rang and it was Tony Marro, the editor of Newsday. He was offering me a job as the paper's book editor. Tony had been my Hempstead Town beat reporter when I was Nassau editor of Newsday and we had remained friends as his career soared— including a two-year stint as a reporter in The Times's Washington Bureau. Under the aegis of my old boss Dave Laventhol who had moved up to become CEO of Newsday's parent company, the Los Angeles Times, the Long Island paper had moved aggressively into the city with a New York edition. I'd be the book editor of the whole shebang and could work out of New York. The only thing I now find strange about this is that I told Tony I'd think about it. Whether from caution, ennui or the concern that, at least in those days, one rarely left The Times, I hesitated. Not for long. My wife, Nella, reminded me that I was coasting and going nowhere. "Do you really want to spend the rest of your life working for people who don't appreciate you, instead of working for someone who does?" she asked. As usual, she was right. I took the job.

I had a great going away party at The China Peace restaurant on 44th Street. My peripatetic existence at The Times moving back and forth among different departments had brought me into contact with a lot more people than I thought remembered me. And many of them showed up. Dick Shepard was the master of ceremonies and made a funny speech about how all of my neighbors and old friends would now hound me about getting their relatives' books reviewed. He wasn't far off. It was fitting that my Times career, which began with meals at the dingy Republic of China around the corner, should wind up at the China Peace. I got notes from almost everyone I ever worked with, or for. Even Arthur was gracious. And Max Frankel, my first boss, who by then had replaced his old rival Abe Rosenthal as executive editor, sent me off with a graceful note and the thought that I could always come back—a welcome change from the bad old days when those who left were rarely allowed re-entry. I was about to begin the most fulfilling period of my career.

My sojourn at Newsday was one of seven fat years and one lean month. The suburban tabloid had blossomed in the 15 years I'd been gone. As part of its strategy to challenge The New York Times on its home turf, the parent Times-Mirror Company, based in Los Angeles, had expanded its cash-cow Long Island newspaper across the city line with a Gotham edition that was in fact a full-fledged autonomous newspaper – New York Newsday. It already had a circulation of upwards of a quarter million and growing. Together with the suburban paper it boasted a combined readership of a million. More than that, New York Newsday enjoyed the most talented staff in the city: a combination of seasoned name columnists—Murray Kempton, Jimmy Breslin, Pete Hamill— together with a storehouse of dynamic young talent: Jim Dwyer, Lars-Erick Nelson, Roy Gutman.

From the late 80's to the mid 90's it was the most exciting place to be doing journalism in New York or, probably, in the country. And, because of the word-of-mouth among newspapermen and women, the paper had people banging down the doors trying to get in. I say, "the paper" advisedly, because that sobriquet was understood to be the property of the fabled Herald-Tribune which had gone under in the mid-60's but whose last city editor, like a survivor of Krypton, was now President of the Times-Mirror Company, CEO of the Los Angeles Times and the moving spirit behind New York Newsday. David Laventhol was determined to resume the battle with The Times that had ceased with the demise of The Herald-Tribune. Of course, he was there to make money and carry out a national corporate strategy of challenging The Times on both coasts. But the imp of revanchism was a demi-urge that drove at least a part of Laventhol's ambition to restore the glory days of the Trib in a new format. Nor was he alone. Many of his writers and sub-editors were survivors of the World-Journal-Tribune (known as "the Widjet")—the Paper's last gasp—as well as outlanders and brigands from the various New York tabloids who'd been conducting guerrilla warfare against The Times for years. They were like Brooklyn fans after the Dodgers left— inveterate Yankee haters looking for an opportunity to stick pins in the balloon of the smug enemy in pinstripes.

The editor of New York Newsday, Don Forst, couldn't have been a more perfect choice. Like Laventhol, he was a survivor of the Widjet as well as a storied rewrite-man on The New York Post in its 50's heyday. He was the first editor of Culture Gulch at The

Times and a specialist in second-banana finesse—he'd edited the L.A. Herald-Examiner and the Boston Herald, both No. 2 outfits in two-newspaper towns. But here, instead of trying to keep a tired hulk afloat, he was commanding a new warship prowling for one of two old tubs, the Post or the News, both of which had been wallowing in the waters for years. Feisty, hip, brazen, Forst was the right man to edit this tabloid in a tutu. The timing was perfect. New York was shaking off the doldrums of the 70's and the recession of the 80's and on the cusp of becoming the emblematic city of the 90's. The strategy was to take away the News's readership in Queens and Brooklyn where the bulk of its circulation was based. Nor did our advertising department fail to notice that 40 percent of the customers in the shopping malls of Western Nassau County lived in Queens.

But if the march across Queens and Brooklyn was the long-term goal, it was important to establish a presence in Manhattan, the city's cultural and financial center. To this end a New York office was established there. At its peak, the New York edition would add 220 people to Newsday's staff of 500. It is amazing in these times of journalistic retrenchment when newspaper staffs are being decimated, to imagine that hardly more than 25 years ago, Newsday was not only investing in a major newspaper startup but doing so in the toughest market in the country. Nor was it just a matter of numbers. Newsday was recruiting a dazzling array of young talent and veteran reporters in its effort to take the city from the wheezing New York Post and the floundering Daily News. It already shared printing, production and circulation costs with the Long Island paper, as well as a common core of foreign, national and state reporters and a formidable sports staff so that projected losses for the startup were easily sustainable so long as the mother ship provided a cash cow in its own right.

In retrospect, Laventhol may be considered a dreamer but in fact he was a pragmatist and his strategy was hard-nosed. He calculated that Long Island, with a shrinking population and a dwindling defense industry, could not sustain Newsday's growth. The only way to expand was by heading west, toward the city. Blocking his way were two aging vessels. Laventhol estimated that there was room for "two-and-a-half" papers in New York: two that were financially healthy and could do strong journalism—The Times and, presumably, a flourishing Newsday; the half being a newspaper subsidized by a wealthy patron with deep pockets who was willing to sustain losses for the prestige of owning a New York tabloid. This would be either the Post or the News. At the

234

time the News was a stepchild of the Chicago Tribune Company that was trying to get rid of it or close it down. The Post was on the verge of receivership with a revolving door of owners from the feckless Peter Kalikow to the repellant Abe Hirschfeld reviled by his own staff. And The Times, in its upscale ambitions, had neglected the outer boroughs—which included anything in Manhattan above 96th Street. (It was only getting beaten and embarrassed on its own turf by this upstart competitor that prodded The Times to resume seriously covering the city.) The moment seemed ripe for a brash new kid to muscle his way onto the block.

Of course, the New York edition was still the tail and the Nassau and Suffolk sections remained the dog, although the tail was getting most of the attention. To make sure that both ends of this act held together was no small feat and the person who managed it was Tony Marro, the editor-in-chief of the entire paper. Juggling the glut of foreign, national and local news that overlapped both editions and meeting the accompanying production challenges was a daunting feat, but more formidable still was soothing the bruised egos of a Long Island cadre that thought it was being upstaged and the fractious personalities of a New York cohort that felt it was being held back. A subsidiary problem was that the cream of the staff wanted to be in Manhattan where the action was, a tug-of-war that caused its own frictions. That Tony Marro was able to hold these centrifugal forces together while winning a brace of Pulitzers along the way was an impressive feat of managerial legerdemain.

I enjoyed the unusual advantage of having earlier befriended all three of these key players. I'd known Laventhol when he first arrived at Newsday and was supportive of him during his early days with Bill Moyers when I edited the Specialists Section, the daily back-of-the-book department that was an innovation of Laventhol's. It was part of his long-term strategy of turning Newsday into a complete newspaper. Don Forst and I were now working together on our third tabloid. I knew Forst at The Post and worked with him on my first go-round at Newsday when I ran the Specialists Section and he was Managing Editor. Tony Marro, as mentioned, had worked for me during my early years at Newsday and we'd maintained our friendship. In fact, he'd asked me to come aboard earlier but I'd vowed never again to work on the Island. This job came with a New York address.

We were parked in the Wang Building on Third Avenue at 48th Street and I had an office on the 26th floor with a smashing view of the East River—easily the best digs I'd ever worked in. My family had moved to Chappaqua two years earlier so it was an easy walk from Grand Central, which turned out to be a blessing when I had to lug all those volumes home in a book bag. The paper was located on two floors, features downstairs, news upstairs, with the aforesaid two hundred-plus people sharing the space.

If Newsday was going to make its mark in terms of news—the subways, the streets, the boroughs, the precincts, the schools, City Hall— it had to be a presence in terms of culture as well. This meant a sophisticated Entertainment Section. Among its guiding spirits were the redoubtable Sylviane Gold who'd go on to work in the Times's Theater Section, Caroline Miller who rose to edit New York magazine and my old friend Tom Wallace who would ascend to become editorial director of Conde Nast magazines. Occasionally it was too much of a good thing. There was sometimes a tension between cultural staffers with cosmopolitan leanings writing for a readership accustomed to a diet of conventional entertainment. But there is no question that their coverage created a buzz in the culture world and, I believe, in time they would have brought most readers along with them. I felt I could overcome such contradictions and provide something for everybody. I'd been brought in to bring the book section up to speed. My predecessor, Nina King, who was succeeding her friend Brigitte Weeks at the Washington Post's Book World, had done a creditable job as editor of a Long Island book section but now Newsday's management wanted to ratchet things up in order to go head-to-head with The Times.

When I had left Newsday, it was an expanding suburban paper with ambitions to be more than just a "housewives read with a good sports section'' as one observer put it. When I returned it had literally crossed the Rubicon or, in this case, the East River, and was making a bid for primacy among the remaining city tabs, but in effect as a hard-hitting broadsheet disguised as a tabloid. Geoffrey Stokes at the Village Voice once wrote that it was America's first transvestite newspaper— a broadsheet decked out in tabloid drag. This dual personality prompted the disparaging quip of the Daily News editor Gil Spencer to dub Newsday "a tabloid in a tutu.'' In a sense he was right. As our Lars-Erick Nelson observed, the souped-up front page suggested to readers that they were getting a tabloid, and it wasn't until they got inside that they realized they had bought a serious newspaper.

This meant beefed-up and intensified coverage across the board. Sections that had once been "good enough" were no longer acceptable. Books was part of this strategy, which is where I came in. Nina's section was respectable but it was insular and staid. Although she had been pushed to hire a few name regular reviewers, too many of her writers were run-of-the-mill, submitting their own list of books for review from which she chose her selections. The copy was loosely edited, the heads clunkers and the layouts uninviting. In all, the book pages looked more thrown together than thought out. I'd inherited a worn, pedestrian section. My task would be to make it a first-rate one.

I knew that changes would have to be made but that Newsday didn't always like making them—a paradox for a paper in a hurry. The fact is, Newsday had two cultures— a penchant for innovation and a paternalism that insisted on moving incrementally. I would have to work within these bounds— particularly in my handling of personnel. I found these limits frustrating but they were part of the challenge that I'd accepted. Over the next seven years I balanced these exigencies with my ambitions to mold the book pages into a distinguished section. I achieved my goals but they took longer than I would have liked and the path was not always smooth. Yet it was certainly the most rewarding professional journey I ever undertook.

A few years before I assumed my responsibilities, David Shaw, the media reporter for the Los Angeles Times, conducted a comprehensive survey of book reviewing in America and here are some of the things he found: Only three newspapers—The New York Times, the Washington Post and the Los Angeles Times— published separate weekly book sections. The rest folded their reviews into Culture or Opinion pages, often at the back of the paper or, worse, in the middle. Some limited their coverage to weekday reviews on the Feature pages. Others used the wire services and some even appropriated the publishers' press releases.

The "staff" often consisted of a single editor, some not even full-time, who lacked the wherewithal to sort through the myriad bags of books inundating them (50,000 a year then printed in the U.S.), much less make an intelligent selection, an appropriate assignment or a proper edit. One editor averred that she felt like "a shipping clerk." The aforementioned big three papers reviewed from 1,500 to 2,000 books annually. At a second level newspapers such as the Chicago Tribune, Miami Herald, Philadelphia Enquirer and Boston Globe averaged from 600 to 1,200 reviews each. The overwhelming majority of books were never reviewed or passed off to other sections (food books to the food editor; ditto with books on sports, business, etc.). Genre books like science-fiction, crime and fantasy, were often cast aside. Reprints forget about. The rare exception were children's books that sometimes merited a roundup.

If the selection of books was haphazard and arbitrary the choice of reviewers was worse. And no wonder. Small newspapers paid nothing; their reviewers got to keep the book. Some paid a modest honorarium. Bigger papers paid $50 to $250, closer to the lower end. The result was assigning a ready-to-hand assistant professor or other local talent. What was in it for the writer was prestige (of sorts), exposure (limited) and a platform (shaky); also an opportunity to gain favor or get even. Many book reviewers interviewed by Shaw said they'd never been asked by editors about possible conflicts of interest. Indeed, some editors encouraged reviewers to write about their friends because they saw their job as getting people into the bookstores. One reviewer, an editor at a publishing company, was assigned a book written by an author from his own house. The demurrer was that an expert on a subject was probably aware of the author and had already formed an opinion of his work. Other editors saw no problem with giving a book to someone who asked to review it without being too concerned about their motivation since it relieved them of the burden of casting about for a writer. Shaw's report makes for some unnerving reading.

I was determined to do better. If this was the competition, I could hardly do worse. But it wasn't. My competition was The New York Times Book Review. I didn't need Shaw to remind me that the TBR was "far and away the most important book medium in the country." I knew. I worked in the building. But having served there turned out to be a distinct advantage. First of all, I wasn't intimidated by the Times's vaunted reputation. (See previous chapters.) Second, by dint of having been there, I felt I could approach anyone. And third, I knew that my effervescent counterpart at The Times was as much style as substance. To her credit, Rebecca Sinkler nee Pepper was quick on her feet, affable and exuded a sense of confidence and authority. Laudable qualities, but they alone do not a seasoned editor make. To my great good fortune, her ascendancy virtually overlapped with mine. Of course. it couldn't be a fair fight but I was determined to win a few rounds before the bout was over. What Becky had in her corner was a dozen preview editors, a copy desk, and the entire book industry at her disposal. But even this could be an advantage for me because all those underlings often tripped over each other and slowed things down. I didn't have to look over my shoulder—Tony Marro had given me carte blanche. I felt it was an even contest.

My family and I were vacationing in Maine in July 1988, the month before I assumed my responsibilities, and I remember feeding quarters into the pay phone outside the Sommesville General Store as I sold A.H. Raskin, a venerable member of the New York Times editorial board, on reviewing for me. Raskin had been the paper's labor expert, the biographer of the union leader David Dubinsky, and was working on a tome about labor since the New Deal, so the book I had in mind, a story of workers' struggles, was something that I thought might pique his interest. I was chatting him up as though I were smoking a pipe in a book-lined room when in fact, I was hovering over two bags-full of groceries, scribbling notes into a pad that I held along with the receiver and praying that I could make the sale before my coins ran out. Mercifully, Raskin was a generous soul and took my $200 and the assignment. It was my first as book editor. I spent the better part of my vacation—my wife and children dutifully put up with me—corralling reviewers for our first few issues since I knew that the larder would be empty soon enough. I had to make a quick impression by introducing my own writers and selections from the get-go. The call to Abe Raskin provided a paradigm for the way I'd operate. I worked full-time, full-speed, no-off-duty. We went for the best writers, paid them top dollar and gave them books they'd want to read and comment on. I used my relationships or created them if none existed, affecting an insouciant phone-side manner to mask my often shaky situation.

My staff consisted of a secretary, a part-time copy editor and two columnists—one about to retire—who had no assigning functions. It was up to me to feed the beast. I decided from the start that I wasn't simply going to fill space, whatever the pressures. Every bullet would count. Moreover, I wasn't just going to assign reviews. They were no longer going to be thrown in at random; rather, there would be a thematic connection shaping every issue.

When I arrived, the Newsday book section was a four-and-a-half-page black-and-white caboose bringing up the rear of a 24-page Ideas Section. The book pages consisted of five reviews, and a feature plus a paperback roundup that was little more than a listing. When I left, it was a six-and-a-half page section in color with a dozen reviews under a variety of rubrics that anchored a 48-

239

page Entertainment Section. What happened in the intervening seven years is the story of my sojourn.

I wrote or supervised virtually every head, every caption, every blurb. We threw graphics onto the pages and streamlined the layouts. I supplemented the illustrations with photos, not just from the books but from the Bettmann Archive, Magnum and our morgue. The New York Public Library had its own graphics division that was available with the imprimatur of a library card.

An old friend, Byron Dobell, who had launched the Washington Post's Book World after it survived the Herald-Tribune's collapse, gave me some critical advice about starting up: "Use your friends." I did. I had more than a few in high places—my toil at The Times had not gone to waste— and I called in every marker. In those early weeks I induced an array of former Times writers to review for me: John Gross from London, Benedict Nightingale on theater, Sam Freedman on Nadine Gordimer, Gene Thornton on photography, Anthony Austin on Russia and Mimi Sheraton on Hong Kong. I had a second set of friends who were not Timesfolk but respected in their own right. This bought me enough time to cultivate my own writers: cameos like Louis Auchincloss, more frequent contributors such as Olivier Bernier and Arthur Danto on art, Eugen Weber on French culture, Jacob Heilbrunn on politics, Philip Gourevitch on social issues, David Rieff on foreign affairs, Philip Lopate on belles letters, and Arnold Rampersad on race. I also found that Newsday had a few first-rate free-lancers whom I kept on and developed as regulars such as Richard Lipez and Wendy Smith as well as Tom Mallon and Susan Jacoby, both of whom went on to have considerable writing careers. And we weren't just reviewing books. We were going to be enterprising as well. When I came across the memoir of School Chancellor Joseph Fernandez and saw that it blasted then Mayor Giuliani, I rushed it out to the city room and collaborated on a front-page story working in tandem with Barbara Strauch, a gifted news editor who would go on to become the Science and Health Editor of The New York Times. This was not a commonplace for most book editors.

Had I been in Des Moines I might have been more laid back but competing against The Times in New York prompted me to go all out. I was determined to be a step ahead of them. If New York Newsday was going to beat them on local stories we were going to do the same with reviews. The S.O.P. of most book reviews was to see what The Times did and follow suit. Or to pretend that The Times didn't exist and go their own way, reviewing what they wanted when they wanted. I couldn't afford to do either. My assumption was that for many of our subscribers, New York Newsday was a second read and, if it was to be a first one, they weren't going to hear that a book had already been reviewed in The Times. I made sure that the minute a book was in the stores, usually a little ahead of its publication date, we reviewed it. The Times could be somewhat more casual about this, and often was. The result was that we generally reviewed books a week or so ahead of them. Considering that they had a lot more space to review a lot more books, this was no small feat. The trick was that we had to pick our spots and choose the right books.

Of course, The Times didn't know it was competing. We were like the Hebrews in Egypt. For us, Passover was a big thing; for them it was hardly noticed. Nevertheless, we started to make a dent, most importantly with publicists from the big publishing houses who began to notice that we were out first with name writers reviewing their best books. They were able to blurb them— often in ads they placed in The Times without ascribing the publication the reviewers had been writing for. It was a practice that I called them on repeatedly and a battle we only half won. But I earned their respect and became a player in the New York game. Newsday's book section became a journal of ideas complementing the front section. Like the larger paper, it strove to be topical, fresh, newsy and surprising. Before long, The Times began waking up to us. I was getting nice feedback from some of my former colleagues. Even Marvin Siegel, who was shoring up Becky Sinkler as her deputy and—surprise—Arthur Gelb himself sent me complimentary notes on the job I was doing.

I began putting together a Reviewers list. The computer slug for this was "Rev" and I started in alphabetical order, by category, with "Rev 1" which consisted of writers on such subjects as American Literature, Anthropology and Astronomy. Eventually, it grew to "Rev 17" with scores of contributors on focused topics. "Fiction," obviously, was in a realm of its own. As I went along, each one of these "Revs" kept growing so that in turn I had to sub-divide them. History, became American History and World History which, in turn, became World History A-M and N-Z. I never counted but, by the end of my tenure I had a list of thousands of names accompanied by phone numbers, faxes and addresses together with notes on my reviewers' preferences, interests, families, backgrounds, likes and dislikes, personal tics, etc. This was before the internet and the concomitant information explosion that has made much of this material available at the touch of a button. In order to build my edifice I had to put it together stone by stone. It was a painstaking process that involved first, word of mouth—recommendations from trustworthy sources, then befriending publicists to gain access to their writers, then scouring rival book reviews for writers who interested me. If they were academics, I would phone their faculty department, chat up the secretaries and call their offices. Ditto with think tanks. If they were unaffiliated, I used the phone book. If necessary, I'd trade names with other book editors.

On one occasion, for a Hemingway biography, I hunted down a specialist named Allen Josephs whose writing on the author I'd come to admire. It was summertime and Josephs, who taught at the University of West Florida, was vacationing in Spain. Actually, he was following a bullfighter through a season's corridas for a book of his own. I learned this after calling his department. They furnished me with nothing further than his wife's phone number. She turned out to be an ex of recent vintage but, acceding to my urgency, she graciously gave me the phone of his girlfriend, Sandy, who taught at the University of Kentucky. Sandy, in turn, provided me with the phone number of an art-dealer friend in Madrid with whom Josephs had been staying. When I called, it turned out, he'd just left and was conducting his own moveable feast from city to city in the wake of the itinerant bullfighter. Every time I reached a hotel Josephs had recently moved on but they promised to forward my messages. Finally, I ran him to ground at a small inn on the coast of Malaga. He was in a hut and they had to bring him in from the beach. He picked up the phone and said: "You're the guy who's been tailing me all over Spain." That was the good news. The bad news was that he'd already agreed to review the Hemingway book for The Times before he left. But, as my late mother said, nothing is wasted. Without missing a beat, I pitched him on a different book and he agreed. Josephs became a frequent reviewer. We had a mutual interest in Spain and got to be friends or, rather, I lived vicariously through him as he followed his bullfighters.

Some years later, I was looking for a writer to review Janet Brown's groundbreaking biography of Charles Darwin. I wanted someone equal to the occasion. I called Jared Diamond, author of "The Third Chimpanzee." He was already working hard on "Guns, Germs and Steel" and couldn't do it but he said the man I wanted was Ernst Mayr, "if you can get him." Mayr was the leading evolutionary biologist of the 20th century who founded the field of the history of biology. He was a professor emeritus of zoology at

242

Harvard at the time and I called him at his office in Cambridge. He was by then 90 but, Diamond assured me, still spry. When I phoned Harvard they told me Mayr was doing research in marine biology in Florida. I got his motel number and the clerk informed me he was somewhere off the coast. I left a message. Two hours later, my phone rang. It was Prof. Mayr, chipper and in high spirits. He assured me that he'd be delighted to do the review. Although the book was a 600-page tome, he submitted it on time, in space. He answered my questions promptly and made the fixes deftly. Like many people of great talent he had the gift of writing prose that was simple, lucid and flawless. Knopf used his Newsday review as a blurb in the paperback edition.

As one can imagine, assigning was a full-time job in itself. The Times had between eight and ten people to do only that. I also did, planning, scheduling, layout, editing, heads, captions and the administration that came with the territory—payment, correspondence, promotion—as well as going through the piles of books that arrived in bulky canvas bags every day. But actually, this was an advantage because I could see the whole picture. Admittedly, I was in a smaller pond, but the writer didn't have to worry about my being second-guessed by a supervisor. We wound up reviewing more than 600 books annually, almost a third of The Times's complement. I sought to compensate for this with writers who were fresh, reviews that were crisp and layouts that were attractive and colorful. In terms of affluence and education, our readership, particularly in New York, could meet The Times head-on, the difference being that we had the cachet of being more hip.

My predecessor had leaned heavily on a narrow base of writers. Consequently, she left a residue of reviewers in her wake, many of whom expected that business would continue as usual. I promptly cured them of this illusion and served notice that hereafter the book editor, not the reviewers, would initiate assignments. Moreover, I swept out the shoddiest of them, gave the intermediary sorts a chance and kept a talented twentieth. I performed this triage firmly, albeit gradually, to avoid a general outcry. Often a polite note would do, sometimes a phone conversation was necessary, occasionally an office sit-down. But I was adamant. I was determined to replace these left-overs with talented writers and recognized authorities.

Although I had a free hand with the contributors I had to tread more carefully with staff reviewers and contract writers. Extracting them from the mix proved more challenging. Well before my arrival, Newsday's top brass, as mentioned, had already prodded Nina to hire a couple of big names to bolster the book pages. She had responded by recruiting Christopher Hitchens and Florence King. Together with Dan Cryer, the paper's chief book critic and an Opinion Page columnist, they served as a quartet that wrote for Newsday's daily book pages, Monday to Thursday, with Cryer and King both contributing a Sunday review as well. Dan was a seasoned critic who could be relied on for a steady stream of solid copy. He could be a bit prickly and I had to be attuned to his sensibilities but, over time, we worked out an equitable modus vivendi.

Corralling Christopher Hitchens was probably the best thing Nina ever did. Hitchens had already established himself in the pages of The Nation and elsewhere as a transplanted gadfly with Oxbridge credentials as well as a scourge of the political Right when he parachuted into Newsday. I believe Nina was dazzled by Christopher's plummy accent and Brit insouciance because she seemed to pretty much give him his head. Or rather, since she wielded a light pencil, it was hardly likely that she'd apply it to Christopher's scriptural prose. But if his copy sparkled, it also bristled with a disdain for what he considered to be the Yahooism, Jingoism and Parochialism of his American hosts. Too often, his reviews were little more than occasions to score points off his political and cultural targets. Hitchens achieved this with panache, for which I gave him points, but he often stretched the facts— indeed ignored them—to make his case. The result is that he infuriated a segment of our readership. I had no problem with a reviewer antagonizing our readers provided that he was fair to the writer and addressed the book rather than his passions. This was not always so, as I adduced from some of his fan mail. To wit:

" 'Simpleton' is what he [Hitchens] labels Pope John Paul I because of 'his doctrine, his politics and his public attitudes' . . . More than a book review comes out when he says that 'nothing is as implausible to me as the theory that there is a benign deity who takes an interest in ours affairs.' Perhaps. But to me and thousands of others of your readers, believing that is very plausible. Respectful disagreement with our beliefs is what I expect from my favorite newspaper, not reading that people who hold them are 'simpletons.' "

More. "It used to be standard practice for a reviewer to approach technical and literary aspects of a book nominally. Hitchens has decided to dispense with such irrelevancies and get to what he seems to enjoy more: using the prestige of a book reviewer's position to proselytize politically."

And More. "Re: Alleged 'Book Review': 'A Man of Many Faces, And All of them False.' You nasty anti-Semitic left-wing son of a bitch."

My task was to maintain Christopher's special voice without his various agendas. Within a month, I had my opportunity. He had reviewed Robin Blackburn's "Overthrow of Colonial Slavery," from Verso, a publisher that was to the Left what Regnery was to the Right. In the review he spent a good deal of time bashing American slavery while cutting considerable slack to his own fellow Brits, much less the French, Spaniards, Dutch, et al. I'd seen the book and pointed out to Hitchens that the author had devoted considerable space to the depredations of European traffickers and slaveholders which he, for the most part, ignored while zeroing in on the Yanks. I said that if we were going to enlighten the reader as to the extent of slavery in the Atlantic, then we'd have to be far more inclusive about its practitioners. I think he was taken aback that I had actually read the book and was informed on the subject. Having been caught out, he didn't miss a beat. Rather I got a prompt revision with a cover note on a Nation letterhead informing me: "Herewith a recast Blackburn." His only caveat was that I refer to him as "Christopher" and he in turn would make sure to not repeat the gaffe of spelling my last name without a "T." The result was less a grudging respect than an amazement that a Yank could actually meet him on his own terms. Hitchens learned to trust my judgment —as I adapted to his tastes —and gradually I got to assign most of the books which, in a way, was a relief to him. I knew that I couldn't break him of his didactic proclivities, nor would I want to because that was part of the moral force that drove his writing. The deal was simply that I pretended to let him write what he wanted and he pretended to ignore my editing.

The coup de grace came a short while later when Hitchens, an inveterate name-dropper, attributed a rare lateness in filing a review to his haste in catching a plane for Karachi to hob-nob with his old friend Benazir Bhutto, seeking to recoup her fortunes in Pakistan. I replied simply "Peccavi." I was referring to the apocryphal message that Sir Charles Napier, was supposed to have dispatched to his superiors on capturing the province of Sindh. "Peccavi"— in Latin, "I have sinned"—was a pun on taking the region which, whatever its actual provenance in Punch, entered into British imperial lore. It also reminded Hitchens that he was late. Christopher was duly amazed and mildly amused that an American could have known this. He submitted his review "forthwith" and never gave me any trouble again.

Although Hitchens had a deserved reputation as a formidable debater and general terrorizer of editors, publicists and TV producers, he was always courtly with me. Of course, he was juggling a host of other assignments during the years he wrote for us and I was awed by, if not somewhat suspicious of, his prodigious abilities to meet all these demands. Truth be told, I'm not sure that Hitchens actually read all or most of each tome he reviewed—my attitude was "don't ask, don't tell"—but he had a knack for getting to the heart of the matter. In looking back at his reviews I am still impressed by how informative, cogent and engaging they are.

For four years, Hitchens dutifully submitted more than 200 high-quality reviews to Newsday without missing a beat, doing some of his best work in an ongoing weekly relationship steadier than he had with any other publication at the time. Moreover, while he was preaching to the converted in writing for The Nation, Newsday took considerably more risk and a lot of flak from its readers in supporting him. I believe Christopher might have found it amusing that his labors for Newsday were generally omitted in the encomiums following his death, disappearing down a media memory hole as void as any conceived by his icon George Orwell.

Florence King was another matter altogether. Florence was a take-no-prisoners Southerner who had opinions about everything, most of them negative. "Feisty" does not do her justice. Florence was an enfant terrible or, rather, an ancien terrible. In her confessional "Reflections in a Jaundiced Eye" she celebrated being a "crazy old maid" as carte blanche for saying anything she damn pleased. Her motto was "Spinsterhood is powerful." Florence reported that her Granny was convinced she'd been twins but had committed fetal murder. Her better half was the one who was done in. She had scads of bete noires—feminism, the nouvelle roman, Southern novels—Gothic and Rural. Her literary hero was the caustic maverick Ambrose Bierce, her muse was Scarlett O'Hara although she made Scarlett seem like a shrinking violet. Her idea of government was that it should deliver the mail and stay the hell out of her business. Florence did not suffer fools gladly. which in her case took in most of humanity. I admired her—we had many mutual antipathies— but together with her contrariness there was a contentiousness that I sensed would lead to trouble.

We first met at an East Side restaurant with Tony Marro, Phyllis Singer, my immediate boss who ran the Entertainment pages, and Howard Schneider, Tony's second in command. I felt as if it were an arranged marriage with the parents nervously hoping that the couple would be compatible. Florence was "on"— she had decided that her job was to divert the Yankees with an onslaught of anecdotes that were a counterpoise to Southern charm. Behind all the cornpone was a formidably intelligent, very belle-lettered lady.

Finally, Florence raised the issue I'd been waiting for—that she expected a wide berth in terms of editing and book selection. She smiled as she spoke but her eyes narrowed. I responded as generally as I could that we'd respect her autonomy provided that it fit the needs of the section. We both had different assumptions of what this would mean but I calculated that the diplomatic ambivalence allowed a certain amount of give and take. As it turned out, there was not much room for maneuver. Florence and I had divergent ideas about her independence. To her credit, she had the courage to fall on her sword early on and save us both a lot of pain. As it turned out, once freed of her contractual obligations, Florence found herself able to write for me again and I put her to good use as an occasional scourge of intellectuals manqué.

Florence King may have been tetchy but she was talented. Our remaining columnist I called The Infant Phenomenon, an heir to Dickens's creatively inept thespian in "Nicholas Nickleby." The Phenomenon was in a league of her own: inventively maladroit, terminally obdurate. But since she was on staff I couldn't simply drop her. All I could do was campaign to remove her. That I had to edit her on a weekly basis was a novel form of torture and a time-consuming one.

Illustrative of The Phenomenon's efforts was her treatment of Matthew Henson, the black explorer who accompanied Robert Peary to the North Pole. In what could only be described as a talent for the perverse she managed to introduce a racial pejorative into a work on the Arctic tundra. In reviewing a book called "The Arctic Grail" she referred to Henson, who shared the rigors of the trip with Peary, as his "man servant." When I pointed out that Henson was indeed an explorer who some believe had come closer to the

Pole than Peary and that it would be not only demeaning but unfair and untrue to call him a "man servant," as if he were some Friday attending Robinson Crusoe, she responded that, although she knew nothing about the journey herself, that's how the author referred to him and that's what she was going with.

I observed that whatever the author chose to call Henson we should call him what he actually was, that John Noble Wilford in numerous stories in The Times had referred to Henson as an explorer, that the National Geographic Society considered him one and, indeed, so had Peary, all of it richly documented. She told me she didn't care what The Times said, averring that "we don't do things that way at Newsday." I responded that the way we did things at Newsday was that we got it right. I showed her news stories verifying that Henson had gone on alone to arrive at what was considered the North Pole. What else would he be but an explorer? When I presented her with clips in which our own science writer, Robert Cooke, supported me, she relented, but only temporarily.

The Phenomenon subsequently sent me a note saying "explorer" in her understanding meant "the expedition leader who secured the funds and backing, planned the route and led the trip." She chose instead to refer to Henson as "the intrepid black American trekker." I was aghast but responded simply that I didn't think "trekker" worked. "Trek," I wrote, "is defined primarily as having to do with migration as in "The Great Trek." "More to the point," I went on, " 'explorer' is the most accurate word for what Henson actually was. It is true in terms of the common-sense and general definition of the meaning: someone who embarks in search of geographical or scientific information—which Henson most certainly did on the trip. It is also true in terms of the entire history of exploration, in which the explorers were surely not only the leaders of the expedition but the men who went with them. Henson was definitely an explorer in the most commonly accepted use of the term. To call him something that he is not, when there is a perfectly accurate term for what he is, is wrong. We have indeed described what the author thinks and that is fair to the author. We should call Henson what he is and be fair to the man."

This interchange involved a single characterization in a single review. There were many such words, phrases, paragraphs, ideas in virtually every piece this person wrote. I had to hand-wrestle over each mote. These labors continued unabated for more than two years when, in response to my entreaties, Tony Marro finally managed to squirrel her from her redoubt.

My last editorial staff writer, Leslie Hanscom, was someone I rather would have stayed on. Leslie conducted the literary interviews for the section. Sadly, he was about to retire. I'd known him in my first go-round at Newsday. He was a fellow New Yorker and I often drove him out to Long Island in those days. Hanscom was that rara avis, the consummate wordsmith. He could make anything sound like poetry. When I first met him he'd come from Newsweek where he'd toiled in the Back of the Book under the whip of the overbearing Jack Kroll. One day, Kroll's acid tongue went a bit too far and, as legend had it, Leslie rose from his desk, squared his shoulders, and marched out the door.

Hanscom, a dignified New Englander, spoke sparely but let his typewriter do the talking. Yet if he liked you Leslie would open up and proved to be a witty and engaging raconteur. He had a wonderful laugh that came bursting out as if he'd been trying to repress it and could no longer do so. After Leslie retired he'd do the occasional piece for us including a moving interview with Katharine Hepburn on the occasion of her autobiography. He was just the man for the job and it showed in every word he wrote. Aside from Hitchens, of all the stable I inherited, Leslie was the one I valued most and he was the first to leave.

During those early weeks, I knew I'd have to buy time before my input made itself felt, but I'd also have to make a quick impression. The way to do this was with layout, heads, pruning the detritus and front-ending my initial assignments. It wasn't until the third issue that my efforts started to kick in. The crime novelist George Higgins, an erstwhile federal prosecutor, reviewed two books on the Cosa Nostra, one of them titled "The Pizza Connection.'' For an illustration I ordered a slice of pizza along whose sides we ran photos of the crime bosses linked in the drug trade. The head: "A Mafia Recipe for Heroin and Pizza.'' Silly, perhaps crude, but journalism isn't high art and it showed that we were going to see things in a different way. That issue introduced reefers to the section, underline heads that referred to inside reviews. The one for the Mafia books read: "A Drug Trail—With a Dash of Pepperoni" followed by a mini slice of pizza pointing to the following page.

By the Labor Day issue, I felt we were coming into our own. The section opened with New York magazine's film critic John Simon reviewing Ingmar Bergman's autobiography. Accompanying this was a large vertical shot of Bergman directing Bengt Ekerot as Death in "The Seventh Seal." The headline: "A Magician Reflects on His Art." For a sidebar, I got hold of an associate producer for "60 minutes" in London and had her report a piece on Bergman's life on Faro, his Baltic island retreat where he'd set some of his movies. This exercise was costly in terms of time and money but I was determined that our pages were going to be more than just another book review. They were going to assume a new personality in terms of layout, graphics, and coverage: assertive, enterprising, singular.

The following issue was our fall preview. This was going to be a major statement that would set the tone not only for the season but for the new section itself. I composed an opening essay to introduce both myself and what we'd be reviewing in the coming months. It was the only piece I wrote in my seven-year tenure and although I'd vowed to let others have the limelight I felt it was important to make this an exception. Finding a theme wasn't difficult. It was an exceptionally fruitful season for biography. There were books on Jack Kennedy, Langston Hughes, Winston Churchill, George Bernard Shaw, Charles Dickens, Barry Goldwater and Margaret Thatcher among others. We just went with it. I had our talented artist Van Howell draw an illustration of all the subjects gathered in a vaulted library with bursting shelves and cathedral windows. The original sketch still graces my wall.

I didn't realize it at the time but I was arriving at the tail end of the publishing business as a gentleman's pursuit. In fact, it was never that. The gentlemen who ran it were invariably out to make a buck, keep writers in thrall and retain as much as they could from the sales of the books they were hawking. Nonetheless, they played by their own rules and one of them was to affect a love of books and a respect for people who wrote and read them. Doubtless the proverbial nod that vice pays to virtue, yet enough of them believed it so that within their clubby precincts one could still talk of literature as something other than product. By then, however, editors were no longer answering to an impassioned albeit arbitrary bookman but to number-crunching media executives whose primary concern was not the readers but the stockholders.

The era of the mega-book designed to make mega-bucks had arrived. The power had palpably shifted from editorial to marketing. And the younger editors were more absorbed in the art of the deal and the quick-selling gimmick than nurturing new writers. Mid-list authors—the reliable rank-and-file of most publishing companies —were being shunted aside for the roulette of betting the house on blockbusters: celebrity authors and "events" whose fascination had peaked by the time the book was published. The fiery independents would wind up shorn or shrouded with their distinctive imprints absorbed as simply a bland division of a bigger label. Along with this, the neighborhood bookstores gave way to Barnes & Noble and Borders, dispensing with the idiosyncratic while reinforcing the big-book mentality. The bookshops were turning into coffee houses and the public libraries into free video stores. And worse was to come. The demise of the beautiful Scribner's book emporium on Fifth Avenue at about this time sounded the knell for the old-fashioned bookstore as redoubt and refuge.

All this happened imperceptibly, over several years, but happen it did. Ironically, this would be looked back on as a Golden Age, or at least a Silver one, given what was to follow. Because these bottom liners and marketers and mega-stores would themselves be swept away by the digital revolution. In less than a generation, they'd be inundated by the internet, swallowed whole in the jaws of Amazon. It didn't matter how ruthless or resourceful a publisher was. If he was in the print medium when reading had shifted from page to screen, he either went over or out.

But in those still-flush days, book parties promoting the wares of a publisher's anointed authors, were still a tribal ritual of the literary world. I doubted the efficacy of these events except as a sop to the writer in the hopes of keeping him or her in the stable, with the added dubious benefit of convincing the outside world that the house was very much in the game and behind the book. For the assortment of freeloaders and hangers-on who showed up—many of them moving on to graze at several events in a single night—it was a chance to schmooze, gossip and indulge in various degrees of Schadenfreude, often at the expense of the guest of honor. I felt that as a new boy in town, I had to establish my bona fides by making an appearance at as many of these functions as I could.

My party rules were strict, particularly if there was more than one event for the evening. They usually took place between 6 and 8, almost all in Midtown Manhattan. I arrived at the first at 6:30 when there was already a critical mass so I wouldn't have to make forced conversation with the author's relatives in a near-empty room. I grabbed a seltzer with a lime twist and advanced directly on the publicist who steered me to the author. I talked about the book for a few minutes, what I found interesting, it's prospects, the writer's tour, his or her next book, and then I shook hands and left. I never ate—it got in the way and the canapés spoiled my appetite for dinner. Moreover, no one can be taken seriously standing around with food in his mouth. I also made sure to be the best-dressed man in the room, particularly with ties and pocket hankies. On the way out, I stopped off to have a few words with the publicists about their upcoming lists, more by way of implicit assurance than seeking information. If there was a top editor, I'd pay obeisance on the season's successes.

As time went on, I got to know the regulars who inevitably haunted these affairs, writers for the trade press, free-lancers, the cycle of recent grads in the lower depths of each house dragooned to give ballast and youthful energy to the party. I made sure to engage in polite but brief chatter with those I recognized as I moved steadily to the door. The important thing was never to wait around for the inevitable speech of gratitude. I was out in 20 minutes which left me enough time to get to the second event, usually still crowded, by 7:30, and decamp before the party wound down. This allowed me to make the 8:22 out of Grand Central to Chappaqua or, on a light night, the 7:52 whereupon I proceeded to pore through the contents of my book-bag on the train.

It was early in my tenure, that I attended one of these events at the home of Corlies Smith. Better known as Cork in the chummy book world, he was a paragon of the old-shoe literary editor. Smith had been one of the young lions at Viking in its heyday, where he had coaxed, nurtured and out-waited Thomas Pynchon through "V" and "Gravity's Rainbow." The glory days were long gone and Cork Smith brought to mind a once-great pitcher throwing junk for a second-division team in August, aware that his best efforts were well past.

Smith's apartment was one of those grand, wood-paneled confections on Park Avenue in the 90's. Everything was low-key, even the noise level which was more murmur than maelstrom. The fulcrum of the party was in an immense room with high ceilings, dimmed chandeliers and wall-to-wall bookshelves that reached to the roof. It was an early evening in mid-fall and even the twilight frosting the windows seemed to enter discreetly. The waiters were unobtrusive, the canapés were spare, the drinks served on tip-toe.

Cork was the editor-in-chief of Harcourt, Brace, Jovanovich, and an elder statesmen of the book world not so much in age but in demeanor: graying, bony, chiseled, wearing something tattersall and bookish. I don't remember a thing of substance we said but the adverbs, "impeccably, graciously, immaculately," come to mind when I recall the impression his bearing made on me. We chatted briefly; he welcomed me aboard but even this was delivered with a touch of irony, given the direction of the book business and his own future. Harcourt was one of the old-line publishers that boasted a pride of literary icons—many of them European and most of them virtually unread in America outside of campuses and a few urban precincts. Dori Weintraub, its publicist, would gamely pitch me on the worthy offerings of her house and its venerable backlist, a brave little sloop sailing into the winds of expediency.

This party was in honor of the critic Irving Howe and Harcourt had pulled out all the stops in terms of the guest list. I introduced myself to Howe and quickly established my credentials as a Bronx Boy and City College striver. I developed a working relationship with Howe who reviewed a few books on Jewish topics for me before he died. I've been to fancier and bigger parties since, but none that caught the quality of the literary world as I'd envisioned it. Discriminating company, good conversation, a premium on the quality of books and the efficacy of letters. As I was becoming aware, it was a Last Hurrah. By then, virtually all the major houses were owned by corporations. The original titans or their heirs, enthralled by the chimera of growth and synergy, drawn by the siren of the blockbuster and the huge advances required as ante, and fired by the passion to compete at a quantum mega-buck level, became strapped for cash and made a Faustian bargain with media giants who supplied ready financing with the bogus promise of independence.

In short order, the venerable houses became little more than satrapies for global conglomerates who forced out the dinosaurs and made the publishers play by corporate rules with their insatiable appetites for a bottom line that kept escalating. This required a shift in command and control from book men to sales operatives. Books were merchandised, editors were marginalized and those who objected were oxidized, but the façade of a literary establishment was maintained. Good for business. Still, it is difficult to change a culture overnight. Writers wrote, editors edited; good books still found their way to the surface, a few publishers hung on and resourceful editors fought honorable rear-guard actions. It was as if a barbarian horde had conquered an ancient civilization but felt it must temporarily accept the superior culture until it was strong enough to impose its will on its fractious subjects. It was this dynastic transition that provided the background to my sojourn in books.

I should emphasize that I had no magic formula for success. I went about choosing books to review and writers to address them pretty much as most of my peers: by poring over the advance reviews in trade publications such as Publishers Weekly and Kirkus as well as scouring the newspapers for relevant items, and plowing through the publishers' seasonal catalogues. Assigning the big books was easy enough; it was picking the ones that might be overlooked which entailed the hard choices.

I found that one of the compensations of flying solo early on presented an unseen advantage: I had a clear perspective of the whole picture and could see patterns emerge. Perceiving the links among what appeared to be unconnected books provided an edge in both attracting reviewers and engaging readers. I cultivated a coterie of writers whom I came to trust, using them not only as reviewers but sources of book assignments. I developed an expanding circle of de facto preview editors who might not necessarily review the books they brought to my attention, but would suggest a path I hadn't seen. These informal one-on-one chats became indispensable in shaping our report.

If competing with The Times on its own turf was a challenge, it also offered opportunities, not the least of which was that we were in New York. As distinct from my out-of-town colleagues, I had direct access to the publishing houses and literary agents, most of whom were based in the city. It was a matter of mutual seduction and need. Once they saw that Newsday was a serious player and I was a book editor who could help their cause, they came flocking. I had no illusion that The Times was No. 1 and would get preference on everything, but if I could establish a niche where I might glean intelligence as well as win respect, I would have achieved my goals. I also noticed that in the gossipy literary world, publicists rather liked the idea of having a modest counterweight to The Times, another avenue for their wares and a sympathetic ear to tell tales out of school about the Great Gray Lady. I got more than an earful of such gaffes as a writer getting a book to review that contained a note from a previous reviewer telling a Times editor that they didn't want the assignment.

While I had to be careful about being compromised by a literary agent pushing a writer or a book, the up-side was that I had access to their authors, particularly those who were hard to reach or, for my purposes, writers on the brink of fame whom I sought to acquire as reviewers before they became household names.

If the literary agents helped stimulate the circulation it was the publicity people for the publishers who provided the lifeblood of the organism. About three months prior to a season—there were usually two, fall and spring—the publishers would unveil their new list of books. Every season would be prefaced with a catalogue in which each house would advertise its wares for the coming cycle. Every book the firm offered received its own page with a capsule summary advertising its virtues—trumpets and fanfare if the author enjoyed most-favored status, all of this gilded with the iconography of author photos and a heavenly chorus of blurbs shouting hosannas to the writer's past and present efforts.

The copy was usually breathless, the covers always slick, bearing the house's colophon—the Borzoi for Knopf, the vessel for Viking, the home for Random House. These brochures—which also included a back list and a reprise of current releases—could run to nearly 100 pages for a busy season, requiring almost an entire commute to thumb through. The catalogues were merely the tip of the iceberg, the end product of editing, production, sales meetings, ad campaigns, strategy sessions, etc. Since there could be dozens of them, given not only the brochures of the big trade firms but those of the small presses, the academic institutions, the art houses and the plethora of other competitors, absorbing the material of these publishers was a time-consuming affair.

This is where the public-relations people earned their keep. They made it clear by winks, nods and body language—and sometimes even straight talk—which books they were flogging and which they were flagging. Ideally, they'd want one to review all their books positively but since this was not possible, they steered book editors to what they considered their "musts," and even this was a crap-shoot. For the most part, heavy hitters from major houses did not take a lot of selling. It was the mid-level authors, the new writers, the chancy books that were the challenge for these practitioners.

Invariably, their work was done over lunch, usually a literary hangout where they could be seen. The best of them were very good at what they did. The class act, appropriately, was William

Loverd who showed the flag for Knopf. Loverd was an immaculate confection who spoke in apercus and dressed in style, a colorful hanky invariably lounging louche-like from his lightly pin-striped suit. I could never imagine him—even at the beach—in anything but his Noel Cowardesque attire. Bill held court daily from his permanent seat in the mezzanine overlooking the main dining room at the Four Seasons from which he had a birds-eye view of the A-list crowd below and a mildly caustic appreciation of their doings. The meal was on the house, an exception I made since eating with Bill at the Four Seasons was akin to dining in his own home.

Lunching with Loverd was like watching a latter-day Thackery ruefully commenting on the foibles of the characters in his own Vanity Fair. Bill's deft barbs did no harm but were rather little amusements that never went beyond acceptable bounds and were usually balanced by affectionate praise for his targets as well. Bill plied his trade carefully. For all his insouciant disdain, he was eager to see who was present and sitting where and mingling with whom else. He was a connoisseur of this ritual kabuki and enjoyed commenting on its nuances.

What impressed me most about Loverd was how well he'd done his homework. No matter how extensive the catalogue, Bill was familiar with each book; and while he didn't pitch every author on the list, if you asked him about someone he hadn't mentioned, he was ready with a helpful response. Loverd also understood that I had done my homework and was familiar with his catalogue so that he could talk in short-hand and cut to the chase. I was surprised at how many publicists were not familiar with some of their books except at a superficial level, so that once you got past the ad blurb they proceeded to bluff their way through. But their smoke and mirrors fooled no one.

The good publicists turned the spotlight on what they thought was important, offbeat or interesting. It was often a matter of eye contact, phrasing, emphasis, a nuance here, a word dropped there, a declension of the voice, a raising of the brow, a flick of the page, a lowering of the flame, or even a burst of enthusiasm. The words didn't change and each book got its due but, based on the code that developed between publicist and book editor, there was a 180-degree difference in terms of conveying the house's wishes, the publicist's tastes and discerning the expectations of what the editor would actually review, much less how it might be received. The pro's could convey this with deceptive ease.

Of course, dining with book editors like myself was a small, albeit occasionally pleasant, part of their duties. These people were responsible for overseeing the publicity campaigns for their house's major books, mollifying disappointed authors, dealing with the whims of publishers, sales personnel and in-house editors, performing damage control on news flaps and subduing a menagerie of neurotic subordinates. It was a draining job and Loverd made it look easy. But behind his casual air was a meticulous attention to detail. Not a month went by without Bill enclosing within one of the company's galleys a hand-written one-line note in his signature purple ink on Knopf stationary. The notes were personal and to the point, calling my attention to a book that he—and the house—felt was particularly worthy of attention. I have kept scores of them, all beginning "Dear Jack'' and signed with a flourish. Here are only a few:

"Nabokov: Cause for celebration." "[Oliver] Sachs: A major and marvelous addition to the Knopf list." "[William] Trevor: One of the true masters." "Speer: Transfixing—A work of the first importance." On Robert Colasso's "Marriage of Cadmus and Harmony" – "Colasso: A literary and intellectual landmark. Wittily original." On Sherwin Nuland: " 'How We Die'—painful and groundbreaking.'' "Naipaul: A major work – extraordinarily resonant." "Marquez: Luminous, quite unforgettable." "[Alice] Munro: A true master." Bill could herald a fresh voice like Cristina Garcia: " 'Dreaming in Cuban': The striking debut of a major new talent.'' And he could gently let down a tired one: "Baldwin: Important, highly illuminating.'' Translation. It's important because of who James Baldwin is, and it's illuminating because it tells us something about Baldwin, if not much else. With such a note, Bill rendered to Knopf what was Knopf's but he damned Baldwin with faint prose and signaled me that if I didn't review this it would be no loss to literature.

Strangely enough, I did not have the same relationship with the editors at these houses. When I've referred to book editors till now, I've usually been talking about newspaper people like myself who oversaw book sections where the publishers' offerings were reviewed. The luminaries at the various firms who assigned, edited and produced the books that each house published were people I met on a secondary basis. Of course, I had the laying-on-of-hands lunches with such editors as Robert Loomis at Random House, but these occasions provided more a rite of passage than a working relationship. The reason for this was that publicists were protective of their turf and, to a lesser degree, of their firm's editors. They tried to steer newspaper types into their own channels so that they could control the flow of what went in and out. The need to be the standard bearer, to assure that the company spoke with a single voice, and to avoid independent players pitching their own books, was a serious consideration in maintaining control.

Nevertheless I developed a few solid relationships with literary editors such as Jonathan Segal at Knopf, Sara Bershtel at Farrar Straus and later Holt, Elizabeth Sifton then at Knopf before she moved to Farrar Straus. I'd known Segal for more than 15 years since I first arrived at The-Week-in-Review and he worked for Travel. As both sections were part of the Sunday paper, we toiled virtually cheek by jowl. At Knopf, Segal was a workhorse producing between nine and 12 finished books a year, which was a considerable number, particularly since many were heavy lifts involving tomes of voluminous size and writers with egos to match. Jon provided me with insights into the culture of Knopf as well as with previews of his own efforts, usually among the big books of the season.

Elizabeth Sifton was not only a doyenne of the industry but also strove to be its conscience, although to the powers that be she may have appeared more as a Cassandra. Sifton was publishing aristocracy, a charter member of the glory days at Viking where she handled Robertson Davies, Peter Maas and Victor Navasky, culminating in 1975 when she edited "Humboldt's Gift," which won a Pulitzer for Saul Bellow, and Roger Shattuck's biography of Proust, which took a National Book Award. Elizabeth bore intellectual lineage as well, as the daughter of the philosopher Reinhold Niebuhr. She carried herself like a queen and told the industry in a much discussed essay why it was going over a cliff. The burden of her plaint, already discussed here, was the bottom-line, blockbuster mentality driven by marketing types who had seized the reins from bookmen in the interests of their corporate masters, a strategy that would ultimately corrode the book business not only morally but fiscally. Elizabeth's stature enabled her to flagellate the publishers with impunity but, since those in authority generally don't like to put up with the hectoring of Jeremiahs, she became increasingly isolated at Knopf and eventually moved on to the more conducive atmosphere of Farrar Straus under the protective wing of Roger Straus, like herself a practitioner of the old school.

Elizabeth and I would meet at the erstwhile Bolo—one of my regular eateries—in the Flatiron District. Graying and gritty,

Elizabeth was a weathered ship that could still fire salvos. But, far more than a scold, she was an astute student of books and those who produced them. I regret only that I didn't tape our conversations but she probably wouldn't have liked that.

Another editor I came to admire was Aaron Asher who had his own imprint at Doubleday. Aaron had been a comrade-in-arms of Sifton at Viking—indeed, he had also edited Saul Bellow, shepherding "Mr. Sammler's Planet" to a National Book Award. Like Sifton, he fought a noble rear-guard action against the barbarians of commercialism at the gates of publishing. Irascible and irrepressible, Asher bounced, or rather was bounced, from one publisher to another. Along the way, he edited Philip Roth. The imprint at Doubleday, where he could call his own shots under the umbrella of a larger house, was a redoubt that he patrolled, breathing fire to the last. Asher was an outsized, opinionated, unreconstructed liberal, giving no quarter and asking none With his shock of white hair and gravelly voice, Aaron would play the grand old man shooting off broadsides against the folly of his colleagues and warning anyone who would listen about the widening pitfalls of the trade. Aaron was an unabashed intellectual and for consolation translated Milan Kundera from the French. I saw him last at a book party where he still held forth, a latter-day Cyrano thrusting bravely at his foes.

Perhaps the closest I came to making an actual friend of a book editor during my sojourn was Sara Bershtel. She'd worked for Andre Schiffrin at Pantheon and then moved on to Farrar Straus when he was fired. Working for Schiffrin was already a giveaway that Sarah saw books as more than just a commodity although she certainly was no slouch when it came to peddling the goods. But Schiffrin had instilled in her—or more probably hired her because it was already there— the belief that books had a moral purpose.

When I met Sarah, one of her writers at FSG was Andre Aciman. A first-time author, Aciman had written a memoir about growing up in postwar Alexandria and the exilic fortunes of his Sephardic family after they were driven from Nasser's Egypt. Sarah sold me on the book. It didn't need much selling. I arranged for a bi-coastal review by the Pulitzer-Prize-winning Richard Eder that would appear on the front page of both our own section and the Los Angeles Times with which we shared a synergistic condominium. Moreover, I found a Jewish family wedding scene from Cairo in the 20's in the photos that had accompanied, but not appeared in, the book. I ran it on the cover with the article. We were the first ones to review "Out of Egypt," a glowing notice that launched its successful orbit and Aciman's career. The Times didn't weigh in till later. Sarah was, of course, ecstatic, grateful and more than a little impressed.

As for the top bananas, the only one I got to know was Roger Straus, probably through the good offices of his publicity director, Helene Atwan, who was always talking me up. I think Straus liked the idea of hobnobbing with newspaper types which appealed to the raffish streak in him. Roger held court at his corner table in the Union Square Café, and lunching with him was more a matter of letting him discourse on a plethora of topics that struck his fancy or piqued his ire. Sporting an outgrowth of white hair, decked out in a natty shirt and blazer, he looked as if he was about to go sailing. And in a way he was because a meal with Roger Straus was a spirited voyage with occasional tempests and stops at various ports.

The old-line publishers might have been tyrants but one of the aspects that distinguished them from their slicker successors was a sense of noblesse oblige. A few months before New York Newsday folded in 1995, I initiated a column called "The Small Press" in which weekly space was set aside for smaller publishers who usually got short shrift. This gave welcome exposure to a considerable number of worthy books that might otherwise have been written off. For my efforts, I got all kinds of kudos as well as lunch invitations from the smaller houses. One of them came, a week before the ax fell on the New York edition, from George Braziller, a venerable name in small—and not-so-small— publishing. Over the years, he'd brought to our shores Nathalie Sarraute, Marguerite Duras, Jean-Paul Sartre, Francois Mauriac, David Malouf and Orhan Pamuk. Braziller, who had started from scratch in the postwar era, virtually introduced the nouvelle romaine to this country. As I struggled to produce a book section while the ship was sinking and I myself was going overboard, I cancelled my lunches but made sure to call up all my lunch dates individually, and put off the commiseration with a mixture of stoicism and gallows humor. I didn't think much of it at the time but a week later, I got a note from the founder asking for a rain check. I never took him up on it—my loss.

In addition to literary agents, public-relations people and book editors, there were all kinds of other flora and fauna that sprouted and snuffled in the literary world: the book stores big and small; award presenters, trade-fair marketers, floggers of annual events like New York is Book Country, book jobbers, literary lawyers, ad agencies, all of who carved a slice out of the floundering whale that was the book business. Among the most common were the trade journals such as Kirkus, Book List and Library News. The colossus in this field was Publishers Weekly and its public face was the long-time editor of its hard-cover trade-book reviews, Sybil Steinberg. I don't know if Sybil ever missed a book party or, in her absence, if it would have been considered one.

Publishers Weekly was to the publishing industry what Variety is to the entertainment world, but without the edge. Its buzz pages, executive tracking, author interviews, trend pieces and news features were required skimming for anyone in the business, not so much to keep up as to get a sense of the conventional wisdom of the moment. The magazine was less trend-setting than validating. A must-read for the trade, even for those who merely riffled through its pages, were the capsule reviews that ran in the back of the book. PW was notably easy on the industry—the rival Kirkus ran tougher and more candid reviews—but a strong notice in its pages sent a signal as did the code language for a clunker written by one of the many anonymous toilers who contributed to PW for a pittance. These reviews covered everything: fiction, non-fiction, hard-cover, soft-cover, mass-market, poetry, you name it. The premier category was the aforementioned hard-cover trade books over which Sybil Steinberg presided.

Sybil knew everybody and enjoyed knowing everyone and everything. Her remarks over canapés were far more caustic than the pedestrian fare that appeared in PW, but she was fierce in defending the pillars of traditional publishing, perhaps sensing that what was to come would leave her marooned in the past. Steinberg lived in Scarsdale and we'd occasionally share a cab to Grand Central to catch our respective trains to Westchester, during which she'd give me a biting assessment of the hand that had just been feeding her. There are some people for whom it is hard to conjecture a role other than the one in which we see them. It was sometimes difficult to imagine Sybil doing anything but making the rounds of book parties armed with drink and hors d'oeuvres. Beneath the fizz, she was a shrewd cookie with an intuitive understanding of the inner workings of the book business.

Florence King's departure was a blessing because it liberated a large chunk of Sunday real estate that had been mortgaged to her, allowing me to bring in writers of my own choosing. It also freed up a quarter of our weekday space, a plus in the long run but an immediate challenge since Florence's precipitous departure left me with a limited amount of time to fill the gap. My strategy was simple. To replace Florence in her weekly slot, I needed four reviewers who would each file once a month for the Tuesday opening. Having inherited three weekday "regulars" I was not going to get hooked into a fourth personality to whom I'd be beholden. I wanted to open up the pages to a variety of opinions. Moreover, with another regular, I'd be more susceptible to run books of their choosing rather than my own. The key to my rotation was that I had to get writers who had Florence's flair without her attitude, preferably women. Given the politically correct politics of the time, then in high season, to replace a female writer with a male in a regular rotation would have left me open to charges of chauvinism—already implicit in my very existence. Luckily, this was not a problem, since there were a host of talented female free-lancers around who were only too happy to have a steady gig at Newsday. I needed a balance of writers who had sufficient cachet to impress the brass, who were familiar to the readers, and who had elegance as well as freshness to catalyze the mix. Most importantly, they wouldn't be ghettoized—reviewing soft novels or entertainment books which was then the fate of so many women reviewers—but rather they'd essay serious nonfiction as well as good novels.

A critical acquisition was Susan Jacoby with whom I probably had the longest relationship, carrying over into my subsequent tenure at The Times. Jacoby was a known quantity who had previously reviewed for Nina but whose real talents had hardly been tapped. She had covered the Soviet Union for the Washington Post along with her former husband, Anthony Astrakhan, as part of a His and Hers team. One of the bonuses I got from Jacoby was also acquiring her ex. An independent spirit, or rather a writer solely dependent on her free-lance fees, Susan was constantly belaboring me about our accounting department's belated payments. Her style was brisk and brusque: "I think it's quite clear that these payments are not being put through till publication, and that is just not acceptable to me. I'm turning in this review because I knew you need it but I'm not going to turn in the next one if I haven't been paid for this review. Tell accounting I don't give credit."

It was in part, based on Susan's hectoring, in part based on my own sense of self-preservation, that I succeeded in getting the accounting department to pay on acceptance of the copy, rather than publication, which could sometimes involve an interval of weeks. The delay was a policy that many other publications invoked in their high-handed treatment of free-lancers. In most cases, the fee was so minimal that it was academic, literally. My payments were serious enough to amount to something.

Jacoby wrote with a fierce urgency that couldn't help but draw the reader along. She didn't so much review a book as seize it, throw grappling hooks over the side, board it and engage, until whatever treasures the prize hid were offered up. Whether celebrating or eviscerating, her enthusiasm for the chase was infectious.

Early on in our long association, I had taken to treating Susan to a pre-Christmas lunch along with her friend, Angeline Goreau who also wrote for us. Angeline may have been a buddy of Susan's but she was a bird of distinctly different plumage. If Susan was meat and potatoes, Angeline was an hors d'oeuvre: cultivated, well-bred, refined to a fault. She was also a perceptive critic and elegant writer who became a staple of our weekly rotation for a year during which she reviewed everything from Gustave Flaubert to Robertson Davies, all with panache and distinction.

Revitalizing the section and keeping it going had me running. I boarded the 6:34 out of Chappaqua in the mornings—it was the earliest train I could get—so it was a longish day but at 50, I had an inexhaustible fund of energy and never seemed to mind it. I read The Times and The Wall Street Journal on the way in to see if there were any news items that would affect our coverage, or trends that might influence my selection of books for review. I saw our section as an active arm of a newspaper, so it was important to be on top of the news. For the first few years, when Newsday was located in the Wang Building, a burnished skyscraper on Third Avenue, I'd wend my way up from Grand Central to the corner of 48th Street where I was usually among the first customers of a feisty lady who ran the coffee wagon on the corner. Armed with breakfast, I'd ride up to the 26th floor where I unlocked the door to the office and made my way to my desk in time to catch the sun as it glinted over the East River. By the time I got settled it was almost 8. I checked the fax machines and was at my computer promptly to see if any copy or messages had arrived overnight.

In those days, before 24/7 internet journalism, the computers were "down" between the time the paper closed in the early morning and 8 A.M. They were literally revved up by an Atex maintenance team led by John McCloud. John was a diligent technician but since I was the first one in the office and eager to get going just as he was starting up, I'd sometimes grow impatient and prod him to move along, which he didn't always appreciate. Luckily, the taciturn McCloud was slow to anger and I learned to curb my impatience so we worked out a modus vivendi. Once the computers were up and running, I'd do a light first-edit of whatever was in or, if articles needed considerable work, I'd call the reviewers and go over my fixes before asking them to resubmit their piece. Our writers were used to getting early calls from me. By now, my valued secretary, Estelle Miller, had arrived and I went over two schedules, the first an immediate one over the next two weeks to make sure that everything assigned was in, or on its way in, or had a backup should it not arrive on time. Rule one was: always have an escape route.

The second schedule was a long-range outline of books that I planned to assign over the next three months and a list of possible reviewers whom I'd approach. The key was to get a lot of this work done early because once the day got going, the agenda was no longer mine. I'd be answering phone calls from bosses, irate readers, writers with problems, fending off ill-considered directives, coddling prima donnas and dealing with an assortment of unforeseen crises that invariably cropped up. Getting the copy, or most of it, safely moved before the onset of this daily flood of distractions, was critical if we were to come out on time. Which accounted for my early arrival and late departure. I found that I got 80 percent of my actual work done in the hour after I arrived and the one before I left, the relative quiet time when I could concentrate undisturbed without the phone ringing and hectoring memos lighting up my screen. When needed, I spent the early hours ringing up writers abroad in London, South Africa and Japan. Similarly, I stayed late to get reviewers in California like the historians Joyce Appleby, Robert Dallek and Stephen Mosher during their afternoon office-hours. By mid-morning the mail started to arrive which, after being screened by Estelle, I sorted through for reviews as well as any epistolary time bombs.

Along with the mail came a deluge of book bags, a phenomenon both anticipated and dreaded. The sheer volume presented a Sisyphean challenge. At least three bags-full containing upwards of 75 books each arrived every morning and a similar consignment came in the afternoon, all dumped on a large stone table-top. If I didn't make a dent in the morning's load, there would be that much more to deal with in the afternoon. Moreover, they all came in parcels that had to be stripped or cut open. Estelle could do some of this but invariably I had to step in and do the bulk of it—labor-intensive, time-consuming, maddening. I knew that my opposite number across town at The Times, with its legions of clerks, was not spending her time with such chores.

To get through this morass involved a system of triage. Most of the books arrived as bound galleys, in effect soft-cover editions on rough paper, often without pictures, indexes and final editing, but sufficient for the reviewer, allowing for a check on any questionable material. The large publishers all bound their galleys in different "house" colors—red for Simon & Schuster, yellow for Little Brown, green for Viking, purple for Putnam and, the elegant gray for Knopf. Also, they usually arrived in packs of bound boxes so that, mercifully, one didn't have to open them individually. The key was that, for the most part, I knew what I was looking for. I had already perused the advance reviews in Kirkus and Publishers Weekly, scoured the publishers' catalogues and been briefed by the publicists on their choice cuts of the season so that those galleys were set aside immediately for possible review. We had a large mirrored closet with sliding doors the length of the office bristling with shelves on which the books were stored by date and alphabetical order in three categories: For definite review, possible review and doubtful. Finally, there were books that were simply cast off, winding up in a slush pile for periodic book sales that raised money for various Newsday charities.

I usually perused the book ahead of time so that I was familiar with it, rather than simply reading the accompanying press release. Moreover, I wanted to be satisfied that it was at least worthy of review. Before making the call, I tried to bone up on the topic if I wasn't already conversant with it. After discussing the review with the writer, we'd agree on a length, fee and due date and I would immediately have Estelle send it out along with a note reprising the essentials of our conversation, copy to me. Once the piece ran and the fee was paid I would never fail to promptly send out a thank-you note praising the writers for their efforts. Being Avis to The Times's Hertz made it vital for me to maintain a special relationship with our reviewers, and a grace note at the end of the process was a helpful way to keep the machinery oiled. Despite the short-cuts triage afforded, there still remained a slew of galleys from smaller publishers or overlooked books from larger ones worthy of consideration, and these I literally skimmed in the office standing at a table perch like a distracted Hamlet. Often there were little gems that came unheralded and would have been consigned to oblivion had I not rescued them.

By now the morning was growing late and I made whatever further assignments I could or tied up any loose editing ends before going to lunch. This was invariably a business meeting with a publicist or editor pitching me on the season's fare, or a treat for a visiting writer or a heart-to-heart with a staffer. Even if I had no lunch date, I tried to get out for half-an-hour. After we'd moved to Park Avenue at 33rd Street, I'd stroll down to the then-seedy Madison Square Park and the magic shops, carpet emporiums and music-box stores that lined this once quirky route. I felt I needed this break just to get my head clear and de-compress from the whirlwind. I would perambulate as far as St. Gaudens's statue of Admiral Farragut in the park and, duly inspired, return to my own version of "Damn the torpedoes, full speed ahead."

The early afternoon was devoted to moving more copy. The week had a rhythm. In the early part I'd edit the four dailies for the following week which went to the Newsday copy desk on Long Island. By midweek, I'd have completed the weekly copy for the following Sunday. Earlier in the week, I'd have addressed the layouts and graphics. If things went well, Thursday was devoted to heads, captions, trims, inserts and minor adjustments. If things didn't—and they usually didn't—they spilled over till Friday morning when last-minute fires were extinguished. This never stopped the daily rhythm of shelving books, making assignments and the painstaking work of expanding and refining our burgeoning list of reviewers. When I got my second wind in mid-afternoon, I'd usually try to make a rush of assignments. I could allot six on a good run and usually managed a dozen over the course of a week which kept us ahead with a little cushion.

Friday afternoon was generally devoted to catching up on the considerable amount of correspondence that needed attending. Looking back at all the letters that I sent and received, to writers cajoling, praising, entreating, criticizing; to readers educating, justifying, mollifying; to the paper's executives lecturing, importuning, defying; to publishers, admonishing, reminding, acknowledging, it's a wonder that I had time to produce a book section. But, in fact, correspondence was a subsidiary exercise, undertaken after the daily scramble. Most important before I left was preparing for the following Monday, which I did without exception, else there'd be chaos when I arrived after the weekend. I'd invariably take a half-dozen books home with me on Friday evenings to decide whether or not to review them. As I rushed for the 6:29, I'd stop to pick up one of the model cars being hawked by the vendors outside Grand Central. They were a favorite of my son. I'd also bring home one of the many children's books that came through to read to my daughter. I promised myself that whatever happened, I wasn't going to sacrifice my family for the job and somehow I found a way to achieve this. I never missed a sports or school event and during this period we took some of our most memorable family vacations.

At 2 Park Avenue I had a bigger office but a lesser view – an interior courtyard whose unvaried bricks and intrusive windows invited regular use of my Venetian blinds. But the limited view was compensated for by a lively walk from the station. Sometimes, I had company. Putnam Book Publisher's was located along my route and Faith Sale, one of its top editors, would occasionally bump into me and we'd talk shop on the way down to work. Faith was another fixture in the publishing world. She had an endless enthusiasm for books and authors that was as genuine as it was infectious. She handled some of the top writers in a very successful publishing house run by the astute Phyllis Grann. Years later she sent me a valued farewell salute when New York Newsday folded. In turn, I attended her memorial service when her flock of writers and a flood of colleagues turned out to honor her. She was concerned about them almost to the end.

Although the dynamics of producing a book section were demanding, they were not worrisome. Each new challenge provided its own opportunity. After Leslie Hanscom retired toward the end of 1988, I was determined to replace him not with another writer but an editor who would act as a deputy. After a brief misfire, I hired Jennifer Krauss. Jennifer had the pedigree of working for two great literary lions Leon Wieseltier at the New Republic and Robert Silvers at the New York Review of Books. She could clearly strengthen our writing pool with top-tier talent from both of these publications. Moreover, Jennifer was a polished writer who could cover the field on a wide range of topics.

The departure of the Infant Phenomenon freed me to turn the daily pages into a serious literary forum. For the balance of the week I could embark on a rotation of my own choosing. Since the women-only pressure that obtained earlier had receded and I'd stabilized my position, I was able to split the difference with two female and two male writers. I chose carefully. I had one bit of luck with the demise of Seven Days, a cooler version of the calcified Village Voice with a more cultural, less political tinge. As often happens in journalism, the misfortune of one venture turns out to be the good fortune of another, in this case, mine. I snatched two outstanding reviewers – Vince Passaro and Francine Prose—from the sinking ship. In addition to selecting Passaro and Prose for the Daily, my two other choices for the regular rotation on Thursdays were Thomas Mallon and Carolyn See, who'd appeared occasionally in Newsday but whose talents I recognized as deserving greater prominence in our pages.

I knew Francine from my erstwhile days at Harvard. She already had a few novels under her belt but was still on the cusp of breaking out as the literary celebrity she was shortly to become. After a sojourn in the Village artists' redoubt of Westbeth, she had retired to the upstate community of Krumville with her two sons, Bruno and Leo, and her artist husband Howie. The steady gig I provided her over the next several years came in handy. I would send the books off to Krumville and she dutifully submitted a review each month, in space, on time, elegantly, almost effortlessly written. Francine was an astute critic, sharp but not sharp-edged. She could be arch but never mean. A writer herself, she had a built-in sympathy for her peers and could at least essay what they were attempting before discussing whether they had succeeded. She usually found something good to say about the weakest of them, although, when exasperated, she could skewer the miscreant.

Francine also had a droll sense of fun. In reviewing a book about an 18th-Century French envoy and military hero who turned out to be a woman, she wrote: "What is it with these French diplomats? What is their problem, exactly? Just when we thought we'd untangled that web of sexual muddle and political intrigue now commonly known as the "M Butterfly" affair, historian Gary Kates has come along to show us that this lepidopterous mix of gender confusion and espionage is certainly nothing new—or, in any case, nothing new to the world of Gallic diplomacy."

Each review came with a brisk note from Crispell Road in Krumville. The missives were spare; the proof was in the writing. On and on, diligently and dependably, year after year. I have scores of these epistles tucked away in my files. In the summer, Francine repaired to one of the authors' colonies like Yaddo or a writer-in-residence teaching program on some bucolic campus. She was an editor's dream, innovative in her approach, judicious in her critique and dependable in her delivery.

Thomas Mallon's father was a glove salesman who toiled unobtrusively in the Garment District for the better part of his life. Mallon took me past his father's workplace on the corner of 35th and Fifth when he wrote a My Manhattan piece about it for me some years later after I'd moved back to The Times. Perhaps it was some genetic legacy of his father's attention to the details of the glove business that gave Tom such a discretionary eye for the nuances of literature and the ability to distinguish between the merely adequate and the very good. I had plucked Mallon from the chorus to which Nina had relegated him. Rather than allow Tom to languish as an occasional reviewer, I brought him into the rotation where his versatility allowed me to use him on a variety of subjects: biographies of William Butler Yeats, Somerset Maughm and Brian Boyd's magisterial life of Vladimir Nabokov, as well as novels by Italy's Natalia Ginzburg and Nathaniel Branden's chastening memoir of his service as an acolyte in the personality cult of Ayn Rand. Mallon had the ability of taking on any intellectual subject and making it accessible to readers without talking down to them.

Tom went on to become the literary editor of GQ as well as achieve esteem with novels such as "Henry and Clara" and "Dewey Defeats Truman." Even after he went on to a wider career we stayed in touch and he'd occasionally do a Weekend article for me when I returned to The Times . The last such piece Mallon wrote was on Madison Square Park – a site he was researching for one of his novels —still raffish before its gentrification a decade later. I couldn't help but think of Tom as some archivist of desuetude, meticulously chronicling waning ages as he'd troubled over the details of the books I'd sent him, teasing out the essence of each for the benefit of a careful reader.

Carolyn See was a product of California, who wrote with an off-the-cuff spontaneity that was a polar opposite of Tom's Apollonian prose and Francine's carefully cadenced sentences. Carolyn just let it rip. I rescued her from the "women's ghetto'' where she'd been languishing when I discovered her. She had been pretty much consigned by Nina to reviewing woman's romances. I saw Carolyn was a lot better than that with a perceptive intelligence informing her down-home, shoot-from-the-lip style. I gave her major authors and threw in political books that she hit out of the park although I occasionally had to reign in her West Coast liberalism which she brandished unselfconsciously.

I owe my good fortune in acquiring Vince Passaro to Pat Towers who'd been the book editor at Seven Days before its demise. I'd known Pat when she was an editor on The Times book section from whence she'd gone off to assist her colleague Richard Locke in his ethereal effort to revive Vanity Fair. It was left to others to breathe earthy vitality into the Conde Nast phoenix and Towers moved on to leaner pastures. Pat was considered one of the great behind-the-scenes players in the literary game. Her counsel was wise, her influence considerable, her taste impeccable. I had already spotted Passaro's reviews in the flagging Seven Days and probably would have enlisted him in any case, but Pat's endorsement put the cap on it. Vince was the most original writer who ever worked for me, incapable of writing a dull line. He was candid about himself, provocative in his views, fearless in his judgments, and he wrote with imagination and flare.

Here he is on the new translation of "The Brothers Karamazov" by Richard Pevear and Larissa Volokhonsky: "Taking on this book—800-some-odd pages of idiosyncratic Russian with a list of characters that fills two long pages—is somewhat like waking up one morning and deciding to clean up the Teamsters Union."

Vince was one of those former near Jesuits who'd been brought up Catholic and rebelled into anti-clerical apostasy but adopted the steely reasoning of his teachers to temper the flame of his dissidence. Passaro had a small following—myself, Pat Towers, Rick MacArthur at Harper's—but aside from the occasional piece for The Times, he never caught on at any of the big shops.

As I had done with our weekday rotation, I was determined to acquire new talent for the Sunday pages and introduce fresh faces to the mix. Although I cultivated a steady coterie of outstanding writers whom we could rely on, I always sought to widen the spectrum with provocative voices and prominent figures who were increasingly receptive to my courting as the book section's reputation grew.

A paradigm of this strategy was our acquisition of the essayist and translator Stanislaw Baranczak whom I engaged with an appraisal of the charismatic Russian poet Yevgeny Yevtushenko whose collected poems were being dutifully published by Holt in 1991 after the Soviet Union crumbled. A professor of East European literature at Harvard who'd translated poets from James Merrill to Shakespeare, Baranczak was himself an accomplished poet and an independent spirit. We couldn't offer him much in terms of money or prestige but, like many such prominent writers whom we attracted, we gave him a book that he'd have something to say about. And indeed he did. Deriding Yevtushenko as "the Soviet Union's equivalent of a court poet" he declared: "To mention him in the same breath with [the Russian expatriate poet] Joseph Brodsky as his editor does is ludicrous, if not obscene. Why? First, because Brodsky has never been a product of the political system whereas Yevtushenko has been precisely that. Second because Brodsky is a genuine poet whereas Yevtushenko most definitely is not.''

Although I spoke with Baranczak repeatedly over the years, I never met him, which was the case with so many writers. The fleeting friendships I developed were among people with whom I had actual contact, whether at lunch, in the office, or at the roundelay of book events. In a way, this made the ephemeral quality of telephone talk more authentic, polished conversation without the patina of physicality. What's left is the core, the writing, which will have to suffice.

At the high tide of the Counter-Culture era in the 60's, Jonathan Kozol published "Death at an Early Age,'' an account of his baleful experience in the Boston School system, which made him a folk-hero to a wide spectrum of educational reformers, Within 20 years, Kozol's nurturing nostrums made his once-radical prescriptions holy writ among many in the Ed School establishment. Several books later, he returned to his original theme with "Savage Inequalities: Children in America's Schools." By now, Kozol had approached the status of near-sainthood and his much-ballyhooed book, in which he did the equivalent of a victory lap through a scattering of the nation's schools, was more of a coronation than a chronicle, albeit in this case he was celebrating the dismal fact that little had changed since he wrote his first book. Part of the promotion involved an ad campaign— a perk reserved for an elite of authors —by his publisher, Crown, which had taken advertising space in Newsday, a bone tossed at our vain efforts to attract more book ads, the preponderance of which went to The Times.

The review was given to Sarah Mosle, our paperback reviewer, who had been brought in by Jennifer Kraus from the New Republic where they'd worked together. Sarah was well-qualified for the task. In addition to having been an actual teacher herself she was a natural investigative reporter with a bird-dogging tenacity in pursuing a lead. Kozol had assumed his book would be ushered in with literary palm fronds by the mainstream media or, at worst, sustain a few predictable brickbats from the marginalized Right. He was not expecting someone from the liberal press to read his book carefully, which is precisely what Mosle did. What she found was that Kozol's grand tour was a perfunctory visit shored up by a clip job providing him sufficient material to justify his assumptions. Worse still, he'd borrowed piecemeal the work of other reporters who'd actually spent time in the schools he cited, without giving them sufficient credit. But let Sarah Mosle tell it:

"Like an undergraduate with a Eurorail pass who tries to take in Rome in a day, Jonathan Kozol appears to duck into a school as if it were St. Peter's. We don't get the sense that he has lingered in any one place for very long. Kozol insists that he wants to listen to children, But oddly, there's really not much sense of children here—only anonymous statistics, and a few blurred faces from Kozol's passing train . . . Kozol appears to have done virtually no original reporting. In each city he culls the local newspapers for anecdotes to support his preconceived notions, which he carries around with him like so many pieces of luggage . . . Nowhere does Kozol adequately indicate the degree of his indebtedness. The pattern repeats itself in each city."

Before the review ran, we asked Crown to withdraw its ad, one of the rare occasions that a newspaper returned advertising money. I had to go round a few times with Sarah to keep the word "plagiarize" out of the review. Kozol was sufficiently cagey so that it might be hard to prove where sloppiness ended and deliberate appropriation began. He had apparently spent more time on eliding the clips than sitting in the classroom. In the end, I convinced Sarah that without using charged language, we had nailed Kozol. The result was a minor contretemps that dented Kozol's reputation but didn't demolish it. His critics, however, never let him forget it. Sadly, Newsday was one of the few publications to criticize Kozol's book.

Many authors had a pocket passion that would induce them to write about a subject not in their field, giving Newsday the aura of the byline and the reader the frisson of a celebrated personality writing against the grain. For instance we got the Harvard biologist Stephen J. Gould, a Yankee fan, to contribute to a baseball section for the Opening Day of the season. We liberated people from categories in which they were pigeonholed to write about their other interests. One such contributor was Shalom Goldman, then a professor of Jewish studies at Dartmouth, who wrote frequently about Jewish cultural and political affairs. Shortly after the first Iraq War in 1991, a spate of quickie books came out trying to explain Iraq to a curious public. They seemed superficial and I wondered if there was something more substantial Newsday could offer. I recalled that Goldman, had written the libretto for Philip Glass's "Ikhnaton," and knew something about Egypt as well as the archeology of the Middle East. He proposed two works written in the first half of the 20th Century, still in print, which might provide better insight into Iraq than the current fare being spun out on the fly. Both books were by Englishwomen: Gertrude Bell and Freya Stark. Neither was a household name in America but each of them had figured as participants in the history of Iraq.

Gertrude Bell was one of the architects of the modern Iraqi state. She helped recruit Lawrence of Arabia for the British campaign in the Middle East during World War I and, as Britain's Oriental Secretary, she was instrumental after the war in placing Iraq's first king, Feisal, on the throne. An intrepid archeologist, she was Indiana Jones before Indiana Jones. Freya Stark, was a British civil servant in Baghdad during World War II who spent the war years countering Axis propaganda in Egypt, Yemen, Arabia and Iraq. Goldman discerningly reviewed the memoirs of both women, Gertrude Bell's "The Desert and the Sown" and Freya Stark's "Dust in the Lion's Paw." Bell and Stark were subsequently unearthed by the media but ours was the earliest mention of them in the popular press, much less together, offering both a context and a linkage for the audience.

While Newsday's New York edition was making headway in the city, three-quarters of our circulation was in the suburbs. Having earlier worked on Long Island for nine years, I'd long ago disabused myself of the patronizing attitude some of my peers in the tonier book precincts had toward the burbs. A quality book section was a source of pride to subscribers on both sides of the Nassau County line. But the common touch was also important; going too high-church would put off readers who wanted to feel included in the conversation. Consequently, Newsday Books addressed the full panoply of popular fiction and lighter nonfiction.

For instance we took sports books seriously and treated sports as more than just fun and games. A special effort went in to the summer game. Publishers traditionally issued a slew of baseball books in time for Opening Day of the season. In the spring of 1989, we reviewed a baker's dozen of books with five reviewers, all female, and all students of the game: the authors Hilma Wolitzer, Susan Jacoby and Roberta Israeloff (Met fans), Diane Cole (Orioles) and Leslie Visser, a sportscaster for CBS. Except for Visser, they were each road-tested as reviewers. The cover art was an illustration from a collection of baseball drawings that captured a play at the plate under the rubric of "Play Ball." What started out as a gimmick turned into a tour de force of solid sports writing and got us accolades from the industry, readers and fans.

The following year, the legendary Mark Harris, author of two of the great baseball classics, "Bang the Drum Slowly" and "The Southpaw," reviewed Robert Creamer's take on the memorable 1941 season and the even-more memorable 1951 year with the Dodgers playing fall guy in both. We twinned Harris out with Stephen Jay Gould, the Harvard biologist who, although a Yankee fan, was eager to review a Ted Williams biography whose author, Michael Siedel, taught the Great Books program at Columbia. In this same issue were reviews of books by Isaac Singer, Alan Furst and Michelangelo's poetry, nonfiction about the fighting in Central America and the fall of the Bingham newspaper dynasty in Nashville.

Matching these books with the right reviewer was three parts alchemy, two parts serendipity and one part instinct: a catch-as-catch-can process that involved friends, flattery, enterprise and a little audacity. Sometimes, it was dumb luck. Anthony Burgess appeared virtually over the transom. I never spoke to the great man himself but to his agent, the flamboyant Gabriel Pantucci. The piece being offered or, rather, heralded, was a defense of the beleaguered Salman Rushdie on the first anniversary of the Ayatollah Khomenei's fatwa against him for writing "The Satanic Verses." Newsday presumably came recommended to Burgess by Christopher Hitchens who was a friend of Rushdie's and connected to the Old Boy network in London. I assumed the essay was either a screed recycled from one of the British journals or something rejected by them as too much, too late. Actually, it was quite a good article, if a bit frothy, which was Burgess's style. Moreover, although this wasn't a book review it was a trenchant essay on the importance of books demonstrated by the impulse to suppress them. It certainly belonged in a literary section as part of the cultural discourse, and the fact that its source was the author of "A Clockwork Orange" was not to be sneezed at. The piece was ours for a mere $900. This was more than triple what I was paying our top writers. Pantucci made it appear as if he were doing me a favor. He talked in flourishes, bringing to mind Parelli, the mountebank barber hawking a hair-restoring elixir in "Sweeney Todd." I admired his cheek and decided to pay the gold to the bridge troll, making economies elsewhere.

The piece ran under the headline: "The Pen Against the Scimitar," with an illustration of Rushdie by Van Howell. Although the cost was exorbitant it was vital not only to know the price of something, but its value as well. Using that criteria, we got our money's worth. The essay was an important one and its author added luster to our list. We could invoke Burgess's name in promoting the section and attracting other top-tier reviewers so his fee was a capital investment. Newsday Books ran a few other pieces by him over the years—always trumpeted with great fanfare by the irrepressible Pantucci—and rejected a few as well to the dismayed surprise of the agent. By then Newsday had an impressive roster of writers and could pick and choose a bit more.

Paul Berman was a horse of quite a different color. By then a considerable figure on the New Left as it edged mid-ward, Berman was eking out a living as a writer for the Village Voice where he toiled in monkish devotion to a calling that apparently required vows of abstinence if not poverty. He maintained a Spartan existence on the still scruffy Upper West Side residing above a bodega. The books I dispatched for review were sent to him care of the store; his copy was often picked up at the same venue. Berman was carving out a niche as an independent thinker, someone who could be unpredictable in his opinions but invariably astute in his criticism. He had spent time reporting in Central America and was an opponent of the CIA-supported dictatorships with few illusions about the revolutionaries who opposed them. Paul dissented with the Neo-Left on Israel but was innately suspicious of the dictums of the Neo-Right. He was a fixture at the major intellectual journals, an aspirant for the mantle worn by such idiosyncratic gadflies as Murray Kempton, but tending more toward social criticism than daily journalism.

I knew Berman from Leftist friends who'd moved further Right and our phone chatter had the congeniality of a give-and-take among acquaintances versed in the same political grammar. Paul was usually busy juggling assignments and reluctant to take on any more but he invariably acquiesced. After I made the pitch, I'd simply let our dialogue evolve into a discourse he gave on the subject, toward the end of which he decided he might as well write a review because he'd just given one. While he was at it, he could read the book. Off it went to the bodega. Paul had a deceptively laconic style in which he appeared to accept a book's premise, then pause to think it over and, after due consideration, find it wanting. Almost reluctantly, he'd proceed to demolish the book, as if he kept stumbling on details he simply couldn't ignore, a gambit that won the reader over better than if he set a strident tone from the outset.

Berman was part of the contingent of Village Voice staffers who from time to time wrote for our book section. While the Voice was no longer what it was during its 60's heyday—the pre-eminent alternative newspaper in the nation—it still maintained enough of its counter-cultural vibes to echo a feisty heritage. Its book editor, M. Mark, represented that tradition. Her monthly edition was one of the few stand-alone book sections in the country. She had attracted a collection of outspoken free-lancers who were only too glad to share their talents with—and receive fees and exposure from—Newsday. Among the reviewers who came from The Voice was the sportswriter Allen Barra, whose contrarian commentary made him a bete noire of the established sports world. Barra would stay with me through my subsequent move back to The Times years later and prove invaluable in corralling a pick-up team of his athlete-writer pals to help me fuel the Times's Weekend Warrior column for several years. Allen was also a movie nut who wrote as passionately about film as he did about sports so with him I got a twofer. Barra finally hit it big with his biography of Yogi Berra, another character who marched to his own drum. The Voice was also a source of several gay and lesbian writers who were important to establish our credentials as culturally cutting-edge. In this category we got such reviewers as Stacey D'Erasmo and Donna Minkowitz, although I had already cultivated my own stable in this area with writers such as Daniel Harris and Jay Weiser.

One of the strongest—and strangest—acquisitions we made from The Voice was Lucette Lagnado. A former investigative reporter for the muckraker Jack Anderson and the author of a book on Mengele's experiments with twins at Auschwitz, Lagnado wrote the Voice's Urban Guerilla column. At some point, Lucette had run afoul of one of the Voice's cultural commissars, who'd developed a personal animosity towards her. Even by the Voice's standards of internecine vendettas, in Lucette's telling her tormenter's antipathy was toxic. Whatever the reason, they were made for each other: he was a consummate bully and she was a perfect victim. On top of this, Lucette's mother, with whom she had an intense relationship, was suffering a lingering death in a hospital. Lagnado was convinced that the doctors were not helping very much. The slim upside to this was that it intensified Lucette's interest in medical issues. She did a few pieces for us on health care. She also wrote a strong review of my old Times colleague

Nan Robertson's "Girls in the Balcony," the story of the women's lawsuit that broke the dam on gender hiring and promotion at The Times.

It must have been a relief for Lucette to have a sympathetic editor who welcomed her copy. I edited her firmly, but with care. Lagnado was looking for an opportunity to escape The Voice and I tried to steer her into whatever avenues I could, including a job at Newsday where I mentioned her to our New York managing editor Don Forst. Lucette had clearly benefited from her apprenticeship with Jack Anderson. She had the makings of a hard-digging reporter. Eventually, Lagnado left The Voice for a more appropriate position as an editor at the Forward. In due course, Lucette broached the health beat to The Wall Street Journal where she became a valued medical reporter. Many years later, Lagnado went on to write about not only her mother but her father in the critically acclaimed "Man in the White Sharkskin Suit." The memoir, about the past of her Sephardic family, made her a star on the book circuit.

At about this time, I'd had a run-in with the AIDS police. During the fever-pitch days of the AIDS crisis in late 1990 Newsday reviewed two books on the topic, "The History of AIDS" and "The AIDS Disaster." I had previously reviewed several works on the subject including fiction by David Leavitt and Christopher Bram and nonfiction by Larry Kramer, Susan Sontag and Paul Monette. Our book section had always been well ahead of the curve on the issue, in keeping with Newsday's general coverage, which was in advance of The Times and most other papers because of the enterprising work of such reporters as Laurie Garrett and B.D. Colen. My deputy, Jennifer Krauss, made the assignment, to Michael Fumento, a gutsy call since he was a known skeptic of the figures bruited about by the activist community, but a good choice since his work was reputable and against the grain.

Fumento's own book, "The Myth of Heterosexual AIDS," had made him persona non grata among AIDS activists. What enraged Fumento's critics was that he brought to bear a formidable amount of research from epidemiologists and the Federal Centers for Disease Control that debunked the conventional wisdom that AIDS had spread from the homosexual culture to the heterosexual world—i.e. that it was a problem for all of us. Fumento showed rather that AIDS, in this country, was still basically transmitted through anal sex, that it was primarily limited to the gay community, drug users who shared needles or heterosexuals

277

infected through drug transfusions. Moreover, even among this cachement, the reported incidents were overblown and the estimates of the disease were actually being lowered. If Fumento was correct then AIDS activists would find it much harder to marshal national resources for what would be perceived essentially as a homosexual problem. Fumento ridiculed the government-financed "Sex equals Death" campaigns which featured low-risk, straight, white people in its ads. He demonstrated that such individuals were at less risk of getting AIDS by participating in casual sex than being hit by a car.

For his pains, Fumento became an object of vilification in the gay community. His book suffered a campaign of suppression that was as chilling as it was effective. After barely managing to secure a publisher he found that his work was effectively banned in virtually every major bookstore in the country. Booksellers, intimidated by gay activists, simply refused to carry it or, if they did, openly display it. The sad irony is that Fumento's inconvenient facts provided an important contribution to the debate over how to respond to the challenge of AIDS. He pointed out that, in terms of national priorities, we were spending more on AIDS than on any other disease even though there were 14 greater causes of death including cancer and heart disease. The latter killed more people in six weeks than died of AIDS in the entire course of the epidemic. And the final irony was that in making this a national emergency, the AIDS lobbyists were diverting attention from the very specific community that was suffering from the disease.

It was in this charged atmosphere that I decided to green-light Jennifer's choice of assigning Fumento the review. I felt that his voice was an important one that deserved to be heard amid the uproar. I also believed that as long as he got his facts right and was fair-minded in the review, we might get some angry letters but that this was part of doing business. I didn't know what I was letting myself in for. The Furies came masked as a farceur in the persona of one Michelangelo Signorile. During the madness of those times, one of the gay magazines that briefly cropped up was a broadsheet called Outweek. As its name implied, it was devoted to "outing" prominent closeted homosexuals. In a self-laceration of the Gay Pride campaign, Outweek argued that everyone should come out and, since those who insisted on their sexual privacy were shirking their duties, the magazine would take it upon itself to expose them. Standing out from the mélange of gossip, innuendo, and rancor that filled Outweek's pages, was Signorile's Gossip Watch which, for sheer vituperation, was in a league of its own. In addition to vilifying his victims, usually for being insufficiently gay, one of Signorile's more inventive ploys was to ZAP anyone who'd run afoul of him. That is, publish the miscreant's name and phone number and unleash his myrmidons in a phone campaign to harass the target. One can only wonder what he would have done in the digital age.

What outraged Signorile about the review was not so much anything Fumento had to say but that we had chosen Fumento to say it. Not only was Fumento's book to be suppressed but all traces of him were to be blotted out. The incongruity of such a Stalinist enterprise in the name of a rights movement was lost on Signorile. In any case he first called a Part II editor, David Herndon, in high dudgeon. Herndon, who was in good stead with the gay community, gave me a heads-up that I'd hear from Signorile and, warning me of his pit-bull tactics, that he intended to attack me in his column. Sure enough, Signorile called, berating my secretary Estelle Miller, shouting that he was on deadline and insisting that I speak to him at once—a sure way not to get someone on the phone. Estelle rolled her eyeballs, indicating she had a nut on the phone and I just signaled that I'd handle him later. Estelle, in her inimitable way, volunteered that it was Newsday policy on such matters to talk to our public-relations director, Chiara Coletti, which was true up to a point but flexible.

Undeterred, Signorile proceeded to keep calling for the next hour. When I finished moving the copy I prudently called Chiara Coletti first, explained the situation and asked how we should respond. Chiara, who knew Signorile from earlier encounters, said it was best to let her handle it. She'd get back to him and cool him off. Fine. As it turned out, she never did, at least not that evening. But I didn't know that. Shortly thereupon, Estelle went home for the day. Before I left, I called Chiara's office to find out how she'd disposed of things. I got no answer and suspected that if she hadn't gotten back to me she might not have reached Signorile. At which point, throwing caution to the winds and not inclined to leave things hanging for the night, I thought I might as well call him myself and have it out. Before doing so, I had the presence of mind to hit my message button and, lo and behold, there was the voice of Michelangelo Signorile, crazed, rabid, frothing, wishing me death. I will spare the expletives but he went on: "Look, I know you think I'm crazy or something, saying I wish you would die but you've got to understand that this community is in shambles and when you see stuff like that in the papers ... well ... IT DRIVES YOU CRAZY. I JUST DON'T BELIEVE THAT PEOPLE LIKE YOU

COULD PRINT THAT . . . YOU FUCKING BASTARD! AND
THAT'S WHY I SAID THAT BECAUSE I DO WANT YOU
AND YOUR FAMILY TO KNOW WHAT IT'S LIKE TO LOSE
SOMEONE AND I STILL HOPE YOU DIE, AND I STILL
WISH IT ON YOU.''

He had, of course, just shot himself in the foot. He didn't want to
talk me, much less interview me. He just wanted to act out through
the pretense of journalism. I realized that this kind of a nut was
best not engaged with. A normal reporter would have waited a
reasonable amount of time for a callback, but there was nothing
reasonable about Signorile. Although his column ostensibly was
about Fumento, what triggered his spleen was that I hadn't called
him back when he wanted. So he threw a tantrum.

Although I kept Signorile's disquistion on tape, the words,
capital letters and all to indicate screaming, were furnished by
Signorile who had taped himself (since I was unavailable) and
subsequently chose to run his monologue at greater length (two
pages of vituperation) which he believed would somehow
vindicate him. His printed rant ended with an appeal for his
minions to Zap me, which over the next month they proceeded to
do. For the following four weeks I got a spate of calls from a
procession of outraged young men wishing me all kinds of painful
death. Most of them came late at night when it was clear that no
one would be around, many of them were slurred, and from the
sound of them it was clear that few had actually read the review or
cared to. Occasionally, a brave soul would call in the daytime and I
made a point of explaining to them why I chose to assign Fumento.
During this period, our security chief asked if I needed any help
but I assured him I didn't.

I was disappointed that none of our writers in the gay community
spoke out for me—the issue was a straightforward First
Amendment one as well as a simple defense of the truth. But I
could understand their anxieties about taking on such a frenzied
mob. I was more disappointed at the pusillanimous reaction of
some Newsday administrators. The Part II editor, Phyllis Singer,
wondered if I shouldn't write a letter of apology to the gay
community. I told her no, but I would accept one from all the
obscene callers and their instigators. Chiara Coletti, who, to put the
best face on it, had dropped the ball on the return call to Signorile,
wondered how we could best effect damage control. When I asked
her what damage had been done to the truth, she bridled. In the
end, we ran a letter from Ira Elliott, who headed the media

committee for Act Up (Aids Coalition to Unleash Power), which had been active in staging street theater and intimidating the mainstream media to promote their agenda. Since Signorile at Outweek was the designated crazy, Act-Up could now assume the role of Elder Statesman and Elliott's letter was relatively subdued. The substance of it was that Fumento was "an ill-advised choice in that his own book advances the dubious thesis that the spread of AIDS in the heterosexual population has been greatly exaggerated."

As Gina Kolata reported in The New York Times the following June, far from spreading, the AIDS epidemic had crested, The Federal Centers for Disease Control had lowered its estimates of infected Americans from 1.5 million in 1986 to 1.3 million in 1987 to 1 million in 1988, and even that figure, according to its statisticians was too high. Moreover, subsequent studies showed overwhelmingly that AIDS in this country was limited for the most part to gay communities, needle users and blood infections. Fumento had been vindicated. For Signorile it may have been a moot point. The same month that Kolata's article appeared, Outweek folded. It imploded in a morass of mutual recrimination, bad debts, acrimony and mass firings.

Well after the dust had settled, I heard from one of our writers, Jay Weiser, whose letter explained the reticence of many who'd written for us in the gay community to come to my defense and speak out against Signorile. Weiser wrote:

"My only regret is my not having written to Outweek to protest Michelangelo Signorile who trashed you even though you were one of the first editors in the mainstream press to review gay-themed books. That was a lack of consideration, or maybe moral blindness on my part, and I hope it taught me something— particularly since that jerk's attacks led to death threats on you. He seems to have mellowed these days, judging from his columns in the Advocate, and become a better writer as well."

I can't vouch for Signorile's writing style, but he'd apparently mellowed enough to become the target of the same tactics he'd employed against me. Several years after I'd left Newsday, I came across Signorile's name in a broadsheet produced by a new generation of militant gays. He was not, however, a hero to these Young Turks but a has-been. These youthful radicals, defying the dictum of Safe Sex, embraced promiscuous anal intercourse which they acknowledged risked death, maintaining that this was at the core of gay life style and that anyone too fearful of putting his life on the line to assert his true gay identity was a cop-out. It was a challenge to the temporizing Old Guard among whom they most definitely considered Michelangelo Signorile. The exchange of letters in this broadsheet was instructive. Here was Signorile pleading with the young militants that intentionally risking death was wrong. They in turn, mocked him for his cowardice. The final irony was that this former incendiary was trying to placate a new breed of bomb-throwers who relished the fact that indiscriminate homosexual sex could be fatal, a phenomenon that was not something to be denied but to be celebrated as a badge of distinction. The wheel had come full cycle.

One of the most gratifying aspects of my job was to develop new talent, a mutually satisfying endeavor since it offered an opportunity to introduce fresh voices at modest fees, providing them a chance to appear in a mass-circulation forum and build up their portfolios. Among the writers who got a leg up appearing frequently in Newsday Books were Philip Gourevitch, a staff writer for the New Yorker who has chronicled the Rwanda genocide; Jacob Weisberg, the editor of Slate; the novelist Brian Morton whose book "Starting Out in the Morning" became a movie starring Frank Langella; Don Guttenplan, a London correspondent for The Nation, who has written a well-regarded life of I.F. Stone; Rebecca Mead, a mainstay at The New Yorker, Douglas Century who has made a career writing about tough Jews, Jonathan Dee, the author of five novels who writes for The Times magazine and Harper's, Updike biographer Adam Begley who served as the chief book critic for The New York Observer, the writer D.T. Max and the critic Robert Boynton, a mainstay of the NYU Journalism School. This is just a sampling of the freelancers who found a home in Newsday Books in the early stages of their careers.

When he first worked for me, Gourevitch was still the Culture Editor of the Forward, a post he was about to leave for the risks and rewards of the freelance world. Philip wrote first on Jewish topics and then, when it was clear that he had broader interests, I widened the horizons of his assignments, giving him fiction, as well as nonfiction. Gourevitch, tall, intense, almost grave, always wrote with a moral compass. Whether addressing the predisposition of the modern state to crush the human spirit as in Eastern Europe, persecute the Jew, or commit mass atrocity—as in Rwanda, Gourevitch never lost his sense of outrage.

The Forward was then under the tutelage of Seth Lipsky, a former Asian bureau chief for the Wall Street Journal who had the knack of cultivating talented young writers who went on to bigger and better things. One of them was Gourevitch's successor at the Forward, Jonathan Rosen. There was, of course, more than a mild whiff of exploitation in Lipsky's approach in which a talented but relatively inexperienced tyro with little support other than moral was allowed to sink or swim. This meant an indentured servitude of long hours and anxious scrambling. Rosen was up to the challenge but not without some uneasy moments. As it happened, The Forward was located right across 33rd Street from our headquarters, so Jonathan had ready access to my office and my ear. Not only did I recognize his talent as a reviewer but— as a seasoned chief-cook-and-bottle-washer myself—I served as a mentor to him in his editorial capacity. Of course, Rosen was doing quite well on his own—the Forward during his tenure produced an impressive Culture Section—but it's nice to have a little outside validation.

One of the books I had Rosen review was "The Mercy of a Rude Stream,'' the rediscovery of a novel by Henry Roth, who had disappeared decades after the publication of his storied chronicle of Jewish immigrant life, "Call It Sleep.'' It turned out that Roth was alive and well in Arizona and the review led Jonathan to interview Roth in a piece commissioned by the Atlantic magazine. This became a turning point in the Roth revival—there was a trove of autobiographical fiction he was sitting on—and Rosen's career as well. Rosen's work has now appeared in The New Yorker as well as The Times Book Review and its Magazine. His criticism for Newsday served as a worthy prologue.

One of The Forward's most successful alumni who wrote for us was Jonathan Mahler, the paper's youthful managing editor during these years. Occasionally, after a haircut at my barber's, located in a warren of shops on the ground floor of our lobby, I'd cross the street to visit The Forward's offices. Mahler himself would greet me half-mockingly, half-meaningfully with: "Is this the famous Jack Schwartz?'' I'd get a little tour of the newsroom and a display of the layouts for the following week's edition, affecting to be impressed by whatever they were doing. Mahler actually did more work for me once I went back to The Times where he wrote a few "My Brooklyn" pieces. He is now a media writer for The Times as well as the author of a best-selling book about the 1976 Yankee season, "Ladies and Gentlemen, the Bronx Is Burning." Some time ago I saw him at a book party and greeted him with: "Is this the famous Jonathan Mahler?"

Jacob Weisberg was a former associate of Jennifer Kraus's toiling away at the New Republic when he first wrote for us before going on to become a prominent essayist and the editor of Slate. We used him to advantage reviewing a spectrum of political books ranging from the first volume of Robert Dallek's magisterial life of Lyndon Johnson, "Lone Star Rising," to Kitty Kelley's poisonography of Nancy Reagan. Here is what Weisberg had to say about Dallek:

"It is difficult to resist the temptation of reading Robert Dallek's 'Lone Star Rising' as an extended reply to the two volumes of Robert Caro's 'The Years of Lyndon Johnson.' Where Caro views Johnson as an almost inhuman villain, Dallek's protagonist wins our intermittent sympathy. Caro the journalist debunks and condemns. Dallek the historian revises and gives credit. Yet to read this biography as a rebuttal does it a considerable injustice.... Johnson's latest biographer replaces previous accounts of LBJ's rise with one that does justice to his extraordinary ambiguities. The tone is measured, generous, mature."

The New Republic of yore, where Weisberg worked, was based in Washington. Like Seth Lipsky, its publisher, Martin Peretz, was adept at attracting fresh faces to his publication. In his case, many of them came from Harvard where Peretz taught and which he used as a recruiting station to fill his ever-revolving ranks. Since Peretz didn't pay much, his legions of whiz kids often went on to more substantial venues once they'd established their bona fides. Book sections like Newsday served as subsidiaries where the more ambitious young talents at the New Republic could have a New York showcase outside of the Beltway. Some of them might not yet be ready for prime time so Newsday served as a handy rung up the ladder. I was happy to take advantage of the interregnum.

The Cultural Commissar of the New Republic was Leon Wieseltier who had decided early in the game that he was not going to move on but, by standing pat he could be sitting pretty. If the New Republic had positioned itself as the conscience of American liberalism—as opposed to the radicalism of The Nation—Wieseltier had established himself as its intellectual high priest. He was a bete noire of the pretentious, a scourge of the conventional, a gadfly who delighted in puncturing intellectual and political balloons. As such, he was resented by more than one cultural luminary whose oxen he'd gored.

Imposing, with an eagle's mane of whitish hair cropping upward from his brow, Leon was the perfect subject for the caricatures that the magazine drew so well in its heyday. Wieseltier thought well of our book pages—he had written a laudatory note to Jennifer, one of his protégés, commending us for being a better section than either the Washington Post's Book World or The Times Book Review, high praise indeed. I had gotten him to review a biography of the culture icon Lincoln Kirstein who'd been instrumental in founding the New York City Ballet and had inspired the legendary literary periodical Hound and Horn. I appealed to Leon's sense of self-esteem. Who, better than he, would be worthy of paying Kirstein his just due?

When Kitty Kelly's hatchet job of Nancy Reagan came out, I thought Jacob Weisberg would be the perfect reviewer. He had a playful side that I wanted to nourish and the kind of salacious Beltway gossipography that Kelley indulged in was an opportunity for Weisberg to let out the stops. First, however, I had to get the book to him. Part of the hype with which the publisher, Simon & Schuster, beat the drums, was a news embargo based on the assumption that the nasty nuggets Kelley had sifted from Nancy Reagan's life were so newsworthy that no book review was allowed to reveal them until the news organization—usually Time or Newsweek— that had paid an exorbitant fee for first-rights to this dish had published its exclusive. If you agreed to the deal you signed a document allowing your reviewer to pre-read the book on the condition that you or your newspaper would respect the embargo. I played the game. Simon & Schuster dutifully sent us a copy which I promptly Fed-exed to Weisberg who was supposed to read the book over the weekend and submit a quick review that we'd crash into the Tuesday paper after the Monday embargo date.

The playing field, of course, was not level. The Times could afford to ignore the embargo because its Washington Bureau was invariably leaked advance copies. This allowed The Times to jump the gun with impunity. Its book editor was off the hook and the publisher could claim innocence while the first-rights news mag sold enough copies to the unwitting so that its squawk was strictly pro forma. All the big players came out ahead and the only ones left holding the bag were the small fry who had dutifully honored the embargo. My policy was to let Newsday's Washington Bureau scramble for the crumbs— a lot of the tidbits had already surfaced—but run my review in the Tuesday paper. I figured by the time the review appeared, the gossip would have been exhausted in the 24-hour cycle and we could concentrate on whether the book was worth anything.

When I phoned Weisberg later that day he said he hadn't received the book. I checked with Fed Ex and they assured me it had been delivered. I called Jake back and, suggesting that it could have been misplaced, I asked him to nose around. He phoned back to tell me that he found the Fed Ex package, which I'd marked "personal" to him, emptied of its contents in Wieseltier's wastebasket. Leon had left earlier for a book party in New York. I got on the horn to Simon & Schuster and leaned on them to get Weisberg a copy from one of their people in Washington. The following week I spotted Leon at a book party. I walked up to him and asked him how he was enjoying the Nancy Reagan book. He looked nonplussed for a moment and then I casually added that someone had torn open Weisberg's personal mail and left the contents in Leon's wastebasket. Did he know anything about it? This was the only time I can recall the usually self-assured Wieseltier look genuinely abashed. He stammered some excuse about not seeing the addressee on the envelope and moved on. Weisberg, as expected, did a nifty job of reviewing the book and we made our deadline.

Another Jake who at the time wrote occasionally for The New Republic was Jacob Heilbrunn. I gave him a lot of work. When I first encountered Heilbrunn he was a fellow at Georgetown's Center for German and European Studies. Since there were always a goodly number of books on Germany before, during and after World War II, I needed to find reviewers who knew the subject but were not jaded by it. Heilbrunn was the best of them: a fresh voice who could write on the topic with enthusiasm and moral clarity. When it came to calling things as they were, I knew that Heilbrunn would pull no punches. I gave him the toughest pieces and he always came through. Among the most challenging was his review of John Fuegi's "Brecht and Company."

After the fall of the Berlin Wall, Fuegi, an authority on Brecht, had found a trove of material in the East German archives that led him to conclude the playwright had appropriated the work of others whose talent he'd exploited as his own. As far as the Brecht establishment was concerned this was an act of heresy and both Fuegi and his book, if not consigned to the flames, were dismissed out of hand which was the secular equivalent of same. The only problem was that Fuegi made a compelling case. I felt that his book should not be ignored and I asked Heilbrunn to have a look at it. Here are excerpts from his review, which ran on our cover:

"Fuegi contends that most of the poems and plays that won Brecht fame, such as 'Mother Courage' and 'The Threepenny Opera," were actually written by three of Brecht's lovers, Elisabeth Hauptmann, Margarete Steffin and Ruth Berlau. Fuegi, the founder of the International Brecht Society, asserts that Brecht's true genius lay in his magnetic personality. Brecht was not so much a creator of original works as a grand impresario who stage-managed his own life. The masterpieces that he wrung from the members of his 'company' were the props that earned him renown . . . . Why did it take so long for the truth to emerge? Scholars played a part. The skill with which East Germany manipulated and intimidated Western researchers who feared losing access if they disclosed the truth, can scarcely be exaggerated.''

That some of these very same scholars, part of the Brecht industry, turned on Fuegi is understandable. That book editors bought into their scheme is less so. For a long time Newsday was, to my knowledge, the only literary section that paid attention to Fuegi's book. Fuegi was, after all, a respected scholar and his work on the subject deserved at least a hearing. But the Brecht establishment closed ranks and the book reviews followed suit. Months later, The Times ran a glowing review of Brecht's journals which, far down in the piece, dismissed Fuegi's book in a paragraph. The reviewer was a man whose own book had been earlier criticized by Fuegi, which alone should have eliminated him from evaluating "Brecht and Company." Years afterward —I had already left Newsday—The Times wrote a news story about Fuegi's revelations, finally giving both sides their due.

It might not be quite accurate to consider David Rieff an up-and-comer since he had a considerable intellectual lineage before coming to work for Newsday. He was the son of Susan Sontag and had spent 10 years as an editor at Farrar Straus prior to our relationship. But in 1989 David decided to leave the cloister of book publishing and strike out on his own for the more contingent vocation of the freelancer. Of course, Rieff had already edited such luminaries as Joseph Brodsky, Elias Canetti and Philip Roth at Farrar Straus and was himself the author of "Going to Miami,'' an illuminating book on that city's Cuban exiles. But there was an aspect of David that sought to cast off his pedigree and establish his own independent bona fides in the hardscrabble precincts of Grub Street journalism.

David wrote for Newsday Books from the early days until just before I left—one of the longest tenures of any of our reviewers. He was first introduced by his buddy Christopher Hitchens. On one of his forays up from Washington, Hitchens called to say he wanted to drop by with a friend looking for some work whom I might find interesting. That evening, the doughty Christopher arrived and introduced me to the chum he had in tow. There was the bespectacled David, towering over the chunky Christopher so that they looked like an intellectual Mutt and Jeff. David was cool and convivial, managing to convey an all-knowing manner that stopped short of being know-it-all. We repaired downstairs to a Dean & DeLuca in the lobby of the Wang building where Rieff and Hitchens held forth in a lively competition of anecdotes, gossip and Schadenfreude about their celebrity friends, an exercise that they had clearly practiced on prior occasions. It was an amusing dog-and-pony act at the conclusion of which we all found one another sufficiently agreeable and I gave David the first of many books he was to review for Newsday.

Others were to follow regularly over the next few years, a substantial achievement encompassing a variety of subjects. During this period, Rieff weighed in on such intellectual heavyweights as Isaiah Berlin, Stanislaw Baranczak and Vaclav Havel, and essayed books on Cuba, Bosnia, Africa and Eastern Europe. Virtually all his criticism took the form of essays in which he would as much discourse on the subject as review the book.

David had cultivated a reputation as a bit of a wild man— brilliant, precocious, erratic—at Farrar Straus. With me, he was a gentleman, honoring his deadlines, solicitous of any changes I wanted, apologetic about going over space and, if he were out of pocket, trusting me to cut his copy without doing injury to his argument. He was often out of pocket, traveling to various exotic locales and leaving word that, in extremis, he could be reached through the intervention of his agent, the redoubtable Andrew Wylie or, better still, through one of his girlfriends, most of whom had somewhat exotic names. His faxed copy would be preceded by notes invariably beginning "Herewith," as in: "Herewith the 1,200 words on Fidel. I trust they will suffice." Herewith is Rieff on a quartet of books about Cuba under Castro, one of the many subjects to which David brought genuine knowledge:

"More and more, Castro's career resembles Cromwell's rather than Lenin's. Instead of creating a society that would last for most of the century, he created a regime co-terminus with his own life span. Like Cromwell, Castro was welcomed at first and then squandered his prestige and his credibility on social experiments, colonial wars and the utopian confidence that people's essential natures could be transformed."

Had David been born sooner he likely would have been a Trotskyite prodded by reality to the all-purpose skepticism of a Dwight MacDonald. He'd often begin his reviews with what appeared to be the presumptions of the Left but halfway through, more in sorrow than in anger, he would lament the failure of one do-good initiative or another and by the end, pronounce it kaput with the finality of any right-wing critic. It was as if he had swallowed an elixir that, against his will, turned him from a progressive Jekyll into a reproachful Hyde.

Beyond these frequent contributors an array of reviewers wrote for Newsday's book section at one time or another before going on to greater things. A partial list includes such current luminaries as the essayist James Traub, the art critics Jed Pearl and Daniel Pinchbeck, Christopher Caldwell, a senior editor at The Weekly Standard whose gloss on Eurabia, "Reflections on the Revolution in Europe," is a must-read on the subject; the writer Terry Golway who served as The New York Observer's political columnist; the author and book critic David Ulin; Michael Tomasky, the erstwhile Voice political commentator, and several reviewers who went on to successful careers at The New York Times including Tina Rosenberg of the Editorial Page, Tony Tommasini, the chief music critic and, most notably, Dwight Garner, who reviews for The Times's daily book pages.

One of the costs of doing business in book reviewing is an author's reaction to a negative notice. Most writers understand that bad reviews are part of the game and, whatever their internal hemorrhaging, they ascribe it to the give and take of criticism and move on to the next book. But not everyone is so inclined and we sometimes heard from irate authors complaining that they'd been misunderstood or maligned by cretinous reviewers with an ax to grand or a reputation to make at their expense. It is understandable that an author, who may have put two or three years into a book, who's been encouraged by his agent, his editor and his publisher, can be somewhat deflated by a bad review, particularly when he's hoping that a good one will boost sales. But it isn't in the province of a book section, whose obligation is not to the writer but the reader, to go along with the program. So there is a natural conflict between the imperatives of the publisher and the book editor.

To insulate myself from the charge of unfairness, I subscribed to a few simple seat-of-the-pants rules: Make sure that the reviewer has no prior congress with the author in terms of negative reviews or back-scratching on the part of either party, or ideological differences. Second, never review a first-time author unless you're going to be mildly encouraging. The exception might be if someone is getting a major hype from a big publisher and the book is worthless, so the review is commenting on the phenomenon as much as the work at hand. Third, avoid reviewers who are notorious hatchet men.

Although these dictums generally saved us from a lot of grief, there was no dodging all the bullets. Often, they came unlooked for. When the historian Lucy Davidowicz, author of "The War Against the Jews," wrote a memoir of her experience as an American scholar during the last days of YIVO in Poland before the Nazis marched in, I gave the book to Shalom Goldman who wrote a sympathetic review. Davidowicz had written for me on occasion and, about a month later, I called on her for a review. The silence was palpable. You could hear her anger through the phone. I asked her what the problem was. She gave me an earful, the burden of which was that she was hurt by the rough treatment she'd received at Goldman's hands, and who was this young upstart?

I was taken aback because, as I recalled, the piece was a positive one. While Lucy ranted, I retrieved the review and, sure enough, it was as I remembered. Except that is, for one line near the end where, after praising Dawidowicz to the sky, Goldman allowed as to how sometimes her style could be a bit murky but this small cavil in no way took away from an outstanding work. I gently pointed this out to her and I also noted that Goldman was a seasoned critic who had reviewed many works on Jewish affairs. But there was no appeasing her. She never wrote for us again.

I can only wonder what Dawidowicz would have done if she got the review that Nelson DeMille received. DeMille, a writer of detective thrillers, was probably the most successful author on Long Island, with a large national readership. If he had a big following, he had a bigger ego. I gave his book, "The Gold Coast," to a young writer, Mark Kamine, whose clips I liked. Kamine didn't think much of the novel and I ran his review as a short piece that I buried in the back. I led the section with a strong review of the American-Indian detective writer Tony Hillerman who was, as Hemingway said, the true gen. I don't know what got DeMille's goat more, being trashed by Kamine or one-upped by Hillerman. In any case, the response came quickly. Actually, it was better than anything DeMille wrote in the book. He demonstrated a healthy appetite for the polemical form. Here, in part, is what he said:

"Who is Mark Kamine? A freelance writer? What's that? I've been writing for 16 years and deserve to be assigned a better reviewer than that. 'Gold Coast,' was picked by the Book of the Month Club as their main selection for June . . . Also, 'Gold Coast' has been on The New York Times best-seller list for 10 weeks and is on Newsday's July 1 list. Obviously, a good number of people like the book but not Mark Kamine. Okay, he's entitled to his personal opinion, but you would think that you would have exercised a little editorial judgment when you were handed a bad review by this man. I mean, the book is not only a best-seller but is written by a Long Island author and is set on Long Island. Couldn't this guy find some charity in his heart? Newsday's book section doesn't do much for its credibility when it runs a negative review of a book that's been read and presumably enjoyed by tens of thousands of Long Islanders.

"For what it's worth, 'Gold Coast' has gotten 16 reviews from all over the country—one bad, one medium and fourteen glowing, comparing it to 'The Great Gatsby,' 'The Godfather,' Edith Wharton's novels, 'Citizen Kane' and 'Bonfire of the Vanities.' You exercised no editorial judgment whatever when you gave it to a non-entity to review, or when you saw the ho-hum review. It has always amazed me that newspaper reporters are edited and their stories killed but critics are given free rein to voice their personal opinion on a complex artistic work such as a book or a movie. I think this review was a disservice to your readership and a gratuitous insult to me personally."

I cite DeMille's letter because he has unwittingly managed to touch on all the major grievances of an outraged author who considers himself ill-used by a newspaper critic. First, that the reviewer is unworthy of DeMille, presumably because the author is so important that only a critic on his own lofty perch merits even consideration of his work. I couldn't help wondering who the other 16 reviewers nationwide were and if they met DeMille's exacting standards.

Second, his book has been chosen by a committee of The-Book-of-the-Month Club. These are the same jokers who passed on "Gravity's Rainbow" and "Catcher in the Rye," a bunch of old fogies put out to pasture who, when they were sufficiently awake, chose a book for its commercial value—score one for DeMille—rather than its literary merit.

Third, he's on the best-seller list. No hard trick for a commercial author with a built-in audience, much less a big-name writer whose publisher grinds out a massive first edition for the beach-book season. And if numbers were a criteria we'd have been giving positive reviews to Deeprak Chopra.

Fourth, the author was a local writer with a local following. Shouldn't he get a break?; No. As a matter of fact, DeMille's fan-base notwithstanding, we owe it to other local readers to warn them about this book before they plunk down their $25.

Fifth, why don't we kill a negative review, the way reporters' stories are killed? A reporter's story is killed because the facts don't add up or there's no story there. Killing a review because of an opinion—most particularly when it would offend a sacred cow—would be the opposite of what honest reviewing should be about.

Sixth, was the review insulting? Yes; was it gratuitous? No. The criticism was well rendered and the writer had no pre-conceived agenda before reading the book, which got a fair appraisal.

Finally, the author's entertaining the thought that his book compares favorably with "Gatsby," "Godfather" and "Bonfire" is all that needs to be said about the grandiose expectations of what his worth merits in terms of criticism. It is little wonder that he was exercised by anything less than a rave.

I later learned that DeMille may have been particularly vexed because, as a local celebrity, he'd been recruited to help promote our 50th anniversary and was upset that the paper whose parties he enhanced took a dim view of his book. I'm told he complained to the publisher. It says something about Newsday's integrity that I never knew about any of this until well after the fact.

Sometimes, the fire came from a book executive vexed that we had spurned a pet project. In fact, this was rare because most publishers rolled with the punches and were not going to stoop to complaining about a review. But occasionally, a publisher, usually a fringe operator with a large ego, a small inventory, and a pugnacious attitude would go into attack mode to question a review or generate one. Such was the case with Donald I. Fine, a small publisher whose imprint carried his name and whose modest output we had reviewed over the years. We chose to pass on his release of a book about Colin Powell—the least in a crowded field—which I felt was an undistinguished tome that did not merit a review. Fine responded by writing to my boss, Don Forst, complaining that we ignored his books. By doing so, he hoped to prompt Forst to get me to run the review. Don simply passed Fine's missive along. I responded as follows, copy to Forst:

"In your letter to Don Forst seeking his help in obtaining a review of the Colin Powell book, you preface your remarks with the statement: 'In the hopes of breaking your record of not being reviewed in New York Newsday forever . . .' Presumably, either your clipping service has failed consistently to apprise you of your reviews in this newspaper or you don't read our book section on any regular basis." I then supplied him with a list of more than half-a-dozen books published by his house that we'd reviewed in the recent past. I continued:

"Your assertion is simply wrong and worse, it is insulting because it shows what little regard you have either for the truth, for getting accurate information on your own reviews or for reading them in the book pages of a newspaper that publishes in the city where you do business. I would think that the amount of attention we have paid to your books is sufficient and respectable. You may not agree, but to suggest that we have been methodically dismissive of you is simply false.

"We make a decision on each book that comes in here on its merits. On that basis I thought your earlier books that we'd reviewed fit our mix. I thought that the Colin Powell book did not. I suggest that in the future, if you have a problem you write directly to me. I would avoid special pleading to other executives at this newspaper, particularly based on false information. It doesn't help your cause, in their eyes or mine." Fine never complained again.

A thornier problem arises when the book editor is caught between two fires—the reviewer and the reviewee. An outraged author like DeMille can be chalked up to a wounded ego, and a disgruntled publisher like Fine can be dismissed as a case of sour grapes. But when two intellectuals lock antlers over a review, the

293

editor is thrust into the unwanted role of referee and awash in a paper tide of claims and counterclaims. The litigants have endless appetite for defending their reputations while besmirching their opponents and the editor must find a way to serve their aggrieved sensibilities as well as his own sense of fairness. Such was the case with Eli Rosenbaum's "Betrayal," a book on Kurt Waldheim's past, reviewed by Robert Herzstein.

Waldheim, as we may recall, was the U.N. Secretary General and later President of Austria whose participation in the Nazi genocide and assorted atrocities as a German officer in the Balkans had been suppressed by both sides in the Cold War for their mutual advantage. When his activities came to light, there was a spate of recriminations as to who was responsible for the cover-up. Weighing in on the debate was Rosenbaum who led the Justice Department's Nazi-hunting unit. His thesis was that not only the usual suspects—the Soviets and the Yugoslavs—had used their knowledge to blackmail Waldheim, but that the eminent Nazi hunter Simon Wiesenthal, a political ally of Waldheim's in Austria, had actively participated in the cover-up. For good measure, he asserted that Wiesenthal's Nazi-hunting was little more than a self-serving tissue of lies.

Although I knew the general tenor of the book, I had not delved into this tome since I simply could not read all of the many books that we reviewed. Rather, I relied on the integrity and authority of the reviewer, upon whom I conferred implicit trust. I assigned Rosenbaum's book to Robert Herzstein, a history professor and author of "Waldheim: The Missing Years," who had previously reviewed for me on the subject. As I always did when assigning a review to a specialist I asked Herzstein if there were any reasons why he should recuse himself from reviewing "Betrayal" and he assured me there were not.

Herzstein wrote a blistering review. He said that Rosenbaum's book was "a polemic" that "fails as history." But his main charge was that "this book is not really about Kurt Waldheim. It is about Simon Wiesenthal, director of the Documentation Center in Vienna, who becomes, in Rosenbaum's hands a self-promoting fraud who built his reputation on the work of others." Herzstein calls "Betrayal" a "demolition derby" and writes: "It is disturbing that Rosenbaum is as impassioned in his hunt for Wiesenthal as he is when indicting Waldheim." Wiesenthal aside, Herzstein accuses Rosenbaum of perpetuating "several myths," most notably that Waldheim was a creature of the Russians, a charge that, Herzstein asserts, gets Washington off the hook. The debate then is over who was more nefarious in white-washing Waldheim's record. Herzstein implicates the U.S. and argues that Rosenbaum is wrong in giving greater weight to Moscow.

Two days after the review ran I got a call from a much-vexed Rosenbaum who told me that Herzstein was a target of the very book that he'd been reviewing. Rosenbaum faxed the relevant material showing me that he had repeatedly called Herzstein to task for his support of Wiesenthal in exchange, he claimed, for Wiesenthal's blurbing Herzstein's work. I called Herzstein and asked if he was aware that he was mentioned critically by Rosenbaum when he wrote the review. He responded that he was referred to in an end note that he hadn't bothered to read. In fact, he had been cited several times, negatively. I told Herzstein that he should have been more forthright with me about any mention in a book he was reviewing. I also sent him a tear-sheet of his lengthy review, which I did pro forma with all my writers. I called Rosenbaum and told him that had I known of the conflict, I would have withdrawn the review. Since it had already run, although Books had no letters space, I'd print his letter in the Op Ed section.

Rosenbaum wrote a lengthy missive that I edited with his concurrence. I thought that was the end of it but, of course, it was only the beginning. Although Rosenbaum had been a gentleman with me, he was less so with Herzstein. He wrote Herzstein a note which the latter wrongly interpreted as my having pulled his review. To complicate matters, Herzstein never got my tear-sheet of his published piece. On top of which, Rosenbaum told Herzstein that we were running his letter in the Op Ed Section. Herzstein then wrote me insisting on a rebuttal to Rosenbaum's rebuttal and evincing shock and chagrin that we would have suppressed his review based on a phone call from a Federal prosecutor. Why he presumed we would have printed a letter in response to a review we never ran is beyond me, but there is no accounting for the irrational when it comes to writers' reputations. My answer to Herzstein is a needful reminder of what full disclosure in reviewing is all about. Here is the nub of it:

"I did not read Rosenbaum's book prior to running the review. My mistake. I did, however, ask you on two occasions if there was any reason why you shouldn't review the book and you assured me that there wasn't. This was the moment to have told me you were discussed extensively in the book. You are cited 14 times in the index. I did not learn of this until after the review ran when it was called to my attention by Rosenbaum.

"It is not my province to enter into the debate between you and Eli Rosenbaum. But it is my province to say that anyone attacked in this manner by an author should in no way be reviewing that writer's book. This is the only issue at hand.

"You had 1,200 words critical of Rosenbaum's book, his work and his reputation—fair enough. Rosenbaum got to reply in about 500 words. Both are fair comment. If you were upset, so was Rosenbaum. Our job is not to declare a winner but to provide a forum. The respondent may get the last word but the reviewer gets more of them."

As it turned out, Herzstein had just written a book on Henry Luce that I sent to Philip Gourevitch who gave it a generally respectful review a month later. L'affaire Waldheim was over.

By now I'd been Newsday's book editor for three years. The section was thriving. We had raised the bar in terms of reviews and reviewers, our pages looked sharper and read better and we'd won new-found respect in the literary community. Our bosses were happy, our readers were engaged, our influence was ascendant in the book world. We decided to give ourselves a party. The occasion was the annual National Book Association Convention of 1991 which was held in New York that year. As part of the week's round of festivities, the big publishers threw a series of lavish parties. Not to be outdone, I thought it would be an opportunity for Newsday to show the flag in New York. I persuaded management to spring for a joint celebration with our counterparts at the L.A. Times Book Section, since we were both owned by the Times-Mirror Company. Together with my opposite number, Jack Miles, at the L.A. Times, we convinced our corporate leaders that this would offer a needed counterweight to The New York Times.

We rented the old Russian Tea Room which still had a few echoes of its literary lineage. I chose a mid-afternoon Sunday hour that wouldn't conflict with any other big parties but would attract a lot of people to a midtown location. I invited every major writer who ever worked for us and many less well known reviewers who had toiled reliably for Newsday over the years. We also invited the publicity people from all the big houses, several name authors, a passel of book editors and the usual suspects from the trades, the agencies and other outliers. It was a memorable event. We'd expected a few no-shows but virtually everybody turned up. The place was packed to the rafters, the banquettes were crammed and the guests were crowded together like one of those book parties in a New Yorker cartoon. New York Newsday's promotions wizard, Diane McNulty, who'd set the whole thing up, had outdone herself. It didn't hurt that our bosses were there from Los Angeles, Long Island and New York to see what we'd accomplished. I made an exception to my public reticence and took a bow. Beware hubris. Within four years it would all be gone.

My reviewing strategy in nonfiction was not to attract stars so much as to develop constellations—clusters of prominent writers and academics who appeared in the more prestigious journals. Columbia University was in Newsday's backyard and we took advantage of the proximity to recruit such reviewers as Stephen Marcus on Dickens and Freud, the Melville scholar Andrew Delbanco on American literature and the Reconstruction historian Eric Foner on slavery. This took a bit of doing but once I had gained the confidence of a few key players we were able to build on these relationships. Thus the network grew and the longer we were at the game, the smoother it got. Since talent recognized talent, I could trust people like Foner for their recommendations.

Columbia alone could have filled our needs several times over with a distinguished cohort on virtually anything. But Newsday Books developed an impressive and wide-ranging roster of academics from other national venues as well such as the Roosevelt historian Robert Dallek. During the years Dallek wrote for us he was working on the first of his two-volume history of Lyndon Johnson. It was overshadowed by the popular success of Robert Caro's biography, but if Caro's was livelier journalism, Dallek's was more even-handed, as we indicated in our review. I had worked with Caro at Newsday before he left to write the book on Robert Moses that made his fortune. Caro had been trained as an investigative reporter at Newsday and he was, intuitively, a prosecutor. Both he and Dallek did prodigious research but I felt the professor's impulse was to get at a complex truth, the journalist's instinct was to build a case. That Dallek's publisher was Oxford University Press brought his book scholarly cachet but also gave it a whiff of academe and was no match for the high-pressure ballyhoo of Caro's publisher, Knopf.

Robert Remini was one of the outstanding historians of Jacksonian and antebellum America. Although Arthur Schlesinger, Jr., is commonly associated with the Age of Jackson, Remini's

297

"Andrew Jackson and the Course of American Democracy" is arguably the finest work on the period and worthy of the National Book Award it earned. And his biography of Henry Clay is unmatched. Although I remunerated Remini as nicely as I could, the real payoff was that I took him to lunch at the Harvard Club whenever he flew in from Chicago. Remini, it turned out, was a Brooklyn boy and although he may have been a Distinguished Professor of the Humanities at the University of Illinois, he missed New York and loved to catch up on the local gossip—politics, publishing, show biz, or simply reminisce about the city of his youth. This was in the days before the internet when newspaper people were thought to have entrée to all kinds of insider poop. So there we were, with me going on about the Compromise of 1850 and Remini harking back to the halcyon days of Ebbets Field. Once again I was reminded that many a scholar, when given the opportunity, wants to discuss anything but his subject.

I discovered the same impulse in Andrew Delbanco who, when we lunched, would just as soon talk about our sons than discuss "Moby-Dick." Stephen Marcus was another such creature, hungry for gossip about the newspaper business. Somehow, academics seemed to feel overly cloistered; that, no matter how illustrious in their field, they were leading a hot-house existence. Access to a newspaperman brought in a gust of air from the blustery outside world. I noticed this during my Nieman year at Harvard when I hobnobbed with the world's leading experts on everything in the Faculty Dining Room and found that they were grilling me on what was going on Out There. It was all a matter of perspective but if it gave me an edge in cultivating reviewers, I was glad to foster their illusions.

Eric Foner became a friend as well. His uncle, Moe Foner, had been a labor official in a Communist-run union and we had a few social links. As I've mentioned, Foner, who became president of the American Historical Society, was instrumental in smoothing my path toward acquiring a cohort of talented academic reviewers. Although best known as a historian of Reconstruction and a Lincoln chronicler, Foner was also an astute social critic. Here he is on Michael Kazin's history of American Populism:

"Kazin's most original contribution is his careful delineation of how post-World War II conservatives appropriated a political language previously associated with the Left. Fearful of democracy and adhering to a hierarchical view of society, traditional conservatives had found populist rhetoric wholly unattractive. But as liberals became more and more identified with the national state, they became increasingly vulnerable to a New Right that drew on widespread resentment against a faraway unresponsive bureaucracy. When the potent issue of race was added to the mixture, conservatives had found a winning combination.''

Many of these reviewing categories overlapped. Reconstruction elided into Civil Rights and so we chose to handle Black Studies not as a separate category but as part of American history. When it came to the experience of black Americans, Newsday was going to have specialists but not segregation. For instance, the Civil War scholar Ira Berlin, a protégé of Foner's at the University of Maryland, could address Emancipation. Or David Garrow, author of the Pulitzer Prize-winning biography of Martin Luther King Jr., "Bearing the Cross," might review Nicholas Lemann's "Promised Land: The Great Black Migration and How It Changed America." At the same time, we attracted a cohort of scholars who represented the gamut of Black Studies, from Henry Louis Gates Jr., chairman of Afro-American Studies at Harvard, to Princeton's Arnold Rampersad.

The battle over segregation was not limited to the U.S. The struggle against apartheid in South Africa was another related topic then generating a cottage industry of books that necessitated acquiring reviewers who knew something about the subject. I decided to go to the source and recruit South Africa's best authors, among whom were several that had either left the country or suffered internal exile under the apartheid regime. These included such authors as J.M. Coetzee ("Waiting for the Barbarians," "Age of Iron"), Andre Brink ("A Dry White Season," "An Act of Terror") and Rian Malan, writer of the aptly named "My Traitor's Heart." Malan was a member of one of the country's ruling Afrikaner families, indeed a descendant of an architect of apartheid, who had broken with his kin to write critically of the regime. We also assigned books on South Africa to homegrown talent such as Richard Stengel who was editing the memoirs of Nelson Mandela and would go on to become editor of Time magazine. I asked Stengel to review "In No Uncertain Terms," the memoir of Helen Suzman who had been the lone voice in South Africa's Parliament to speak out against apartheid. Here is what Stengel wrote:

"The most famous resident of Houghton, the tony, tree-shaded Johannesburg suburb that Helen Suzman represented for 36 years, would not have been permitted to live there when Suzman was a member of Parliament. But Nelson Mandela, Suzman's old friend and new neighbor, was barred for two very simple reasons: He was black and he was in prison. The fact that Mandela is now free, the resident of a smart northern suburb and the odds-on favorite to be the first black president of South Africa, owes something to the plucky persistent political courage that Suzman demonstrated as one of the few voices raised against apartheid from within the South African system."

When it came to the business of business, I dropped the imperative of even-handedness and picked characters who wrote like sports writers. I felt a little attitude would keep people awake as long we were up-front about where the reviewer was coming from. Alan Sloan, a Newsday columnist who would later move on to Newsweek, fit the bill. I had met Sloan 25 years earlier in my first go-round at Newsday when he toiled as a fellow night-side beat reporter. Back then, Alan was forever worried about missing a story or getting a fact wrong, thereby constantly second-guessing himself. Sloan was not cut out for beat reporting but he was a terrific columnist. He left Newsday briefly for a turn in the South where he got outside validation and the confidence that went with it. By the time we reconnected, Sloan was a formidable business pundit. He had undergone a complete professional and psychic makeover. The tone was self-assured, bold; nervy rather than nervous. His reviews were feisty, informed, pungent. Here he weighs in on Donald Trump's ballyhooed autobiography:

"This is one of the most boring books I have ever run across. The only reason I read it to the end is that the imperatives of reviewing required it of me. So in the space I have left let me give you an idea of why you shouldn't waste $22— or 22 cents—on this book. And why Random House should be chagrined to publish it, even though massive publicity and the Trump name will doubtless put the book, such as it is, on the best-seller list. The book should probably have been listed as fiction because Trump seems to have made most of it up as he went along."

We tried to maintain this lively approach whether in the social sciences or the physical ones. The crucial factor was to make these sometimes off-putting categories accessible and jargon free. Central to this undertaking was presenting an entire reader-friendly package in terms of heads, art and layout. In reviewing James Trefil's "Dark Side of the Universe" in 1988, one of the first popular books to essay the concept of "dark matter," the physicist Laurence Marschall, who had written lucidly on the cosmos in

"The Supernova Story," offered a luminous introduction to the subject. Jutting into the review from the upper right-hand corner of the page was the artist Gary Viscupic's illustration of the cosmos with galaxies and planets spinning off into a darkened void; in the foreground was a large pair of hands—a la Michelangelo's God creating Adam—working a cat's cradle out of which sprang the heavenly swirl. Image and story ran under the headline: "The Dark at the Top of the Stars."

My efforts at attracting first-class freelancers notwithstanding, I might have filled the pages of Newsday Books with star talent and never gone outside the newspaper. Without pressing, I could come up with more than two dozen writers whose credentials and abilities would have graced any other book section in the country. I hesitate to cite only a few who wrote for us because it would diminish those exceptional talents whom I must perforce omit. But in the spirit of the editor's watchword "kill your darlings"—cutting a passage beloved by the writer that embellishes but does not advance the narrative—I must consign some gifted staff contributors to the cutting-room floor.

Even paring this list leaves us with such Newsday writers as Murray Kempton, Jimmy Breslin, Pete Hamill, Jim Dwyer, Richard Eder, Sydney Schanberg, Lars-Erik Nelson and Roy Gutman. I cannot leave out at least a mention of reviewers such as John Anderson—at the time far and away the best film critic in New York; our music critic Tim Page, a polymath whose passions took him well beyond his field to resurrect the reputation of the novelist Dawn Powell; the elegant feature-writer Lynn Darling, who brought her deft style to the book pages; the award-winning Laurie Garrett who wrote on science and health; the witty fashion connoisseur Frank DeCaro; the sports writer Stan Isaacs who used humor to prick the balloons of the athletic establishment, and Len Levitt, probably the finest police reporter in the business, who focused on the cops as much as on the robbers. Even our second-stringers, such as Gene Seymour on movies, were better than the chief critics at many papers. The array of talent we had to choose from and the range and depth they provided was dazzling.

I first met Pete Hamill through friends shortly after he'd started at The Post. Hamill's story has been told many times in his memoirs and those of his comrades-in-arms. My own memory of him, as relates to this account, is merely a refracted fragment of his adventure. Our experience at the Post was strikingly different, and telling, in terms of our careers. Pete had arrived after a hitch in the

Navy and, under the tutelage of the Post's managing editor, Paul Sann, as well as members of its fabled rewrite bank, he became a larger than life presence on the New York tabloid scene. As I've noted earlier, my experience at The Post was, in the grand Hobbesian tradition, nasty, brutish and short.

The next time I encountered Hamill professionally was during my first go-round at Newsday when I was an assistant night city editor and he had decamped from the Post—an on-again-off-again love affair that was to last another three decades—lured to Newsday as a columnist by Bill Moyers during the latter's reign as publisher. Pete's assignment took him to Washington in hopes of energizing the national coverage. In the crazy-quilt logic of Newsday where I was responsible for Nassau, Queens and the world, my duties inevitably brought me into contact with Hamill. The fact is we already knew each other from The Lion's Head, the watering hole for New York's newspaper crowd. Pete was a celebrity but I had gotten there on the ground floor and was well-connected with a lot of mutual friends from The Post and Newsday, so we had a relationship which, if not close, was based on a certain assumed camaraderie.

Over the next few years, after I'd gone on to The Times and Pete had gone on to greater glory, we'd run into one another at the Head or a few parties, where we'd affect a hale, how-you-doin' familiarity. So it was no surprise, with Newsday trying to corner the market on the big-name columnists in its bid for legitimacy as a New York tabloid, that Hamill would be lured back yet again by his old New York Post pal Don Forst, this time to share the spotlight with Breslin, Kempton, et al. It really was a Murderers' Row of the best in the business with a street-smart, urban flavor. One of the calumnies that the Daily News's hatchet man Fred Drasner tried to put over in his assault on New York Newsday was that the stale and staid News—owned by a native of Canada, edited by Aussies, peppered with Brits who had a tin ear for the city—was New York's authentic newspaper and Newsday was a suburban upstart. The sad fact is that he succeeded, in part because the L.A. Times pulled the plug before Newsday could establish its image. The best friends the Daily News had were in Los Angeles. But I am getting ahead of myself.

It was exciting to see these big-name players competing with one another and inspiring the younger staffers. It was also a pleasure simply to have them around. And since I had a prior relationship with some of them it was easy for me to approach them for an assignment. The trick was to choose stuff that would tempt them.

I had no past relationship with Jim Dwyer. This was, in part, because Jim didn't have much of a newspaper past. He was a scrappy young reporter out of the Bronx by way of Fordham University. He'd been given the subway beat, something then beneath The Times and beyond the News. Dwyer virtually invented the beat and covered the underground to a fair-thee-well, which led to his first book, "Subway Lives." When an early-morning subway train crashed downtown with fatal results, Jim led the coverage under a team steered by Barbara Strauch. We were all over it with a 16-page Extra that hit the streets the same morning. The Daily News, "New York's Hometown Newspaper," missed it completely and didn't have a story till the following day. Dwyer—and the paper—won a Pulitzer in 1992. A year later, he led the coverage of the World Trade Center bombing in 1993 out of which came his book, "Two Seconds Under the World"—a foreshadowing of 9/11—in which Dwyer and a Newsday team prophetically detailed the blunders of officials who allowed Islamic terrorists into the country and ignored a smoking trail of clues that pointed to a conspiracy to commit mass slaughter on American soil.

I first met Dwyer searching for clips in the Newsday morgue when we were still working in the Wang building on Third Avenue. He said he'd be interested in writing for me and I told him that if something on his beat came my way, I'd think of him. Quite a few things came my way and Jim responded in succinct and straightforward prose that became a hallmark of his writing.

Lars-Erik Nelson was one of the most respected journalists of his day. He wrote with a moral authority that few other peers could match. He covered national affairs for us out of Washington, after a career that took him from Moscow to the capital. Before meeting Nelson, I had known his father who had taught an art-history course I took at City College that filled one of the gaping holes in my education. Like Hamill, Nelson was also one of those itinerants who bounced back and forth among the tabs, in his case between The Daily News and New York Newsday. And he did weightier pieces for The New York Review of Books. I particularly enjoyed assigning reviews to Lars because it often involved a lively discussion of whatever political contretemps had caught his fancy that day.

When New York Newsday folded in 1995 Nelson was part of the exodus, in his case returning to the Washington Bureau of the Daily News where he continued to do outstanding reporting. He died young, at 59, living just long enough to see George Bush elected in 2000. I attended Lars's memorial service at which an elite of the newspaper fraternity gathered in his honor.

Tim Page was Newsday's chief music critic. Another refugee from The Times, Page was someone whom I'd known since his early career there. Tim was a gifted music critic with a wide range of enthusiasms both within and beyond the music field. He'd been treated shabbily at The Times which fobbed him off as a stringer until he finally left for Newsday where his talents were better appreciated. I first encountered Tim after he had hardly been at The Times for a week when he stumbled upon a trove of unpublished Gershwin scores locked in a trunk in a New Jersey warehouse. It was a front-page story, an intimidating prospect for a young critic who'd probably never written a news story, much less a front-page article for The New York Times. I shepherded Page through, assuring him all the while that things would turn out right, as they invariably did. So Tim's near-debut at The Times came not with a short review buried in the back of the Culture section but with a front-page byline.

Page had a splendid career at Newsday, serving not only as a critic but also as an ambitious reporter. Tim loved getting the drop on his former bosses at The Times, which he relished relating to me, knowing that I'd savor a scoop on our erstwhile employers. He was also very generous in fostering the careers of developing freelancers. At Newsday, he touted the talents of a young Boston critic named Tony Tommasini who reviewed for us. Later, as chief music critic for the Washington Post, Tim provided behind-the-scenes support for such aspiring critics as Jeremy Eichler and Anne Midgette who succeeded him at the Washington Post. As I mentioned earlier, Page had a variety of interests, one of them being the novelist Dawn Powell who was virtually forgotten until Tim reclaimed her reputation in a fascinating biography, and almost single-handedly reintroduced her books.

John Anderson, our chief movie critic, looked younger than he wrote. His criticism had the weight of someone more seasoned, but the lightness of a young counter-puncher feeling his oats. Anderson was quick with a quip, which sometimes made him appear glib but he knew his movies and his assessments were astute and engaging. Here he is on two biographies of Janis Joplin.

"Although linked by what seemed like simultaneous deaths 20 years ago, Jimi Hendrix, Jim Morrison and Janis Joplin have ended up with wildly disparate accommodations in the cheap hotel of public imagination. Upstairs is Hendrix, the genius. A little less comfortable is Morrison who, thanks largely to the adolescent fantasies of Oliver Stone, is thought of by some as a cross between Bacchus and Blake. And down in the lobby, looking for a fix, is Janis Joplin, the poster girl of 60's excess, whose appetite for sex and narcotics has forever overshadowed the music she made."

Anderson hung on for a while after the New York edition folded, but there was no kick in the booze anymore. I see his byline from time to time in various guises but not in the prominent forum he deserved. This is a misfortune because John was an original talent just getting up a full head of steam as a top-of-the-line film critic.

Murray Kempton was in a class by himself. Working with Murray was the newspaperman's equivalent of saying one had clerked for Justice Brandeis. Kempton was probably one of the few intellectuals who had managed to attract a large tabloid following. He did so by hiding his erudition beneath a carapace of street-wise skepticism, jazz-age aphorism and principled criticism, together with a voice that could sound patrician while appealing to the plebian in his readers. Kempton was a maverick whose respect everyone seemed to seek whatever their political stripe. An unreconstructed liberal, he was on intimate terms with the conservative icon William Buckley and had a soft-spot as well for other right-wing columnists such as Westbrook Pegler. What Kempton and Buckley admired about one another were the sparks their brains gave off.

Kempton's appeal was that he was unpredictable; unlike so many of his fellow pundits, you never knew quite where he was going to stand on an issue. Or rather, while you knew where he stood—he was, after all, a Man of the Left—you could anticipate an unexpected insight that gave pause to the certitude of your convictions. Murray had the ability to go simultaneously High and Low, much valued in that cultural climate. While he churned out his columns for the tabloids, he was also a valued contributor at the New York Review of Books although, to my mind, the sprint rather than the long-distance run was where his strength lay. Kempton had made his bones at the old New York Post in the days of its liberal owner Dorothy Schiff so that by the time he moved on to New York Newsday he could well be considered the Grand Old Man of the tabloid game. Murray was always up for a book he could sink his teeth into and I was careful to assign him reviews that set his juices flowing: biographies of political rascals, mavericks and larger-than-life characters like Mayor James Michael Curley of Boston, Fiorello LaGuardia of New York and John F. Kennedy. Kempton's talent was to bring a certain grandeur to the doings of mortal men while not neglecting the banana peels on which they often slipped.

Although Kempton spent his career working for tabloids, he never wrote down to his readers but brought them up to his own demanding level making them all the richer for it. Ironically, one of the most difficult moments in my sojourn involved Kempton and, like most troubles, it came unlooked for. Times Books had persuaded Murray to gather together a collection of his columns, essays and reviews over the past 30 years which it presented in 1994 as a tribute to his career. I assigned it to John Judis, himself a Man of the Left who'd written for Mother Jones and was a regular contributor to our pages. On rare occasions, should the situation warrant, I might indicate in advance to a reviewer that if they really hated a book, to send it back, whereupon I'd either shelve it or reassign it. In Kempton's case, because the writing was so good and the writer was so respected, I never thought to do so. What Judis submitted was nothing less than a demolition job. I could not imagine what perverse motives prompted him to do so on what was clearly a salute to this newspaper's most venerable writer without at least calling me after he'd read it, indicating his feelings and asking me how to proceed. Judis took shelter later under the rubric that he was an independent spirit who didn't need an editor's imprimatur to voice his opinion of a book. True enough, in theory, but common sense might suggest otherwise. There was a protocol that any reviewer understood in addressing this kind of situation. The gist of his review was that Kempton was a lightweight whose work didn't measure up to the more serious journalism of his time.

While allowing that Kempton was an outstanding columnist, Judis wrote that after a day or a week his observations "begin to flicker" and, damning with faint praise, Kempton's essays "are a notch below writers like Norman Mailer or Dwight MacDonald whose musings still seem fresh and provocative long after they were written." Judis dismisses Kempton as "a local writer" and describes his prose as "often difficult and even rococo." Citing various examples of what he considers Kempton's stylistic flaws, Judis goes on to attack his lack of substance: "Kempton fails to convey a compelling understanding of the period . . . his view of history is nowhere to be found." Judis conjectures that Kempton's brief romance and later disillusion with the Communist Party in the 30's left him with "a fascination with the form but an allergy to the substance of political commitment. . . . In abandoning Communism and Marxism, Kempton seems to have abandoned any attempt to systematize his own point of view. Like other refugees from the hothouse 30's he seems to have rejected not only ideology but also theory. . . . Kempton's profiles are deeply intelligent but they remain lacking in reach, and will probably not outlive readers' interest in the particulars he describes."

In sum Judis's objections to Kempton are 1) that he is not an ideologist. Guilty as charged. Kempton's career was devoted in good part to dissecting the pretensions of theory and warning against the dangers of ideology; and 2) that he is not writing for the ages but rather is local and topical, which is exactly what the task of a daily journalist should be. Kempton was doing his job. Judis is not addressing his work but faulting him for not having done something else: the longer magazine form of a Mailer. As for Kempton's "rococo" proclivities, those flourishes are precisely what endeared him to his readers and distinguished him from the run-of-the-mill hacks who wrote for the dailies.

Judis, of course, is entitled to his opinion but this book was not a tabula rasa. The widely read and politically sophisticated Judis had to be familiar with at least some of Kempton's journalism and knew that much of it would reappear in this collection. If he had previously formed a negative opinion of Kempton's work he should have recused himself before accepting the assignment. That perhaps there might be some redeeming material in 30 years worth of writing that would alter his attitude, is unlikely. The decent thing to do was to have apprised me of his problem with Kempton. He did not do so.

Judis's sanctimony put me in a bind. If I killed the review, I'd be accused of special pleading in favor of one of Newsday's own. If I ran it, I'd be participating in a mean-spirited and ill-deserved attack on a colleague whom I respected. Why, after all, run a tribute to one's own, simply to attack it? Murray, of course, would be too honorable to fault me for it publicly, but he'd remember. I had soured relationships on reviews with friends before but I always felt I was on solid ground. This time, I was not. I could show the piece to Murray and let him know what he was in for or, at least, indicate a bad review was in the offing, but this was the worst option because it would make both of us complicit. I could edit the review but the gist of it was so damning that there was no way I could pare it without altering the substance. I decided that none of these alternatives was good. I called Judis and told him that his piece was unacceptable and I felt unfair as it was. Would he consider having another go? He refused to change a word and was indignant that I'd asked him to do so. I told him in that case, I was killing the review and would send him full fee for his efforts.

I thought this was the end of it but, of course, Judis was going to get his own back. Our interchange was brought to the attention of Howard Kurtz, then the media columnist for the Washington Post, the gist of which was that Newsday had quashed Judis's review. I got a call from Kurtz—who declined to name his source although it was not hard to figure out the identity—and I told him briefly why I'd killed the piece. I felt a response was in order but the less said, the better. The result was a short item in Kurtz's media column, which began: "When Newsday asked freelance writer John Judis to review a new book by its much-acclaimed columnist, Murray Kempton, Judis figured the paper wanted an independent assessment. But Newsday promptly killed his negative review of Kempton's collected essays, 'Rebellions, Perversities and Main Events.' Judis says Book Editor Jack Schwartz told him the piece was 'a demolition job' Judis adds: 'I was annoyed. If a book review expects a reviewer to take a certain line, they should either warn the person beforehand or they shouldn't assign it to someone who is independent.'

Schwartz says he simply didn't like Judis's review. 'He's free to write what he likes and I'm free to run what I like.' Schwartz added: 'I think this was an unfair piece, period.' ' "

Kempton, of course, had heard about the contretemps and came to my office a bit out of sorts, for Murray, which meant that just a touch of choler was added to his ruddiness. After the fact, I don't think he wanted to be associated with killing an unfavorable review. I explained what I did and why, giving him some idea of what Judis had written. As far as I was concerned, it was like pulling a piece by a reviewer who had failed to disclose that he had an adverse attitude to a writer's work. When Kempton heard the whole story, he seemed appreciative of my position and we called it a day. I reassigned the book to the essayist Philip Lopate, a tough critic himself, who gave it a good review, as it deserved.

The last time I saw Murray was the day New York Newsday folded. The next contact I had, in a manner of speaking, was at his funeral. By then, he had attained the status of a local Orwell and everyone who was anyone in journalism was there, not a few hoping to assume his mantle.

And then there is Richard Eder. Dick and I worked together in three venues. This was the second, sandwiched between two stints at The New York Times. It was in my years during Eder's sojourn as The Times's chief theater critic in the late 70's that I came to know him well. Dick wrote with an impish charm. He spoke as eloquently as he wrote giving off playful sparks of wit. Eder's lightness of tone belied considerable heavy labor. He sweated over his copy. Those were the days in which reviewers came back from the theater at 11 P.M. and dashed off a thousand-word review for the late edition of the next morning's paper. Richard would bang it out arduously and hand it to me in takes, a page or two, or three paragraphs at a time, which I'd edit and mark up before rushing it to the printer so that by the time he was on his last paragraph most of the story was set in type with the headline written. My job was more hand-holding than editing, with a tactful reserve of patience, based on hope as much as confidence, to resist pressing him as the clock ticked. There is nothing in journalism like the mutual experience of writer and editor working in tandem under the Sword of Damocles to affect a bonding experience. This one developed into a friendship that we maintained throughout our careers.

Our paths crossed once again when I became book editor. Newsday's corporate owner was The Times-Mirror Company and Eder, as chief book critic for the Los Angeles Times, was one of the jewels in its crown. Our own chief critic, Dan Cryer, had done the job for 14 years. He arrived at Newsday's Op Ed Section after I'd left for The Times and shortly thereupon segued into the niche of book critic. I had no quarrel with Dan's work—he'd credit any book section and had done a commendable job for us. I simply thought Eder could do a better one and I determined to bring him aboard.

My opportunity came in 1992. The corporate zeitgeist at the time was "synergy,'' combining the talents of both the L.A. Times and New York Newsday to create a greater energy source on both coasts that would challenge the august New York Times. Although it may now seem quaint, if not zany, the idea was viable at the time. By 1992, Jack Miles had been replaced as L.A. Times book editor by Sonje Bolle and I raised with her the idea of a joint condominium with Richard Eder as chief critic for both our sections. I'd already suggested it to Dick who was only too delighted to have a venue in New York, particularly going up against the former employers who'd driven him out. Sonje was enthusiastic about the idea—it gave her a leg in New York as well, featuring her premier reviewer. We joined forces to convince our supervisors that this was an innovation that would redound to everyone's benefit. They didn't need much convincing. Don Forst, the editor of New York Newsday, agreed that we needed someone of Eder's stature as our chief critic, Tony Marro valued my judgment and supported my decision. Dave Laventhol, the Times Company's CEO, was only too glad for the opportunity of showcasing a Pulitzer-winning critic in New York.

By the fall I had put all the pieces in place. Eder's reviews would appear simultaneously in both sections, Sunday and daily. Since Dick chose his own books, Sonje and I didn't have to worry about assigning him different reviews. Any discrepancies could be worked out. The key was that Sonje and I liked each other and worked well together, or else the thing never could have come off. The same held for the editing process. First of all, Dick hardly needed editing; secondly, if slightly different edited versions ran in both papers, it wouldn't matter to the readers; in effect, we usually helped one other if each desk caught something and passed it on to Eder. And it was easy enough to run one or the other version on the Times-Mirror wire syndicate. Finally, it didn't cost Los Angeles or Newsday any more money except that Eder got a slight raise which both papers shared. Dick came to New York in September and met with me, Tony, his deputy Howard Schneider and Newsday's Culture editor, Phyllis Singer. We gathered at Tropicana, a faux Latino restaurant at the top of the escalators in Grand Central—now a Citibank—where no one from Newsday would notice us. Dick charmed everyone and it was a done deal.

I called Cryer in to give him the news. I had kept a pretty tight lid on this and I wanted to make sure that it came first from me. I told Dan that he'd done a fine job but he'd been at it for 14 years and it was time for someone new. However, we still valued him and wanted to make sure that he maintained a prominent place in the book pages. With Eder reviewing on Sundays and Thursdays what I offered Dan was to maintain his Monday review at the head of the week and alter his Sunday presence to an author interview. At first he appeared chagrined but when I gave him a rundown of some of the luminaries I wanted him to interview, he perked up a bit. We were going to create a special column for him called "Talking With." The more Dan thought about it, the more he realized what a good deal this was. For the same salary, Cryer had to read only one book instead of two. An interview was a lot easier, more fun and gave him access to a host of interesting literary people. Plus he could pick his own subjects the way he chose his own books. Naturally, Eder would have first dibs on book reviews but there was plenty to choose from. As it turned out, Dan enjoyed his new career as an interviewer where he did some fine work.

As for Richard Eder, investing him in Newsday was an achievement. He brought intellectual cachet, cosmopolitan taste, authority and discernment to the book section. His arrival was the final touch of validation that capped my effort to make Newsday Books second to none. Working with Eder over the next three years was the most rewarding experience of my career. Dick's presence provided a critical bonus: the awareness that I was dealing with a kindred spirit. Although intangible, such a feeling is vital to the relationship of editor and writer and ultimately to the success of a section. By the time I recruited Laurie Muchnik as my deputy the following year, I had fine-tuned the operation so that it was the smooth-running, dynamic, prestigious enterprise that I'd dreamed of when I took the job. I only had little more than a year to enjoy my success but a good year is more than many people get.

Eder was terrific from the start. Of course, he wasn't really starting but rather extending his mandate from the L.A. Times to our own pages. From his first piece—a review of "Memories of the Ford Administration"—John Updike's elegiac transition from the Rabbit Angstrom saga—to the last under my aegis, a problematic story collection by Rick Moody, Eder didn't merely write about the book but went beyond it to the work's core and the writer's intent. Today, his reviews read as fresh as when they were written.

One of the many other bonuses that Richard Eder conferred on me was recommending his friend Anna Mundow as a freelancer. Anna was an Irish expat who wrote about the States for the Irish Times and picked up extra change contributing to American publications. She was one of the hundreds of freelancers who wrote for Newsday Books. They usually appeared under the italic identifier, "reviews frequently for Newsday." Through trial and error, I had built up a pool of trusted writers who were the equal of any reviewing staff. None of them were celebrities nor, to my knowledge, did many achieve fame or notoriety in later years. But, like craftsmen who toiled on the Gothic cathedrals, they were indispensable to the shape and substance of what emerged. That they didn't attain more status, is the genre's loss, because so many of them were talented writers with a passion for books and a gift for engaging them. One of them was Anna Mundow.

At the time, I was looking for a fresh face with a sense of humor who could have a little fun with name authors and big books that required needling but not trashing. Leon Uris, a bit long in the tooth since the appearance decades earlier of "Exodus" and "Battle Cry," had just written "Redemption," a novel about "The Troubles" in Ireland. I mentioned this to Eder who said he had just the writer for me: Anna Mundow. I called her and we hit it off straightaway. I warned Anna that she wasn't getting William Trevor but, in the spirit of Grub Street, she wasn't fussy and indeed, welcomed the chance to have a go at Uris's foray into the Irish troubles. Here is what she wrote:

"Leon Uris is back. The setting of 'Redemption,' Uris's first novel in seven years, is Ireland. The date is the bad old days when real men are constantly on the run and real women insatiably on the boil. Ripped bodices and smoking pistols litter the Irish hillsides. Landlords sneer, peasants cower, grooms limp and infants mewl. Look—there's noble Parnell, scheming Churchill, the Famine, the Easter Rising, World War I and . . . Ben Gurion? Well, why not?''

I found that, unasked and unsolicited, I attracted a fringe of writers who saw me as confessor, sounding board, devoted listener, tireless recipient of bulletins, wayward friend and the subject of an intimacy that was as unsought as it was at times unsettling. Perhaps it was their very neediness that made me so wary—and fond— of them. The prototype for this was the brilliant, quirky Richard Elman. Richard was the consummate luftmensch. He wrote fiction, poetry, criticism and did anything literary that would come to hand. He taught at the State University at Stony Brook which provided the Long Island connection. He also had gigs at colleges ranging from Bennington—a magnet for scholar gypsies—to Notre Dame where this migratory melamud must have been a rara avis.

Elman was a great sender of postcards, all of them obliquely or ironically linked to whatever message he was trying to convey. He was a master of the witty card in terms of juxtaposing the unintended weirdness of the picture with the zaniness of whatever he was writing on the reverse side. I have postcards of Harpo Marx at the typewriter (signed "Harpo''), Arthur Rimbaud from Paris,

Marianne Moore's Greenwich Village living room, a double-shot of both the young and aging Ezra Pound atop of whose anti-Semitic visages are scrawled in blue crayon the words: *"Ich hub nisht kein gelt!"*—he doesn't have any money. This, in one of Elman's many not-so-subtle appeals for work and breadwinning. It didn't help that he had terrible handwriting so that I had to struggle to decipher the code in which he wrote. Tummeling aside, Richard was a good reviewer and, had he left it at that, I probably would have used him more.

Elman had been working for some time on his magnum opus, "Tar Beach," a reference to the rooftops where working-class New Yorkers would sun themselves in the years on either side of World War II. It was a coming-of-age novel that gave him a chance to re-imagine the Brooklyn of his boyhood with his ear for the argot and feel for the shtick of his wised-up characters. I don't think there was a radio jingle of the time that he didn't throw into this tzimmes of a novel whose temperature was overheated and characters overdrawn, but which caught the moment in a seat-of-the-pants freewheeling way. It fell under the rubric of "experimental" which was, indeed, the world in which Richard operated. He would have done better in Europe where there was an audience for writers like Marguerite Duras and Nathalie Sarraute. He was not going to get a big readership—or big bucks—in America. His publisher, Sun & Moon Press, was one of those small houses that specialized in such fare. I gave the book to Vince Passaro who was receptive to experimental writing and would at least appreciate what Elman was up to.

Try as one will to avoid pigeon-holing reviewers, the imperatives of survival mandate that we classify writers into categories so that, in response to a certain genre, the Rolodex in our brain churns out a few apposite names that provide a necessary context for the harried book editor. Such it was with the illusive rubric of humor, which implied both the slippery slope of taking send-ups seriously and the prickly path of twitting pretentious books without being brutal. This was an art from in itself, involving equal parts craft, cunning and generosity and, most important, a sense of humor that could at once evoke laughter while treading lightly. Such reviewers were not easy to come by, but one of the best was Judith Dunford.

Despite her very Episcopalian surname, she was actually Judith Schwartz from the East Bronx, a contemporary, who had grown up not far from me on Southern Boulevard. We had gone to similar public schools with their uniform curriculums, teachers and mnemonics. Unlike me, however, Judith had not gone to City College but had vaulted to Yale where she acquired the Dunford surname by marrying the son of one of her professors. Ultimately, Judith dropped the marriage but kept the surname. As things turned out, she wound up with a City College boy, Alfred Kazin, his fourth and last wife. Alfred was no picnic either but, although demanding and cantankerous, there was no denying his talent and affection. In any case, with a history like Judith's a sense of humor was a necessary survival tool.

In the fall of 1991, I received a resume and some sample reviews from Judith and I was taken at once with her sly, diffident humor. I called Dunford and asked her to write for us. I learned we had the same last name—or at least that hers was originally the same as mine.

What I liked about Judith was that, although, through Kazin, she flew in pretty high-altitude circles—The Century Association, Philip Roth and the like—it never went to her head. She moved in this milieu as something of a subversive, like the Marx Brothers at a banquet. She would relay her impressions in a burst of hilarity mingled with embarrassment at having been part of the scene she was skewering. Judith's sense of the ridiculous was perfect for the kind of fare I'd assign her. Here she is on Robert James Waller's "Border Music," a failed attempt to capitalize on the phenomenon of his earlier "Bridges of Madison County":

"Even the hardest-core Waller fans may be disappointed by his new book; he is still trying to write a novel. His hard-stomached hero comes to the rescue of a stripper who is being pawed during a performance. The folksy dialogue of hero and heroine smells of the SEARCH button on Waller's word processor, so relentlessly are the G's dropped. As he is from Texas and she is from Iowa it's hard to figure out why they are talkin' the same—but maybe the G's were shed along with the G-string."

Richard Lourie would have made a fine police reporter. He had the look and the lingo. Like certain of his Boston Jewish brethren he affected a streetwise insouciance together with a roguish charm. The voice was Duffy's Tavern but the words were knowing and succinct. In a manner of speaking, Richard actually was a crime reporter. Except that the cops he covered were Russian, the perp was a serial killer and the writing appeared not in a tabloid but between the covers of a book. Somewhere along the way Lourie had mastered Russian and become an astute observer of Soviet affairs. His nonfiction book, "Hunting the Devil," was the story of a Jewish detective who spent years tracking a killer who murdered scores of children in the pre-Glasnost Soviet Union but whose crimes were never reported because there was not supposed to be any crime in the Workers' Paradise: therefore the public never knew that a maniac was on the loose.

Lourie was a natural raconteur and an incipient boulevardier whose Boston colloquialisms failed to hide a formidable intellect. He was the biographer of Andrei Sakharov, the father of the Russian H-Bomb who became the Soviet Union's leading dissident. Lourie's description of Sakharov's principled exile in the provincial city of Gorki won him a National Book Award nomination. He reviewed several books for us on Soviet affairs, always with a tongue-in-cheek, wise-guy flavor no matter how weighty the subject, leavening the black bread of Russian affairs with a yeasty sense of the absurd.

Lourie, handsome with white hair and mustache and a radio-announcer's voice that resonated with an off-hand authority, was a natural bon vivant—he would later apply his flaneurial talent writing for me at The Times after he'd emigrated to New York and I'd moved back to 43d Street. At the time, Richard had been recommended by Don Forst, who'd used him during an earlier tenure overseeing Boston magazine, and who recognized a kindred spirit. Not long ago I heard from Lourie in a photo email showing him dancing with a chorus girl in a Havana nightclub on New Year's Eve just 60 years after Castro came to power. Right out of "The Godfather."

The 50th anniversaries of the end of World War II in Europe and Asia coincided with the end of my career as book editor of Newsday. We were fortunate to cover the flood of books devoted to these events with Eric Bergerud, an extraordinary military historian. Bergerud was not widely known as a reviewer but I was impressed with a book he'd published on a U.S. division in Vietnam. It was written with sympathy for the GI's in the field, respect for their foes and a broad understanding of the big picture. Bergerud's writing was lucid, vigorous and made a moral point without moralizing. Whenever I spoke to him I got an education. Eric taught at Lincoln University in San Francisco and his sensible views on military history—and indeed, the American military—did not make him popular in the revisionist circles of academe, much less in those of the radical waters of the Bay area. Perhaps for that reason, he jumped at the chance of not only writing for a big eastern newspaper but in providing the benefit of his considerable knowledge to its book editor.

One of the most valuable rewards of my tenure at Newsday Books was the learning experience I derived from my phone conversations with our many knowledgeable contributors. It was a Renaissance tutorial where, by showing just a mite of interest, I could major in a spectrum of subjects. Bergerud was one of my best instructors: articulate, voluble, passionate. I would let him go on beyond the time required for the assignment because he was conducting a graduate class that I was happy enough to audit.

Which brings us to the final stage of World War II, Hiroshima. The 50th anniversary of the dropping of the atomic bombs on Hiroshima and Nagasaki produced a flood of revisionist history asserting that the attacks were unnecessary, that the Japanese were ready to surrender and that the chief purpose of the nuclear bombings was to intimidate the Russians rather than bring Tokyo to heel. In effect, rather than the final blow of World War II, this was the first salvo of the Cold War. According to this line of reasoning President Truman's justification that Hiroshima and Nagasaki avoided a long and bloody invasion that would have taken far more lives on both sides than the bombings was invalid. Rather, such an assault would have involved relatively light casualties and even this was unnecessary because strategic bombing and a blockade would have done the job. If this were true, Truman was a mass murderer and America was guilty of war crimes that bordered on genocide.

Leading the charge of these revisionist historians was Gar Alperovitz whose "Decision to Use the Atomic Bomb and the Architecture of an American Myth," had become Scripture to a generation of true believers brought up on the debacle of Vietnam. In addition to Alperovitz's tome and other like-minded volumes, there were books that took a more measured view of the political, diplomatic and military events that influenced the decision to drop the bomb. I sent them all to Bergerud and let him sift through them. The result was a 2,000-word essay, to my mind, the most important piece Newsday Books produced under my aegis.

In modulated tones, Bergerud proceeded to carefully examine and systematically demolish all of Alperovitz's claims using fact, documentation and the tools of the historian rather than the lawyering of a polemicist. It is not the province of this profile to reprise the details of Bergerud's essay. But a short summary paraphrasing his main points would be instructive of his approach. Most critically, he observed that Alperovitz's book ends on Aug. 6, 1945, the day of Hiroshima. Consequently, it ignores the crucial drama of what was going on in Tokyo. In effect, it takes the Japanese military out of the picture and thereby removes them from any responsibility for the subsequent events. What Alperovitz failed to address was that at this point the zealots of Japan's military junta were virtually running the country. The so-called "peace party" led by Prince Konoye had as much influence on events as anti-war activists did on Richard Nixon.

And even their feelers—which had to be done surreptitiously — insisted that Japan retain its conquests in Korea, Manchuria and Formosa and that war minister Tojo and his allies, who had plunged the world into two decades of devastation, be allowed to stay in power. Moreover, their appeal was not to the Americans but the Russians in the hope of splitting the Allies.

The Japanese military, as was clearly documented by their own records, had no intention of surrendering. Rather, they were bringing back 800,000 troops from China as well as raising a home army of a million men plus squads of kamikaze planes for a fanatical defense of the home islands. Their strategy was that American losses would be so great in an invasion of Japan that the U.S., already exhausted after four years of war, would be forced to negotiate a peace that would leave the military in power, ready to fight another day. The first atom bomb on Aug. 6 did nothing to shake them. It was only the second bomb at Nagasaki that altered the balance. Even here, the vote for fighting on at the imperial council was still a 3-3 tie. It was the intervention of the emperor after the second bomb that tipped the balance. Nagasaki was not redundant but crucial in breaking the will of the Japanese leadership to accept unconditional surrender with the understanding that the emperor would remain on the throne under American suzerainty until Japan could govern itself.

In regard to the light casualties of 30,000 that Alperovitz cites, Bergerud reminds us of the bloody price the U.S. had paid on Okinawa alone. We can only imagine what the toll would have been invading the home islands where the Japanese were preparing a suicidal defense involving the entire population in the cities, guerilla warfare in the rugged mountains and the use of gas stockpiles. In addition to the half-million American casualties in a planned invasion projected by U.S. Army medical authorities, millions of Japanese would have been slaughtered in the ensuing protracted warfare. President Truman was rightly concerned about saving the lives of as many Americans as possible. It was the central motivation in his decision to drop the bomb. Bergerud's judgment is that, horrible as they were, the atomic bombs saved far more lives than they took.

As I stated earlier, I was able to cite only a few of the many talented regular free-lancers who provided the sinew and bones of Newsday Books. I could have written about many more who were not only outstanding reviewers but outsized personalities. I regret their banishment from this stage but the proscenium is already crowded. By way of atonement, I will take the liberty of mentioning just a few souls who will have to stand for the rest: Nick Jenkins, the Yeats scholar who wrote so beautifully on Wordsworth and Coleridge; the elegant stylist James Marcus who went on to became Executive Editor of Harper's magazine; Linda Simon, then director of the Writing Center at Harvard, who graced our pages with polished prose, as did Maureen Corrigan who became book critic for NPR's "Fresh Air," as well as two memorable Brits, the Guardian's Martin Walker and Ben MacIntyre of the Times Literary Supplement, two elegant wordsmiths and accomplished authors in their own right. I apologize to the countless reviewers whom I exclude, but were I to list them, I would have to apologize more to the reader.

As important as attracting outstanding reviewers was packaging the report so that it would be accessible and inviting to our readers. I wanted to match the influx of talent with a comparable sense of innovation. We expanded the section on a variety of fronts. One of these was in the domain of Coffee Table Books. Hefty, handsome volumes on art, photography, fashion, architecture and the like, they had been relegated for the most part to Christmas season roundups where they were dispensed with in de facto gift-for-the-holiday coverage. I decided to take them seriously and treat them not as annuals but perennials. They were, after all, on the shelves year-round. We addressed them on their own merits, one at a time. In so doing, we were able to attract better reviewers who might have been put off by a roundup. We decided to come right out and call the space "Coffee Table Books." The advent of the streamlined Culture Section Fan Fare and the introduction of color in the spring of 1991 offered new opportunities to present this material. The review was squared off with the words "Coffee" and "Table" making a right angle in the top, left-hand border of the package. This design held throughout, whatever the rubric, whether Spy / Thrillers or Talking / With. The type was set off against a rose-tinted or maize-hued background and in the center was a picture from the book. It was an eye-catching affair providing a nice balance with the surrounding pages.

Since Fan Fare was in color we took full advantage of this, using the front cover as an introduction to the rest of the section. We led with a major review graced with a color illustration. Down the side were three tiny picture "reefers" with short one-line heads and captions highlighting what was running inside. We often tried to connect the over-lines on the teaser photos with the headlines of the reviews that ran on the inside pages. For instance, a roundup of policiers featuring female sleuths might be illustrated with a thumbnail drawing of a 19th-Century heroine detective under the heading "The Lady Vanquishes." It referred to an inside review under the headline "She Snoops to Conquer."

One of the most intractable categories to deal with was Paperbacks. I finally came to the realization that paperback reviewing was probably not where Newsday Books shone best. I decided to dispense with it altogether, treating new soft-covers as we would hard-covers. Indeed, in terms of price, there often wasn't that much difference. Moreover, we were now reviewing up to a dozen books a week so there was more room to incorporate new soft-covers into the mix. Where we could make a difference was by paying attention to books that came off the small presses, which often got short shrift from reviewers but were important to dedicated readers. Thus came into being the Small Press column. Every week, we gave a full column of reviews to books from such publishers as Coffee House, Serpent's Tale, Steerforth, Milkweed, Dalkey Archive, Baskerville, Braziller, Overlook, Catbird, Bridgeworks, Mercury and god knows how many more. The response was impressive. We probably never got so much mail from publishers. These houses had long been neglected by the mainstream press—including the august competition across town. This improvisation also enabled us to introduce some fresh young reviewers who were more receptive to experimental voices. It was one of the most successful innovations we'd made and brought us a lot of points in the industry.

Probably the most enterprising category we introduced—or retrieved —was that of the literary interview. Strange as it seems, the Times Book Review didn't then run interviews and, for that matter, neither did most other book sections, whether for reasons of space, manpower or policy. When I first arrived, we had actually run interviews. They were conducted by the incomparable Leslie Hanscom but the function ended with his retirement. We used the debut of the paper's weekend Fan Fare section to resume the category. But this time, I was going to spread the wealth around a bit more. This was important because, although unheard, the voices of different interlocutors were quite distinct and injected variety into the space. Moreover, multiple assignments gave us the flexibility to run the freshest pieces. The other advantage of The Talker was that we had the choice of using it in lieu of a review or to whet the reader's appetite in advance of an important book, or call attention to one that might appear only in the weekday section.

Dan Cryer had pride of place in this arrangement. As noted, Cryer was an outstanding interviewer and took to it with relish. On those alternate Sundays when Dan wasn't doing a Talker, we had a cohort of writers such as Lauren Picker and Wendy Smith who demonstrated a knack for getting authors to open up. The result was an impressive array of interviews under the rubric of "Talking With." Among the many literary figures who appeared in our pages were Isabel Allende, Margaret Atwood, Paul Auster, Russell Banks, Julian Barnes, Joseph Brodsky Peter Carey, Carlos Fuentes, David Grossman, Oscar Hijuelos, Norman Mailer, Tim O'Brien, Philip Roth, William Styron, and Scott Turow.

One of the most gratifying aspects of being book editor was not only selecting appropriate reviewers but also communicating with them, a task accomplished via the exchange of correspondence as well as through the editing process itself. I enjoyed hundreds of such encounters during my stewardship. I will take the liberty of citing only one, by Elie Wiesel. I first met Wiesel at a Newsday book lunch in 1991 where I prevailed on him to write a review of three books on children of the Holocaust, the first on Jewish youth in Nazi Europe, the second on the last days of Anne Frank and the third, a memoir, "I Remember Nothing More," by Adina Blady Szwieger, a nurse in the Warsaw Ghetto's children's hospital. We worked together till the end of my tenure in 1995. During the intervening years Wiesel contributed what was no less than a series of moral lessons. He never turned down a book. He would submit his review in French accompanied by a brief, note. After his review was translated, I'd edit it and send it back to him. The last piece Wiesel did for me was a review of "Konin," an effort by a British documentary filmmaker, Theo Richmond, to re-create his family's Polish shtetl swept away by the Nazis. Wiesel, in his review, could have been speaking about his own community of Sziget.

Over the course of my seven years, we reviewed upwards of 5,000 books. Not all of them involved such an exchange but more than a few did and it was at the core of what I strove for. What appeared in the paper was the proverbial tip of the iceberg. What didn't was equally important. I engaged in lengthy correspondence on numerous assignments that, for one reason or another, failed to pan out. I can only be humbled by the time and care my various correspondents took in telling me why a book was not suitable for review, after dutifully reading it. We paid a kill fee for such endeavors and, if I thought the effort considerable, we offered full remittance.

In addition to my other duties, there was correspondence with young writers helping them to find work at other venues, letters in support of applications for grants on behalf of our various academic contributors, and the many applications—with attendant clips—to review for Newsday Books. I tried to respond to every one of them. Perhaps most satisfying of all was a note from a reviewer relating how much pleasure they'd gotten from a book we'd sent them. The satisfaction of knowing that I'd touched something in a discerning reader that, for a moment, made them a kindred spirit, was a special delight that made the arduous hours of book editing worth the candle.

On July 17, 1995, a Monday, I was invited to attend what could justifiably be described as a memorable occasion in the publishing industry. On the cusp of its centennial in America, Oxford University Press was moving to new quarters in what was the northeast corner of the old B. Altman Building on Madison Avenue at 35th Street only a few blocks from our own offices. To celebrate the event Oxford had assembled the Press's governing body, delegates from the university's staff as well as the top tier of academic luminaries who produced the publishing house's 600 annual volumes. Several of them had been reviewed by and written for us such as the Roosevelt scholar William Leuchtenberg, and a few greeted me as old friends. What made this event special, however, was that prior to the cocktail party and speeches in the marbled sanctuary within its portals, Oxford had lined up an array of scholars in serried ranks outdoors and marched them majestically in full regalia for a block along a closed-off Madison Avenue. No other publishing house—no matter how big—could have carried this off. Oxford University Press, founded in the 15th century, was right back there with Gutenberg, and it knew how to do tradition. Decked out in their ceremonial robes, the assembled academics gathered in the twilight of a pleasant summer evening and strode with stately step and measured self-consciousness in solemn procession. In fact, it was serving as my own valedictory. On the previous day New York Newsday had published its final edition. I knew that this would be the last of such events that I'd be attending. In retrospect, with the recessional of print, this moment takes on ever more the aspect of a final salute, the dipping of colors, the lingering haze of a sunset.

The demise of New York Newsday has been well documented; it can be researched easily, and needs little further elucidation here. I offer merely a brief synopsis as context for how its closing affected my own fortunes. The seeds of the paper's downfall lay in its creation. It was fostered by a corporation and it was closed by one. As mentioned earlier, Newsday, and its New York edition, was a subsidiary of The Times-Mirror Company which owned a chain of papers throughout the country. The company was run by the Chandler family which had two branches, one headed by Otis, the other by his cousin Philip. It was Otis's branch that turned The Los Angeles Times from a parochial, right-wing sheet into a leading newspaper with national ambitions. And it was under Otis's influence and those of his executives that New York Newsday was hatched in an ambitious plan to challenge The New York Times in its own bailiwick.

Instrumental to this was the aforementioned David Laventhol, Times-Mirror president and former Newsday publisher and CEO, who was the chief booster and architect of the New York edition. But just as New York Newsday was picking up steam, Otis was being edged out of the picture by his conservative cousins, the sons of Philip Chandler. The Shakespearian echoes of family strife aside, the Wrong Chandlers, as I choose to call them, were more interested in the bottom line than in the romance of newspapers. It didn't help that the overheated California economy was starting its implosion, pulling the L.A. Times down with it, a decline abetted by a series of disastrous business decisions by Times-Mirror. This gave the corporate bean-counters the upper hand at the very moment that Newsday's New York edition was on the cusp of breaking even after a 10-year struggle. With a modest staff cut and other cost-saving measures it projected a loss of less than a million dollars in 1995—pocket change for Times-Mirror—and a slight profit the following year. Given the amount of time it then took for a start-up publication to turn a profit—witness Sports Illustrated— New York Newsday was on track to be in the black in good order. But the Chandlers and their hirelings had no interest in waiting, nor little love for an upstart, liberal, Eastern newspaper. In May

1995, they hired a new CEO as hatchet-man, one Mark Willes, an executive with General Mills where he had developed a successful strategy for marketing Hamburger Helper.

Willes arrived in New York to kill the paper, and the cost-cutting proposals of Newsday's executives to save it fell on deaf ears. The cereal killer, as he came to be known, had already made up his mind. Willes and his corporate patrons in L.A. had decided that, given the buffeting Times-Mirror papers were sustaining from a recession and the competition of two tabloids sustained by vanity owners with deep pockets, it was time to pull the plug. On the second day of a pro forma two-day tour, Willes pronounced the New York edition dead. The news came on a Friday afternoon, July 14—Bastille Day. I was at my computer completing a list for the following week's section when we were summoned to gather in the newsroom. As it happened, I was standing next to Murray Kempton when we got the news. I remember Murray turning to me and saying: "Jakie, I've had three other horses shot out from under me but at least in the past, the owners themselves had the decency to show up and give us the bad news. It's the first time I've ever been fired by strangers. We are living in a new era."

Technically, the verdict was announced by Ray Jansen, Newsday's publisher, but in fact, the ax had been wielded by Willes, fronting for his keepers in L.A. Kempton, of course, was old-school. He'd been used to an era of personal ownership where publishers at least felt the responsibility to lament the passing of an institution before they tossed the toilers into the street. The only obligation Willes had was to the numbers. And indeed, Times-Mirror stock soared after New York Newsday's obituary was announced. As it happened, this was a Pyrrhic victory for the Chandlers whose cost-cutting strategies led to an erosion of growth that eventually sapped the company's energies and sent its stocks tumbling once again. Willes, after being embarrassed by a variety of scandals and mishaps was sent packing. It turned out that he was as much fall guy as hatchet man. But he had served his purpose. New York Newsday was no more.

Ironically, with the boom in the second half of the 90's, had New York Newsday managed to hang on, the improved economy might well have given it a profitable new life. From a business perspective, Willes may have pulled the plug at exactly the wrong moment. Mulling this in retrospect provided little consolation for those who were displaced by its loss. Admittedly, the paper could have done more to help its cause. Perhaps a block-by-block invasion of Queens and Brooklyn from the east, eroding the Daily News's base, as Tony Marro advocated, instead of a frontal assault on Manhattan, might have been more prudent and, ultimately, more successful. And we certainly could have fought back harder at the canards of The Daily News that we were a bunch of hicks and they were the hometown paper. Considering we had a great New York staff that demolished them on local coverage and they were a demoralized outfit run by the detritus of the Commonwealth, it was no contest. But we never succeeded in getting our message across.

It was probably in the eulogies that our worth was best evoked: As the New Yorker wrote: "New York Newsday was the best, by far, of the city's three tabloids, promoting a consistent combination of investigation, accuracy, speed, civility and humor. The Newsday staff was the one that regularly beat The Times or gave it a close run on major stories in the city. In some ways New York Newsday had become the leading city paper. In fact it was no slouch in national and international reporting. Certainly, there has been no paper since the old pre-Murdoch Post that had such an impressive and varied array of columnists: Jimmy Breslin, Pete Hamill, Jim Dwyer, Les Payne, Gail Collins, Sheryl McCarthy, Lars-Erik Nelson, Sydney Schanberg, Dennis Duggan, Jonathan Schell and —the greatest columnist since Mencken—Murray Kempton. On Sunday, the bell tolled for Newsday. Our newsstands are poorer, our city a diminished place."

As I observed at the outset, Newsday's fate was dependent on a corporate parent and when nemesis threatened the mother ship, the New York edition was tossed overboard. Survival in a newspaper market depends on commitment, staying power and the iron will of an owner to remain in the game for reasons beyond the bottom line. Newsday's tabloid competitors had two such proprietors, Mort Zuckerman at the News and Rupert Murdoch at the Post, a private fief whatever its corporate trimmings. It's worth remembering that The Post had actually folded before being exhumed by Murdoch with a little help from his friends in Washington and, just two years earlier, the News was floundering—dumped by its corporate owners at the Tribune Company and fleeced by the mountebank Robert Maxwell—before Zuckerman salvaged it at bargain prices. New York Newsday could have survived, and probably flourished, with a 10 percent staff trim and some other cutbacks, well under the 13 percent cut in labor costs the News had undergone in 1987 or the later slashing of hundreds of jobs by Zuckerman. Moreover, during Newsday's ascendancy, both its rival tabloids suffered bitter strikes – the News in 1990-91 and the Post in 1993, leading to further labor concessions. In the end, pragmatic union leaders, unwilling to kill the goose that laid the eggs, if not quite golden ones, proved to be more far-sighted in keeping the News and the Post afloat than the expedient corporate management in Los Angeles in traducing New York Newsday. Had these beleaguered tabloids had to answer to the market during their travails, as Newsday did, either likely would have gone down and Newsday might have won its long-shot bet. But contingency intervened and both Zuckerman and Murdoch, for their own reasons, were willing to sustain losses to keep their papers afloat. Newsday had to answer to stockholders; the Post and the News had only to satisfy the whims of their well-heeled owners. The outcome was inevitable.

Just two months before the cereal-killing, we were celebrating two Pulitzer Prizes. The atmosphere in the newsroom was heady. There were staffers who were convinced that the Pulitzers would somehow insulate us from the imperatives of the market; that no one would dare shut down an award-winning enterprise. Our merit was proof of our success, a shield against fortune. But as that great philosopher Mae West observed: "Goodness got nothin' to do with it." True, yet it was this goodness that was the saddest aspect of Newsday's demise. I have worked for two other papers that folded, deservedly so. They were aging, creaking, decrepit. But the passing of New York Newsday was akin to the death of a young person in full flower.

History happens to people without them being aware that they are part of it. I was caught up in a great historical drama, the gradual eclipse of newspapers which were just coming to the end of a Golden Age, a window of 40 years in which they were the predominant form of news dissemination. Although the internet was still on the horizon the tectonic plates were starting to shift and the fallout from the implosion of Times-Mirror —which killed New York Newsday—was a harbinger of things to come.

The great diaspora began and I was part of it. Except that I was not among the evacuees thronging the de facto employment bureau that Newsday had set up in its New York headquarters. I had decided that after almost 40 years in the newspaper business, it was time to call a halt and take stock. As I wrote to a friend: "Staying on would have made me feel like a Paul Scott character hanging about India after the Raj. I saw no reason to fight a war of attrition after the game was up."

Of course, my decision to leave the fold was as premature as it was precipitous. But at the time, I wanted to do some of my own writing and the buyout looked good. What I knew I didn't want to do was stick around and administer an enervated book section that I was certain would be ever more circumscribed as time went on. Tony Marro would try to look out for me but even he could do only so much under the circumstances and who knew how long he'd be around? I felt that I had built something special and I didn't want to be there to see it picked apart.

In practical terms, I must have been crazy. With two kids on the way to college, the belief that I could become a country squire—even with a surgeon for a wife—was delusional. What I advise anyone who has ever asked me, is that their current job is a golden passport to their next port of call. Perversely, I failed to take my own advice. What I should have done was made a beeline for The Times Book Section where I probably could have found a haven. But who knows how that would have worked out with my being used to running my own show and having to work in a milieu I did not altogether respect. Nevertheless, it would have kept me in the book world, a realm I knew and enjoyed. After many vicissitudes, I was fortunate to wind up back on The Times at my old stomping ground in the Weekend Section. Reality had cured me of the illusion of cultivating my garden and, after little more than a year of the contemplative life and some freelance reviewing, I was back in the traces.

I handed over the reins to my No. 2, Laurie Muchnick, a solid deputy and one in whose hands I felt confident that I could leave Newsday Books. In fact, if Laurie wasn't so dependable, I might have remained since the only thing worse than leaving the section was leaving it in disarray. As it turned out, Laurie toiled in the vineyards for another 12 years, doing a laudable job under what must have been increasingly trying circumstances. By then Newsday had been sold by Times-Mirror to its new corporate owner, a cable company.

Sometimes I see a name pop up on the internet—Jan Harayda, the former book editor of the Cleveland Plain Dealer who created her own literary blog—and feel as if I'm watching from a shard of Krypton as other splinters of the planet whirl out to the ends of the universe. Reading such blogs from people whose enthusiasms I fed off is like trying to guess the age of a distant star by its fading light. Jan's stewardship influenced the reading habits of many people in a large American city unified by a newspaper that provided common ground for its subscribers. But now she was a voice among thousands in the blogosphere, distinguished only by the ability to attract attention on this digital runway. When I think of all the awful writers I prevented from appearing in Newsday, I am convinced that we need gatekeepers. As has been pointed out, having an opinion does not a critic make. What I seem to have lost was not just a book section but the climate that sustained it. Not long ago, The Washington Post closed Book World. To my knowledge, this leaves The New York Times as the last remaining major newspaper with free-standing book pages. I don't think such literary forums can be replaced by twitter or the hucksterism of the internet. The higher literary journals soldier on but this leaves what used to be called the general reader to the confusions of the web. In my humble opinion, we're the lesser for it.

In my last year at Newsday, I had a conversation with a savvy young woman, the book editor at the St. Petersburg Times. She said that within 10 years the then burgeoning internet would put many of us out of business. I assured her that her obituary for print was premature. I also thought New York Newsday would sail on till I retired, which shows you how good a prognosticator I am. She was right, of course. But even so, I occasionally fancy an alternative ending where the New York edition had somehow managed to dodge the bullet and not face the music for another 10 years. I most certainly would have remained and, in all likelihood, retired as an elder statesmen with a modest stature and a measure of acclaim in the book world, together with the knowledge that I'd brought the ship safely to port. Moreover, I would have been in good company since most of those writers—the Dwyers and Hamills— would likely have stayed at Newsday and not melted away. But as another great philosopher, Leo Durocher, tells us: "Would-a, could-a, should-a don't win ballgames."

After Mark Willes declared the New York edition defunct, Jim Dwyer and a few others negotiated with him for three days in a vain attempt to save the paper as an independent entity. When this final bid failed, Dwyer wrote a memo to his colleagues informing them of his last-ditch efforts. It ended in a tribute to the paper and its staff. I will let it serve as a memorial for the Book Section as well.

"For the last three days, with the help of many staff members, I have spent virtually every waking minute seeking help from politicians, investment bankers, friends, lawyers, business people, the broadcast and print news companies. The goal was to press Mr.

Willes to seek better alternatives. It was a long shot. That effort has failed. The public has filled my phone mail and mail box, called my home and offered every kind of support under the sun. Priests have said mass; two separate millionaires have pledged their fortunes if that would help. I have not had time to call them back. New York Newsday didn't need additional investment. It threw off enough money to run at a small profit margin; perhaps a larger one if some expenses were trimmed. But this shutdown wasn't about making money at an actual business. It was macho stagecraft for the stock market. One final thought: A day from now, or ten years from now, if some future boss wants to know about anyone here—in any department, any job—I'll be glad to tell them what a high and mighty honor it was to work with the people in this newsroom. If this sounds magnanimous, you shouldn't be fooled. It's just everlasting pride at having moved in these circles."

After about a year of "retirement," I realized that I had to get back to work, both for reasons of finance as well as mental health. The ivory tower of solitude, that I'd sought during the hurly-burly of my working years, turned out to be an unlooked for quarantine. But once off the train, getting back on is not so easy. Tony Marro was generous enough to offer me a part-time gig on Newsday's Long Island copy desk, a position from which I'd graduated 30 years earlier, but at least it got me back in the game.

I had been at this endeavor for several months when early in 1997 I got a call at Newsday from my old colleague Pete Hamill who had also been part of the Newsday diaspora. He'd been hired by Mort Zuckerman to run The New York Daily News. What Hamill wondered was would I be interested in being his book editor. Pete had a romantic vision of revamping The News so that it would regain its stature as a scrappy tabloid with a blue-collar readership that, under his aegis, would speak to a new generation of immigrants. He talked enthusiastically about revitalizing the News, energizing a young staff and putting out a paper that would not talk down to its readers. An upgraded and expanded book section was part of Hamill's design and he felt that I, like himself, being a city boy of immigrant stock and a veteran of its tabloids, would be ideally suited for the job. The cultural venue for this was going to be a streamlined Sunday magazine slated for the spring and, in addition to my book duties, I would double as the Deputy Sunday Magazine Editor. The Editor-in-Waiting was Orla Healy, an Irish import, whom Pete described as a great gal, full of enthusiasm and ideas with whom I'd get on famously. She'd been plucked from the fashion pages and hadn't had any newsroom experience which is why my stabilizing presence would be so important and why we'd make such a great team. What did I think? I told Pete I'd think it over.

Hamill's pitch, and my position, not withstanding, I had reservations. First of all, I had misgivings about Zuckerman. I remembered how he'd gone after Jane Perlez for the profile she'd done on him in The Times about his real-estate wheeling and dealing. I also recalled that he'd canned the News staff when he grabbed the floundering paper at a fire-sale price and only hired some of them back. Zuckerman had a reputation for being arbitrary, willful and intrusive—the morale at The News was considered to be Dickensian. And he went through editors like office-temps. One of them was Don Forst, my recent boss at New

York Newsday, who lasted only a few months before he'd had enough and went on to run The Village Voice. While there were no guarantees in the news business, Hamill's tenure—and thereby mine—was, at best, up for grabs. Also, there was my residual grievance against the News for its nasty attacks on New York Newsday that helped lead to the demise of a far-better competitor.

And then there was my concern about working with an editor who was an unknown quantity with no newsroom training. Orla Healy's elevation was ostensibly due to her overseeing a hot style section, which left a lot to be desired. The powers that be presumably believed that the dynamism that she'd invested in covering street fashions would energize a broader format. What she didn't know she could learn along the way. That the management would entrust such broad responsibility to someone with so limited a resume as Orla gave me pause about exactly what sort of a product Zuckerman had in mind. Moreover, my last taste of working as the No. 2 to a fashion type was during my tenure as Deputy Style Editor at The Times, an experience that I'd vowed never to repeat. I also knew that, as well-meaning as Pete was, he'd have a lot on his plate and, once I was into it, I couldn't keep running to him, so the chemistry would have to work.

Orla called me at Newsday, and then at home, and turned on the charm. Nevertheless, I told Pete about my reservations but he was upbeat about the job; he assured me of his support, and his enthusiasm was infectious. Like all people with charisma, Hamill was a natural salesman. And he confided that Orla was thrilled to have me and would value my input and experience. I agreed to meet them and the interview went well. Orla seemed delighted at the prospect of working with me. I tossed out a few ideas to which she appeared receptive and Pete reassured me that we'd complement each other's strengths.

My concerns notwithstanding, I felt the opportunity was too good to turn down. I accepted the offer and, having done so, I threw myself into the task on all 12 cylinders. Though I was not due on board till middle-March, by mid-February I began making plans for the section, calling in my chits with many of the writers who'd reviewed for me at Newsday and peppering Pete and Orla with ideas. Herewith is a passage from one of my memos which clearly states the kind of section I envisioned:

"Dear Pete, As I understand the job, I'll be functioning as Orla's deputy in the new Sunday section. I think it's important to detail

330

the functions of this job so that One, there are specific responsibilities and Two, people don't go stepping on each other's toes or, conversely, that nothing falls between stools. There is clearly a need for a deputy but to function as one while running the book section is a full plate and it's best that it be focused.

"Speaking of books, I presume what we're doing here is scrapping the current book coverage and starting from scratch. If you want a prestige book section that will get some attention, it will take money and space. Presuming that we have at least three pages for a Sunday section, this means that we can have four pieces—reviews, profiles, columns—in that space. Reviews will have to be the heart of the section. I think I can get good people. I've submitted separately a three-month schedule over the spring. This is flexible but it gets us in play, on target and sends a message to readers, writers and publishers. Obviously there's lots of adaptation that will be involved but it's important we agree on the basics. The critical thing is to assure that the essential concept is a good one.''

Orla turned out to be a terrific actress, in fact a diva. Her greatest role was playing the part of an editor. She made nice to me for the requisite honeymoon period. Pete had wanted me so she had accommodated him. As it turned out, my fears came to pass.

My sojourn at The News can be divided into two halves: pre-Orla and Orla. Although she was putatively my chief throughout this whole time, during the pre-Orla weeks, because she was distracted and I was involved with producing a book section for Spotlight, the waning Sunday section, we had relatively little congress and she had virtually no direct supervision of what I was doing. The second part of this period, from early May to mid-August, when Spotlight was converted to Sunday Extra, was very definitely "Orla." As it turned out, we had little contact over this duration as well, albeit for different reasons. Looking back, I now consider pre-Orla a halcyon time. The problems were mechanical and administrative but manageable. The Daily News was notorious for leaving people to their own devices with little support. But this was merely technical and it was comparatively blissful given what was to follow.

During the pre-Orla phase I had considerable autonomy. I was working with the feature assignment editor, Ron Givens, a cultivated man who seemed glad for my input and appreciative of my professionalism and the quality of my report. In effect, I was being asked to jump-start the book section. There was nothing left in the can which was just as well given the nature of what had come before. Within two weeks I turned things around and engendered a steady flow of solid reviews. This was the high point of my tenure. While reviewing popular fare for The News— biographies of Bogart, Raymond Chandler and Stephen Spielberg, as well as baseball books and thrillers— I also managed to essay fiction by Thomas Pynchon, Philip Roth and Cynthia Ozick and nonfiction on subjects as diverse as the massacre at Srebrenica (reviewed by David Rieff) and "The Kidnapping of Edgardo Mortara," the Italian Dreyfus case (reviewed by Andre Aciman). I brought to The News such reviewers as Francine Prose and Alfred Kazin. I managed this while limited to three pages a week. It was a brief rewarding period. Hamill loved the report.

The tone of the section was very much what Pete and I had agreed on before I took the job. We believed that The News could provide solid book pages that would not talk down to its readers. I was very specific in the memos I sent Pete and Orla about what I wanted and needed for the book section and what my vision was in shaping the Sunday magazine. What I encountered, however was a 180-degree turnabout.

It was Pete's idea that I'd provide a balance. Orla did not have balance in mind. I saw myself as both an elder statesman and a junior partner. Orla saw me as a junior. Partner was not in her vocabulary. The sad thing is that she needed all the help she could get. Orla manifested an abundance of gaps, some of which she masked, others in which she basked. She knew little about the venues where most of her readers lived—in a story on horse-racing she talked about sending a reporter to "the Beaumont." But the less she knew, the more she exuded the confidence of the heedless.

As for my bailiwick, let us say we had two different ideas of how to run a book section, the difference being that I had done so. Alas, Orla didn't really want a book section and her systematic decimation of the book pages bears this out. She cited the publisher as justification for reducing the book pages from three to two, for limiting them to commercial fiction by and for women, for cutting them to one review and a light "feature," for introducing all kinds of bells and whistles framed by white space that further diluted the room available for reviews. By June she had eviscerated the book section.

It was clear from the beginning of my tenure at Sunday Extra that Orla had no intention of working with me in any capacity. From Day One there, it was as if a switch had been turned off. I wanted to meet with her to begin mapping out the first issues. I warned her that unless we had three sections ready to go and were working on the fourth at launch time, we would be hopelessly behind and playing catch-up ball thereafter. She never listened and took my warning as an affront rather than reasonable advice. The result was that Sunday Extra lurched along from week to week, unplanned and virtually unedited. The more I asked to meet with her, first casually, then more formally, the more she resented me, finding ways to avoid me, at which she became increasingly inventive. Probably most telling about Orla's attitude toward me is that I never knew the name of the section until it was out in print.

The turning point came when Orla got Kevin Hayes, a capable and decent young fellow from the Sunday section, to be the third member of our team. Ron Givens—who indicated to me that he'd be unable to work with Orla in the new operation and opted to go back to writing—had already dropped out. Once Kevin was aboard, Orla had her preferred No. 2, an editor familiar with production who would do her bidding. She no longer had to pretend she needed me and her attitude was now actively hostile. She addressed all her remarks to Kevin, fed all the reporters to him, gave him all the assignments and made him her confidante. Whether at a staff meeting or on rare forays into the office I shared with Kevin she acted as if I wasn't there. Now that she could drop the façade, the gloves were off.

The handwriting was on the wall but I persisted in thinking I could stick around if I made myself useful. I kept sending Orla memos and story ideas that went up in smoke. I waited until the third issue of the new magazine hoping that in the give and take of producing the actual section things would improve, but they only got worse. It was clear that Orla wanted me gone.

Feeling that I could go no further with her, I met with Hamill and apprised him of the situation. Pete knew what I was talking about but he didn't want to take her on. Rather than locking all three of us in a room and talking some sense into her, he told me to talk to her myself. Predictably, she didn't respond to my overtures but about a month later attacked me for talking to Pete, calling it "inappropriate." I told her what was inappropriate was her high-handed behavior and gave her chapter and verse. I then asked her, in a final effort, if there was a way we could work things out. She refused to respond.

The irony is that I was actually a good fit at the Daily News. I liked it and grew to respect and appreciate the people I worked with, and they repaid the compliment. My only problem was with Orla, but the house had put its chips on her. I should note that when I decamped virtually the entire features staff came by and told me how pleased and honored they were to work with me.

I sent a final memo to Pete telling him what I thought were the problems with the section and its editor. Herein are a few passages: "Pete: As you're aware, things weren't working out between me and Orla. She didn't want me as her deputy, fair enough, and she had no need for a serious book editor. She does pictures, I do words. Perhaps she is right and graphics is the wave of the future with a light once-over on the content side for décor. I think this is a mistake for people who still buy newspapers and want some meat with the potatoes.

"To my mind, the section has some very serious problems. Basically, it is not a Sunday magazine in any accepted sense but an agglomeration of whatever comes in the door. It appears to be virtually unedited. It lacks content, focus and relevance. The gaffes are egregious and it seems to be produced without any serious forethought. I know that a magazine can't be judged by its startup content, and that it evolves, but the tendencies I've seen are being reinforced rather than amended. What we have is Content Lite. Nothing to disturb the attention of the reader, who is encouraged not only to go on but never stop. In a way it is a perfect vehicle for a shopping guide, suited more to the flip-through sensibilities of a fashion magazine than the more arresting qualities of a newspaper. I took this job to preside over an expanded book section that wouldn't talk down to its readers. Instead we have a contracted one that patronizes them. The result is not a book section but a book presence. There is no reason to have a serious book editor attending to such a travesty."

I spelled all this out to Hamill because I didn't want to leave any gray areas about the circumstances of my departure. As things stood, I advised Pete that I didn't think I could function there viably any further. I suggested I'd be receptive to another place at The News if he could find one. We talked about it a week later and decided it was best for me to cut my losses, so I left.

It should have been clear from the outset that I was the wrong man for the job. Orla knew it and, for her own reasons, strung me along. What I was offering was serious journalism. What Orla produced was not a feature section but a fashion runway—a façade of attitude and posturing without substance. The idea of my serving as a mentor, much less a counterweight, to anyone as headstrong and willful as Orla demonstrated a misreading of my personality and her character.

Not that Pete wasn't sincere when he said he was determined to bring the Daily News upscale and that I would be an ally in this endeavor. But, in fact, he handed the reins of the Sunday magazine and its book section to someone who would not only take it downscale but was determined to dumb it down literally beyond words. Whatever Orla's disclaimers, Pete should have understood this. He also should have known that bringing a quality book section to a racy tabloid was a long shot under the best of circumstances. For all his street-smart guise Hamill was a romantic who took a gamble on a fanciful notion. It certainly wasn't his intent, but once hard reality set in he was unable to support me.

As it turned out, Pete was having his own troubles with Zuckerman. By then his days were numbered. I had hardly decamped when he followed me out the revolving door of Zuckerman's editors. After more changes, the mantle eventually fell to our mutual friend Ed Kosner. Pete had fought the good fight but it was a losing battle. I was collateral damage. As for Orla, I'd primed Kosner on what to expect from her. Ed didn't need any input from me to come to his own conclusions before their ways parted.

BACK TO THE FUTURE

There is a photo montage in my living room of the Culture staff of The New York Times circa the early 1980's. It is a copy of an original presented to Clara Rotter, the longtime drama secretary, on her retirement. Virtually every member of the Culture Section from the most illustrious – the critics Vincent Canby, Harold Schoenberg, Hilton Kramer— to the most venerable – Howard Thompson, Abe Weiler, Thomas Lask—to the most humble— Fernando the coffee vendor, Charlie the front-desk man, the young news clerk Rosalie Radomsky— is accounted for in this display. It is a photographic record of The Times in its heyday, with Culture being one of the jewels in its crown. When I returned, about 15 years after the montage was assembled, almost 50 of those 60 faces were no longer in the building. Most had moved elsewhere, some had retired, a few were dead; more were to follow. I had returned to a different place. The aura of triumphalism was gone, the city room was somewhat more subdued, the people who were once knocking at the door were now gatekeepers, new faces predominated—no surprise—but the sense of exuberance had somehow evaporated. In many ways, it was now better run, more workmanlike, more rational, calmer. There was less institutional craziness yet the inspired madness that went with it seemed to have gone as well. A few of the old faces were still there—islands of reassurance in uncharted waters. But the familiarity was deceptive. A sense of apartness prevailed. The computer enabled critics to write at home and mingle less with the staff. It was the same and not the same. And I had changed as well. My ambitions were altered, my horizons diminished, my expectations limited.

I had thought that my return to The Times would have been a post-script, a soft landing in the ocean where I'd coast along on a rubber dinghy until a friendly stream brought me gently to rest on a final shore. I should have known better. As Bogart's Sam Spade observes, "You never get nothin' for nothin'." The price that I paid for being plucked from the sea was to be put to sundry uses by the paper. When John Darnton bumped into me in Grand Central after my stint at The News and offered me a way back into The Times at my old post on Weekend, he knew he was getting a bargain. I had no illusions about glory. Promotion was out of the question. I was pushing 60 and The Times wasn't known for advancing the careers of people my age. Which meant that I was going to be a utility infielder, but no more.

My restoration was effected by the serendipitous bifurcation of Weekend into two sections, one devoted to the performing arts, the other to the visual arts. The copy traffic was too heavy for the current editorial twosome, my old colleague Myra Forsberg who now ran the section, and her deputy Wendy Sclight. The heady currents that swell such an expansion—driven by the prospect of more advertising— created a brief window in which a bullish management indulged in growing the staff. It didn't hurt that the guru in this case was Gene Roberts, the outgoing managing editor, who saw the refurbished section as a capstone of his career and was quite willing to spend the paper's lucre on what he fancied would be his legacy. We didn't know it at the time but these were the magnificent sunset years of the mainstream media and, whatever the future augured, The Times was still top dog in this arena. Amazon was a blip in the Northwest, the Internet not yet ascendant, and Craig's List was still in the future. The Times was yet pre-eminent in Culture, Weekend was its cash cow and the free-spending ways of yore still obtained. If it was a Fool's Paradise, the Garden was well-watered.

Not only was the Weekend Section being renovated but so was the work space wherein it was located. We were housed in temporary quarters on the fifth floor so that I found myself jammed into an archipelago of stations that formed the Culture copy desk. This turned out to be an advantage since I knew most of the crew who were helpful in re-orienting me to the re-jiggered digital system in what was a sink-or-swim operation. For me, editing copy was far preferable to the technology of actually processing it. As the craft unions disappeared, the editors assumed greater responsibility for their technical input. This gave a subtle edge to editors whose talents were more digital than editorial, the early stages of a phenomenon that triumphed a decade later with the ascendancy of internet producers and their cybernetic counterparts. For the actual launch of our maiden two-part issue the system crashed and remained down for several hours while the computer experts tried desperately to solve the problem as the clock ticked well beyond deadline. I remember Gene Roberts himself coming down to ascertain the state of emergency— and being absolutely helpless in terms of fixing it. This was a "2001" moment. It was clear that the power was shifting to the digital world.

The paper was in a hybrid stage where, though most of the work was done on computers, we still "closed" in a composing room albeit the tasks there were mostly make-work. What had once been a humming labyrinth was now an echo chamber, its scattering of printers a rear guard holding a last redoubt before disappearing over the border. My boss Myra Forsberg, in her diligent way, insisted on checking the very last pages as they were processed in the proof machine—although this was redundant as they had already been double-checked upstairs. The upside was that standing around doing nothing except trying to look busy enabled me to listen to the dwindling band of printers as they talked about the relative merits of their forthcoming buyouts and the fortunes of their retired pals who'd already moved to Florida. In six months, although I caught little more than an occasional typo, I gained a valuable insight into the dynamics of obsolescence.

As a venerable member of the team, I thought that I would be included in the inner circle that motored the input of the Daily Culture section. Anticipating this role, I had prepared several ideas that would bear fruit in the coming season. My initial enthusiasm turned out to be premature. I attended the first few meetings with John Darnton and his new deputy, Martin Gottlieb, at which John was unfailingly polite but non-committal regarding my suggestions, Marty less so. This is not to say that all my proposals were brilliant but I knew that some of them were worthy of consideration. The truth of it was that Gottlieb—a solid company man who'd been recruited from the city room to act as the easy-going Darnton's enforcer—did not welcome any competition. And who could blame him? He had an eye to the future of the section and I was part of the past. I had my uses, but taking part in management councils wasn't one of them. The Deputy's task was simply one of many stations where Gottlieb would be posted on his ascent up the ladder. Not to put a fine point on it, I had already done the job. I had scars as the de facto Deputy Culture Editor under the much more demanding regime of Arthur Gelb, I was the only member of the staff who'd worked all three Culture Sections—Daily, Weekend and Arts & Leisure, I'd run a book section, I was a known quantity, with a firm grasp of the field, a solid record in hard news and features, familiarity with the staff and proven administrative abilities. No wonder Marty didn't want me around.

The denouement came when I learned of a fire in a venerable Bronx Catholic church whose blue-collar parishioners had banded together to refurbish it for the Christmas season when they would hold their first service in a partially restored chapel. It would make a perfect lead for our annual Christmas Music special. It had everything: poignancy, faith, urban grit, local appeal, great graphics and, most of all, a natural story that didn't have to be "manufactured" for the Christmas issue. Gottlieb was palpably unenthusiastic and Darnton politely tabled it. A small item announcing the event ultimately ran as a brief in the Christmas Music roundup that led off with a predictable piece of pap. I knew that if I couldn't make the case in this instance, I couldn't convince them of anything. I thereafter devoted my energies to Weekend.

Myra and Wendy ran a tight ship, perhaps too tight. It was nose-to-the-grindstone, elbows-to-the-wheel. No one could quarrel with the result: Week after week, the section appeared on time, in space, under budget. Myra set the course and Wendy served as executive officer, attending to the technical details, trouble-shooting and monitoring the staff. The copy was invariably solid, crisp and, for the most part, readable. Reporters and critics generally liked writing for them, the ads flowed in and the trains ran on time. For all the efficiency, there was an austere atmosphere on board. It was like living with two straight men— Abbott and Abbott. The result was an office dynamic that could at times be somewhat labored. All this being said, Myra left me alone. She did her job well and allowed me to do mine and for that I was grateful.

Although I was putatively an assistant editor on the Culture Desk with a single responsibility—to process copy for the Weekend Section— over the next eight years I wound up doing a spate of different jobs for a half-dozen editors. These tasks simply blended into the great maw of the Culture Section, materializing as part of a seamless whole with little notice as to their provenance. At one time or another I supervised Arts & Leisure's Architecture Section, the Weekend Warriors, My Manhattan, metropolitan excursions, a Dining Out Guide, New York is Book Country, a Celebrity Letters column, the TV Weekend Grid, the Daily Culture reviews, maps, corrections and the erstwhile movie critic, Elvis Mitchell—itself a fulltime job. This does not count such forays as bolstering the Ideas Section and other ad hoc exercises. Needless to say, none of these assignments relieved me of my primary obligation to the Weekend Section where I shared the labors for virtually everything that appeared in its 48 pages from the front covers to the listings with particular attention to such columns as Books, Television, Antiques, Family Fare and alternate duties in areas such as the Broadway and Movie columns.

I volunteered for none of these auxiliary assignments but somehow they seemed to find me. Typical was my involvement as progenitor of the Weekend Warriors. The concept materialized early on at a weekly planning meeting. During those heady days, the Advertising Department, in a bullish mood, fantasized that the Weekend Section could attract sporting-goods ads with the come-on of a weekly feature on different sports activities that weekend athletes might engage in. The idea, of course, was hare-brained, but that didn't stop us from forging ahead. Myra bruited the proposal, emphasizing that it would make most sense for a single editor to be in charge. After a long silence, Myra averred that, since I was the only male in the room, and sports was a guy thing, I would be the most suitable candidate for the job. That this was a bit of reverse sexism passed unnoticed. I responded that the only sports with which I was familiar were baseball, basketball and football—the basics, which did not seem to be the province of this feature. Beyond that, I was equally in the dark with everyone else in the room. To no avail. Myra, with the little grin she gave whenever dragooning me into a project, handed me the baton. I believe at the time, Myra herself thought this was a management trial balloon that would, in short order, float away. But, as it turned out, the Warrior column took on a life of its own and became a popular feature. Myra, of course, had been right in saddling me with the job. Once chosen for the task, I threw myself into it.

I proceeded to get hold of my old sports contacts who had reviewed for me at Newsday. My key player was Allen Barra, who wrote a sports column for the Voice and the Observer. Not only did Allen know lots of writers but he could distinguish the wheat from the chaff. My problem was that most sports writers—including Allen—are not athletes. And most athletes can't write. I needed the few who could do both and, in the bargain, were willing to engage in all sorts of esoteric sports—many of them do-it-yourself— that would be of ostensible interest to like-minded readers. Barra got me started with a few sources and before long I had built a team of writer-athletes who were up for everything from spelunking to rock climbing, hang-gliding to kayaking, wind-surfing to ice-fishing. I had a core of regulars such as Allen St. John (on lawn tennis, building a jump shot, ski training, tandem bike-racing, improving your serve, swimming for beginners); Jerry Beilinson (on Frisbee, hang-gliding, roller blading, adaptive skiing, camping and canoeing); Chris Ballard (on lawn bowling, roller basketball, co-ed hoops, Thai boxing, racquet ball, billiards); and Peter DeMarco (darts, cricket, stickball).

Once the column got going, the volunteers came from everywhere. My star, however, was Joe Glickman. Over three years he did more than 20 pieces for us on subjects as varied as mountain biking, sculling, wilderness tracking, fencing, triathlons, tandem canoe-racing, tree-climbing, scuba-diving and—one indoor lark—a computer workout. Considering that I didn't go much beyond stickball in my own athletic repertory, this was an eye-opener for me. During that period, I got to learn more about esoteric sports and their idiosyncratic practitioners than I ever hoped to know. In order to edit these writers I had to absorb something about the sports they were talking about and to develop a certain enthusiasm for them. It didn't always work. To this day I still don't understand the niceties of cricket. But my obtuseness led the writer to clarify the rules until at least they made some sense to this troglodyte.

Over time, I got to know some of these writers fairly well in addition to providing a forum for their work in The Times and a generous fee for doing what they enjoyed in any case. Jerry Beilinson's articles eventually helped him get a job at National Geographic and Joe Glickman's feats led to a solid free-lance career topped off by a book on climbing the highest peaks in all 50 states. The Warrior columns ran weekly for more than three years, from October 1997 to February 2001. They could have gone on for the duration. I had no trouble feeding the beast and the rich variety of sports and people who could write about them engagingly proved inexhaustible. But end it did. The curtain fell when Jim Gorman, the Circuits Editor, decided to leave his indoor job for the outdoors and was given a Nature Column in the Weekend Section that replaced the Warriors. Although editing Gorman was easy I was actually sorry to see the Warriors go. So were my various charges who by then were making a nice piece of change courtesy The Times and enjoying the exposure. Of course, the Warrior never produced a single sporting-goods ad but, as often happened at The Times, once the ball was in play, people forgot why it started rolling in the first place.

At about this same time, I was also asked to oversee the Eating Out column. As with most of these assignments, they began as jobs that were to be spread around but that de facto devolved to me. I was given the Hobson's choice of carping about the imbalance in the work load —bad form—or simply hunker down and get on with it. I chose the latter. Eating Out, with its accompanying Diner's Journal, was a holdover from the days when Restaurants was one of the popular columns in Weekend featuring such doyennes as Mimi Sheraton whom I'd edited in her heyday. Subsequently, the Dining reviews were moved to the Living Section. Whether as a sop to Weekend or a strategy to cover all bases, it was decided to keep a residual Dining presence in its pages. This accounted for my editing Eating Out, which operated on a simple premise. Every week, Eric Asimov, the second-string Food critic, condensed his earlier takes on a dozen different restaurants into a capsule paragraph each, and we assembled them thematically —Al Fresco, Middle Eastern, Pasta, etc. This string of eateries— numbered 1 to 12 in alphabetical order and, accompanied by ratings, phone numbers and addresses— was preceded by an introductory paragraph that unified each column. For instance, on Valentine's Day we dished up a survey of romantic venues, on July 4, All-American restaurants, on New Year's Day, brunch places. Agreeing on a theme—fireplaces, desserts, breakfasts—had its challenges, particularly in avoiding a recent repeat of the same French restaurant that might appear under the rubric of "Quiet Nook" and materialize shortly thereafter under "Bastille Day" and yet again under "Bistro." It was impossible to avoid repetition and there was occasionally a minor tussle between myself and Eric over how frequently we could recycle an eatery. For the most part, however, our relations were cordial. Eric, the son of my old Newsday colleague, Stan Asimov, bore not only a physical resemblance to his father, but had also inherited Azzy's forbearance, which made working with him fairly effortless. Our affiliation lasted for several years until he became The Times's chief wine connoisseur devoting himself to writing about the grape.

With Eric's departure, the column's fate was sealed. It wheezed along for a while under the auspices of Kris Ensminger, a news assistant in the Food Department, while I administered last rites, monitoring the weekly themes. But before the paper pulled the plug, I'd supervised more than three years worth of columns on topics ranging from late-night eateries to smokers' havens, sandwich places to tea parlors, barbeque joints to noodle shops. Actually, Eating Out provided a helpful service and probably deserved a better fate. It was subsequently resurrected in bits and pieces in other parts of the paper but never to the good effect that it had in Weekend. Similarly, well after I left, the Warrior resurfaced fitfully as a flaccid "Urban Athlete," a shadow of its former self, in one of The Times's periodic forays into reinventing the wheel.

One task that naturally fell to me was to oversee a set piece that led the section for New York's annual book fair. Weekend was event-oriented and, like the rise and fall of the Nile, one of the occasions it covered with fanfare was New York is Book Country which recrudesced every September in step with the fall publishing season. Anchoring our panoply of service listings and maps that indicated what was being hawked, was a free-form literary essay, loosely linked to the pleasures of reading, by a prominent writer. Given my background in books, I was assigned to recruit the appropriate celebrity, which sounds easy enough given the clout of The New York Times. In reality, it had its own hurdles. First off, I had to beat back the suggestions of my colleagues, all of whom had famous friends or thought of writers who were currently on sabbatical in Ulan Bator. Then, I had to come up with a sufficiently warm and willing body, distinguished, available and preferably tied to New York. It is amazing how many writers are off communing with their muses or nature or busy meeting publishing deadlines over the summer. To furnish a piece by Labor Day meant beginning the search after Memorial Day, the work of a long hot summer. My first acquisition in this enterprise—which I kept at for eight years—was concordant with New York's centennial as an incorporated metropolis, so I needed someone who could write about literary life in the city through the prism of their own experience. After a mild crucible of trial and error, I hit upon Grace Paley, an accomplished author, passionate activist, consummate New Yorker and fellow Bronxite.

While I gave Grace leeway to write whatever she pleased, I stressed that I hoped she would address how the city had served her as a personal muse and what it was about New York that got the creative juices flowing. Naturally, she didn't do this. The piece that came in was a nostalgic, autobiographical resume of her life in New York moving from the Bronx to Greenwich Village with the various literary way stations en route. So I undertook to finesse it, focusing on what was relevant while massaging Paley's sensibilities in a joint literary effort with as little of my fingerprints showing as possible.

Grace was a skilled and engaging writer but I had to fit her deftly into the Book Country template—which was after all the reason for the piece—without bruising the fruit of her labor. She began, "Once my New York City was the Bronx . . . '' and went on from there at some length, never mentioning the occasion for the essay until the finale. I moved her ending upstairs and altered it slightly so that the lead now read: "This weekend, New York, our big, noisy, contentious, world-engaging town, is being celebrated as book country. For most people, that's Manhattan. But once, my New York was the Bronx." The piece picked up from there as she'd written it with my emendations and her responses, often in barely legible faxed-in scrawls. Yet by deadline we'd negotiated our differences, and the essay took pride of place in the Book

343

Country package. In subsequent years I recruited such writers as Jamaica Kincaid, Jonathan Rosen and Richard Eder for the book-fair essay.

Sometimes the missions I was assigned actually were impossible. But this was not ascertained without a crucible of trial and error. As part of an effort to spruce up Arts & Leisure, it was decided to anchor its Letters Page with an Op-Ed component. To be known as "Forum," this would feature a provocative opinion piece by a respected cultural figure on any subject that excited their interest. In tapping yours truly to manage this affair, John Darnton assured me that it wouldn't interfere with my regular duties and should take no more than a few phone calls a week. Having handed me the baton, Darnton turned me over to John Rockwell, the Arts & Leisure Editor, and wished us well.

Once on the high seas, Rockwell indicated that the course had changed slightly. Rather than assign knowledgeable people in the Arts who might actually have something to say, he wanted me to focus on celebrities who would add "buzz" to the section. The problem is that most celebrities can't write, are not readily accessible and generally prove to be unreliable. More to the point, to model Forum on the Op-Ed section was specious reasoning since the latter was anchored by a brace of Times columnists supplemented by a flotilla of free-lance contributors with an interest in promoting a point of view, as well as a full-time staff to solicit them. When celebrities did appear, such as Henry Kissinger and Arthur Schlesinger, they were not only articulate but eager to grind an ax on the Op-Ed page. Show-biz personalities, on the other hand, were not polemicists who needed us and would meet our deadlines. Moreover, entertainment luminaries were insulated by an array of handlers so that even getting to them entailed the obstacle course of negotiating their entourage. Nevertheless, the ship was sailing so I tended the rigging as best I could.

This enterprise got under weigh in June '98 with the goal of a landfall by October. I prepared a tentative roster of about a dozen theater people whose shows were making a splash that season. To sate Rockwell's appetite for marquee names, I offered up Alan Alda, Elaine May, John Leguizamo, Eric Bogosian and Marsha Norman. In movies, I nominated Jonathan Demme, Nora Ephron and a young Michael Moore who was just beginning his career as a political provocateur. For heft, I included Neil Gabler, who was writing a book on celebrity culture in Hollywood. In television I proposed Don Hewitt, Candice Bergen and Larry David before his enthusiasm was curbed. I also tossed out such generalists as Wally Shawn, Spalding Gray and David Sedaris, all of whom had one-man shows or various stagings at the time.

As September rolled around, I had a lot of promises but few commitments. As we approached the starting line we were spinning wheels with no gas in the tank. Although I had kept Rockwell abreast of events as they developed, we were now at a critical juncture and I decided it was time for a wake-up-call in the form of a memo that would get his full attention and also put everything on record so that, if the ship foundered, at least there would be a log indicating that I had flashed warning signals.

I don't know if it was the efficacy of my letter, but cooler heads prevailed and Rockwell threw in the towel. I considered myself lucky that both Johns were reasonable men. If that had been Arthur Gelb, the ship may have actually sailed. And who knows? It might have worked. Like all great men and maniacs, Gelb had the Churchillian impulse to forge ahead: The results were often disasters like Dieppe and Gallipoli. But then there was the Battle of Britain. And that's what most people remember.

The Op-Ed fiasco may have died aborning but Arts & Leisure had use for me yet. Forum had hardly wheezed its last when Darnton called me into his office once again. Whenever John summoned me, my heart sank. Basically a decent man, Darnton was actually very humane about these moments. Each top editor has a different style in delivering the bad news. Gelb would bluster with faux enthusiasm as if he were offering you a rare opportunity that you ought not miss. Darnton was more straightforward. He would take you into his confidence, let you know there was a problem and that you were the best candidate to solve it. In neither instance was there ever talk of a raise. In Arthur's case he was doing you a favor; in John's variation there was the perennial budget crisis but he'd try to make it up in some way when things got better. They never did. Over the eight years of my return, there was little prospect of a merit raise.

The problem once again was Arts & Leisure. It seemed that the paper's Architecture critic, Herbert Muschamp, ostensibly responsible for producing the Sunday Architecture section, was temporarily hors de combat. Would I step in and rescue them? As per usual, this was in addition to, not instead of, my normal duties. Since the paper could not allow A & L's Architecture Section to go dark, the understanding was that I would fill the breach while Herbert recuperated.

But there was more to the deal. As Darnton explained it, Muschamp would still be responsible for filing as many columns as he could over the next few months so that the burden shouldn't fall entirely on me. In fact, John said, not only would Herbert be glad to do so, but he would also "oversee" my choices to make sure that nothing untoward got into the paper. I told John I didn't need overseeing, especially from Muschamp. As a matter of fact, I had edited the A & L Architecture Section during my last go-round at The Times. But then the Architecture critic was Paul Goldberger, who filed regularly and dependably with occasional fill-ins from Joe Giovannini. This new gig would be a whole other ballgame with me having to come up with a list of architecture writers from scratch and scrambling to fill the weekly space hole.

Then came the zinger. Darnton ruefully acknowledged that Muschamp was to have de facto veto power over my choices. Without saying so directly, John indicated that his hands were tied. I told him flat out I wouldn't accept the job under those circumstances, nor would any other editor. We then had a long negotiation in which Darnton promised that, in effect, it wouldn't come to that. Muschamp would be glad to stay away from the office. As it turned out, John was half right. When it came to holding up his part of the bargain, Herbert was virtually AWOL. In the five months that I ran the section I accounted for 18 pieces, Muschamp for two, coming near the end of both my tenure and my tether. We met once in the lunchroom at the outset of this enterprise. Herbert, somewhat bedraggled but more defiant than contrite, was making sure that I wouldn't pee on his hydrant which, among other things, consisted of the city of New York. "There's so much going on in the rest of the country," he enthused. I pointed out that The Times was based in New York, which was undergoing a building boom.

He countered that there was nothing really interesting in town and that the exciting stuff was happening west of the Hudson. As a sop, he threw me a couple of names, almost none of which turned out to be of any use. I was on my own except that Muschamp was a chain on my leg. To be fair, he pulled rank only once—but it was once too often—when I enticed the essayist Philip Lopate, an accomplished architecture critic in his own right, to do a piece for us. Muschamp objected to the story but his real aim was to keep Lopate—a genuinely original talent and therefore a threat to

Herbert—from appearing in our pages. I went to Rockwell and then Darnton, but they were of no help. I would have walked away but by then I had developed relationships with several writers whom I didn't want to leave hanging or, worse still, exposed to the ministrations of a recycled Muschamp, so I bit my lip and soldiered on. I told Lopate exactly what had happened. He was aware of the situation at The Times and affected to understand my predicament but I know it rankled him.

Although Muschamp did not repeat this behavior I learned from talking to a wide range of architecture writers how he kept competitive voices from appearing in the paper and how he fawned on a rarefied set of clients and patrons and marginalized whatever talent lay outside this circle. I also found how many gifted contributors there were who were more knowledgeable and far-ranging than Muschamp, and how foolish The Times was to have put all its eggs in his fragile basket.

I got the assignment in mid-December to fill the first hole for the issue of Jan. 3. I remember driving uptown on a wintry weekend, spotting a magazine store near Broadway and 72d Street and pulling over to double-park. I scooped up every architecture magazine on the rack—Architecture, Architecture Digest, Art in America—brought them home and began poring over them. By Monday morning I was making assignments. The first one I made, however, was not to a specialist but to our European Cultural Correspondent, Alan Riding. I didn't have time to take a chance or explore the terrain. Riding was the consummate cultural reporter: cosmopolitan, unflappable, resourceful, accommodating and fast. Based in Paris, he roamed Europe coming up with novel, offbeat pieces on the arts. He was available for hard news assignments, able to parachute in anywhere at anytime, and ever-ready to help out an editor in need. While lots of people were on vacation during the holiday season Alan, like the lifesaver he was, would be around.

I rang him up in Paris and said something to the effect of: "Alan, I've just been given this 'plum.' I need something fast in your bailiwick that says 'architecture.' What've you got?" He didn't miss a beat before coming to the rescue. It turned out that there was a new state of the art museum in Dijon designed by a hot young architect with all kinds of techno bells and whistles. Alan could have the piece by week's end, just in time for our close, with great pictures. Riding was as good as his word. He delivered a splendid piece, engaging, informative, readable and, most important, timely in every sense of the word. Riding's good offices had bought me sufficient time to build up just enough of a backlog so that I could have breathing space. Within a month, I had a cluster of my own writers, an inventory of a half-dozen pieces and more on the way. After that, they just kept coming. I never had to worry about filling space again. And the quality was good.

Turning adversity to advantage, I realized that the ground rules which made New York out of bounds implicitly extended my reach to the rest of the nation and beyond. I interpreted it as an elastic clause that would open a window on the world. I gathered a new set of writers from a variety of sources. First, I went to my friends. Stephen Marcus at Columbia recommended his colleague Gwendolyn Wright who taught architecture there and became one of my most effective collaborators; my pal Nora Kerr in the Culture backfield volunteered Tom Hine, a feisty architectural freelancer from Philadelphia; Sara Bershtel, an erstwhile publishing ally at Holt, connected me with Mike Davis, a dissident voice on urban design who wrote from Las Vegas; Philip Lopate championed Lisa Germany, a talented young protégé from Texas, and Richard Sennett, a major figure in urban planning, although otherwise engaged, nominated his wife, Saskia Sassen, herself a significant presence in the field.

I also leaned on my Times relationships such as Todd Purdum in California who did an article for me on the rebuilding of a neighborhood in South Central L.A. after the riots there, and Sarah Lyall in London who went up to Glasgow to do a well-turned piece for us when it was named the United Kingdom's City of Architecture and Design. The virtue of Times writers was that they needed very little work.

Then, there was a pile of applications that had been moldering on Rockwell's desk from a slew of candidates who wanted to write for The Times but had been held in limbo by Muschamps's cordon sanitaire. I dutifully sifted them, choosing a few who'd contribute gainfully. Among these were Cheryl Kent, who wrote for the Chicago Tribune, and James Russell of Columbia, both of whom were regular contributors to Architectural Record. Between Russell, who taught urban design, and the aforementioned Gwen Wright I had two of the most prestigious people on Columbia's architectural faculty whose talents had been overlooked by A & L, albeit they published widely in design magazines and wrote for our Real Estate section. Though I wasn't allowed to comment on New York's architecture no one said I couldn't utilize its writers.

Almost all of these specialists had the added virtue of coming up with an abundance of stimulating ideas, with which I could fill the section several times over. In my earlier morphology, I had pretty much let Paul Goldberger generate the ideas; this time I was responsible for them. One of the unspoken rewards of being an assignment editor is that it affords a seat-of-the-pants tutorial on a wealth of topics at the hands of an erudite faculty. In order to engage them you must not only be interested in their subject, but sufficiently knowledgeable so that they are addressing a receptive audience. Whatever the topic: Health, Style, Film, a good editor becomes an autodidact in a crash course on whatever is under discussion and, in short order, an instant expert or, rather, a brief enthusiast, which is just as good for assigning purposes.

One can't cover architecture in this country without writing about Chicago, where the skyscraper was virtually invented. And this is where my stewardship fittingly started and ended. Cheryl Kent, one of the writers whose resume was on Rockwell's slush pile caught my attention with solid clips from the Chicago Tribune and I called her to send along some ideas. She responded promptly with a few proposals. The first was a story about a commission given to Rem Koolhaas to design a student center for the Illinois Institute of Technology. The campus of Illinois Tech at Chicago University had been designed by the master builder Ludwig Mies Van der Rohe who had directed Illinois Tech's architecture program for 20 years. Koolhaas's commission would be passing the torch from one of the pillars of modern architecture to a new generation. It was also a story about rejuvenating a decimated part of Chicago with the choice of Koolhaas serving as a metaphor for both continuity and innovation. But Koolhaas turned out to be taboo, one of the rising stars whom Muschamp had appropriated, so that this story was sidelined. I found other venues for Cheryl, however, one of them in nearby Milwaukee, a zany piece about Harley-Davidson's new bells-and-whistles "college" for salesmen with a vast showroom where Wild Ones from everywhere could journey to spin their wheels on a specially built ramp to nowhere.

But I wasn't through with Chicago yet. Shortly before the end of my tenure, I heard from the above-mentioned Saskia Sassen who was teaching there. A few months earlier we had tentatively discussed an article on the renaissance of downtown Chicago. But as she hadn't gotten back to me, I'd pretty much written off the idea, assuming she'd let it slide. Then, in May, just as I was preparing to turn back the baton, I got a call from Sassen. It turned out she'd been doing research on the story, which had developed into something more focused: the renovation of Chicago's great office towers into lofts for living space. This hyper-urbanity was taking place not in old industrial warehouse districts like Manhattan's TriBeCa but rather in skyscrapers still surrounded by other office towers. Although I had more than filled my quota for the transition, I sent off a note to Rockwell attesting to Sassen's bona fides and urging that this was too good a story to miss: the city of the Big Shoulders becoming the city of the White Shoulders. I no longer remember the disposition of the piece but I cite these two Chicago stories for the intellectual energy that good ideas can generate. The electricity between an editor and a writer when they spark an idea is the closest thing a sedentary deskman may ever get to sinking a buzzer-beater. In this context, I was fortunate to be handling architecture because it is the only art whose mandates are both social as well as esthetic, bringing together the imperatives of design, sculpture, engineering, urban planning, public space, politics, social policy, lifestyle and fashion. So, although I came to this assignment with the usual quotient of misgivings, despite all the headaches, I rose to the bait.

And make no mistake, there were plenty of headaches. Many of my correspondents wrote well enough for the specialty journals but were not professional newspaper reporters. Consequently, they needed a good deal of editing which took considerable effort, particularly for material that was going to appear in The Times culture pages, one of the best written sections of the paper. With virtually all of these contributors, I had thick files on every piece consisting of the initial assignment, a marked-up first draft that invariably needed restructuring and more reporting, a second draft often requiring more reworking and additional questions, then a third draft with yet more pencil editing, followed by fine tuning involving much back-and-forth over the telephone, then comments from Rockwell on this "finished" copy, which led to penultimate negotiations before a "final" version—that in itself was subject to last-minute trims for space and yet another flurry of phone conversations before the piece ultimately ran.

As draining as this process sounds, it was actually far less arduous than the toll exacted by other Sunday sections such as the Magazine whose group editing I've alluded to earlier. The advantage with us was that the writer was dealing mostly with the sensibilities of a single editor. I made every effort to keep as much of their work as possible, seeking simply to refine and clarify it so that the narrative was smooth and the prose graceful while still retaining the writer's voice. The key was to make them believe that the final product was theirs.

Most vexing of all was that my labors were seen as counterproductive by my Weekend overseers, Myra and Wendy, who considered my work for Arts & Leisure as subsuming my responsibilities to Weekend. Of course, they had a point. My duties for Rockwell were at least half-a-job. I tried to compensate for this by working on Architecture during limited down time, plus arriving early and leaving late. I also tried to avoid doing any Arts & Leisure work on Wednesdays and Thursdays when Weekend closed. But given the pressures of the task this could not always be avoided and I could see Myra and Wendy bristle when I took an architecture call on "their" time. The worst moments came when I had to use our mutual printer to get an architecture piece that might come in at some length. Standing in front of the printer waiting for the story to finish with them glaring at me was no fun. It was as if I were working for The Daily News. From where they sat, I might as well have been—my primary responsibilities had to be to Weekend, not a job in another department. From my point of view, the other department was at The New York Times and I was solely responsible for accomplishing the task. I finally went to Darnton and told him to rein them in or get another patsy; that it was impossible to do his bidding furtively. Although they never said anything, Darnton must have spoken to them because they let up on me.

At the best of times, nothing came easy with the architectural copy. Jane Holtz Kay was the architecture critic for The Nation and the author of "Asphalt Nation" and "Lost Boston." She was an expert on the reclamation of America's fading downtowns. I assumed that as a regular writer for a leading magazine of political and cultural criticism, she would have a felicitous prose style. Not quite. Jane's original printouts are dotted with fixes. My pencil work on her first drafts were moot because she usually went off in a different direction so that the story had to be edited anew. Each time it took a while until I discovered the substance of the story somewhere inside the piece. I abided this because Jane's subjects were important, she put considerable effort into reporting the story and I liked her.

Editing Jane provided a paradigm for a working relationship between writer and editor. The basis was trust. Jane was confident I could make her work better, and that I was on her side— that is I was looking to enhance her, to make her envision possibilities in her story that she might not have seen in the throes of writing. This might simply involve bringing up a paragraph, filling a hole, clarifying a statement, smoothing out a rough passage or finessing a sentence by changing a word. Or it could mean shifting the emphasis of the story or teasing out a tantalizing fact that lay submerged deep in the piece. I was there to protect Jane and she was grateful for my catches. But the greater task was to strengthen the story—a mutual undertaking. A good editor has the advantage of distance and knows how to use it wisely, re-ordering the material if required but always aware of the reporter's sensibilities. The writer, after all, is the one who has done the work and it is his or her name that will be identified with the story. Therefore the editor has to proceed nimbly, balancing the writer's vulnerability with the need to show the piece to its best advantage. It is important to be knowledgeable about the topic at hand or at least to show an active interest in it. And it is helpful to know something about the reporter. The key is to create a sense of intimacy so that when the crunch comes the writer is assured that the plane will land safely.

It took years to perfect this but, once refined, it could work across the board, with veterans who needed only a few brush-strokes or with writers whom I'd never met before, such as Victoria Newhouse. Victoria had arrived through Muschamp's auspices. She was the only one of his picks I ever used. To her credit, Victoria knew a lot about the design of museums and she had access to the people who ran them. She took direction like a class in deportment. With Victoria, I was courteous to a fault, in fact uxorious. Newhouse did two pieces for us, one on a pair of refurbished natural-history museums at the Jardin des Plants in Paris, the other about Amsterdam's new science museum in the city's harbor. Victoria had a beautiful phone voice: gracious, capable, confident. She was consummately professional about responding to questions and taking editing—she was not Sy Newhouse's wife for nothing. Victoria accepted editing well, which I was deft in administering. It was a workable pas de deux.

The Paris piece required some refurbishing. Victoria was pleased with my efforts but she had some changes to my changes, submitted by her assistant. As we went back and forth, pleasantly, like tennis between two old friends on a grass lawn, I affected an unflappable air, channeling Noel Coward while Myra frowned at me for putting off my Weekend work. The article ran and Victoria was delighted. So much so that she volunteered her second piece, this one on the Dutch museum that, despite its innovative design, was having financial and identity problems. I will cut to the chase.

Here is Victoria: "Amsterdam's new Metropolis Science and Technology Center adds a startling new presence to the Dutch city's harbor. Nicknamed the Titanic, the wedge-shaped structure clad in green pre-oxidized copper evokes a giant, mystery ship. This fantastic apparition just across the Oosterdok from the 17th-century city center houses a new breed of museum: science centers are dedicated to the exhibition of processes rather than objects, the application of ideas rather than the preservation and exhibition of precious objects." The piece continues in this vein at some length.

My revise: "Looming up over Amsterdam's harbor just across the Oosterdok from the city center is a fantastic apparition—a wedge-shaped structure clad in green copper that could be mistaken for a giant mystery ship. Although harkening back to the city's fabled seafaring past, it is actually very much an edifice of the future: the new Metropolis Science and Technology Center designed by the versatile Italian architect Renzo Piano. But despite drawing upwards of 625,000 visitors since it opened in June 1997, the new enterprise has experienced a rough passage. The ship-like building, which fits in well with the moored sailing craft belonging to the nearby Maritime Museum, has been nicknamed The Titanic and the name may prove fatefully prophetic. Notwithstanding its architectural flourishes and technological seductions, the Metropolis is struggling with problems endemic to science centers: identity and money."

My efforts almost came to naught when Rockwell wanted to know why we were doing a piece on a foundering ship. Which is why I introduced the business about other beleaguered science centers and had Victoria broaden it with a few more generic examples, that made this a ripple if not a trend. Rockwell bought it and the piece ran. Victoria was grateful.

Probably the only thing of lasting value that came out of my sojourn in A & L was meeting Patwant Singh, the editor of India Architecture magazine who did a piece for us about Corbusier's Chandigarh on its 50th anniversary. Patwant was an extraordinary personage, a man who lived many lives, working as an engineer in South India, building a hospital, running a cultural magazine, thriving as a bon vivant and world traveler, and, most importantly, being a historian of the Sikhs for whom he was a fierce advocate. A man of great cultivation and charm, he was a voice for reason and moderation and a rare human being. Whatever I sustained during my sojourn, befriending Singh was worth the trouble. As for Muschamp, he recuperated and by May was back in the fold. My services were no longer needed.

Perhaps my most rewarding task of this period was responsibility for "My New York," a column that alternated with a metropolitan excursion series. Both were usually featured on the front of the second section of Weekend. The first was subdivided into the various boroughs being covered—"My Manhattan," "My Brooklyn," "My Bronx." The second had an elastic reach that was basically the corridor from Boston to Washington, which dovetailed with the Northeast edition that The Times published. Each of them offered opportunities to run a mini-section assigning my own writers — many of whom had worked for me at Newsday —and coming up with my own stories. To this nucleus, I added a burgeoning cluster of talented free-lancers as well as an array of Times staffers. The bonus for everyone was that not only were the contributors handsomely paid but they were prominently displayed in one of the best-read sections of the paper, which meant national exposure. Writers constantly told me about getting mail from correspondents in all parts of the world in response to pieces they'd written. This, of course, was just before the advent of the Internet, when such global fan mail on a local piece was still an experience that was as unusual as it was flattering. More than one free-lancer confessed that their relatives in California never took them seriously until they saw their byline in our national edition. Both the "My New York" column and the excursions ran for the better part of my tenure, from almost the beginning until about a year or two before the end. The Our Town series ended a little earlier than the Out-of-Town forays, but each provided contributors with a decent windfall and a desirable forum while they lasted. The ideas were bountiful and the writers virtually assigned themselves which meant that I merely had to pick and choose and then shape the piece once it arrived.

The thrust of the "My New York" column was to offer a mini-Baedeker focused on a single site, like the northern reaches of Central Park, or a simple theme, such as venues made famous in film. An accompanying box would offer specific locations mentioned in the essay with directions on "How to Get There," and perhaps a "While You're There" sidebar on local eateries and related attractions. It was conceived as a service piece on how to spend part of one's weekend. But I turned the concept on its head and used the service aspects as an occasion to justify an essay on an offbeat slice of New York life. Since many of my writers came from the book world, the columns had a literary bent. One of our earliest pieces was an essay on Bernard Malamud's New York—the shabby streets that his characters walk in the downcast boroughs of the Depression. The downbeat theme was actually catnip for affluent readers receptive to a dose of virtual nostalgia. Selecting a writer was critical. For Malamud, I chose Jonathan Rosen, a former culture editor at The Forward who was familiar with Malamud's work as well as an author in his own right and a deft stylist. Timing was equally important. The article had originally been planned for the release of Malamud's collected works. Then the usual snafus delayed publication. But I learned that Symphony Space on the West Side had scheduled a reading of Malamud's works by Laura Linney with no less than Alfred Kazin and Irving Howe introducing the subject. I made a successful pitch to Myra that we run the piece in conjunction with the reading so it looked as if we'd planned the whole thing.

At about this same time, I sent Andre Aciman, the author of the memoir of exile "Out of Egypt," to take a ride on the M5 bus. Aciman, who taught Proust, had shown me an essay he was writing for The New Yorker on the statue of Memory in Straus Park near his home on the Upper West Side. Andre spun an imaginative fantasy on how riding along Riverside Drive in the snow was evocative of Paris. It was a confection of gossamer, a memory piece held together by the writing that conflated the mundane beauty of a bus ride along a snowbound Riverside Park with a re-imagined Paris where Aciman had spent his youth. As it turned out, Andre would use this journey as the setting of a romantic novel upon which he had already embarked that he was to complete many years later. I used Aciman for several stories set in the recesses of the West Side. One of them conjured up an old curiosity shop tucked into a recessed ground-floor doorway on a quiet inlet of Riverside Drive at 100th Street, the workshop of the luthier Joseph Tanen, a repairer of stringed instruments. Inside, was a collection of violins, violas and cellos—literally unstrung—in the process of reparation by a latter-day Dr. Coppelius. Aciman had a meticulous eye for the details of the shop, the nuances of Tanen's craft and the interchange with the various clients concerned about the care of their instruments. He also brought a novelist's gift to a reporter's observations.

The result was no longer your average Baedeker. The writing was so good and the pieces so engaging that they took on a life of their own and evolved from service vehicles to evocative essays on the life of the city whose bounds were limited only by the imagination of the writer.

Over the years we published essays on a Bronx Public Library that had opened a literary world to a young girl who became the essayist Vivien Gornick, a barber shop that gave what was arguably the cheapest and best haircut in the city—attested to by the writer Michael Shapiro, the quiet spirituality of a Quaker School on East 16th Street in the midst of a bustling city recollected by one of its alumnae—the author Francine Prose, Sandee Brawarsky's visit to what may have been the oldest reliable floating mah-jongg game in New York, Susan Jacoby's paean to her favorite mystery book store, and Philip Lopate's farewell to the Fulton Fish Market in a dawn visit to the fated landmark.

To be sure, I paid heed to my bread and butter: Places that readers could actually visit, that still formed the bulk of the report and which kept my supervisors satisfied. Sam Freedman—a former colleague at The Times and a future one at the Columbia Journalism School—did an evocative piece on the re-opening of Ellis Island where his grandparents had landed. The historian Christine Stansell, wrote about Greenwich Village in its radical heyday at the turn of the 20th Century—a subject about which she'd recently published a book. The journalist Rob Boynton limned the wonders of the Transit Museum capped off by a ride to Coney Island on an old subway train. And the writer Lynn Sharon Schwartz conducted a sampling of her favorite street-food vendors.

Like many things, this column began almost as an afterthought. At a brainstorming session early on, Darnton suggested that Weekend do a piece about how poets find inspiration in New York. The notion simmered for a while and when John asked what we'd done about it, Myra passed it along to me. The idea was to find a poet who could do journalism and write about the city—not as easy as it sounded. But I managed to run down Ron Padgett, who had rhapsodized on that very subject and who was willing to give it a go. He did a nice enough essay on Frank O'Hara along with some of the other usual poetic suspects —Marianne Moore, e.e. cummings, Edna St. Vincent Millay— as well as a take on how the city served as his own muse. A little editing, a box and voila! From there, a lot of ideas that had been floating around coalesced under a convenient rubric.

While we generally had a destination in mind, the sites weren't always predictable. Judith Dunford celebrated her favorite greasy spoons. Jonathan Mahler provided a guided tour of the Gowanus Canal—an erstwhile Mafia dumping ground before its later gentrification. Speaking of the dead, Mahler traveled to the sites of the former Polo Grounds and Ebbets Field, echoes of which appeared in his later successful book on baseball and a Bronx in distress. Douglas Century essayed the still gritty Brooklyn waterfront. The author Thane Rosenbaum did a study of gargoyles poking out of West Side buildings. And the critic Jeremy Eichler wrote an evocative piece on the great dead buried in Woodlawn Cemetery.

All things come to an end and, after Darnton's departure in 2002, a new Pharoah arose who knew not Joseph. Darnton was eased out by the executive editor, Howell Raines, who arrived the previous year and wanted more energy in the section as well as his own man at the helm. Raines chose Steve Erlanger, a foreign correspondent who he believed would breathe fire into the department. Erlanger, although cultivated, did not know much about the Culture Section and went through the usual bumpy learning curve. He was to lean on me in a variety of ways but, in going forward, he decided that "My New York" had run its course. As he told me (or, rather, told Myra to tell me), there were just so many different stories in the city and our particular forum as a means of telling them had reached its limits. I would submit that Erlanger was wrong. There were countless good stories to tell and "My New York" was an engaging way of doing so. I got calls and letters from everywhere lamenting what a loss it was. The only one who gained from this was my old colleague Connie Rosenblum from the City Section—not in Erlanger's purview— who alertly appropriated the concept as well as several of my writers (I was glad to help her, and them). She thrived on the idea for many years in barely disguised form. Erlanger eventually went back to being a foreign correspondent where his true talent lay as evidenced by his outstanding coverage of the Middle East and Europe. But by that time the damage was done. Since my departure, I've noticed that Weekend occasionally reactivates an enervated "My New York" in another guise, but the effort is slapdash and perfunctory, lacking consistency and a guiding vision. Weekend can do this with impunity now since not only is Erlanger gone but so is the City Section.

The Metropolitan excursions, because they were more straightforward service pieces, had greater longevity, surviving almost to the end of my tenure. Not only were they helpful guides for short weekend outings to nearby sites and cities—a precursor of the Travel Section's globalized "36-hour" forays into foreign venues—but they provided a handsome stipend for a coterie of venturesome freelancers like Diane Cole. Diane wrote for me at three different newspapers: New York Newsday, the Daily News and The Times. She was there from almost the beginning— reviewing a baseball book in which she disclosed allegiance to her former hometown Orioles—to near the end when she did a nostalgic return-of-the-native tour of Baltimore.

Perhaps the most venturesome of my travelers was the team of Michael Crewdson and Margaret Mittelbach. Like so many of our contributors they were holdovers from New York Newsday's book section. They were offbeat nature writers who had combined on a book called "Wild New York," which celebrated the abundance of plant life that flourished amid the urban pavement. Their counter-intuitive investigation turned up a variety of flora that materialized not only in parks but parking lots as well as all manner of cracks and crevices in the city's sidewalks. The duo's approach put a zany spin on the pedestrian genre of nature walks. Their forays for Weekend included crabbing in Canarsie, the bucolic Bronx and a visit to the migratory pit stops of Monarch butterflies. Fish or feathers, Crewdson and Mittelbach were on the case: They were up before dawn to cover pigeon racing in Pennsylvania and catching bluefish off Coney Island—during which Michael turned blue from the tossing waves. They trekked along the bosky "Blue Trail" in Staten Island and returned there for a piece on bird-watching with a nod to the borough's population of martins.

The twosome ranged far afield, from exploring New York's tallest trees (Alley Pond Park) to its geologic sediments. They had no problem sending up the conventions of nature writing, and themselves as well, with an ascent to the highest points in each of the city's boroughs. In Manhattan, after scaling to the top of an overlook at Fort Tryon Park, the intrepid pair were chagrined to find they had been beaten to the summit by a grandmother pushing a stroller. They could breathe life into bird-mating visits and, in the winter months, come up with indoor treks such as birding at the Metropolitan Museum, an imaginative tour of the avian life depicted in the Met's great paintings. I didn't often get to work with a team and I gleaned that Michael was the entrepreneur and Margaret the writer because when I had trouble with a fix, it was Crewdson who said "we'll be right back to you" and Mittelbach who made the change. They were a delight to work with, bringing a wry approach to the earnest trek through the nature genre.

Then, there were the sidewalk excursions, itineraries through a neighborhood or along the length of a thoroughfare seen anew with the practiced eyes of a keen observer. It could have literary overtones, such as Dawn Powell's Manhattan timed to the publication of a new biography of the author; it might be a nostalgia trip—the small wonders of a nondescript block like 20th Street limned river-to-river by the writer Blake Eskin who'd grown up on its Eastern fringe before moving to its Western reaches, or the delights of Russian Manhattan—Moscow on the Hudson—by Richard Lourie. Richard, who had written more seriously at Newsday on Glasnost and Perestroika, brought a cosmopolitan air and the insouciance of a boulevardier to his peregrinations through the city. A homesteader on the Hudson edge of Canal Street, Lourie wrote a series of little essays for us about his favorite TriBeCa cafes as well as providing bon vivant tours of Carmine Street, Elizabeth Street and Spring Street when these gentrifying venues were still in the process of becoming.

The trick for these Weekend walkers was to make the reader feel venturesome without being put off. Also, it was important to be a step ahead of the curve. We were all too aware that in a short time anything we wrote about would be deluged, which invariably came to pass. But even in that case, Lourie had the gift of pouring new wine into old bottles. While so many who attempt the Baedeker form wind up sounding like tour-bus guides or breathless enthusiasts, Richard came across as a boon drinking companion, a knowledgeable but louche connoisseur who was going to casually initiate the reader to a neighborhood's finer points.

Perhaps my most rewarding relationship in these urban "walkers," as we called them, was with Sandee Brawarsky. I had known Sandee since she was doing publicity for Times Books before taking the leap into a full-time freelance career. She could hit to a lot of fields. One of them was exploring New York's less celebrated recesses such as the delights of Chinese Flushing or the Bukharin culture of Forest Hills. Sandee spent a lot of time in Queens, after Staten Island then perhaps the city's most overlooked borough despite its rich ethnic mix. Her most notable celebration of Queens was a colorful ride on the No. 7 train, which rumbles through the heart of that borough and, because of its Asian flavor, is known as The Orient Express.

Sandee was also a master of the long-distance walker— a piece that would encompass a lengthy stretch of the city. She excelled in such forays as an excursion along 57th Street at

Christmas from the East River to the Hudson or a walk along Upper Broadway in the early hours. Sandee was skillful at describing how the light at different times of the day or night altered the contours of the buildings she described. Most representative of this was a piece she did on the Bowery where her father had owned a fixtures shop. A few blocks below Cooper Union the street opens up to a landscape of low-roofed houses, appliance stores and craggy tenements that shimmer under a hot afternoon sun, casting bolts of shadow, a De Chirico devoid of menace. Sandee was able to evoke the characteristics of such a neighborhood in a stroke at once instructive and inviting.

Although, for the most part, I went with known quantities in this endeavor, I did manage to introduce some new faces and, in the process, jump-start a few careers. Among these was a young fellow named Seth Kugel whose specialité de la maison was New York's Hispanic sub-culture. He reported for us on the salsa scene in the Bronx—a relief from our Manhattan-centric coverage and its Brooklyn clone. I made it a point of honor as a Bronx boy to remind our readers that there were five boroughs in New York. By then, western Brooklyn had become an annex of Manhattan just as Washington Heights might as well have been in the Bronx as far as the paper's Culture coverage was concerned. When people referred to "The Heights" they meant "Brooklyn." Seth lived in the other Heights and did some well-crafted pieces for us on the art scene in the South Bronx, Mexican nightclubs in the North Bronx, Dominican lounges in Washington Heights and an interesting story on Hispanic entertainers who moonlighted in different Latino venues—a moveable fiesta. Seth has since used his taste for adventure to become the Times's Frugal Traveler.

My most successful young protégé was the aforementioned Jeremy Eichler. When I first heard of him, he was winding down as a free-lance music critic for Newsday which was casting off most of its non-staff talent. Jeremy was scraping by editing a music web called Andante. His Newsday clips were impressive and, after his well-rendered piece on Woodlawn Cemetery, I assigned him several others: a visit to an antiquarian book shop, an evocation of the Christmas-tree scene on the Upper West Side when whole swathes of the neighborhood are turned into late-night forests of fir trees for sale, and a melodic piece on Barge Music and its feisty impresario, Olga Bloom. The work he did for me called Jeremy to the attention of Darnton and led to a job as a music critic. So I was eventually able to edit Eichler in a genre that was his true calling. Jeremy went on to become chief music critic for the Boston Globe.

The "walkers" were so successful that they attracted the notice of several Times staff members who volunteered their services. Among the many reporters who contributed to the column was Wendell Jamieson, a Brooklyn native who did pieces on a colorful old waterfront bar called Montero's as well as a history of the quirky apartment complex Cobble Hill Towers. Jamieson, did his work with the brisk professionalism of a deskman. It was not hard to foretell that he'd one day become the Times's Metro Editor. We also got contributions from my old Newsday comrade-in-arms Barbara Strauch, the paper's health editor, on an excursion to Block Island; Jan Benzel, later to become Weekend editor, on the trials of a soccer mom, and Dinitia Smith on the charms of Columbia's Morningside neighborhood. I sent young staffers like Tina Kelley to explore the wonders of Jamaica Bay, and Patrick Healy to rhapsodize on the beauties of Manhattan's bridges.

Over the course of time, I had more than fifty writers appearing on these pages. They ranged from the comic (the novelist Colm Toibin's lark on being an Irish ringer in the chorus of a Hispanic Catholic Church on the West Side) to the lyric (the memoirist Susan Shane Cunningham's homage to "Grains and Trains": the Botanical Gardens' Christmas display of skyscrapers made of foliage traversed by electric trains) to the panegyric (the author Susan Jacoby's paean to the quiet consolations of Central Park's Conservatory Garden). Some of these contributors wrote only once, several from time to time, and quite a few appeared frequently. Although produced on-the-fly, their work reflects a panoramic snapshot of New York culture at the turn of the 21st century.

Like Gaul, the Culture Section was divided into three parts: Daily Culture, Arts & Leisure and Weekend. Ostensibly, I worked for the latter but, as heretofore noted, I was hired out to Arts & Leisure to midwife Forum and manage the Architecture Pages while still responsible to Weekend. All that was needed to complete the trifecta was a tour on the Daily Desk. Given the fact that the Daily backfield was perennially short-handed, it was not surprising that Darnton would look to throw me into the breach. I had de facto run the Culture Desk 15 years earlier so I could be called in by John at a moment's notice. The backfield had grown since I'd last done the job. In addition to Darnton and his deputy, Martin Gottlieb, there were a few more bodies: Nora Kerr who did trouble-shooting, Marty Arnold who did kibbitzing, and assorted other players borrowed from the copy desk to fill in as needed. It was inevitable that my turn would come, as soon it did. Of course, it was understood that my time on the Daily backfield was in addition to, not instead of, my Weekend duties. At first, I was asked simply to fill in during vacations or illnesses but by early 2002, the last year of Darnton's tenure, I was committed to the Daily backfield on a more-or-less regular basis, a duty that continued through three more years and two more editors.

What this meant was that I was bifurcated into a Daily backfield editor in the morning and a Weekend backfield editor in the afternoon. My responsibility on the Daily was to shepherd all of the incoming reviews into the paper. This involved keeping track of the assignments, making sure the critics wrote to space, and moving the reviews—sometimes upward of 20 a day—onto the copy desk, all by about 1 P.M., when I would turn into a pumpkin, leave my post on the Daily backfield and shuffle back to my desk on Weekend where I'd return to my normal duties. A consolation was that since this was a command performance for the Daily, I was not to be trifled with and Myra and Wendy had to respect my autonomy. And because all of the review copy had to be over by midday, they knew that I'd be back in a finite amount of time. To be fair to them, they were good about this, even showing a bit of sympathy for what was clearly a double burden, leavened by a soupcon of relief that they weren't called upon to bear it. I got a "day off" on Thursdays when Weekend closed, but this only meant that, since many Daily reviews ran in the Friday Section, I could move them as well from my Weekend perch—a win-win for both the Daily and Weekend—without missing a step.

The Weekend staff got in early on Thursdays—we were there by 9 A.M.—to begin moving the copy, a process that would last steadily till the 5 P.M. deadline. I arrived not much later on the other weekdays as well to set up the schedule for Darnton's 10:30 daily staff meeting (moved up to 10 by his rigorous successors). This engendered a daily race from home to drive my teen-age son and daughter to high school, arriving there at 7:35 in order to make the 7:53 express to arrive at Grand Central at 8:44 and hoof over to The Times—then on 43d Street past Broadway—by 9 o'clock. A dawdling teen-ager or a blocked railroad crossing could throw the entire day into chaos. Like Waterloo, it was a near-run thing.

My first task on the Daily after arriving was to consolidate the schedules from the several departments – music, theater, film, dance, TV, books, etc., and revise them according to date, then to see what had already been filed by the various critics and what was still outstanding, whereupon I'd call up those writers who still owed us copy to make sure they'd submit it promptly in the space required. Based on this, I put together a daily schedule broken down by departments with top billing given to music. Left blank on top were News and Features, the responsibility of the Culture Editor and his Deputy except for the Saturday paper where the same duties were filled by the editor of the Ideas Section, Patricia Cohen. So I was there, in effect, to put together the B-Matter, the masonry of reviews which served as mortar for the edifice of news and features that took pride of place on the dress page, the ad-free opening page of the section.

In order to "energize" the Culture pages under the aegis of Howell Raines, a premium was placed on developing newsworthy stories. The days of "Reviews are News" were over. All this notwithstanding, the façade of features had to be balanced upfront by reviews. It was my job to recommend the best of the lot for the front of the book. Indeed, when we had a major opera, an important film, a hot TV program, a big opening night, or any event that a critic considered significant, it would often lead the section and, on occasion, be a candidate for a front-page "reefer"—a one-sentence teaser on the front-page referring to the inside review. I was expected to alert the Deputy Editor, Martin Gottlieb, on such occasions. In effect, I wrote him a weekly note, usually updated, recommending what I considered to be the most likely candidates for the dress page or pieces requiring any other special attention. I also suggested the reviews that had to run the next day in order of priority. These notes were invaluable in that they saved Gottlieb the trouble of sorting through the entire directory of reviews to ascertain which ones could be fronted.

Each review in the schedule was labeled with a "slug," or title, the writer's name and a capsule description, together with a size in inches. But the length of the piece was what had been assigned, not what was submitted. This meant that the makeup editor had no realistic idea of what actually fit on the page and the copy desk had to scramble late in the game to make the piece fit, sometimes without consulting the writer, which frayed tempers. By the simple expedient of going into the electronic directory, I ascertained the exact size and listed it on the schedule so that whatever cuts were needed, which I often made, were trimmed at the outset of the process rather than at the end. This obviously took a lot of extra scut work but I didn't see a better alternative.

In a similar vein, I posted the date that every review was written so that the backfield could see at a glance how long a piece had been held over. This was a simple adjustment but without it, the backfield had little idea of what they could and couldn't hold, except in a seat-of-the-pants way and, with more than two dozen reviews piling up from all departments, it was easy enough to be confused. I was often troubled by the cavalier manner in which some backfield editors consigned over-held reviews to oblivion. This rarely happened with major artists but was rather the fate of lesser fry where attention was most needed. Keep in mind, this was before the ascendancy of the Web, when permanence was still defined by print and The Times was the Paper of Record.

The saving grace in all this was that our contributors were The Times's Culture critics, probably the best concentration of writers on the paper. So when the copy came in it was, for the most part, clean. Otherwise, there would have been no way that a single editor, or a brace them, could handle more than 20 reviews a day. The staff consisted of such stalwarts as Holland Cotter on art, Tony Tommasini in classical music, John Pareles in pop, Ben Ratliff in jazz, Stephen Holden in movies and Julie Salamon on television. This was a Silver Age, not like the Golden Age I'd experienced with critics such as Vincent Canby in film, Harold Schoenberg in music, John Russell in Art and John Gross in books, but exceptional nonetheless. The hardest part came in trimming and, since most of the reviews were tight, this could often pose a challenge. It's easier to cut from 3,000 words than 300. The worst problems were technical ones, like hunting down a lost story, but such glitches were far preferable to the agita on other desks that came from personality clashes, writing problems, or assignment issues, virtually none of which obtained in this exercise. I had worked with most of the staff in my earlier run on the Daily desk and, despite the added load, I was pleased to be editing them again.

After John Darnton departed in 2002, the usual chaos prevailed in the transition and Steve Erlanger leaned on me to hold the fort during the interregnum. Bill McDonald, John Rockwell's No. 2 at Arts & Leisure, became Erlanger's deputy. But before McDonald— a good newspaperman who went on to become The Times obits editor—could move over there was a gap that, along with a few pickups, I filled for several weeks while Steve got himself oriented. I soldiered on at this station until McDonald came aboard and then continued, on and off, as the situation warranted. In another year Howell Raines was gone—sunk by the Jayson Blair scandal—and, shortly thereafter, so was Erlanger. He was a little off-putting but essentially a decent man who tried to do the right thing as he awkwardly felt his way in an alien environment. As someone once observed of Steve: "He's nicer than he seems." Erlanger was replaced by the Metropolitan Editor Jon Landman—whose star was then rising for having sent up warning signals on Jayson Blair. I continued my backfielding under Landman for a short while before he proceeded to restructure the Culture operation. But that is another story.

Although the Monday-Thursday news and features list was the purview of the Daily backfield I was deeply involved in the Friday production for Weekend and I also had a little piece of the Saturday features package with a foot in the Ideas Section. Presumably, Saturdays afforded Times readers the leisure to reflect on the deeper thinking that Ideas proffered. More irreverent observers suggested that it was simply a good way to fill the yawning Saturday space hole. Whatever the reasoning, I'd been recruited along with a few cerebral types to serve as catalysts for what appeared in the section. The editor, Patricia Cohen, formerly a staffer on Newsday's Opinion pages, had been part of the diaspora that eventually found its way to The Times after the New York edition folded. Cohen was relatively new to The Times and it was felt that a little support from senior hands might be a steadying influence. Our brain trust consisted of Ed Rothstein, Judy Miller, Janny Scott, Sarah Boxer and myself. Judy was the star, brought in for her political skills and global experience. She was a lively presence and I enjoyed her company. Her contributions were always grounded in good sense and modestly presented. I think she was relieved to be in a room with colleagues who were there simply to bat around ideas, and where she could be herself without having to be "on." She would later leap from one controversy to the next culminating in the Iraq missile imbroglio and her imprisonment for refusing to name the source of a government leak, the fallout effectively ending her career at The Times.

Janny Scott was by far the smartest person in the room. She was newspaper smart, which meant that she could quickly compress a lot of disparate material into concise narratives, get to the essence of a story and present it in lucid detail. She was also a pleasure to work with —anticipating an editor's question before it was asked—and very good at turning high-concept thumb-suckers into viable features. She had been involved in some of the paper's prize-winning long-term projects—most notably, a series on race in America—and had developed a specialty in sociological reporting which is what brought her into our realm. She was particularly good at numbers-crunching, gleaning fresh meaning from staid figures and turning a skeptical eye on the received wisdom of publicized "facts." She was a voice of reason in what was sometimes an exercise in hapless brainstorming. To my mind, Janny would have done an outstanding job of running the section.

Which brings us to Patricia Cohen, who operated the shop and presided over these ceremonies. Patti was lively and engaging, a quick study with a gift of palaver, an opinion on everything and no shyness in projecting it. But I couldn't help feeling that she'd learned to play the caroms rather than ply her craft. Patti went on to have a solid career in the Culture Section as theater editor. After that gig ended she proceeded to cover the intellectual beat which returned her to brain terrain, except in this case it was the best of both worlds: writing about ideas without running an Ideas Section. She could virtually do her own assigning and reporting minus the administrative headaches. Patti had achieved relative autonomy on her own terms. I have to hand it to her. I'd misread Cohen as a surfer when in fact she was a shrewd survivor.

Although Patti preferred to run her own ship, there were times—whether she was overwhelmed, inundated, or otherwise engaged—that I'd be called in to edit some of her pieces. Typical was a brace of articles I was asked to handle in the late spring of 2000. One of them was by Robert Boynton, an accomplished writer who, like several of her contributors, had once reviewed for me at Newsday and was later to become the director of the literary concentration at NYU's Journalism Institute. Boynton wrote a compelling article about a controversy over two competing versions of Freud's works that were being published simultaneously. I offered a few suggestions about shaping the story for which he wrote me a gracious thank-you note. Even a good writer can use some editing and the best appreciate it. During that same period I edited other Ideas pieces, from Sarah Lyall's London dispatch on the writer Alain de Botton's feel-good nostrums posited in his "Consolations of Philosophy," to Somini Sengupta's interview with Kathleen Cleaver, ex-wife of the former Black Panther icon Eldridge Cleaver. My byline never appeared in the paper but my imprint was there.

Then there was my real work. The mission for which I'd actually been hired, a full-time job that was still my primary responsibility: serving on the backfield of Weekend. The section, redolent with ads, came out 48 pages every Friday. It was divided in two halves, the first containing movies, theater, music and dance; the second the arts pages and television. Each part led with a cover consisting of either a major review—a Broadway debut, a big movie, a blockbuster art show, a hot TV program—or a feature story by a prominent staff writer keyed to an important cultural event occurring that weekend: a jazz festival, a gallery opening, a book fair. Since Weekend contained Culture's news coverage for Friday, there was invariably a breaking news story or two that dropped late in the afternoon. To fill the interstices were the usual complement of reviews flowing in from all departments which, as noted, I'd set up during the course of my Daily duties. In addition, there were the listings -- capsule summaries of earlier reviews -- together with service information tethered to reviews and features.

Virtually every performance review was accompanied by a cast box prepared by the departmental news assistants which required careful editing since this served not only to check on the accuracy of the names in the review but was also a place where mistakes could be made if the tiny agate type was not read carefully. Most certainly, the copy desk performed Herculean labors in catching glitches, preventing their appearance in the paper. Enough cannot be said of their unsung efforts in saving the day. Still, the backfield was the first line of defense and, if an error got through, we'd be held responsible.

Although the work was divided among all of us and accomplished in an "as needed" manner, there was a de facto sub-division with Wendy and myself sharing the Arts pages, a fourth member of our crew reading the theater and some movies, and Myra "reading back" on all of us before the material was moved on to the copy desk. This is only a rough approximation since I handled Books, TV and Anna Kisselgoff on dance as well as alternating with one of my partners on the Broadway, Movie and Children's columns. Usually, one of my features dressed up the front cover of the Arts Page, so I'd shepherd that through as well.

Prominent among these were David Dunlap's walkabouts of architectural gems hidden in plain sight. In effect, they were disguised architecture pieces by Dunlap who wrote for the Real Estate section. David had a keen eye for seeing the beauty in sites that people passed every day, and a deft touch in evoking their esthetic qualities. He wrote numerous stories for us ranging from the seminal works of Cass Gilbert to the traces of what was once Automobile Row to a morphology of Harlem churches—an expanded version of which became a book. The last piece David did for me was a journey through the bowels of The Times from the subterranean floors where the presses had once rolled to the top of the tower where few employees had ever ventured. As it turned out, this was a farewell to a journalism of typewriters, copy spikes and linotype machines as well as a valedictory to the Times Building which was sold a few years later. By then I was gone.

The weekly cycle began again on Friday afternoons with the arrival of early copy—simple things like the "Eats" column. We usually tried to move most of the listings although strays were always straggling in later in the week. Myra was formidable at making the trains run on time and by our 3 P.M. staff meeting on Tuesday, a fair chunk of the copy had been processed. Wednesday was our crunch day, with the bulk of the report flowing in, often keeping us late until the last piece had moved. Thursday was closing day which was usually reserved for a cover piece, a TV show, the Broadway column, a few late reviews and whatever breaking news occurred. The other work involved reading proofs, closing pages and cleaning up. By the 5 P.M. deadline we were drained but Myra kept me around until the last page was closed in the composing room.

Although the Culture writers, as noted earlier, were the cream of the staff, they were not without their own idiosyncrasies. One luminary was not always rigorous when it came to names. We had to pore over every title in her review. Worse was that she would on occasion go back into the directory after her piece was off the copy desk, ready to be launched, and make a few "improvements," which raised the possibility of error exponentially. Under the upgraded digital system, if someone "restored" a story after retrieving it, they could hit the wrong button and lose it altogether. This was a mortal sin. She was caught a few times and reprimanded but occasionally recidivated.

Generally, if someone was error-prone, we could take defensive measures. One ebullient critic was a good example. She was a perceptive observer with a robust prose style but accuracy was not her forte. In a way it was flattering that she had such confidence in her editors that she let us concern ourselves with the details. And she was always grateful about the saves we made, effecting a charming air in acknowledging a catch. The trick was to insist that her reviews arrive early on a closing day allowing sufficient time to give it a careful read. She was diligent about respecting this ukase. Once I had the copy in hand, I would check every fact. The copy desk did likewise.

Well after my departure the system changed, not for the better. Weekend was basically decimated together with its backfield, the copy desk was reduced and, because of pressures from the Web, it was forced to work at ramming speed, moving more copy in less time. The result was less attention to each piece, including the work of writers who needed all the attention they could get. I was chagrined but not surprised to learn recently that one writer had made a gaggle of errors in a single piece, a gaffe so egregious as to send tongues clucking about the imminent demise of The Times's standards. The fact is that they hadn't changed. But the support system that provided a safety net in years past was no longer functioning as it once had.

Then, there was Anna, by which I mean the chief dance critic. I don't know that any of us referred to her by her last name. Anna Kisselgoff was the last of the grand chief critics who had dominated their fields in The Times's glory days. She was a walking font of dance history, intimate with the likes of Ballanchine and Agnes DeMille. Anna was deservedly celebrated but, for all her achievements, she was a technophobe of the highest order. Kisselgoff balked at having anything to do with computers. Which meant that she would call in her review on Thursdays to the recording room whereupon it was transferred to a computer screen by a typist and sent along to us. I would then edit it, make a printout of my edited version and send it back to her by fax. The recording room was a vestigial organ of The Times, a holdover from analogue days but still used by those few troglodytes who were computer challenged or, for one reason or another, not linked to the internet. Since the recording room didn't open until 10 A.M., we never got Anna's copy before 11. To facilitate matters, she would phone in her review in "takes," pages of a few hundred words, as if this were a late-breaking story in the days of the Front Page when copy was rushed to the composing room for an Extra edition. Presumably, this would give us a jump on the review, allowing me to send it on to the copy desk in pieces.

This cumbersome arrangement often led to Kisselgoff's recorded voice mail getting lost or a fax to her home not going through so that she would blame technology for the tardiness of a review. After Anna phoned in her copy she'd call me promptly to ascertain whether it had arrived in my directory although it wasn't possible for the recording room to have processed it. But this established that she had "finished" with that take so that the ball was in our court. By this stratagem she managed to turn the game around, demanding to know why we were lollygagging when the material

369

was clearly in hand. We solved the problem by the novel expedient of bringing Anna in on Thursday mornings and plunking her in front of a computer that was set up so all she had to do was bang out her review as if she were on a typewriter.

At the other end of the pole was Anne Midgette, a young music critic who was only moderately late with her listings but profusely apologetic. Anne was not on staff but reviewed regularly for the music section. The distinction was not apparent to readers who saw her byline but it was important for the writer. As a "stringer" Midgette received no benefits and could be terminated at a moment's notice. Moreover, she usually got second-desk events that the Chief Critic, Tony Tommasini, assigned to the scrubs. Since the venue was New York and the vehicle was The Times, this was still pretty good and made it worthwhile for aspiring writers to put up with all the guff that was their portion. I grew to recognize Anne as a critic of some talent: perceptive, stylish and knowledgeable. I could also see that her hopes of making staff were dim. I counseled her as best as I could in maintaining decent relations with the editors and keeping her options open.

I offered similar advice to Jeremy Eichler, also a music stringer, whom I had befriended. Eventually, both Eichler and Midgette left The Times, Anne becoming Chief Music Critic for the Washington Post and Jeremy ascending to a similar slot at the Boston Globe. Both have since enjoyed impressive careers in music criticism for two of the most prestigious newspapers in the country. Being forced to go outside brought them rewards that they couldn't hope to have achieved had they remained at The Times.

More successful in navigating the narrows of the Culture Section was the TV critic Julie Salamon. She had come from covering television for the Wall Street Journal so she knew her way around a big newsroom and had a good feel for the corridors of corporate power. She also had a winning personality and an indulgent attitude toward the hubristic foibles of The Times. Julie was not only a good writer but a keen social observer as evidenced by her book "The Devil's Candy," which deftly chronicled Brian de Palma's kamikaze effort to bring "The Bonfire of the Vanities" to the screen. She would eventually go on to have a career as a best-selling author. Since Julie was a natural reporter eager to venture outside the TV ghetto, she wrote several pieces for me that were featured in the front of the Arts Section. One of them was a story about perhaps the least visited of New York's cultural sites, the Hispanic Museum. The story was keyed to the Sixth of January,

"El Seis de Enero," when children throughout the Latin world celebrate the Wise Men bringing gifts to Baby Jesus on the Twelfth Day of Christmas. The museum, sited on 155th Street in what had become a scruffy Latino barrio, was conducting a Nativity ceremony for the neighborhood kids and I thought this would be a good occasion for a feature.

The building's location had made it a destination not often frequented by tourists or, for that matter, New York's gentrified. The museum was originally part of an ambitious Beaux Arts complex which, in the early 1900's, was envisioned as the hub of a cultural center in Upper Manhattan. Instead, the neighborhood went to seed—less Western Civ than West Side Story—and most of the center's members, such as the Numismatic Society, decamped for safer climes downtown. Among the refugees was the American Society of Arts & Letters which, until it fled, conducted a hurried annual awards ceremony whose recipients arrived and departed by limo leaving the place deserted like an intellectual Brigadoon until it wakened the following year. The lone holdout was the Hispanic Museum. Its recondite status was not helped by the musty exhibits and its failure to mount any major shows. After all, who would come? But for the hardy soul who rode up to the 155th Station on the No. 1 train there were treasures enough. The dusty paintings on the museum's second floor included Goyas, Murillos, El Grecos and Zurbarans as well as a flock of lesser but fascinating Spanish and Creole artists. When the Met held a show of Iberian art it would often borrow some of these works.

The complex was set in a vast plaza sheltered from Broadway by a stone wall so that once inside, a visitor could have fancied himself in a Spanish square, surrounded by equestrian statues contemplating granite facades with the names of Cervantes, Lope de Vega and other literary greats chiseled in bas relief,. It says something about the popularity of the museum that its administrators were going to close up shop for Christmas but opted to keep the place open when they heard a reporter from The New York Times was planning to do a story. Julie caught all this in her piece—with a glowing description of the Epiphany celebration. The story briefly brought a flurry of visitors to the museum but in subsequent visits I've found it as reassuringly empty as ever.

I should pause here for a moment to sing the praises of Anne Mancuso, the once-and-future news assistant of Weekend. In less politically correct times, Anne would have been called a news clerk. The term had a fittingly Dickensian ring to it, which did not

371

stand the test of time when its form and function changed. As its responsibilities grew, "news assistant" was considered more dignified. The term also affected an employee's pay scale. In an earlier era, the job provided a lifetime sinecure for grown men who used it to accumulate power and perform a variety of auxiliary roles such as de facto bookmaker. There was a middle period during which the job went to ambitious young men, the brightest of whom, attaching themselves to powerful editors—"Reston's clerk," (Steve Rattner), "Rosenthal's clerk" (Rich Meislin)— went on to successful careers. By the late period, news clerking was no longer a path to advancement, at which point, the current nomenclature of "news assistant" came into play. a more respectable moniker with appropriate pay. The news assistant jobs—while ostensibly staffed by both sexes—contained a sub-category of women who chose not to enter the corporate lists but, for their own reasons, to enjoy a secure job allowing them to have a life outside The Times yet still bask in its aura. While reporters and editors came and went, they formed a permanent bureaucracy, essential to the operation of every department. New editors quickly learned to depend on them to oil the machinery that made the section run. Anne Mancuso was one of the most curable, and her contribution was incalculable.

Anne's responsibility was basically to do "everything else." She gathered the material for, and wrote, most of the service boxes that accompanied our stories, put together the listings, answered the phones (no mean task) and performed a myriad other assignments as well, not the least of which was putting together our various seasonal sections culminating in the annual roundup of Christmas music which she assembled since Weekend began in 1976. During Anne's sojourn, she has endured the quirks and quibbles of a wave of editors and commiserated with an archipelago of writers who worked under them. She came to the Weekend Section virtually straight out of City College—she is the president of its Alumni Association—and remained there till she retired, the glue that held the section together, not only physically but socially. Over the years, Anne became the Culture Section's institutional memory. Long after people left, she kept track of them. She organizes an old-timers dinner and also hosts a small series of lunches for her fellow news assistants—"the girls" —at which I am an honorary member. These women were gatekeepers as well as keepers of the secrets of their supervisors. And most knew more about their fields than some of the editors brought in over them, many of whom were just passing through.

Another cluster of unsung players were the copy editors. I bristle when someone refers to them as "copy readers," ostensibly mechanics whose job it is merely to fix typos and catch minor errors and spelling mistakes on the proofs. Such a portrayal only betrays ignorance about the nature of the editing process. A good copy editor could virtually rewrite the story of the reporter who got credit for it. At the very least the copy desk saved writers from themselves, making catches that would have embarrassed the author, often altering the tone of the story to its considerable improvement, reshaping content as well as syntax, much less catching the innumerable errors of fact and spelling that any story is heir to. This is not due to the writer's incompetence but because of the intense time pressure and other exigencies that go into reporting a story for a daily deadline.

Most journalists were grateful for the saving graces of the copy desk. But there were always a few convinced that the desk was out to fracture their pristine prose. One leading proponent of this school was a prima donna who would regularly cavil at the desk for the liberties it had taken with her copy. Nor was she bashful about lobbying for more space and badgering us about when her story would run and whether it would be prominently displayed. She avowed how she loved working with me because I was "different" but I took her praise advisedly. At the other end of the scale was a backfielder, a former copy editor, who once shared duties with me. He was the inverse of the prima donna. He often seemed to act on the premise that most writers were a collection of whiners, wayward children who had to be disciplined for their own good. He wielded a heavy pencil and conducted his editing like a drill sergeant which did not endear him to his charges. Both the martinet and the prima donna could have used a term in the other person's shoes.

When readers think of a newspaper editor they often don't distinguish between top editors and copy editors. The former are the big-picture people who set the tone of the place in terms of coverage, direction, overall supervision and assuming a public face. The latter are responsible for actually editing what goes into the paper. A common path for many senior editors is to move directly from reporting to the upper echelons. A trial-and-error process, it has produced many a glistening star as well its share of wayward meteors. Copy editors on the other hand are charged with fixing and fine-tuning: shaping, sharpening and often cutting stories on deadline without doing harm to the integrity of the piece.

The best copy editors always had respect for writers. They could be firm, like Don Caswell, or softies like John Storm, but they appreciated the reporter's dignity. Caswell, touchy and short-tempered, could blue-pencil a story to a fare-thee-well but reporters on deadline knew that with "Caz" they were in good hands. Storm was a courtly soul who would keep at an ambiguous point until it was clarified, or patiently question an unsubstantiated statement till it was supported or removed, or wonder gently about what turned out to be a gaping hole in the story or a lead buried in the tenth paragraph. These editors were masters of their trade and I fear their like may vanish in a speeded-up digital universe where there is neither the time nor the urgency to practice their craft. We seem to be living at a moment where there is a false dichotomy between accuracy and "traffic," as if responsibility was a hindrance to posting first on the internet. The acolytes of such digital alacrity might do well to remember that before the advent of 24/7 journalism newspapers printed several editions plus re-plates without sacrificing professionalism to bragging rights. The impetus to "get it first" was part of the game but could never trump the mandate to "get it right." Without it we had no credibility.

Speaking of credibility, one of my more challenging tasks was to write corrections on errors we'd made. Since I moved a considerable chunk of the copy, it fell to me to handle an equivalent portion of corrections. Although I've evoked this Sisyphean undertaking earlier, it might serve to remind the reader how the game was played and to illuminate some of its strictures. The first rule was pragmatic enough: avoid denial. We were usually informed of our misfeasance by an alert reader, an irate subject, a know-it-all editor or one of the squads of self-appointed critics who regularly pored over our pages hungry to pounce on an error.

Considering I was responsible for more than 16,000 words of copy a week—most of it dribbling in as bits and pieces or flooding over late in the day, it was a miracle that we had no more than one or two corrections a week. Most of this was due to the Herculean efforts of the copy desk, the diligence of a seasoned reporting staff and, perhaps least, to my own good fortune. Nevertheless, there was danger everywhere, most critically when least expected. A casual phrase, an extraneous fact, an added word to fill out a caption, the wrong numbering on a map, a last-minute fix (the most devastating because the least checkable). Any of these could cause a fatal error that would lead to the dreaded exercise of a correction or a "CX" as it was known. On being informed of an error, I first had to determine that a mistake was made, whether of omission, or commission; then whose fault it was, a slip on the reporter's part or something introduced by an editor with a quick pencil looking to "improve" the copy. The worst crime was if this improvement was done without checking back with the writer: a hanging offense. Once I established the nature of the inaccuracy and the culpability I had to write the CX.

This was an experience that had all the discipline of Chinese calligraphy with none of the esthetics. It required a short sentence, no more than two, stating the conditions under which the mistake was made but never repeating the error, an exercise that was Zen-like in its use of circumlocution to assert what was right without mentioning what was wrong. It was an art form that a few souls on each desk had mastered and so it fell to us to perform the ceremony. The reporter, even if he or she had made the error, rarely had to write the correction. I imagine the reason for this was that the bullpen, which supervised corrections, preferred to deal regularly with a single backfielder who knew the drill rather than with an unruly crowd of writers.

Which brings us to the Zen Master of this ceremony, Allan M. Siegal. Al was the major domo of the bullpen and the ultimate arbiter of all style questions on the paper, a function that he'd turned into a fiefdom where he was the unchallenged overlord. So, let us say, an obituary stated that the deceased, the movie actor John P. Manley, was 87 when he was 78. The Correction would read: "An obituary last Friday of the movie actor John P. Manley incorrectly stated his age. It was 78." If the obit had multiple errors, citing the subject's Philadelphia birthplace as Boston — which would catch Siegal's eye— it would read: "An obituary last Friday of the movie actor John P. Manley, who starred in such films as 'Dawn Patrol,' incorrectly stated his place of birth and age: He was born in Philadelphia and died last Wednesday at 78."

If there were multiple errors or if the mistake was particularly egregious or embarrassing, Siegal would write back, "Who?" in his green-penned notes, known as the dreaded "greenies," and an investigation would be made to ferret out the guilty party. The worst thing that could happen to a backfielder was to introduce an error into a correction. Let us say the actor John P. Manley had died Thursday and not Wednesday. In that case the new corrective would have to read: "A Correction yesterday, incorrectly stated the date of death of the Philadelphia-born actor John P. Manley, a star of 'Dawn Patrol,' who died last Thursday at 78." God forbid should we learn a week later that Manley had starred not in "Dawn Patrol" but "Lost Battalion," a second correction would read: "A Correction last Friday about the Philadelphia-born actor John P. Manley, who died Jan. 10 at 78, incorrectly stated one of his roles. He starred in 'Lost Battalion.' " This happened on rare occasions and the offending Correction writer was duly drawn and quartered.

The above example is a simple one. Often the Correction was more complicated involving verbal gymnastics to avoid mentioning the original error or introducing a new one. Worst of all was the endless Ping-Pong between the backfielder and Siegal on the exact wording of the Correction that had to be as economic as possible. It was a paradoxical process whereby The Paper of Record stated it was making a Correction yet never mentioned the error itself.

Sometimes, the process bordered on farce. On one occasion I had to write a correction on a caption that ran under a photo of The Lone Ranger. The original error involved an incident about the origins of the Ranger but in writing the CX I had to identify the character who played him and, because the original photo information was ambiguous, we were uncertain as to just who was that Masked Man anyway? Clayton Moore who played the Lone Ranger on TV from 1949-51 and again from 1954 to 1957? Or John Hart, who replaced him from 1952 to 1953? And since the figure in the photo was masked—that's why he was called "the Masked Man"— there was sufficient ambiguity so that it could be either actor. Not only were the desperados scratching their chins about this Ranger's identity, but so were the rest of us. I was then caught between the pressure to run a Correction or cite the Wrong Ranger, thereby requiring a fearful second correction.

Al Siegal, or AMS as he signed his notes, was a veritable Rhadamanthus, belching fire from the Underworld for us to get this straightened out. I managed to hold him off pleading the necessity for accuracy in our correctives. I suggested to my colleagues—it had now become an office joke—that we keep our ears to the ground in hopes of hearing the thundering hoofbeats of the truth. Our picture editor, Ray Paganelli, spent another two weeks bird-dogging this quarry until he finally uncovered the identity of the masked man. It was Clayton Moore. Or was it? Who knew? But Ray came up with enough circumstantial evidence to make a reasonable case for Moore so that if anyone challenged us we were effectively off the hook.

Actually, I got on well with Al, who usually went relatively easy on me. He knew I was often the fall guy for other people's gaffes. Behind his gruff exterior lay a sense of decency. Given the exigencies of digital journalism, I understand that a lot of copy goes out raw on the Web these days and it is often left for citizen journalists to catch mistakes. Whatever my reservations about the old system I believe that, for all its faults, it was still conducted by professionals and went through a rigorous process of validation. There was no "gotcha" factor nor the passion of a partisan outlier nor the enthusiasm of an amateur gadfly. Most importantly, we could judge what was worth a correction. Maddening as it was, I think our system was more responsive, and more responsible.

As I've noted, while a few reporters had to be watched, we were fortunate in having a seasoned cadre of writers. Then, there was Elvis Mitchell, in a class by himself. Mitchell had been hired by Howell Raines, presumably with the aim of getting the view of someone cool, hip and "downtown." There was the added laudable goal, long overdue, of bringing a black critic into the mix of what was till then a virtually all-white critics roster. The question was, whom to hire? Candidates weren't lacking, not the least among whom was Gene Seymour, a first-rate movie critic I'd worked with at Newsday, whose taste and prose were impeccable. Seymour was playing an honorable second-fiddle there to the outstanding John Anderson but John simply wasn't in the running in this contest. Allowing that The Times could pick the best and the brightest in Culture, its failure to do so was a source of bemusement, to me. It let Peter Marks slip away to the Washington Post in Theater. It turned up its nose at Michael Riedel who covered Broadway for the Daily News because he'd once taken on Frank Rich, allowing Riedel to regularly beat the pants off our rotating succession of new faces who were simply passing through the theater beat on their way to other posts. Riedel, whom I edited at The News, went on to an enviable career at The New York Post. That John Anderson never got to display his talents at The Times was a travesty. Tony Scott, who got the nod, developed into an outstanding critic, but at the time the decision was made, Anderson was the more seasoned reviewer. Many Times readers often assumed that once a critic was anointed, he or she was the best candidate. What people failed to realize was that there were often better qualified talents whose gifts were never realized at the paper. While The Times has certainly recruited a distinguished staff for its Culture pages it has also had its lapses. Elvis Mitchell proved to be a problematic choice, a round peg that never quite fit into the paper's very square hole.

377

Credit where it's due, Mitchell was indeed hip and unquestionably cool. He hailed from the Detroit Free Press and I'd first heard of him when he interviewed for the movie critic's job at Newsday. Or rather, Newsday paid for his travel and hotel expenses to New York but Elvis didn't show for the interview. Yet if Mitchell was a bit of a scamp he was a charming one, and he knew his onions. He could be both delightful and maddening. The thing about Elvis was that he was eminently likeable with a puckish sense of humor. Insouciant, easygoing, affecting an offhand, laid-back style, he sported dreadlocks that made a fashion statement which only casually suggested a political one as well. Mitchell also had a profound understanding of movies and a breadth of cinema knowledge. He'd seen everything, from the classics to trashy exploitation flicks and had a keen appreciation for the whole shebang. The problem came with writing. Not that Elvis couldn't write. He wrote with flair. His loose, free-form style was a refreshing change from some of the more austere prose that passed for criticism at The Times. At his best, he could be funny and mordant, flashing a devastating wit that deservedly skewered some clinkers and sacred cows. When he was good he could be good indeed, but when he was off he could be challenging.

The point of a movie under discussion was often buried well into Mitchell's review, together with what he thought of it. Elvis had a discursive style suited to the longer essay form in such counter-cultural magazines as Rolling Stone. And he chose to presume that The Times audience was as hip as he was—or should be—so his reviews were salted with inside jokes and references suitable to a film class at NYU, but that were lost on the general reader. Consequently, he would open his review with a thought or image indirectly related to the movie and meander on from there until he got around to the film under discussion. This might work for the Village Voice but I'm not sure The Times was ready for Elvis. Nevertheless, he saw himself on a mission of education. He was going to liberate Times readers from their cultural ghettos, lighten up the content and open the reviewing to a more freewheeling, spontaneous, streetwise brand of criticism. Some of this might have been a breath of needed fresh air but too much of it was simply confusing. The abstruse references became self-referential, the distinctive style itself became a cliché and Mitchell's grand experiment ultimately became a wearying one. It devolved into a war of attrition between Elvis and the desk. This wasn't helped by Mitchell's penchant for slipping risqué allusions into the copy, like a naughty pupil trying to sneak something past the teacher. More troubling still was his flagellating Whitey for all kinds of crimes and misdemeanors, some legitimate, others less so.

Most vexing of all was not Elvis's prose style but his personal one. He would file his copy by email and then vanish. He was invariably off on a speaking engagement—in Detroit or Houston or San Francisco or God knows where. His home number was useless and the mailbox of his cell phone was usually full making him de facto incommunicado until he chose to materialize, usually by midday Wednesday just prior to our copy deadline, so that the subsequent tussle with the backfield was conducted under unnecessary last-minute pressure. Often, he was responsible for a second review which doubled the agita. A "three-Elvis day" was a trifecta of anxiety.

When Mitchell came aboard, he was assigned to my no-nonsense backfield colleague, Diane Nottle. This was like a contest between Miss Jane Brodie and Superfly. Never were editor and writer so mismatched. Diane was a stickler for form and substance. She would brook no mischief from a writer, particularly a new one. Elvis viewed her with bemusement as a prissy Miss Anne whose high-handed rigor and manifest distemper would be contravened by guile, faux compliance and cheeky repartee. The fustier she got, the cooler he became. Diane's solution was to throw Elvis's reviews back at him, demanding he rewrite them. This was pointless since he'd only alter them in a manner to cause her further apoplexy. Their dance went on for almost a year before Myra separated the two.

Which is where I came in. The understanding was that Diane and I would take turns sharing Elvis, alternating periodically. That didn't happen. Elvis and I got along so splendidly that I became his editor for the duration. We got on because I understood that Elvis was a trickster and he knew I knew it, although we both pretended otherwise. If he was going to be cool, so was I. Our encounters were informed by humor and repartee—Elvis doing the "dozens" and I using my Bronx give-and-take. My other advantage was that I also knew movies so I could pick up on his trivia. Having benefited from Diane's ordeal, I proceeded to approach Elvis with a light but firm touch. Rather than toss the copy back at Elvis and leave the options to him, I made the fixes myself and presented him with a fait accompli that we could negotiate. But we were already on my ball field.

This, of course, took a toll. Mitchell had not changed a whit, nor did he intend to. All of the impulses that drove my predecessor mad still obtained. I just tried to approach them differently. Ultimately, however, Elvis could wear down anyone. Good intentions and psychology were not enough. Mitchell's habit of simply leaving town without telling anyone didn't help matters, The powers that be took no notice of this. The day-to-day headaches were mine.

Not the least of them was a trail of errors dropped like breadcrumbs through Mitchell's reviews. On a simple Critic's Choice of a vintage French film like "Pepe le Moko," starring Jean Gabin, Elvis wrote: "Gabin, who runs the criminal empire in Morocco . . . " I noted that Morocco is a country but Algiers, where the movie is set, is a city which, in any case, is in Algeria. Whatever his geographic problems, Elvis should at least have guessed right since in his lead he refers to "Algiers," the slick American remake of "Pepe le Moko." In this same piece Elvis indulged in one of his favorite pastimes, the extraneous aside, presumably to show how much he knew about the fine points of the film. Describing Gabin's tough-guy appearance, he wrote: "Gabin's irrepressible suavity—how many men could make one suit so peerlessly right?—created an aura that influenced the fashion designer Hedy Slimane—who seems to have taken his name from both Hedy Lamarr and the dogged police inspector from 'Pepe.' " The reference was to the leading lady in the American remake and the surname of the character who pursues Gabin. So in a short piece where every word counts, we are told in a peripheral clause that Gabin's couture influenced a fashion designer having nothing to do with the movie and then, in a subordinate clause in the same sentence, what the designer's exotic name conjures up in the reviewer's mind. Mitchell devotes hardly more than a paragraph to what the movie is about: that what makes it memorable, and far more than a gangster drama, is that it is a tale of love and longing. Instead we get a parade of references to other movies that influenced, or were inspired by, this film, leaving readers baffled.

Probably the most unnerving encounters we had came over race. Not that it wasn't an important issue and Elvis brought sensibilities to the subject that might have been overlooked by another writer, but he often dragged in race out of left field. introducing it gratuitously, thereby debasing the coinage. While I respected his experience, I refused to concede the moral high ground and I made him justify his sly allusions and bald assertions as relevant to the review. Typical of this was a go-round we had over "Windtalkers," a World War II drama focusing on the tension between Nicolas Cage, a Marine sergeant, and Adam Beach, a young Marine who, with other Navajos, has been chosen to transmit messages in the Pacific fighting because the Japanese could not break the code of their language. That I had to rework the opening paragraphs so that the reader could make some sense of what the film was about, was par for the course. The tension came when Elvis went on to attack the film's premise: that the Navajos were a precious commodity who were there to be protected by their fellow Marines (like Cage) or killed if faced with falling into enemy hands, to safeguard the code.

Mitchell wrote: " 'Windtalkers' taunts the Navajos. It short-sheets the real-life premise: Imagine becoming a Marine, the selection of the selection of U.S. soldiers, only to be babysat and kept from becoming part of the action. This becomes another instance of the patronizing attitudes of the white man towards Native Americans, which must have created some ire; how do you prove you're a patriot if you're treated like a second-class citizen?"

Clearly, Mitchell was reacting to the racist treatment of black soldiers during World War II who, with a few notable exceptions, were often limited to supply or custodial duties in a segregated Army. This, however, had nothing to do with the situation of the Navajos. I responded as follows:

"You are saying that the Marines were wrong to want to protect their code-talkers and that this was condescending, and that the movie fails to call the Marines on it. But if the code-talkers had special value, whatever their ethnicity, it would have made military sense for the Marines to protect them. No one expected the code-breakers at Bletchley Park to hit the beach at Normandy when their task was to break Enigma. It was their role – not the need for heroics – which was the only thing that counted for the military. As for not letting personnel with sensitive information fall into enemy hands, cyanide, suicide and more were part of a brutal war – informed not by ethnicity but necessity. Moreover, the code-talkers are in combat. They're risking their lives and are not sitting home in the States. Native Americans fell and fought bravely in the Pacific campaign, not the least of them raising the flag on Mount Suribachi at Iwo Jima. To suggest that the Marines 'coddled' them for racist reasons is absurd, and bad history. This doesn't make military or dramatic sense. Rethink, rewrite or delete." (I note for the record that about a dozen code talkers were killed in action and survivors were honored by President Bush with Congressional Gold Medals the year before the film was released.)

The movie had obviously hit a nerve with Mitchell and his review was studded with land mines, factual, logical and racial. Cutting through this thicket was unnerving. To make matters worse, this was a three-Elvis afternoon, by end of which I was drained. Sometimes I won our battles, or at least, deflected the most troubling of what was originally offered. Sometimes, when Mitchell was completely unheard from, I sent my edited version to the desk— copy to Elvis. At which point, he'd materialize before closing and attempt to reinsert much of what I'd removed or altered, with mixed success. I might have made a fuss but I felt I'd done what I could and, if the copy desk saw fit to let Mitchell reassert his prerogatives, providing that it wasn't erroneous or libelous, that was its privilege.

One thing I finally did make a fuss about was Elvis's unavailability. I'd hoped things would have stabilized but they only got worse with time. In the end I was working around him, as he probably was with me. On the cusp of a Labor Day weekend, he performed his vanishing act one time too many, leaving me holding the bag with a Critic's Notebook, and I apprised John Darnton in writing. I got a note back from John thanking me for my efforts and patience and indicating that he'd speak to Elvis. By then, however, Elvis was past talking to. The denouement came with the fall of Howell Raines and Gerald Boyd after the Jayson Blair affair. Boyd, in line to be The Times's first black editor-in-chief, instead followed Raines out the door. Shortly after Boyd's exit, Mitchell resigned.

Elvis was replaced by Manohla Dargis, whom I inherited as well, or rather appropriated. Manohla, who hailed from The Los Angeles Times, was the real McCoy. She knew her movies, wrote well and brought a creative intelligence to her criticism. I didn't always agree with her enthusiasms but I enjoyed the way she argued them. Dargis was an original and I gave her room to push the envelope. I also gave her some helpful advice regarding the pitfalls of working for the paper—the kind they don't provide in orientation. The L.A. Times allowed its critics a lot of leeway in their style as well their substance. The New York Times held the reins tighter, particularly with new and relatively young critics. It was important to get off on the right foot with the top editors and the copy desk so that the new girl in town did not outlive her welcome. The newcomer had to strike a balance between being distinctive and being refractory. Manohla was strong-willed and was ready to fight the desk on changes she considered arbitrary but that they saw as necessary. I provided a little practical guidance on when to back off and when to go to the mat. I assured her that once ensconced she could call her shots, but until then it was best to tread easy. I won her trust by the simple expedient of using a judicious pencil. Manohla was to be my last project.

I was well past 65 and it was time to move on. The paper was moving on as well. Jon Landman, the eighth of my nine editors in the Culture Section, was himself ready to pass the baton to the winner of a contest between his dual and dueling deputies, Sam Sifton and Jim Schachter. In the meanwhile, he had overseen the creation of a universal Culture desk, a goal that had eluded generations of former Culture editors. What this meant was that— except for the top editors and their deputies —the rest of the editors at Arts & Leisure and Weekend were transposed en masse to a general Culture backfield or onto the Daily desk itself. This was traumatic for several editors, particularly in Arts & Leisure, who had long been sequestered from the rough-and-tumble of daily journalism. For me it provided no hardship since I had been working mornings on the Daily in any case. It was just a matter of changing my seat. What it did mean, however, was that I would leave Weekend and spend the last months of my career working exclusively on the Daily. Goodbye to Myra and Wendy. Well, not quite. As it turned out, when Wednesdays and Thursdays rolled around, I still wound up handling a chunk of the Weekend copy.

Still, the principle of a universal desk was established. To compensate for the loss of the departmental editors in Arts & Leisure, Landman instituted a regime of specialty editors who ran herd on the various cultural subsections and allotted their stories to the troika of Daily, Weekend and Arts & Leisure. Balancing all this required some coordination but, though the buggy wobbled at times, once it gained momentum it moved well enough. Under this new system, my load actually lightened since, as part of a general backfield, I had no specific responsibilities. Myra could borrow me but she didn't own me. It was quite liberating, certainly the lightest duty I had since I returned. I came to know some of the new backfield editors such as Steve Reddicliffe in television and Mike Cieply in movies, who seemed to be glad for my input and respectful of my experience. And I got to keep Manohla. There was a general understanding that I was her go-to guy in the backfield. She was apprehensive when I retired but I left her in good hands, turning her over to my old comrade-in-arms, Andrea

Stevens. One of the positive aspects of the universal desk was that Landman had molded a team of five editors as the core of a Daily backfield so that my services trotting out the Daily schedule were no longer needed. In fact, my services in general were no longer needed. Although I was still actively engaged I chose to see it as a well-earned easing down after a long journey.

When I came back to The Times eight years earlier in 1997 I anticipated puttering around in the Weekend Section until retirement, a little seeding here, perhaps some weeding there. I never expected the variety, intensity and sheer weight of the work I'd be doing. But looking back, I was glad for it. While the paper was never going to give me any titles, its editors knew they could count on me to do the heavy lifting on whatever projects arose. It was a left-handed compliment, but I took it.

Shortly before I left the paper, my wife and I visited Antwerp, among whose treasures is the oldest printing house in Europe. The building, which dates to the 16th century, houses its original print shop containing a cornucopia of type in a dazzling array of styles, fonts, musical notes and you name it. A tour of the premises takes a visitor through the various stages of the printing mechanism. This includes the copy desk, a high altar festooned with galley proofs bearing markings not dissimilar to those I myself made in earlier days. The busts of copy editors adorn niches on the wall, a distinct improvement in immortality over anything their current-day heirs may expect. The final stage of the process took us through the hand-press, onto the mat and finally to the printed page. I noted that, with the exception of the linotype machine, very little had changed between the 16th century and my own early days in journalism. A Renaissance printer would have recognized that the rotary press, although mechanized, operated on the same principle as the hand-press, only bigger and faster. I realized that between the invention of the printing press and the first half of my own career in hot type, not that much had altered. Then, everything changed. And I had been around to see it.

When I left The Times there were no more printers and the presses were rapidly becoming a thing of the past. We had recently changed to a streamlined system which digitalized everything so that a single person at the keyboard could do the work of a dozen people — backfield and copy editors, make-up editor, copy-cutter, linotype operator, make-up man, lithographer, pressman, as well as picture editor, paginator and God knows what else to come.   And that was probably becoming obsolete. As was the whole idea of paper and print itself, which seemed to be going the way of the Dodo—presses giving way to platforms, copy to content and the newspaper game to a recombinant journalism of online media, aggregation desks and contributor networks, twittering, gawking and buzzing into a digital future. I came to understand that, while not fossilized, I was a living fossil, a creature that had undergone the geologic stages of all these momentous changes. The craft I entered was, in spirit, much closer to the Era of Gutenberg than the Age of Amazon. I seek neither to celebrate this epoch nor mourn its passing but simply record it.

When I entered this business in the late 50's, except for the august Times and a number of like-minded broadsheets, many newsrooms were still infused with the racy atmosphere of tabloid journalism whose practitioners were, for the most part, a raffish, seedy lot—witness the popular Daily Mirror (two-million Sunday circulation) where I started. It wasn't until the 60's that the general run of newspapers—and its practitioners— gained respect with the Civil Rights and Vietnam coverage, enterprise stories and investigative reporting culminating in Watergate when many Americans grew to distrust politicians but most still believed their newspapers. It was the heyday of the mainstream media, three dominant networks and big cities with competing papers. This turned out to be a Hegelian moment in which the seeds of imminent demise were built into the illusion of transcendent success. Between the communal erosion of the culture wars and the technological assault of the internet abetted by the inroads of cable and the advent of social media, the world of the front page imploded. It was already dissolving at what appeared to be its apex, and with it went a brief sense of popular cohesion and national unity, collateral damage in a seismic shift of apprehending the world. In retrospect, it was a window of hardly more than 40 years. I had the good fortune to be there. As my old Times colleague Frank Clines observed: "We had the best of it."

I bowed out early in 2005. I walked out on my own steam. It was just before the Deluge. I took no buyout nor was I part of any mass resignation to meet a company cost-cutting deadline. There was no joint leave-taking with everyone crowded into a single tumbrel. I left alone. I was almost 67 and had been in the newspaper business for nearly 48 years. It was time. I got a nice sendoff. No gold watch, but the farewell was all my own. I pretty much filled up our newsroom. A lot of people whom I'd worked with came from all over the building, a goodly turnout. A few of them made funny speeches, generally keeping with the irreverent tone of such occasions. Among the speakers were my old pals Joe Berger and Larry Van Gelder as well as my new and last boss, Sam Sifton. I observed that I had retired to leave the field to older men—a chestnut from Max Beerbohm that I'd appropriated.

I was pleased enough with a decent valedictory. The banter was accordingly light-hearted with just a touch of feeling. In the end, we are a bunch of rank sentimentalists. My wife, Nella, and daughter, Molly, were on hand to bask in the glow of my sendoff. My colleagues had passed the hat for a few bucks toward some books to smooth the path of my retirement. I also got a cake. I stepped into the elevator for the last time, pressed the button and bid a final salute to the guards in the lobby. Within a year, not only would I have been gone but so would the lobby. The paper moved to new quarters, the building was sold—predictably the new owners turned it over for a fat profit— and all traces of The New York Times that I knew had disappeared. And with it, the journalistic world I inhabited, as well. I had left at the right time. And, indeed, I'd had the best of it.

Author photo The New York Times

Jack Schwartz worked for five New York newspapers, the Paris Herald-Tribune and two metropolitan dailies during a career of almost 50 years as an editor and reporter. He has taught at the Columbia School of Journalism and New York University as well as serving as a mentor at the Writers' Institute of the CUNY Graduate Center. He lives with his wife, Dr. Nella Shapiro, in Westchester County. This is his first book.

Cover illustration: The author at The New York Times Week in Review, 1973, and a marked-up copy of a story

Made in the USA
Las Vegas, NV
26 February 2021